D0991441

Against the Grain

Against the Grain
Memoirs of a Western Historian

Brigham D. Madsen

Signature Books • Salt Lake City

On the cover: *Brigham D. Madsen*, oil by Alvin Gittins, 1976, original owned by the University of Utah. Used by permission.

∞ *Against the Grain: Memoirs of a Western Historian* was printed on acid-free paper. Printed in the United States of America.

2002 2001 2000 99 98   6 5 4 3 2 1

LIBRARY OF CONGRESS CATALOGING-IN-PUBLICATION DATA
Madsen, Brigham D.
Against the grain : memoirs of a western historian /
by Brigham D. Madsen.
p.   cm.
Includes index.
ISBN 1-56085-113-9 (cloth)
1. Madsen, Brigham D.   2. College teachers—Utah—Biography.
3. Utah—Biography.   I. Title.
CT275.M446693   1998
979.2'03'092—dc21
[B]   98-17518
CIP

Contents

Preface. . . . . *vii*

1. My Mother's People: New England Stock 1

2. My Father's People: Roots in Wales, Scotland,
   and Denmark 11

3. Dad, Mother, and Five Little Madsens 33

4. Growing Up with Callouses 57

5. Missionary to the Mountaineers. 73

6. "Building" the Church in North Carolina 95

7. Utah Student, Idaho Teacher, 1936-38 115

8. Graduate School at Berkeley and the Shipyards
   of World War II, 1939-43. 135

9. Infantry Rifleman, 1943-45. 151

10. Third Army Historian in Germany, 1945-46 167

11. Ph.D. and New Professor, Berkeley and
    Brigham Young University, 1946-51. 185

12. My Years at Wilkinson's BYU, 1951-54 207

13. The Smell of Sawdust, 1954-61. 229

14. Utah State University and the Peace Corps,
    1961-65. 249

15. At the University of Utah: Dean and Deputy
    Academic Vice President, 1965-67 269

16. Administrative Vice President, 1967–71 279

17. Librarian and History Chair, 1971–75. 303

18. The Smell of Chalk Dust and Pencil Shavings,
    1975–84 319

19. An Active Retirement, 1984–90 339

20. A Writer at Work. 367

    Appendix. *383*
    List of Publications *385*
    Index. *389*

Preface

I began writing my autobiography about 1984 as a project to acquaint my children with aspects of my life and their family heritage about which they might be unaware. My professional life has swung back and forth between building construction and teaching, with other stints in the Mormon mission field, school principal, military service, the administration of the Peace Corps, author, and university administration. All of these ventures have been challenging and interesting and, I hope, productive and worthwhile.

If this book had remained only a family project, I still feel that it would have been fully worthwhile, but two friends asked to read it, then strongly urged me to revise it for a larger audience. Their unexpected encouragement and a keen sense of the challenges involved prompted me to make the effort. I have stood at intriguing and sometimes contradictory frontiers—at the border between manual labor and the academic toil of research and writing, at the intersection between being a story-teller and a fact-seeker, at the crossing between consistent participation in Mormon congregational life and personal agnosticism, on the divide between deep-rooted idealism and hardheaded practical skepticism, and among the parental paradoxes of being a protective and loving father who protects best by equipping his children for hard times and loves them best by releasing them to their own lives. Perhaps there are patterns in my own life that will help others of my generation understand themselves, and help those of later generations to understand the forces that produced mine.

I have had the great good fortune, not available to everyone, to give my life to my loves. The first of those loves—in terms of time, if not in terms of priority—has been my work. If I were to look at myself from the outside, I would probably first characterize myself as an always-busy, energetic man who has lived by the maxim, "See what needs to be done and then do it." Carrying out this maxim has required some creative imagination, a willingness to work hard, and a high sense of duty toward the responsibilities I have undertaken. Sometimes impatient with others' slowness to respond, especially when I was younger, I hope I have mellowed somewhat as maturity and better judgment have taught me additional lessons.

My driving nature has taken me to a number of different activities, most of which have rewarded me financially and brought me a certain amount of public recognition and validation. There is no question that my work has been one of the great loves of my life. But these activities have also taken me away from the true core of my life—my family. I have always been available to and involved with my children, but I know that they have not always come first in my attention. Too often I have let my ability to provide comfortable and stimulating opportunities for them substitute for expressing the tenderest feelings of my heart for them.

One of my greatest rewards as a parent is to see the close and loving relationship that our four children, Karen, Linda, David, and Steven, have with each other as adults. They get together as often as they can, communicate by phone or fax, and provide a solid combination of thoughtful critique and enthusiastic cheerleading for each other. This blood loyalty has survived moves and marriages, the addition and subtraction of in-laws, and the demands of careers and parenthood. With delight, I see the same loyalties building between and among our grandchildren.

Perhaps I did a better job of communicating my love to Betty, my companion and partner in fifty-eight years of marriage. I became who I am now because she accepted me for what I was. I could not have asked for a more loving or supportive wife, a more skilled and creative homemaker, and a more intelligent and caring mother. These qualities could have left her merely a sugary centerpiece, however, and Betty was a real person, a whole person, and a strong person. She was adaptable to new conditions, conservative in financial matters, stoical during difficult times, and endlessly interested in new places, new ideas, and new growth.

My fourth love is my country. The United States is still the hope of the world. I volunteered as a soldier in World War II. I take citizenship as a duty very seriously and taught that expectation to my children and students. Democracy, for all its failings, is still a shining example for other nations to see and emulate. My passionate love of history and my passionate outrage at the failings of the United States are both rooted in my ineradicable love for this country.

My final love is for my individual freedom—for the independence to think and act as I decide. These pages reflect that hunger for latitude and longitude in the wide boundaries of action which I have always sought and tried to protect. Sometimes my independence has crossed the border into coolness or aloofness—and I have suffered the consequences—but it has always been my choice. I have never regretted taking the steps which have assured me that independence. Perhaps that quality will be my legacy, together with the productive and happy lives with which my children will honor themselves and their parentage.

I.

MY MOTHER'S PEOPLE
New England Stock

I was destined to be a worker in wood. In both my mother's and father's families were carpenters and joiners who made their livings by constructing dwellings and small buildings. In my early years, I fought against the idea that I, too, should follow the carpenter trade and eventually found another career in teaching—but only after many years devoted to nailing studs into walls. Even then I have continued to build occasionally, and my life as a scholar has been greatly influenced by the construction business.

But the beginning involves different kinds of roots than those that interest carpenters. The roots that have dominated my life are family roots and religious roots. They have, furthermore, been inextricably tangled since one grandfather and three sets of great-grandparents espoused Mormonism. Their lives were changed and influenced by conversion to the strange new doctrine taught by Joseph Smith, Jr., Mormonism's founding prophet. (See Appendix.)

One of my maternal great-grandfathers was Hosea Cushing, born April 2, 1826, in Boston, Massachusetts, a member of the numerous descendants of Englishman Daniel Cushing, who arrived in the Commonwealth in 1630. Several Cushing men served as soldiers and commanders in the American Revolution, thus making me eligible to join the Sons of the American Revolution, an opportunity I have carefully avoided. Hosea's parents were Philip A. Cushing, born May 3, 1798, in Hingham, Massachusetts, and Mary C. Rundlett Cushing. Philip moved his family to Hingham while Hosea was still a small boy. At age sixteen, in 1842, Hosea was sent to Boston to serve an apprenticeship to a carpenter until age twenty-one. But only a few months after his arrival in the city, he heard an Elder J. Adams preach the Mormon gospel and, "much impressed," according to a journal he began shortly afterwards, "investigated this doctrine and found it to agree with the doctrine taught anciently. I believed it true."[1] On February 4, 1844, two months before his eighteenth birthday, Adams baptized him into the new church. Brigham Young and Lyman White ordained him an elder at an LDS conference in Boston seven months later.

The young man's conversion changed his life forever, and the first effect was dispossession. In a large volume devoted to the genealogy of the Massachusetts Cushings written in 1884, the author usually spends at least a page on the parentage and life of each member of the clan; in the case of Hosea, the notation is severely brief: "Went West with the Mormons."[2] After young Hosea spent a short stint as a missionary with an Elder Lloyd, Mormon apostle Wilford Woodruff counseled him to move to Nauvoo, Illinois. He arrived there April 8, 1845, ten months after Joseph Smith had been killed by mob action in nearby Carthage, and was promptly put to work as a carpenter on the imposing temple which Brigham Young, new leader of the church, was attempting to complete before moving the Saints to the Great Basin.[3] It is interesting to me that, when I was given a patriarchal blessing by William A. Hyde of Pocatello, Idaho, on April 22, 1931, when I was sixteen, the knowledgeable old patriarch, aware of my family connections with building, predicted that "thou shalt lay

---

1. Hosea Cushing, one page of excerpts from his journal, n.d., in my possession. Location of journal unknown.

2. Ibid.

3. In the Mormon temples are performed rituals called the "endowment," meaning an endowment of power and blessing, including sacred pledges to keep God's commandments. Separate but related to the endowment are various ordinances. One provides salvation for the dead through vicarious baptism. Couples married in Mormon temples are "sealed" for "time and eternity" in an eternal marriage that also includes an eternal relationship with the children born to them. This ordinance is also performed vicariously for the dead. Latter-day Saints who have been endowed are authorized to wear temple "garments," sacred underclothing with special markings which promise the wearers security from the ills and dangers of the world.

thy hands to the building of the great temple of the Lord."[4] Now, more than sixty years later, it is evident that this is one prophecy which will not come to pass, either because my faithfulness to the gospel has not measured up or because the old man's blessings were no more than wishful thinking.

After four months' work on the Nauvoo temple, Hosea Cushing was engaged to help build a house for Heber C. Kimball, second in command to Brigham Young in the church hierarchy. It was the beginning of a close relationship with Kimball who soon accepted Hosea as an "adopted" son. The young man received his "washing & anointing" and his "endowment" (traditional temple rituals of commitment and promise) in the Nauvoo temple on January 10, 1846. With this important process completed, Hosea then joined the refugees streaming out of Nauvoo and crossed the Mississippi on February 15, 1846, "on the first part of my journey toward the West. I drove Heber C. Kimball's family."

During the next year, we have no information about Hosea except to assume that he probably engaged in his trade of carpentry to help the beleaguered Saints at Winter Quarters, Iowa, try to provide housing for themselves. At some point, he courted Helen Jeannette Murray, twenty-two-year-old daughter of William E. Murray and Helen Sarvis Murray. They were engaged when, on April 18, 1847, Brigham Young assigned Hosea to the "Ninth Ten" company of the original pioneer party headed for the Great Salt Lake Valley. He was under Captain Howard Egan with Heber C. Kimball and William Clayton as members. Hosea drove one of the Kimball wagons across the plains and arrived in Salt Lake Valley with the other pioneers on July 24. The next day Heber C. Kimball gathered fourteen men to give them advice about planting crops and building homes. Howard Egan noted in his diary on August 7, "Hosea Cushing made a hay rake today," probably the first constructed in the valley, and continued on August 19: "It was a warm and pleasant day. Hosea and myself

---

4. Patriarchs, one per stake, are senior holders of the Melchizedek Priesthood who pronounce blessings by the laying on of hands, one per recipient, that declares the person to be a descendant of one of the twelve tribes and that usually includes promises and admonitions about the person's future life.

were engaged part of the day in drawing [hauling] gravel with which to cover houses."[5]

Because Hosea Cushing's name is inscribed with the other pioneers on the famous statue of Brigham Young at the southeast corner of the Salt Lake temple, I have often remarked to my university classes that the original Brigham Young party to the Great Basin has sometimes been compared to the Pilgrim Fathers' arrival at Plymouth. Many Americans who have no right to do so have, nevertheless, claimed a connection with one of the first pilgrims, to secure whatever status that would bring. So many have done so that, it is joked, a whole fleet of *Mayflowers* would be necessary to deliver these so-called ancestors to America. I usually ended my comment by suggesting that the only reason I raised the point was to furnish an opportunity to tell the class that my great-grandfather was a member of the original Mormon pioneer party to Utah but that "a man's worth should be measured by his own accomplishments and not because his family tree contains some firsts, especially when some of the firsts may well have been horse thieves."

After about a month spent in Salt Lake Valley, Hosea departed on August 27, 1847, with Heber C. Kimball and the rest of the Brigham Young party on the return trip to Winter Quarters. His was the first name listed of the fourteen men of the Kimball group. On August 30, 1847, at Bear River, as the group organized to recross the plains a second time, Hosea was assigned to the thirty-sixth and last wagon, also the temporary home of William A. King and Carlos Murray. Murray was a relative of Hosea's fiancée, Helen.

Hosea and Helen were married on February 14, 1848, in Winter Quarters. The next year, expecting their first child, Helen and Hosea traveled to Salt Lake City where Hosea built a small log house a block north of Temple Square. During the next few years, his carpenter skills were in great demand as new homes sprang up. Helen provided board for men like Thomas Bullock, Brigham Young's clerk, who recorded in his journal on August 29, 1848, "I supped with Hosea Cushing and

5. Qtd. in Journal History of the Church of Jesus Christ of Latter-day Saints (chronology of typed entries and newspaper clippings, 1830-present), Aug 7, 19, 1847, LDS Church Archives.

wife where I had all my food."[6] Hosea and Helen had three sons: William Ellis born in December 1848, my grandfather, Hosea Philip Cushing, born August 27, 1851, and Samuel Roswell, born in May 1853.

Hosea was named one of the seven presidents of the Twenty-fifth Quorum of Seventies on May 9, 1853. Three months later the Walker War, a series of guerilla attacks by Ute Indians on Mormon settlers in central Utah, led to a proclamation of Governor Brigham Young on August 19, 1853, warning citizens to "fort up" and mustering the territorial militia, called by the nostalgic name, the Nauvoo Legion. Five days later, according to the History of Brigham Young, "Lt. Col. [William H.] Kimball and Dr. [William M.] Andrews joined the [Thomas Callister Cavalry] company, which was organized by the appointment of the following officers: Thomas Callister Captain, H. M. Alexander, John Alger and Hosea Cushing Lieutenants." The company was sent south to reconnoiter the area around Spanish Fork and Spring Creek from July 22 to August 25, 1853.[7]

Hosea evidently continued his military activities into the next year when he was sent on a scouting expedition with a man named Ging in May 1854. The two men became lost in the desert for three days during which they had neither food nor water. They managed to find their way to help, but Hosea never recovered from the ordeal and died in Salt Lake City "on the 17th inst. [May], of consumption."[8] He was twenty-eight. His widow eventually married Norman Taylor, a polygamist, in 1867, and thereafter made her home in Santaquin, Utah. My grandfather lived in Santaquin until his death on September 23, 1919.

Fifteen-year-old Hosea Philip saw cavalry action in the Black Hawk War, inflating his age by a year to enlist in Captain A. G. Conover's Cavalry Company on May 1, 1866. Between then and the war's end in 1869, he served seventy-nine days. He left no personal account, but the militia record states that he "was in constant service. Made expeditions against the Indians to Fort Gunnison, Fish Lake,

6. Ibid., Aug. 19, 1848

7. "History of Brigham Young," Bancroft Library; "Military Records Concerning Service in Indian Wars in Utah," Utah State Archives.

8. Journal History, May 17, 1854; *Deseret News*, May 25, 1854.

Henry Nisonger,
my maternal great-grandfather, born in 1814.

Grass Valley, Circle Valley and Rabbit Valley." He received $13.00 a month plus a monthly clothes allowance of $3.50, for a total compensation of $59.40. On September 14, 1909, at age fifty-nine, he signed an affidavit attesting these facts and began receiving a veteran's pension of $15.00 a month. Another private in the same company was Chester Nisonger, whose sister Phoebe Hosea Philip married five years later.[9]

My maternal grandmother's family, the Nisongers (sometimes spelled Niswanger), were probably of Swiss-German origin and may have immigrated first to Botetourt County, Virginia, where a John Nisonger was listed in the U.S. Census of 1810.[10] My great-grandfather, Henry Nisonger, was born October 2, 1814, in Fairfield County, Ohio, the son of David Nisonger and Nancy Gunder Nisonger. As early as 1788, they pioneered in Ohio, part of the great migration to that area after the American Revolution. In the mid-1830s Henry married Sarah Slusser, daughter of Peter Slusser and Mary Dean Slusser. She was born April 26, 1816, at Clear Creek, near Cincinnati, Ohio. One of Sarah's descendants pointedly remarked, "When she was quite young she met and married Henry Nisonger and from that time on she led an unsettled life."[11] The couple had nine children between 1837 and 1854, born in five different

---

9. "Affidavit Concerning Service in Indian Wars Within the State of Utah and of Service Relating Thereto," No. 137, Utah State Archives.

10. "Phoebe Nisonger," Ancestral File (computer software), Ver. 4.17, copyright 1987, July 1996 by the Church of Jesus Christ of Latter-day Saints.

11. N.a., "History of Sarah Slusser Nisonger," n.d., typescript, 1 p.; photocopy in my possession.

Ohio counties, a fact that supports the picture of a very mobile family. The second youngest child, Phoebe, my grandmother, was born February 4, 1851, at Cincinnati, Hamilton County, Ohio.

Probably in the fall of 1854, while the family was camped in the forest outside of Cincinnati cutting wood for winter, they were visited by two Mormon missionaries and soon joined the new faith. Following the advice of their new religious leaders, Henry and Sarah moved their family to St. Louis to procure funds for the move to Utah. Henry cut wood for a railroad company while Sarah worked in a shirt factory. After two years' effort, they had sufficient funds to purchase two wagons, eight head of oxen, and adequate supplies. They traveled with the Captain Milla Andrews Company and reached Ogden, Utah, in the fall of 1856 where the family spent the winter in one rented room. Phoebe Nisonger was five at the time. The following spring they rented a house on the bench overlooking Ogden while Henry began constructing a dug-out. This project was interrupted when he was enrolled in the Lot Smith Company and assigned to defend Echo Canyon against a federal army sent by President James Buchanan, who believed the Mormons to be in rebellion against the United States, in the summer of 1857.[12]

Left in a damp dug-out for the winter of 1857–58, Sarah and her children soon exchanged it for a brush shack in Payson when the Ogden Saints were moved south to escape the troops. Once Colonel Albert Sidney Johnston's army finally settled at Camp Floyd west of Lehi in July 1858, Henry moved his family near the army cantonment where Sarah washed clothes for the soldiers and peddled home-made pies. Eighteen months later they were again on the move—this time to a ranch at Pelican Point on the west side of Utah Lake. She was alone much of the time with her two youngest daughters, the nearest neighbor ten miles away. One day a party of about ten Indian men came down the road towards the house. Sarah, who was weaving woolen

---

12. The troops, led by Colonel Albert Sidney Johnston, were stalled in Wyoming during the winter of 1857-58. A peaceful settlement was negotiated the next spring and summer through the mediation of Colonel Thomas Kane, a friend of the Mormons. Brigham Young, after evacuating the northern settlements, allowed Johnston's army to march peacefully through Salt Lake City and make a camp forty miles to the south.

cloth at the time, placed her flintlock gun on the loom, prepared to defend herself and children. When the Indians looked in the door, they were highly amused and slapped their legs, laughing at the sight of the courageous woman. When the family sheep dogs and the Indian dogs began fighting, Sarah grabbed a bucket of water, went outside, and doused the fighting animals. This second display caused even more merriment on the part of the Indians who soon left. I remember hearing my grandmother's account of the incident. She was about eight at the time—and frightened.

The family soon moved once again, this time to Santaquin where they finally settled for a period of ten years. Henry Nisonger, like most of his neighbors, farmed and did whatever else he could to bring in some cash. When the Union Pacific was extending its line down Echo Canyon in the winter of 1869, Henry saw a chance at real money and wrote to Brigham Young who had taken a contract to build the roadbed for the new railroad:

> Henry Nisongers Camp
> Feb. 15 '69 Ogden City
>
> To President B Young
>   Dear Sir I have been on your contract on the Railroad since June last helping to complete the same I am now about finishing the peice I am now at work on which is about 3 miles below the Mouth of Web Kanyon - if you have any more contracts to let I would be glad to work a Mile or so if this meets your mind Please send me a few lines in care of John W Young [Brigham's son] and you will much oblige your humble Servant and Brother in the Gospel of Truth and Right
>
> Henry Nisonger
> My home is in Santaquin Utah Co[13]

At the bottom of the letter, perhaps in Brigham Young's handwriting, is the note, "Write to J W Young to give him work on the west somewheres ask him to apply to J W Y." In their later life, Henry and Sarah moved to Diamond in Tintic Mining District. During the last two years of her life, Sarah lived with my grandmother, Phoebe

---

13. Brigham Young, Letterbooks, Reel 62, LDS Church Archives.

Cushing, "as the rest of the family wouldn't care for her," according to the unidentified descendant who wrote her short biography.[14]

Hosea Philip Cushing and Phoebe Nisonger, both twenty, were married in Santaquin on September 7, 1871, by David Holladay. They set up housekeeping in a small home where they lived their entire married life and where they raised to maturity ten of twelve children born to them.[15] My mother, Lydia, like Phoebe, the second youngest child, was born December 11, 1891. My grandfather was a small farmer and later became a "horse doctor" who was in great demand to treat sick animals by the use of a wonderful ointment whose formula was given to him by a German immigrant. The Cushing family has always called it "Pa's Salve," and this marvelous elixir is still being made in small batches by Aunt Myrtle's children from the closely guarded secret formula. All of us use it for cuts and bruises and any other ailment which will not respond to treatments by today's doctors. I have two jars in my medicine cabinet; I don't want to run out!

---

14. "History of Sarah Slusser Nisonger."

15. No author, "Cushing Family History," n.d., typescript; photocopy in my possession.

2.

MY FATHER'S PEOPLE

Roots in Wales, Scotland, and Denmark

The union of my mother, Lydia Cushing, and my father, Brigham Andrew Madsen, had roots that led into three European countries. Perhaps the most colorful of these ancestors—certainly the one I know most about—is James Crane, the father of my father's mother (my great-grandfather). He left an autobiography which reads as though it could have come from the pen of Charles Dickens.[1] James was born April 1, 1830, an illegitimate child of Elizabeth Harris, of the village of Penally, near Tenby Pembrokeshire, South Wales. As James wrote, "My father's name was George Crane, so my mother said, of Brighton, England, but was never married to my mother, but was engaged to be but died before fulfilling his engagement. ... Some of the people doubted this statement of my mother and when I grew up told me of it. But my mother was always silent to me on the subject."[2]

At the age of three weeks, James was placed in the home of a family by the name of Thomas, "the officers of the Parish paying for my keep." Elizabeth Harris, evidently, had no more interest in the child she had borne. James lived with his foster parents for the first six years of his life on the island of Colda (Caldy) and in the town of Tenby. Mr. Thomas was drowned while crossing from the island of Colda and

---

1. James Crane, *History of James Crane* (n.p.: Crane Family Genealogical Committee, 1949), 40 pp.

2. Ibid., 1.

James Crane,
my paternal great-grandfather, born in 1830.

left his widow with four sons and James to care for. When she could not pay the rent on her house, the landlord threatened to "pull down the house on our heads" and actually began to undermine the house using a pick and shovel. James very early displayed his initiative and determination and remembered, "crying all the way I went and raised the neighbors in our behalf, so that the man was so ashamed he had to quit."

But the respite was short-lived. Six-year-old James suffered a broken hip which was not set properly by the local baker, leaving him with a life-long limp. Then Sarah died suddenly, and parish officials assigned him to the care of a widow, Sophia Howells, who lived in Penally, where James's mother then resided. As James recorded, "My mother was married by this time, but she had no interest in me." He remembered, "The first six years of my life is nearly a blank. ... The first time I knew myself, I was a little, dirty, ragged, barefooted, hungry boy, having no one that seemed to care anything about me."

Mrs. Howells treated the boy kindly and did the best she could to provide for him on the parish allowance of two shillings (fifty cents) a week. Two charitable ladies named Bond paid his school fees, so he was able to learn to read the New Testament. When James was eight, a poorhouse was built in Pembroke and he was sent there with other destitute and homeless children. The governor, a Mr. Large, was "very kind to all." James also learned to write a little and do some arithmetic. He was ill for almost two of the five years he was at Pembroke; as I count up the many times he was sick, due mostly to undernourishment and exposure, it is understandable why he died at age fifty-six.

At age thirteen, James ran away from the poorhouse to escape punishment for riding a visitor's horse that he had been assigned to hold. He fled to the home of a blacksmith named Evans who had taken an interest in him and who placed him with a farmer named James in the village of Rafter-bridge. After six months he became so homesick for Tenby that he pleaded with his mother to take him in. She did so reluctantly because, with seven other children and a husband who earned only seven shillings a week, James was "a very unwelcome visitor and they were not long in showing it." His mother "had no more parental feeling for me than any stranger on the street." She threatened to send him back to the poorhouse and relented only when he was able to find a job herding cattle for "six cents" (he uses the American sum). He gave the entire amount to her but she remained hardened toward him. "While the other children sat at the table, I was given my piece in the corner. I got to be very thin and puny and between hunger and lack of clothing, I could scarcely walk the earth. I was worse off than when I was in the poorhouse by far. And had it not been for the timely interference of friends it seemed I must soon die."

His mother finally turned him out, and he sought refuge with his employer. One of the women who worked in the fields at the farm agreed to cook his food while three others told him they would take turns to wash and mend his clothes. For six months, with the help of these women and the six cents a day he earned as a herd boy, he was able to survive "almost entirely" on bread and coffee, with an occasional square meal from one of his friends. The farm owner, a Mr. Watters, contracted with him for one year, for two cents a day and board. James worked for Watters until he was twenty—a seven-year term of comparative security during which he "grew to manhood, forgot all the sorrows of my early youth, got to be as saucy and troublesome as anybody, used bad language, kept bad company and did many things that were no credit to me."

Then, in the winter of 1850-51, James Crane had an experience which changed his life. He met a Mormon missionary, William Hire, who held a series of meetings in Tenby. James Crane always "had religious feelings" but had no use for the churches in his neighborhood, especially the Church of England. He called it an "easy religion to live and the greatest qualification a member needed was to be a first class hypocrite." Hire's first sermon "sounded to me better than anything I ever heard." He continued to attend the meetings, despite ridicule from the townspeople, and "got quite expert at defending the Elders." After three months he had read the Book of Mormon and gained a desire to be baptized. Learning that a local woman was to be baptized in the ocean, he arrived on the seashore just as the woman was being led out of the water and asked the elder, "'Sir, ... I suppose you would have no objection to baptize me in the same water.' He looked straight at me with a look that went through me and in an instant he said: 'Yes sir,' and led me into the sea and baptized me." The date was March 21, 1851. The elder was Thomas Noot. Fully committed to his faith, James gave the poverty-stricken Utah elders, who were traveling as missionaries "without purse or scrip," six of his seven suits of clothing.

James Crane's friends were horrified at his conversion, and Mr. Watters refused to renew his contract. James began working in a stone quarry near Tenby, was named presiding elder over the Lydstys Branch, two miles from Tenby, in September 1851, and attended meetings at the small Mormon branch in Pembroke ten miles away, sometimes three or four times a week. He walked the ten miles in all kinds of weather, often running most of the way to get back for work the next morning. He also began proselyting. He gave his first public sermon "with trembling knees" but soon became such a staunch defender of the faith and so adept as a debater that the missionaries and other members began to call on him to meet the challenges of opponents.

Once a man approached him from the crowd and with a reaping hook attempted "to strike me with it ... but he had no power to [hurt me.]" The missionaries prevailed upon him to travel to a nearby town where "a very troublesome fellow was disrupting the meetings." In another confrontation a disturber "marched out of the crowd to lay hold of me. I gave one step back and then braced myself, pointed my finger at him, looking him straight in the eye I said, 'You dare lay a hand on me. I have an instrument in my pocket that will put you in prison so fast you will be astonished how you got there.' He stepped back quicker than he came forward and turned as pale as death." These missionary activities transformed James Crane into a forceful and fearless expounder of his faith.

Determined to gather in Utah's Zion with other Saints, he starved himself, living "on barley bread and water for three months." His work at the quarry involved "lifting large rocks. I used to spit up blood every day from the heavy strain." He succeeded in getting the last pennies for his passage together only two days before he embarked on the square-rigged *S. Curling* on May 19, 1856, with 707 passengers headed by the colorful Welsh missionary Dan Jones.

James was doubly fortunate in his passage. He had no food or money, but provisions were included in the passage, and Captain Sanders Curling, a "generous, courteous, and philanthropic" man, had his crew take special care of the sick. James was ill for most of the thirty-four-day voyage. They docked in Boston harbor on June 23.

James and three others set out to find work but did not have the single penny necessary to pay the toll over a bridge into Boston. He eventually found his way to New York City. His first job was with an Irish contractor laying blocks in the streets of nearby Williamsberg. The Irishman, "Teddy Mack-wiggin," turned out to be an abusive slave driver who worked his men eleven hours a day. "In my young days I had become very much taken up with America," James recalled. "I had read the history of Columbus several times and my ideas and anticipation of America were great. But when I got amongst this crowd, I really thought I had landed in the wrong place, for I could see no beauty in it." After a short time James took work with a farmer on Long Island at twelve dollars a month. But the farmer also "trotted us through from sunrise until dark, in July, and when Sunday came we were hardly able to walk." He stayed at this job only five weeks, then returned to New York City. He spent two years in the state but does not describe other jobs.

In the spring of 1858, he moved to Iowa City, Iowa, with Joseph and William Davis and their sister, Alice Davis.[3] Their parents were John Davis and Elizabeth Cadwallader Davis near Tenby who had become Mormons in 1849 and 1852, respectively. Alice and her siblings were baptized in 1855 when she was twenty-one. James had agreed

---

3. *A History of the Three Wives of James Crane: Alice Davis Crane, Elizabeth Stewart Crane, Rachel Briggs Crane* (n.p.: Crane Family Genealogical Committee, Alice Davis portion published in 1951), 2–31.

to send passage money to Alice; and Joseph, living in New York, had made the same agreement with his brother William. James and Alice were married in Iowa City on April 5, 1855, so poor that they had to borrow a dollar to pay for the marriage license. Because there were apostates "in about every other house," James and Alice agreed, in the spring of 1859, to work their way across the plains to Utah come what may. James signed on as a teamster with a small Mormon company, and they left Iowa City on April 3, 1859, under the leadership of Joseph W. Young, Bishop Frederick Kesler, and Orten Haight. James was made a captain of ten. Their three months' journey was uneventful, and the company reached Salt Lake City on September 1, 1859. James and Alice had five cents "between us. We bought a melon and was square with the world once more." They had no children.

James worked for Brigham Young for the next year and a half, then, in the spring of 1861, began farming in the Salt Lake Valley "on the shares of Daniel Cahoon. Worked hard for six months. Lived hard, but never went hungry." In the fall he bought a house and five acres in Sugarhouse Ward in Salt Lake City. At thirty-one, the wandering James finally had a home and became a "producer on my own hook."

In 1862 he joined a company of minute-men in Salt Lake City, called out to oppose Colonel Patrick E. Connor and his California Volunteers who supposedly were threatening to arrest Brigham Young. Crane described how Connor and his cavalry made a demonstration march through Salt Lake City but returned to Camp Douglas when faced with the Mormon militia.[4] James Crane later joined the Nauvoo Legion in which he served as a second lieutenant until the

---

4. Brigham D. Madsen, *Glory Hunter: A Biography of Patrick Edward Connor* (Salt Lake City: University of Utah Press, 1990), 92. The Union government sent Colonel Patrick E. Connor and his California Volunteers from California to Utah in the fall of 1862 to secure the trails and mail lines in the Rocky Mountain and Great Basin region. An open opponent to Mormonism, Connor bypassed Camp Floyd, located forty miles south of Salt Lake City, and established Camp Douglas on the "bench" east of the city, with the avowed intention of keeping an eye on the Mormons as well as repelling any Indian attacks on the transcontinental roads. A cold war soon developed between the Mormons and the soldiers. James, in this incident, was gathering with others to defend Brigham Young when rumors spread that Connor was going to arrest him.

territorial governor disbanded the outfit. He does not explain where he learned to shoot, but he claimed he "could put three bullets in a rabbits head at one hundred yards."

Elizabeth Stewart Crane,
my paternal great-grandmother born in 1846

Alice was still childless; but as a loyal Latter-day Saint, James would no doubt have accepted polygamy as both doctrine and practice anyway. On February 3, 1865, he married Elizabeth Stewart, my great-grandmother, on her nineteenth birthday. Scottish born, she was the fourth child of William Stewart and Sarah Thompson Stewart's family of eight. My grandmother, Annie Crane, was the fourth of *their* eight.[5] In 1868 James took charge of a company of men who spent a year building roadbed for the Union Pacific Railroad in Echo Canyon. "We had a good time and made good wages and lived our religion ... and returned with honor," he summarized with satisfaction.

On March 18, 1869 the family moved to Herriman, Utah, in the southwest corner of Salt Lake Valley, where, on March 28, James also married Rachel Briggs, who became the mother of seven children.[6]

By 1877 Crane, now forty-seven and the father of eleven, was the bishop and leading citizen of Herriman Ward. He was appointed a member of the Territorial Board of Trade, subscribed to the *Deseret*

---

5. These eight were James (1866), Heber (1867), William (1869), Annie (1870), Brigham (1872), Franklin (1875), Mary (1876), and Fannie (1878).

6. Rachel Briggs was born in Lancashire in 1853 to John Briggs and Ruth Butterworth Briggs. Her children were Alice (1870), Charles (1872), Rebecca (1873), Esther (1875), Hyrum (1878), Sarah (1880), and Carrie (1884).

News to keep himself informed of national and world affairs, and read the Book of Mormon and the Bible from cover to cover each year. He built a long, one-story house of three connected apartments with three front doors for his large family. The house is still standing in Herriman, still used as a home. In 1882 he appraised his personal practice of polygamy: "We get along pretty well generally and have been quite a credit to the principle of plural marriage, but many times by giving way to the tempter, we are not as good as we ought to be and do many things unbecoming saints; but by the mercies of the Lord and humbling ourselves before him, he forgives us and we feel encouraged and press on."[7] James Crane died July 6, 1886, and was buried in the Herriman cemetery.

My great-grandmother, Elizabeth Stewart, the second wife of James Crane, was born February 3, 1846, in Greenoch, Argylshire, Scotland, to William Stewart and Sarah Thompson.[8] William Stewart's family were wealthy landowners in Argylshire with a stable of riding horses and many servants. William, born in November 1814, made the mistake of falling in love with Sarah, a maid seven years younger in the Stewart household. He married her secretly and never revealed the date. They fled to Ireland where he learned the paper mill trade and, after three years, returned to Greenoch where they were reconciled to William's family. Elizabeth, the fourth of their eight children, was born February 3, 1846. William and Sarah moved to Glasgow where working conditions were better; but Sarah died in June 1857, "troubled because all her children had not been able to see the light of the gospel." Sixteen-year-old Annie, the oldest daughter, took over the care of the younger children. Elizabeth, eleven at her mother's death, was baptized by James Crane the day before Elizabeth became his second wife.

The second son, Samuel, immigrated to America in 1861 at seventeen, and worked for two years as a plumber to pay for the passage of his father and brother and sisters to the New World. The eldest son, who had married, decided to stay in Scotland. Eighteen-year-old

---

7. Crane, "History of James Crane," 34.
8. *A History of the Three Wives of James Crane,* 32–42.

Elizabeth, who was engaged, also planned to remain; but the night before the family left, she returned home from assuring her young man that she was going to stay in Scotland to find her father in tears. He had promised her dying mother that he would keep the family together. Elizabeth, overcome by the reference to her mother and by her father's tears, agreed to emigrate. She never saw her betrothed again.

The Stewarts sailed from Liverpool aboard the 1,518-ton ship *General McClellan* under Captain G. D. J. Trask, on May 21, 1864, and landed in New York on June 23 after a passage of thirty-three days. The vessel carried 802 Saints under the supervision of Thomas E. Jeremy. The family took a steamer to Albany, a train to St. Joseph, Missouri, and an ox team for Utah under Joseph S. Rawlins. They left July 15, 1864, and reached Salt Lake City on September 20, 1864, the children walking most of the way.

Elizabeth worked in the home of Truman Angell until her marriage on February 3, 1865, to James Crane. At their home in Sugarhouse, Elizabeth bore three sons, whom the first wife, Alice, ever after known as Auntie, adopted as her own. The two wives got along very well, but James's marriage to Rachel Briggs in March 1869 and the move to Herriman injected more strain in the family. Elizabeth's biographer has written:

> As was the custom of the men who lived in polygamy, James would buy a bolt of material and expected his wives to all dress alike. This was always a source of annoyance to her. ... Many is the time she rode to Salt Lake City on a load of wood, and returned on the running gears, to sell some of her berries and beautiful handiwork. With this money, Elizabeth used to buy clothing for her children.[9]

Elizabeth Stewart Crane was a well-organized, hard-working, meticulous homemaker. She loved her children but was physically undemonstrative with them. Her fifth child, Brigham, died of whooping cough at age three; but my grandmother Annie, who was twenty-six when he died, remembered him and named my father for him. The

---

9. Ibid., 39.

name, passed on to me, creates an emotional link to this great-uncle I never knew. I confess that I perpetuated this questionable custom by giving my oldest son "Brigham" as his middle name. Elizabeth was "proud, independent, reserved, and very modest." She was simultaneously "hot tempered" and very good-hearted. One son saw her sneaking across lots to the house of a neighbor who had greatly wronged her, carrying a pan of flour covered by her apron. Elizabeth "knew of their need and couldn't allow them to go hungry while she had bread to eat. He said never in his life did his mother appear more wonderful to him than at that moment."[10] Elizabeth died at Herriman on December 7, 1915, at age sixty-nine.

Her first daughter, Annie, named for Elizabeth's older sister, Annie, who had been a mother to the younger children, was born on August 30, 1870, at Herriman. Annie inherited beautiful red hair from her father, and passed it on to my sisters, Ann and Phyllis. It must be a dominant gene; when I attended a Crane family reunion in the early 1950s in Herriman Ward, about half of the 200 or so people there had red hair. I have always admired my sisters' beautiful hair, but they have resented looking "different" in a way that attracted unwelcome jokes.

Annie Crane at seventeen accepted a marriage proposal from a young man and prepared her wedding dress; but when she saw him with another girl, she indignantly called off the wedding. A few months later, she met Carl Madsen, a Danish immigrant, who was doing some carpenter work for the family for whom she was doing housework. They were married on November 30, 1887, despite her mother's disapproval. Carl, thirteen years older than Annie, was a widower with two children. Elizabeth and the other two wives of James Crane told Annie that they would never take her part against her stepchildren. They needn't have worried, because red-headed Annie showed no favoritism for her own ten children over the two; in fact, when shopping, she always gave the stepchildren the first choice of what she bought. I was a grown man before I discovered that Uncle Charley and Aunt Mary were not Grandma's children. Carl and Annie had a devoted, though not demonstrative, marriage. They were both industrious, pragmatic, and excellent managers, certainly a necessity in rearing their

---

10. Ibid., 40.

twelve children. My grandfather was the undisputed
head of the Madsen house-
hold, and both had fiery tem-
pers; but to some extent,
they balanced each other.
Grandmother skillfully managed family relationships and
intervened when Grandfa-
ther's explosions became
dangerous to others.

Carl Madsen operated a
small farm in Riverton and
built houses and small buildings while his growing
family helped in both en-
deavors. Annie had the typical hard work and cares of a
farm wife of the late 1800s
and joined her husband in
insisting that all of their
children learn the advan-
tages of industry and dedicated work habits. As her

*Carl Madsen
as a missionary in about 1898.*

biographer wrote, "Grandma was a very particular housekeeper—almost to the point of being a fanatic about it."[11] For example, if she
found a spot on a dish, the errant dishwasher was forced to do the
whole batch over again. Annie was just as particular about her own
appearance and that of her children. Also, "she liked to get done in a
hurry." One of her children remembered that when the butter delayed "coming," she "raised her voice to it." The losing of her temper
and the coming of the butter always seemed to coincide, so her children can be forgiven for thinking there was a causal connection.

Like her mother, Annie was well organized, a good manager, and

11. Lorena Madsen Smith, "Annie Crane Madsen," 3, n.d., typescript, 9 pp.;
photocopy in my possession.

very generous. All of her children remember carrying a particular red bucket filled with food to a neighbor in want. Danish immigrants who knew Carl frequently stayed with the family for a month or two while they found a location in their new country.

Near the turn of the century, Carl was called on an LDS prose-lyting mission to Denmark. Neither he nor Annie apparently thought it unusual for him to accept this assignment, leaving Annie, who was on crutches from phlebitis, to care for nine children and a heavily mortgaged farm. Carl advised Annie to borrow money from her well-to-do sheep-ranching brothers for living expenses, promising to repay them when he returned from his missionary labors. Instead, Annie took in washing, made ice cream and peddled it to nearby towns, and operated the farm. "When grandpa returned from his mission he was very much surprised to learn that grandma had *not* borrowed money from her brothers but she had kept her family, had kept grandpa on his mission, had paid off the mortgage on the farm, and had some money saved to help him get started again," wrote Lorena Madsen Smith, a granddaughter.[12] But my father remembers the bitter experience of being "farmed out" at the age of seven to Annie's brother Will and his wife, Rebecca Miller Crane, in Herriman during these two years as Annie tried to reduce the burden of feeding and caring for nine children. He remembered that when she came to visit him he would cry and beg her to take him back home. It must have been a heart-wrenching experience for her too. Such experiences forced her to make hard choices. No wonder she opposed the practice of wasting money to place marble headstones at the graves of relatives. "She felt there were people living who needed help and money should go to them instead," wrote Lorena.[13]

I came to know this remarkable woman because in 1928 when I was thirteen, my father sent me to spend the summer with his parents in Riverton, Utah, because I was not "going to be allowed to lie around all summer like the lazy boys of the neighborhood" in my little village of Alameda, Idaho. During those three months, I learned to

---

12. Lorena Madsen Smith, "Carl Madsen," n.d., typescript, 31 pp.; photocopy in my possession.

13. Ibid., 4.

love Grandma Madsen very much and to admire and respect my stern and hardworking Grandpa Madsen. I particularly remember Grandma's "parlor" which I was allowed to enter only on the sabbath. It was meticulously cleaned and arranged, and I sat on the old horsehair sofa during these periods of reverence, usually listening to Aunt Desna, about age eighteen, play appropriately subdued pieces on the piano.

My grandfather operated a farm of five acres and, that summer, was also building a large barn for a neighbor. I worked with him every day either doing carpentry or cutting and hauling hay and other farm chores. We worked from sunup to sundown six days a week but never on Sunday.

Annie Crane died at age fifty-eight on May 19, 1929, after suffering from a heart ailment for ten years. She was fifty-eight. My sturdy Danish grandfather outlived her by another seventeen years, dying at the age of ninety.

Carl Madsen was born November 14, 1857, at Meilby, a small village about four miles from Randers, Jutland, Denmark. His father's name was Mads Bradt and, according to family tradition, Carl Madsen Bradt changed his last name to Madsen when he arrived as an immigrant in the United States.[14] I'm glad he did; otherwise I would carry the name of Brig Bradt, and a name that sounded like "Brat" would have made me an automatic target for dreary jokes (and worse) in elementary school.

Mads died when Carl was six; three years later his widowed mother, Annie Nielsen Simonsen Madsen, was forced to place him in a home where he earned his keep by herding cattle and sheep. The family with whom he lived was very kind; but at age fifteen he was "forced to leave"—he doesn't say why—to begin a four-year apprenticeship as a carriage-maker in Randers. Carl disliked his master so much that he never recorded his name. During this period he received only his board, room, and a small clothing allowance.

When he was eighteen, he attended a Mormon meeting with his brother Anders and another youth. He confessed that he

[went] more for an evening of mischief and amusement than anything

---

14. Carl Madsen, "My Conversion to Mormonism," 3.

else.... It has been nearly sixty years since then, but the feeling of wonder and amazement which I experienced at that time has always stayed with me. As I listened to the Elder preach, I said to myself, "What's the matter with me?" It seemed as though every word that he spoke went right through me with a force I shall never forget.

Anders and the other boy, unmoved by the sermon, departed at the close of the meeting, but Carl stayed behind, asking the missionaries how they could be so certain that Joseph Smith was a prophet and that the Mormon gospel was true. Their answer was that he should ask his Father in Heaven who would reveal to him whether Joseph Smith was a true prophet or not. Taking them at their word, when he reached home, he knelt by his bed and implored God to let him know if Mormonism were true. "When I had finished," he testified, "to my astonishment, I was enveloped with such joy and happiness that I find words inadequate to express the reality of it to my readers."[15]

The news that he had accepted this new and quite disreputable religion prompted his mother and stepfather to send for him to come home. There they and his seven brothers and sisters warned him he would no longer be considered a member of the family if he should join the Mormon church. He was particularly sad because he loved his mother tenderly, and it cut him to the heart that she should join with the others in condemning him. "Many hours I spent crying to myself," he wrote, but he finally asked for baptism. At midnight on January 20, 1877, for fear of a mob, the ceremony was performed in the Guden River, about two miles from Randers. Soren Jensen, who was baptizing him, asked if he had brought any clothes in which to be baptized.

I answered in the negative and explained that I wished to go into the watery grave & be born into the Kingdom of God in the same manner as I

---

15. Ibid., 4; Lorena Madsen Smith, "Carl Madsen," 5. I have also used Carl Madsen, "My Conversion to Mormonism," n.d., edited by Robert Carter to correct his spelling and usage, 17 pp.; photocopy in my possession. I recently became aware that Carl Madsen's original autobiography, the basis for the above-cited accounts, had also came into Robert Carter's possession and that he is now editing it for publication. "A short Histori of the Live of Carl Madsen Bradt," n.d., holograph, 164 pp. with twelve addenda.

was born to mortality, as free from clothes as at that time. In this manner was I baptized a member of the Church of Jesus Christ of Latter-day Saints. ... A faith that God lives & that I am a member of his true church came to me that night which has been with me ever since. I firmly believe that if the penalty of death should have been pronounced upon me for my act of obedience that night, it would have had little effect on me. The news spread rapidly that Carl Madsen had joined the Mormon Church and "it seemed as though all hell was turned loose upon me."[16]

The family gathered again and, in two lengthy sessions of a "terrible schooling," tried to get him to renounce his new faith. When he steadfastly held to his convictions, "my step-father and oldest brother were quite cruel to me, & I was knocked around & beaten up rather badly while other members of my family stood around & spat in my face. I was then thrown bodily out of the house."

The family's next tactic was to ask his employer to keep him locked in his room on Sundays. Carl tells how he once found the key and started to leave the shop. His employer saw him, "grabbed me and threw me on the floor. While we were wrestling I told him that he could kill me if he liked but until he did that I was going to assist & be with Mormons as much as I could. When he learned how determined I was, he loosed me & cursing shoved me out the door."

For the next few months until his apprenticeship ended, he continued to endure the ridicule and ostracism of his family and employer. As soon as he was a free man, he moved to Aalborg, forty miles from Randers, and secured a job as carriage-maker. Only two weeks later, he contracted typhoid fever and for two months "lingered between life and death." Of course, he lost his position. Weak and penniless, he wrote his mother who sent him enough money to return home. She pled with him to leave the church; when her entreaties failed, they agreed to "turn over to me everything they owned if I would promise to leave the Mormons alone." As he wrote later, "when this glittering prize was offered me, I gave in to the tempter." He was granted the farm and the home, and was given enough cash to set himself up as a carriage-maker.

---

16. Lorena Madsen Smith, "Carl Madsen," 6; Carl Madsen, "My Conversion to Mormonism," 6.

His new business was successful beyond his expectations, and his new prosperity led him back to his old associates and habits, including tobacco and drink. He was twenty-one at the time. For the next year, he abandoned his activities in the Mormon church, led a free and easy life, and might have gone on this way for some time if his mother had not died after eighteen months of suffering with an infected leg. During the last weeks of her ordeal, Carl was at her bedside "day and night" to help nurse her. During these months "of gloom and sorrow ... my condition became unbearable." He came "to his senses" and began to pray again. "One night in January, 1879, I went out into an open field & lying flat on the ground, buried my face in my hands and pleaded with the Lord to free me from my painful & terrible condition. My prayers were answered, but it cost me my mother." She died two days later.

She had been his only strong tie to the family, so he signed over the farm, the house, and his carriage-making business to his older brother, Anders, taking only enough money for his passage to New York. He also received $50 from Mary Harder to pay his railroad fare from New York City to Salt Lake City. Mary was a young woman whom he had known in Denmark who had immigrated to New York City. Apparently the two had had a romantic attraction, since Mary later became his wife.

Under Danish law, Carl had already been drafted to provide the years of military service required of all young men. Reluctant, he wanted to evade the authorities if he could and emigrate, but the mission authorities convinced him that, if he were captured, he would bring disgrace to the church. So on May 1, 1880, he entered the army and was sent to Amager, near Copenhagen. After several weeks of drill and training, Carl and another man were chosen to be servants to higher officers. It meant freedom from drill and watches while he prepared breakfast for his officer, made the bed, and brushed his clothing. His officer, furthermore, was "a very kind & genial middle-aged man" who allowed Carl leave during the afternoon and evenings. Carl spent this free time working with the Mormon missionaries in that vicinity. In one final stroke of good fortune, in a traditional drawing held for the draftees after several months of service, "again the Lord blessed me." Carl drew a free number, releasing him from army service while the rest of the men in his company had to serve another six months.

On August 29, 1881, he sailed for England with 1,300 other Mormon immigrants from northern Europe. Only two days later on September 1 in Liverpool, he was one of 644 LDS passengers who boarded *Wyoming*, a ship of 3,832 tons under Captain C. Rigby. James Finlayson was in charge of the emigrants. They reached New York on September 15. Carl describes the voyage as pleasant, despite picking up a thriving colony of lice, but many of the other steerage folk suffered in the smelly holds where much seasickness did not improve appetites. The company left New York the evening of the *Wyoming*'s arrival by train and reached Salt Lake City on September 21.

The next day Carl Madsen hired out to Bishop Peter Barton of Kaysville. The Bartons were very kind to him, and Sister Barton, after his day's work on the farm, would sit up late with him, teaching him English. The local boys mocked and ridiculed him. They would draw a ring around him, poke him in the sides, and abuse him with "all kinds of vulgar language" which he could not understand but the meaning of which he grasped. The situation was so unendurable compared to his idealistic visions of Zion on earth that he again turned to the Lord. He recorded: "One early Sunday morning I walked to a point about a mile above Kaysville, and lying down among the sagebrush with my face in my hands, I pleaded with my Heavenly Father to release me from the torment which had hold upon me. I can truthfully testify that my unhappiness left me, & I became again a normal individual."

During the winter of 1881-82 he worked as a section hand for the Denver and Rio Grande Railroad. On March 16, 1882, he married Mary Harder. According to Carl's autobiography,

[Mary] was working at that time for Emaline B. Wells. I spent some happy evenings there for a couple weeks in which time we made up our mind to get married. We made arrangement [sic] for the big affair of our wedding day which was a very humble one indeed. ... We rented two little rooms somewhere in the eighth ward. And I admit it only took a little to fill them. So all we bought with the little money we had, not going in debt, was a little bedstead, a little table 20 by 30 inches, three chairs, a small stove with two holes, a few plates, cups and caucers and a couple knives and forks. ... Emaline B. Wells cooked our wedding supper. I had the honor of siting [sic] by the side of Daniel H. Wells, counselor to President Brigham Young. ... We was married in the old

Endowment House by Daniel H. Wells and in his house we had our wedding supper.[17]

They set up housekeeping in Riverton, their home for the rest of his life, where Carl worked at his trade as a carpenter. Mary bore two children, Carl (Charlie) and Mary, but died on January 24, 1885, before their third anniversary. Carl later wrote, "She died in my arms. It was an awful shock and unexpected."[18] Until he remarried three years later, he was forced to place the children with relatives or hire a house-keeper/caregiver.

Carl's version of how he overcame the opposition of Annie Crane's parents to the difference in their ages and the burden she would be assuming as a stepmother is an interesting lesson in human relationships. Carl described the event:

> Op north [Clarkston, Utah], a brother to Annie's mother he happined to come down to Heriman on a vesit wright at that time. So Annie's mother laded the matter before him about us young people, and got him to be the Juch, she made him aquainted with both of us, that is just by sith [chance?], i was building a House at Herriman at That time and i used to ride a gray Horse To Herriman every morning To work and i can see them now in my mind, as The whole Family standing out side The House, waiting for me to come, as i rote through the gate up towards the stable, and all looking at me, acorse i didn't know what They were up to—and after That Onkel of Annie's had taken a good look at me and my grey Horse, he turned To his sister Elisabeth Crane Annies mother, and sated Lize as he caled her, There is the man for your girl and after that everything went along, OK.[19]

Carl and Annie married in the Logan temple on November 30, 1887, and spent a two-week honeymoon with Annie's relatives in Clarkston before settling down in Riverton. Throughout his life Carl Madsen maintained his strong faith in his church, raised twelve children, operated a successful farm and small building business, and even-

---

17. Carl Madsen, "A Short History of the Life of Carl Madsen Bradt," n.d., corrected version edited by Robert Carter, p. 24, photocopy of holograph.

18. Ibid., 27.

19. This account is a single untitled, undated holograph page which I found among some scraps of Carl Madsen's notes given me by my aunt Jean Madsen.

The family of Carl Madsen and Annie Crane Madsen.
Back left: Alice, James, Malinda (Lynn), my father Brigham A. Madsen, Carl,
Keturah, and Alonzo. Front left: Mary, Annie, Annie Crane Madsen, baby Jean,
Carl Madsen, Desna, and Charley.

tually served three missions to Denmark. He converted an older
brother Niels, who immigrated to Utah in the fall of 1886 and also settled in Riverton. He was the only other member of the family to become a Mormon.

Annie, in addition to raising Charley and Mary, had ten children
of her own: James Emanuel, Malinda Annie Elizabeth, my father
Brigham Andrew, William Carl, Etty Keturah, Alice Fanny,
Frankland Alonzo, Annie Johanae, Desna Gwendolyn, and Delilah
Jean.

He was strict but fair, hard-working, a man of integrity and
honor. He also had a fiery temper. I remember one day when a young
heifer, that he was training to enter a stall, balked. In sudden exasperation, he jabbed her with a pitchfork, shouting, "My soul, I'll teach
you to do what I want you to do." The heifer immediately jumped
into her stall, and I immediately decided never to cross Grandpa
Madsen.

He was opposed to the silent movies of the time, believing them to be not only frivolous but a menace to moral values. It was with some trepidation, therefore, that his two youngest daughters, eighteen-year-old Desna and sixteen-year-old Jean, and I sneaked out through a basement window to see Rudolph Valentino in *The Sheik*. To my great relief, we were not apprehended. I was, however, caught one sabbath afternoon after church swimming in the canal with three cousins. I was confined to my room for the rest of the day without supper, although Grandma was able to get cookies and a glass of milk past his vigilant guard.

Grandpa did not observe his church's precepts in one particular. He just could not give up his taste for Danish beer, and Grandma indulged this peccadillo by often sending me to the village store to get a half dozen bottles of his favorite brand, always packed in a large grocery sack so the neighbors would not see what they already knew. I rather enjoyed these weekly journeys into sin in behalf of my otherwise circumspect grandfather.

When I was in the LDS Mission Home in Salt Lake City in July 1934 for a few days' training before I left for my mission to Tennessee, he drove the twenty miles to Salt Lake City so that I could spend the day with him at Riverton. It was early Sunday morning. There wasn't much traffic, and Grandpa barreled through every red light and stop sign, both coming and going, for the whole twenty miles. When I expostulated the first time that he shouldn't break the law this way, he answered, "My soul, there aren't any other cars in sight and besides this is the way I always drive in Riverton." That was a harrowing experience.

I sat in the adult class of Riverton Ward's Sunday school that day and watched my grandfather with amusement and admiration as he took on the entire class, contending that the Holy Ghost, or Comforter, was actually our Mother in Heaven, the wife of God the Eternal Father. He would neither shut up nor sit down, much to the teacher's exasperation. I have some of his religious notes which include such self-imposed questions as the following: "After we have gained our Salvation, and are worthy to mingle with the gods, shall we again become Mortel, and go Throu Life Exspirience, like our Father Adam," "in given a Revelation, could there be any chance of making a mistake when it is not given verbely," and "is it reasonable

To believe That God is the actsuel, or reall Father of The Billions of spirit That has lived on This Earth."[20]

Carl Madsen died in 1947, surrounded by most of his numerous family, and secure in the knowledge that there was a place waiting for him in heaven where he would be reunited with his two wives and where he could continue preaching the everlasting gospel. My father told me that about an hour before he died, he asked to go to the bathroom. My father and his younger brother assisted him to the toilet where Grandpa relieved his bowels. My father handed him a goodly portion of toilet paper, but Grandpa immediately tore off a single sheet and handed the rest back to Dad, exclaiming, "My soul, there is no need to waste things!" All of Carl Madsen's descendants treasure this little incident as utterly typical of Grandpa.

This look at the heritage of my immediate ancestors has perhaps gone on too long, but it has helped explain me to myself and even helped explain some of the qualities and characteristics of my children. The reader has no doubt noted that I have a great deal more information about my Madsen forebears than I do about the Cushings. This is because the Madsens have always been sufficiently devout Mormons to keep genealogical records, while the Cushings have approached their religion with a certain insouciance that has stopped short of worshipping at genealogical shrines. The standards and expectations that became guides for my own conduct are largely drawn from my parentage. Family traditions help explain who I am and give identity to my aspirations. These strands of hard work, Mormon devotion, an ingrained love for the scent of sawdust, and a considerable fund of stub-

---

20. Carl Madsen, undated and untitled page of notes. Mormons believe in a Godhead of three separate personages—the Father, Jesus Christ the Son, and the Holy Ghost. A few members agree with my grandfather that the Holy Ghost is our literal Mother in Heaven, but the 1995 excommunication of Janice Merrill Allred, who also advanced this view as her strictly personal opinion and not as church doctrine, indicates the nervousness of the institutional church in contemplating this possibility. (See her "Toward a Theology of God the Mother," in *Mother in Heaven and Other Essays* [Salt Lake City: Signature Books, 1997].) Mormon doctrine teaches that God the father is a personage of "body, parts and passions," the literal father of our spirits, which enter earthly bodies of flesh and bone at birth. The doctrine of "eternal progression" also holds out the possibility that worthy male members of the LDS church may some day become gods themselves, accompanied by their wives.

bornness came together in the early lives and marriage of my own mother and father.

3.

DAD, MOTHER,
AND FIVE LITTLE MADSENS

My father, christened Brigham Andrew Madsen, always hated "Andrew" so much that he never used it and was known universally as "Brig." He was born September 28, 1891, in Riverton, Utah, the third of my grandmother's ten children. I have an enlarged photograph of him at about age six with his brother Carl Jr., who was a year and a half younger. They are dressed in stiffly starched Little Lord Fauntleroy suits, long curls hanging nearly to their shoulders. This picture is quite deceiving and probably represents what their mother wished they were like. In reality, my father was a hardworking farm boy who received very little schooling and, from age seven to nine, was placed with an aunt and uncle in Herriman, as mentioned, working for his room and board while his father did missionary work in Denmark. As he wrote in a short autobiography of this period, "[I] used to get in to mischief like all boys do & on Sat when mother would come up to see us I used to get a whipping just as sure as Sat came. I used to be broken hearted. I didn't think I could stand it but I had to."[1]

There is no question of blaming my grandmother, who was coping in the best way she knew how, but I think of that little boy, longing yet dreading to see his mother for two years, and my heart aches for both of them. My father must also have longed for the return of his father,

---

1. Brigham Madsen, "My Life Story," 3, Jan. 25, 1958, Sacramento, California, holograph, 37 pp.

when the family could be united again. Yet whatever emotional satisfactions might have come, his life did not ease. Father and Carl were directed to clean out all the irrigation ditches on the Riverton farm and
"from then on it was nothing but work no play. all work. We couldn't
have a dog or a gun or we couldn't go fishing just work."

Nor was their family life the sentimentalized and nostalgic version
of the nuclear family that the ill-informed think of when they envision
the nineteenth-century family. My grandfather saw no need to control
his temper with his children and saw every harsh economic reason for
getting as much work out of them as was humanly possible. It was the
way he himself had been raised. I was raised with the same emphasis on
work, but my father never played the overbearing taskmaster with us.
Every year Dad and Carl were kept out of school for the spring planting for four or five weeks and then were sent back to class during the
last two or three days of school when the exams were given. My father
always did his best, but Carl rebelled one year and played hookey during exam week. When my grandfather found out about it, in a rage he
started for him. His mother told Carl "to run for his life" until Carl Sr.
got over his terrible anger. When my father was about seventeen, a
neighbor woman accused him of having gotten her daughter pregnant. He absolutely denied it and refused to run from his father's exploding temper. My grandfather picked up a buggy whip and gave my
father a terrible whipping on his bare back. Finally my grandmother, a
big, strong woman who towered over her husband, pinned my grandfather's arms to his side until he subsided. Another youth in the neighborhood later confessed to the moral offense.

At thirteen my father ended his fragmented schooling and began
working as a carpenter alongside his father who kept his wages as a
matter of course. My father never had control of the money he had
earned until, at seventeen, he left home to work with his older
brother, Charley, at Magna, Utah. They were helping to build a new
smelter for the copper company. My father began as an apprentice carpenter at $3 a day but was soon raised to $5 a day when his boss recognized that he was a skilled journeyman. With this newfound wealth,
he began his lifelong love affair with any kind of vehicle which had
speed and power, in this first instance a handsome horse and buggy.

After a few months he moved to Lark, Utah, a short distance
above Herriman to work on another mill and boarded with his par-

ents. His father was building a schoolhouse at Lark at the time, and Carl was working for him. Although my father was eighteen and on his own, my grandfather still expected instant obedience, leading to the following incident:

> One Friday night we [Carl and Brigham] wanted to go down to Riverton to the dance & Dad told us not to but we went anyway with my horse & buggy. So the next day was Sat Mother & him went home for Sunday & he was so mad because we went to that dance that he took my horse & Buggy home with him. ... I got the boss to let me off I hired a Saddle horse & went down home to get my horse & buggy & when he saw me he wanted to know what I was doing home when I should be at work. I told him I had come after my Horse & Buggy. But his dainish got up & he called the Sherriff & told me he would have me arested if I tried to take the horse & buggy. Mother put her arms around me and begged [me] to go back without the Horse & buggy so thats what happened so a week or so later I got it back.[2]

The incident is instructive for several reasons. In the first place, of all my grandfather's sons, Dad was most like him in disposition and determination, though not in temper. Once my father felt himself independent, they were a standoff. Second, as I was to learn, my dad's horse and buggy, or later his shiny new automobile was sacrosanct. And last it seems to me that Grandmother Madsen must have spent a good part of several years physically restraining either her husband or her son so that they would not commit mayhem on each other. They never did come to actual blows as adults; but after the horse and buggy incident, Dad began boarding with his maternal grandmother, Elizabeth Stewart Crane, at Herriman.

In the fall of 1909, my eighteen-year-old father went to Logan, Utah, to enroll in the Utah State Agricultural College, a land-grant institution, as one of a class of thirty-eight freshmen. His preparation for college had been skimpy, to say the least, but the first year at many small colleges in the early 1900s consisted of college preparatory courses—what today would be included in high school. He was determined to get a college education; and as far as I know, he was the only one of his brothers and sisters who had this lofty ambition. He had saved enough

2. Ibid., 6-7.

money to pay for his first year; but just after Christmas he contracted typhoid fever, spent three weeks in the hospital, and was forced to return to Riverton when his finances were exhausted. He received no help or encouragement from his father who thought he "should be home any way I was just waisting my time." I can understand why my father, from my earliest memory, insisted that I should get an education and always gave me every kind of support to achieve that goal.

He did not give up his dream; but after he recovered, he went to work, saved his money, and enrolled in the LDS Business College in Salt Lake City in the fall of 1910. Through his sister Mary he obtained a place to stay with a wealthy family named "Sailsberry." In exchange for room and board, he tended the furnace and did yard work. His sleeping quarters were in an attic "which was awfull. They treated me like I was a Poor Dog. So I stayed there for about 2 months till I couldn't stand it any longer." He moved in with Charley, who had married his wife, Pearl, and was living in the Sugarhouse neighborhood of Salt Lake City. Dad finished the quarter but again ran out of money and was forced to go back to carpentry. Determinedly, he saved enough money to return to Utah State College for the winter quarter of 1912. It was his last attempt to complete a college degree, but he always regretted his failure.

The day he died, November 5, 1959, at the age of sixty-eight of acute coronary occlusion, I wrote a tribute to him:

> My father was a man's man, a strong personality who demanded and received the respect of others and who was fearless when he thought he was in the right. A man of high integrity and morality, his word was his bond and he was scrupulously honest. His two chief loves were his work and his family. As a builder, he devoted himself energetically and with consuming interest to his work. He never asked any man to do any more than he did; and in all my life, I never met anyone who could match him in fierce energy and determined effort. He was an acknowledged leader in the field he loved best and usually and quite naturally assumed command of any building situation with which he was connected.
>
> His other love was his family and here he was gentle and devoted, often quite sentimental in his attachments. His chief concern was that his sons and daughters should be useful, straightforward, and law-abiding citizens. To this end, he sacrificed his own interests to see that they received as much education as they desired. He supported four of his five children on missions for the LDS Church. He taught them the meaning

of sacrifice and hard work; and as they measure up, so will he measure up.

In the final analysis, perhaps his finest attribute was his high sense of responsibility. When he tackled a job, he gave it the very best that was in him and never quit until it was finished.

To balance out this picture of esteem, I need to acknowledge that my father could be as blunt and direct as a bulldozer, especially if he felt he had been wronged. He tried to manage his children's affairs, even after we had families of our own; but Dad certainly exercised more self-control and more respect for others than his own father. I have a sense that he had reflected on his father's personality and made a conscious choice to have a different kind of family life. Obviously, he held the same firm opinions about the value and necessity of hard work, but any money we earned was ours, a very different arrangement from that practiced by Carl Madsen Bradt.

After leaving school for the last time, my father moved back to Riverton and entered a partnership on equal terms with his father in building a store in Magna. From this time on he followed the carpentry trade with occasional stints of farming. The partnership lasted for a year—1913. One of their projects was to buy a lot and build a three-room frame house in Magna. It is still standing in a run-down neighborhood of the generally improving town. Dad bought out Grandpa Madsen's interest in the house and rented it to Charley and Pearl, who moved to Magna in May 1913. Dad became their boarder, a satisfactory arrangement to all concerned. In July Dad was chopping wood in the backyard for Pearl, when his lack of a musical education attracted Mother:

> I was humming the chorus of some song ["My Wild Irish Rose," according to my mother] & that was all I knew of the song and Lydia my wife now was working for Mrs. Brown She ran a boardinghouse she [Lydia] was washing dishes & she called to me and asked me if that was all I knew of that song. And that started our romance. That night the Japanese that worked at the mill were putting on a fire works display So I asked her if she would like to walk with me up the hill to see the fireworks display She agreed From then on we kept company with one another. I had my horse & buggy there so we used to go riding at nights I remember one night it was moon light we sat in the buggy talking & she said she was getting tired frying eggs for those boarders over at Browns

My parents,
Lydia Cushing Madsen and Brigham A. Madsen,
on their wedding day, November 12, 1913.

So I said if she would like to come & fry eggs for me and she said she would like to So that night we decided we would get married on the 19th day of Nov.[3]

On November 1 Dad took my mother to Santaquin so he could meet her family and ask her father for her hand in marriage. Grandpa Cushing replied that "yes she sure could be the mother of a big family." My father, writing "My Life Story" forty-five years later, warmly testified, "And it turned out that she was the sweetest & best mother of 5 of the finest children that ever lived." They were married in the Salt Lake temple on November 12, 1913, Alvin T. Smith officiating. Charley and Pearl had already moved to a farm in West Jordan, so Mother and Dad set up housekeeping in the Magna house.

As is often true in successful marriages, my mother's nature was quite different from that of my father's, and the two complemented each other. Lydia Cushing was born in Santaquin, Utah, on December 11, 1891, the eleventh of twelve children born to Hosea Philip Cushing and Phoebe Nisonger Cushing: Philip Hosea, Chester Samuel, Henry Ellis, Sarah Helen, Heber Carlis, Phoebe Jane, Lucrishey

---

3. Ibid., 10.

Lydia Cushing, my mother, as an elementary school student.
She is in the back row, fourth from the left, wearing a ruffled white pinafore.

[Lucrezia] Vilate, William Heaman, Mary Emma, Charley, Lydia, and Myrtle. When Mother had completed the eighth grade, her principal was so impressed with her intelligence and academic potential that he made a special visit to plead with my grandparents to send her to Brigham Young Academy in Provo, Utah, a few miles away. His pleas were fruitless because the family could not afford it. Like my father, she always encouraged me in every way to "get an education."

Her family was close-knit and affectionate. They enjoyed each other's company and got together on every possible occasion to sing and have a good time. My mother never received any formal training on the piano but very early learned to "chord" and to accompany anyone who wished to sing. She was thrilled when Dad surprised her with a piano—I have no idea where he found the money—and we spent many an evening after supper singing the latest songs or the old favorites with Dad taking the lead, Mother playing and singing alto, while the rest of us chimed in as best we could. Mother taught us some ballads, folk songs, and old vaudeville tunes, my favorite being "The Preacher and the Grizzly Bear" which I have sung to my own children and grandchildren. I have always received the keenest pleasure from listening to any kind of music.

Dad enjoyed singing, but he was more of a storyteller. One dark and rainy night, he concocted a ghost story which came to a climax when, just on cue, an upper cupboard door unaccountably and silently swung open. Even Dad paused for a long moment, and we children pressed close to him, our eyes wide as saucers. He never told another ghost story that I can remember. Lacking a radio or television, I also resorted to storytelling to entertain the younger children when Mother and Dad went out in the evenings, which they did about once a week. One night I ventured a little magic by tying some dark thread around my ankles and then fastening the other end to the front legs of a dining room chair. The eerie effect of the chair, slowly "following" me along the hardwood floor as I backed away created even more fright than Dad's ghost tale. Even I didn't like it.

But our principal babysitting game was hide-and-go-seek confined to the house. This game also came to an end after I had the bright idea of hiding in the wooden clothes chute leading from the bathroom to the basement. I couldn't be found, but I also, unfortunately, couldn't get out. I was stuck fast. In a moment of inspiration, I had Annie sprinkle a cup of flour on all sides of me. It provided enough lubrication that the four of them, standing in the basement, could yank me on through at the count of three. I swore them to secrecy, but the flour would have given me away even if the temptation hadn't been utterly irresistible.

My mother was a hard-working homemaker who kept her house orderly and her children neat and clean. She had a rare ability to manage her strong-willed husband and a wonderful sense of humor. She was absolutely ferocious if anyone ever took advantage of her children. I shall never forget a minor difficulty I had with a neighbor boy whose mother called me an "alley rat." She barely escaped my hard-charging mother by locking the door before my mother could reach her.

But with these rare flashes of temper, Mother was a congenial, friendly, and hospitable person whose first greeting to any visitor was, "Will you have something to eat with us?" She fed anyone or anything that looked the least bit hungry. She adapted very easily to new situations and had a quiet strength. She mostly followed Dad's lead; but when she took a rare stand, my father fell into line. She was very tender-hearted; when I left home at age nineteen to serve a proselyting mission in Tennessee for the LDS church, she was broken-hearted at my departure. I remember her exclaiming to Dad, "It seemed like we were driving him away from home like a dog." She certainly wanted me to go and no pains had been spared in making a ceremonial fuss over my departure, but her tender heart was wrung at this first departure from the family circle.

The Cushings and Madsens were very different in their outlook toward life. Both were independent and self-sufficient; but while the Cushings looked upon money, wealth, and property as the means toward good fellowship, a satisfying life, and generosity toward others, the Madsens considered wealth and property as an end in themselves—a status symbol. If the two families had ever philosophized a little, the Madsens would have asked why the Cushings didn't want to get ahead and build up an estate, while the Cushings would have asked why the Madsens didn't want to enjoy life instead of money-grubbing every blessed minute.

As I review my life, it seems clear that I have gravitated between these two points of view with quite happy results. I followed my Madsen traditions long enough to accumulate a little substance but finally returned to my Cushing roots to enjoy the daily pleasures of family life, friendships, and work that is satisfying as well as remunerative.

On October 21, 1914, eleven months after their marriage, I arrived at our Magna house. I was named Brigham for my father and Dwaine as a middle name. "Dwaine" is what my family and friends still call me, but the U.S. Army's custom of using everybody's first name regardless of preference means that most people who met me as an adult know me as "Brig."

My birth came just one day after my father was laid off from his carpentry job building the Magna smelter. As he wrote later, "Mother and I had a tough time." Following the construction trade is a hit-or-miss affair but it does teach resilience and fortitude.

My earliest recollection is being given a piece of ice by the ice man who made his daily rounds with a horse and wagon to fill the household refrigerators. As he drove slowly down the street, I hitched a ride

My first official portrait, Brigham Dwaine Madsen, with my parents,
Brig and Lydia Madsen, in early 1915.

on the back step until my mother, yelling at the top of her voice, stopped the wagon and retrieved me. I must have been about two.

I remember our three-room house well and also our first automobile, a Dart touring car that my father purchased on the installment plan. I was present when Dad tried to teach Mother to drive one evening on a country road outside Magna. My mother backed the car into a ditch while trying to turn it around. Dad, completely exasperated, had to hire a nearby farmer to pull the vehicle out. Mother never did become a skilled driver, although she could drive in an emergency.

My sisters, Annie LaRae (she later went by Ann) and Phyllis, were born in the Magna home on April 14, 1916, and November 26, 1918, respectively. Dad was still working at the smelter; but after Uncle Charley was almost killed in an accident there, Dad quit in the winter of 1918-19. "I thought I wanted to be a farmer," he confessed.

He purchased a small acreage on the "flats" above Riverton but soon found out he "didn't know much about farming." My mother always claimed that he failed because he couldn't make the irrigation water run uphill, and it was true that his driving nature lacked the patience required by maturing crops. A vignette is revealing of his personality. When a stubborn cow refused to come in, Dad angrily set off in pursuit, ignoring the fact that he was riding bareback and that I was behind him. I was four, and I remember the wild ride, clutching Dad desperately around the waist. Mother, horrified, shouted at him to put me down, but Dad grimly rode through the canal and over fences until he corralled the critter. I would have voted with Mother on her proposal, but I needed both hands to hang on, and I reflect with a certain amount of

I was a chubby and happy toddler in the fall of 1915, about one year old.

pride that I neither fell off, got bounced off, nor let go in panic.

I later learned another vignette completely typical of Dad from an old Magna friend. When Dad was still working at the mill in about 1916, the foreman, who was also a big man, had been "riding" Dad and, during one lunch break, said something which prompted Dad to challenge him. The bare-knuckles encounter continued for about fifteen minutes. The two fell on the conveyor belt carrying ore to the crusher but wouldn't stop fighting. The other men had to drag them off the belt before they entered the crusher. It was a draw, but apparently the foreman treated my father with greater respect after that.

In the early fall of 1919, after Dad gave up the farm, we moved to a rented house in Riverton where Dad got a job helping to build a flour mill. After it was completed, the same construction company offered Dad and Uncle Carl, who by now had married Dora Hibbard, jobs building another flour mill in Pocatello, Idaho, then the second largest city in Idaho—population 15,000. We moved there during late

November 1919 and rented an apartment on north Arthur Street. Dad did not actually work on the Pocatello mill but was shifted instead to the Bannock Hotel, also under construction in Pocatello. During my youth it was the finest structure in town at the time. After a few weeks we moved into the back two rooms of a rented house in the Greek-Italian section of the town on the east side near the St. Anthony Hospital.

My father then became ill with smallpox and for about two months hovered between life and death. This was probably the low point in my parents' lives. Mother was alone in a strange city with no money and a desperately ill husband. The Greek owner of the small store across the street took pity on her and advanced groceries to her, an act which can only be described as compassionate charity in light of the odds against my father's recovery. One day Mother found me sitting on the curb in front of our home, eating the peelings from an orange which a more prosperous little boy was passing to me as he ate the orange.

Dad finally struggled out of bed and returned to work, although he was so weak that, on his first day back, the foreman put him in the basement of the hotel with instructions to hide out for a couple of days. It was a rough and ready form of sick leave—and another act of compassion to get Dad on the payroll again.

In the fall of 1920 Dad went to work for the Union Pacific Railroad as a carpenter on the "rip track." His duties were to repair railroad cars and to go out with the crew when there were wrecks along the line. He purchased a small house on north Garfield Avenue, where my brother Mack James was born on November 26, 1920. We lived in the back two rooms and rented the front two after Dad remodeled it into a duplex.

That fall I entered first grade at the Lincoln School, a few weeks before my sixth birthday. I was a shy, timid, introspective little boy and must have been a great disappointment at the time to my outgoing, aggressive, and self-confident father. One morning when Dad was at home, I dawdled so long at breakfast that Mother knew I would be late for school. But Dad insisted I eat every morsel before being allowed to depart. When I reached the school, classes were already in session. I was afraid to go in, so I turned around and went back home. But that was like jumping from the frying pan into the fire because Dad at once marched me back and stood in the hall until I crept into the awful stillness of my classroom.

After a year on Garfield Avenue, Dad sold the newly-remodeled house for a good profit, rented a house for four months at the packing plant north of Pocatello, bought three contiguous lots on Park Avenue in the small subdivision of Fairview on the northeast section of the town, and built a small temporary three-room house near the back of the central lot. By this time Dad was working steadily for local contractors. He was earning a dollar an hour—very respectable wages for the time—and the bank loaned him enough money to build a large house—at least for that time, although it looks rather small to me today. Charles Rodney (he went by "Rod"), the last child in the family, was born in this house at 243 Park Avenue on June 16, 1923.

A very candid shot of the family in early 1921. May father is holding Phyllis on his knee and baby Mack in his arm, flanked by face-making Ann and me, squinting. We were in the doorway of our home on Garfield Avenue in Pocatello, Idaho.

My memories of the family's fifteen years in this house are always colored with comfort, cleanliness, and the smells of good cooking. Built in the traditional bungalow style of the 1920s, it had a big front porch with a swing that provided hours of entertainment. My parents slept in one of the main floor bedrooms, my sisters in the other. In the basement Mack and Rod shared one room while I had the dignity of one to myself. Our single bathroom was on the main floor, along

I am holding the cake for my eighth birthday at our house on Park Aveue, Pocatello.

with a small living room and an even smaller dining room. But the place where we lived was the large kitchen where a coal-fueled Monarch stove provided a warm focus around which we gathered. Dad later installed a coal-burning furnace in our basement.

Monday morning was devoted to the laundry, with Mother working away at our wringer washing machine in the basement and hauling baskets of damp clothes upstairs to be hung on the outdoor clothesline. Monday afternoons she traditionally baked six or seven loaves of bread.

Mother's bread was delicious, and we devoured it at every meal along with a good helping of No. 1 russet potatoes: fried, scalloped, boiled, baked, or mashed. When there was nothing else to eat, there were always potatoes. Later when people asked how I grew so tall, I always rejoined, "Idaho spuds!" Every Saturday afternoon my parents made a shopping foray to O. P. Skaggs or the Piggly Wiggley in downtown Pocatello. A week's food cost about ten dollars. If we ran short during the week, Mother would send one of us over to Reed White's small store a block away on Wayne Avenue where a loaf of bread cost a nickel.

Fairview was soon transformed into the Village of Alameda, with a separate city government and its own police force in the person of Constable Ira Stokes. Our closest neighbors were the Bentleys, the Reynolds, and the Coffins. Ellis Bentley and H. C. Coffin were some

of my first boyhood friends. Alameda was a pretty, little, tree-lined settlement but a poor one. Many of the residents were "hill-billies" from
the Cumberland Mountains in eastern Tennessee who had followed
the Union Pacific Railroad to a new start in Idaho. Most worked for
the railroad, and the sounds of train whistles from the nearby yards
lulled all of us to sleep each night. When I first left Pocatello, I was
lonesome for the long, mournful night sounds of the engines.

I attended the newly-constructed Roosevelt School at the edge of
Alameda for second and third grades, but have virtually no memories
of those two years. At the end of third grade, my mother, to her shock,
received the report that I would be "returned" for a year. When she
visited my teacher to discover what was wrong, the teacher told her
that I had spent the past year staring out the window. Mother persuaded the teacher that I was mentally competent, and I was passed
into the fourth grade. I would never underrate my mother's powers of
persuasion, but my private theory is that the teacher could not face the
prospect of my vacant face for another year and was glad for an excuse
to pass me on to someone else.

That someone else turned out to be Miss Phillips, one of only five
teachers in my first fourteen years of school whom I can still remember
after the passage of sixty years or more. I have always felt it a tragedy
that I had so few effective teachers that I could count them on the fin-
gers of one hand; and perhaps this fact had something to do with my
own lively interest in the art of teaching when it became my own career. Miss Phillips took an interest in me, discovered that I had the be-
ginnings of a brain, praised me when I led the class in learning the
multiplication tables, and transformed me into something of a scholar.
Miss Holbrook continued this revitalizing work in the fifth and sixth
grades. By the time I was ready for junior high school, I had discovered
my identity. I had the sense that I could, by mighty efforts, make
something of myself. I even discovered classical music from Miss Holbrook who tutored a few of us so we could participate in a district-
wide contest to identify correctly composers and representative pieces.
I named every one correctly and proudly brought home an engraved
certificate. My parents, who always encouraged my efforts, shared in
my victory.

Of the many sensitive and kind things which my mother did for
me through her long life, I remember one especially which was so

typical of her and recorded it in a short essay at the invitation of Carma Wadley, a *Deseret News* staff writer. It was published with the contributions of six others as "From Christmases Past, Gifts That Make Memories," on December 18, 1980:

> I grew up in Pocatello, Idaho; the oldest child in a family of five children and with parents for whom I had the greatest love and respect. My father and mother did not have much formal education, and although we never starved or froze, we certainly were not wealthy.
>
> From so far back that I can't remember, my parents encouraged me and my brothers and sisters to "get an education." It was easy for me to respond because I have always loved books and have been an inveterate reader. But, except for a "doctor book," and a few other miscellaneous volumes, my parents' library was composed of two books: Swift's *Gulliver's Travels* and Scott's *Ivanhoe*—that's all. As a boy I read each of them several times, and they still remain my favorites today. But I was starved for reading material.
>
> My mother recognized this longing in me; and although we couldn't afford it, one Christmas while I was in the fifth or sixth grade, she contracted to purchase by the month a set of encyclopedias, *The Book of Knowledge*. I thought at the time it was the most wonderful present that I [and my siblings] had ever received.
>
> The books opened up a whole new world to me, and I sat down and read all 20 volumes. The illustrations of the Vikings' ships and the pyramids and "Washington Crossing the Delaware"—all these plus much more, excited my boy's imagination and created my first interest in history—an interest which I finally adopted as a lifelong profession.

As a sad and revealing postscript, I should add that, after several months' possession—and fortunately after I had been through them—my mother was forced to return them because she could not keep up the monthly payments.

Dad did not profess much interest in religion during my childhood although he made no attempt to conceal his identification as a Mormon. Mother usually took us children to Sunday school and Primary (a weekly meeting for children up to about age twelve or thirteen). Mormons were a distinct minority in Pocatello during the 1920s, but there were still enough to make up six congregations of about 200 or 250 each. We were members of the Fourth Ward, the poorest of the lot.

Dad considered Sunday "free" time, meaning free to spend on one of his own projects. Usually he worked on houses for himself,

which he built, then sold, or for someone else. He and Mother socialized with his carpenter friends, most of whom were non-LDS and
often non-religious.

As a railroad junction, Pocatello was also a strong union town and
Local Union No. 1258 of the United Brotherhood of Carpenters &
Joiners of America had about thirty or so members. Dad was proposed
as the president of the local but declined because he was terrified of
speaking in public meetings. Instead, he was its secretary-treasurer for
two or three years. Our social life was very much tied up with the
members of the union. The annual Labor Day picnic was one of the
big events of the year for our family, and I still have a photograph,
taken about 1924, of the members and their families, the men in straw
hats and ties, the mothers surrounded by their coveys of children.

Mother and Dad also socialized as a couple with other carpenters
in the union and their wives. Because the Roaring Twenties offered
new freedom from the prim Victorian values under which they had
grown up, my parents partied a lot until Mother decided things were
getting out of hand. The final straw for her came when some of the
other wives began making passes at Dad, who was tall, handsome, vigorous, and not above flirting back. He never stepped over the moral
boundaries of his strict Mormon upbringing, but Mother did not like
the trend. Since I continually and loudly announced that I didn't want
to attend church but wanted to work with Dad, Mother decided it was
time to lay down the law. I must have been about twelve—ready for
ordination to the Aaronic priesthood—when she announced that she
would not attend one more party and intended to have no more to do
with the carpenter crowd. I remember overhearing part of the discussion that followed.

For one of the few times in his life, Dad had met an ultimatum.
Would he socialize without Mother? It was as much as announcing
that the marriage was ending. Could he change her mind or work out
a compromise? The thought may have crossed his mind, but it soon
withered under Mother's implacable determination. Dad made his decision and, with his usual bluntness, told his friends he would have no
more to do with them although he remained a dues-paying member of
the union. He cut his social ties to them cleanly and irrevocably. The
crisis was over. Mother had won, and Dad started to go to church. Our
lives were changed from then on.

In this new phase Dad became a committed churchgoer, but he retained a goodly amount of skepticism. Just a few months before his death, he decided to read the Bible, which he had never even looked at before. Each weekend as I visited him, he gave me reports about where he was in the text. Finally, one Sunday he announced that, when he reached the story of Jonah and the whale, he decided that the Bible was nothing but baloney and slammed the book decisively shut. To my knowledge, he never opened it again.

He was not a well-read man but had a good share of common sense which he was not afraid to exercise at appropriate times. I shall never forget my embarrassment when, as a twelve-year-old, I sat in our ward's priesthood quorum and listened to a discussion of the Word of Wisdom—a Mormon dietary law forbidding the use of tobacco, coffee, and alcoholic beverages. One good brother rose to testify that he never drank coffee whereupon my father arose to announce that he *did* drink coffee and wanted everyone to know it, unlike the previous speaker who was a pure hypocrite because my father had seen him drink coffee on numerous occasions. In retrospect, I am less embarrassed and considerably prouder of my father's forthrightness.

When rumors began to spread through the ward that this same man was having an affair with the wife of another member, Dad took direct action. As Dad and I entered the chapel one Sunday morning, this man was at the front door welcoming the members. Without even an opening "hello," Dad asked, "Is it true, Brother [_____], that you're keeping company with Sister [____]?" I wish now I'd waited for the answer. Instead I hurriedly sneaked into the chapel and hid in the corner.

Mother found it easy to work in church positions and adapted well to the life of a congregation, including a term as Relief Society president. In addition to his lack of diplomacy, Dad was terrified of speaking in public. As a result, despite his obvious leadership ability, he refused all efforts to give him a teaching or leadership calling.

Fourth Ward met in a small warehouse-type frame building which had to be separated into Sunday school classrooms by drawing curtains. It was large enough for basketball games during the weekly Mutual Improvement Association (MIA) meetings, and we also held dances there. Eventually, as economic conditions improved somewhat, my father was chosen in 1934 to build a new chapel. Again I was his chief crew and ran the concrete mixer and helped with carpentry. The new building was not finished by the time I left on my mission, and I made my farewell speech from the rostrum of the old, somewhat dilapidated building.

Although I was an active member of Fourth Ward, I spent a great deal of time attending other churches as well. Nearly all my close friends were Baptists, Presbyterians, or Catholics. With Sam Garrett, I attended BYPU (Baptist Young People's Union) services almost as often as I attended my own MIA meetings. I went to Presbyterian church services with Raymond and Baron Pearson and heard my first Catholic mass with Maurice Remington. By the time I had finished my second year of college, I was quite ecumenical as far as religion was concerned.

But the dominant feature of my youth was work. Work has always been central in my life. My father's constant aphorisms to me were: "You'll never learn any younger"; "If a thing is worth doing at all, it's worth doing well"; and "Hurry up and get the damn thing done." He would come into my bedroom about 6:00 o'clock every morning and say, "It's time to get up and get the stink off you."

One of my earliest recollections is the morning when I was seven when Dad announced that it was "high time you learned the trade." I knew just what he meant, gleefully picked up my hammer, and followed him up the ladder to the roof of the house he was building next door where I enthusiastically started whacking nails into shingles. Mother stood at the foot of the ladder expostulating that I was too young, that the roof was too steep, and that I would kill myself before I learned anything. Her not unreasonable concern made no impression on Dad, and I have been assembling construction materials into organized chaos ever since.

There was always something to do around the house and yard, especially for the oldest son who was considered a man from a very early age. We always had a large garden which I was expected to weed and irrigate. And then there were the chickens, rabbits, and family cow to feed and take care of. I learned to milk the cow at about age twelve and can still remember how comforting it was to snuggle up to the old Jersey's flanks on a frosty morning when our breaths filled the stable with steam. I was also responsible for feeding the chickens and rabbits.

Dad loved rabbit meat, but Mother thought a skinned rabbit car-cass looked too much like that of a cat and refused to eat the meat. I was ten when Dad first told me to go kill and dress a couple of young rabbits. Mother intervened, pointing out that I was only ten. Why didn't my father take care of that chore? Dad answered, "He won't learn any younger." Between tears I clubbed two of my pets on the head behind their ears, then skinned and cleaned them. The truth was, as I learned later, that Dad was too tender-hearted to kill the rabbits himself. I was the rabbit butcher for three or four years until we stopped raising rabbits.

During the winter months, my time after school and on Saturdays went into helping Dad build, first our home at 243 Park Avenue, and then houses on the two flanking lots. In 1928 Dad bought an old frame house; he and I tore it down and hauled the lumber to the rear of our home. I spent an entire winter pulling nails from the lumber and stack-ing it up each evening after school. By using this wood, we con-structed a new house on the lot south of our home with only $350 worth of new material. From about age fourteen on, each evening and Saturdays I was kept busy lathing the walls, painting, and doing what-ever else was necessary. A year later we repeated the process by tearing down an old bowling alley and using the lumber to construct a house on the north lot. The younger children were also harnessed to work on the second house. There was never much time to play until dark-ness brought a few hours to engage in "Run, sheepy, run" or some other outdoor game.

The summer I was nine, two other boys and I were hired to herd some cows gathered up each day from various families in the village. We would collect them every morning about 8:00 o'clock, drive them about a mile away to the grassy banks of the canal, allow them to graze all day, and then return them to their owners by 5:00 P.M. This wasn't work but pure fun. We ran around like naked aborigines all day, swimming, sun-bathing, and having a glorious time.

For about a month one summer in my early teens, my sister Ann and I picked peas with Mexican field workers to buy our school clothes. The strains of the song "Ramona" always remind me of that venture. Every fall some schools took a two-week recess so that the students were available to pick potatoes after a plow had turned them up to the surface. It was back-breaking work, picking the spuds into a basket, and then pouring them into sacks, but I seldom passed it up. The cash was too tempting.

My first "real" job outside the family occurred when I was about eleven. (Dad remembered that I was only eight, but I think time exaggerated his memory of my youth.) Dad decided to get me a summer job on a farm so I wouldn't be lying around with the "lazy" neighborhood boys. Part of one summer, my friend Claris ("Cassicks") Johnson and I accepted an arrangement—probably engineered by the Johnsons—to thin and hoe a large field of sugar beets for a farmer about six miles away. We received $4 an acre for thinning and $2 an acre for each of two hoeings. The job took much of the summer. We rode our bikes out each Monday morning, lived in a tent at the edge of the field, and ate mostly sandwiches and food our mothers prepared on the weekends. When Grandmother Cushing visited the family for a few days that summer, she exclaimed to my mother, "Bless my soul, are you so poor that you have to let him go out & work on a farm to make a living?" Dad thought it was good for me and would teach me independence and how to be self-sufficient. I didn't have much choice in the matter; still I felt rather proud to be considered competent and confident enough to be on my own. I was also glad to have the chance to earn my own school money and not be dependent on someone else for it. Still, the sight of a short-handled thinning hoe brings twinges to my lower back.

The next summer, when I was twelve, Dad convinced a local drugstore owner who also ran a large farm outside of Pocatello that I was a competent farm worker and could run a hayrack. The truth was I had never been even close to a horse and knew nothing about putting up hay. But meeting my dismay with his usual argument— "You'll never learn any younger"—the next morning he deposited me bright and early at the farm with a large crew of hay hands. The foreman pointed out the team I was to drive, showed me where the harness was, and left.

Several of us were working side by side in the barn getting our teams harnessed. I placed the first collar around the neck of the nearest horse—upside down. The man next to me glanced over, then asked, "Hell, kid, haven't you ever harnessed a horse?" When I answered in the negative, he helped me get the team ready and hooked to the hayrack. By this time the foreman had also noted that I was a useless greenhorn, but he did not have a replacement, so he was stuck with me for the day. Fortunately, the horses seemed to know where to go and followed another wagon out to the hay field.

I didn't know anything about holding a tight rein on my frisky team. They hit the corrugations of the irrigated fields at a good clip and bounced one of my hay pitchers from the rack. By sheer good luck, I was able to deliver the first load to the stack without mishap but lost half of the second load when I approached a ditch crossing at an angle. The foreman cussed and fumed but kept instructing me in the intricacies of managing a team until, by the end of the day, I was a passable hay hand. I worked for a week or two until the hay was in the stacks. Dad was right; I couldn't learn any younger. I guess the fact that I didn't get myself killed convinced him that I was ready to spend the next summer, when I was thirteen, in Riverton with his parents, working with Grandpa. I survived that experience, too.

By the time I reached Benjamin Franklin Junior High in Pocatello, I had somehow become an inveterate reader. In addition to *The Book of Knowledge,* I devoured several Wild West magazines each week, trading copies with a group of like-minded boys who thrilled at the action stories of Max Brand, Clarence Mulford, B. M. Bower, and others. I was quite disappointed later in my boyhood to discover that B. M. Bower was a woman. I naively puzzled over how such a thing could be. What did a woman know about rustlers, and ranchers, and gunfighters? I'm pleased to say that my respect for women's abilities to write authentic history and authoritative fiction has improved considerably from that initial disillusionment.

I made a wonderful discovery at Franklin Junior High. Just a block away was a small one-room frame library. I don't think I realized before this that such institutions existed. Furthermore, I could take out four books at a time—about a week's reading. Here I discovered Tarzan of the Apes, endless adventures, animal stories, and westerns by authors such as Zane Grey. I'll admit that I was not much attracted to Shakespeare, Thoreau, or John Stuart Mill, but the improbable tales on which I gorged myself corrupted my soul only a little and certainly taught me to be the rather fast reader I am today.

Franklin Junior High also introduced me to a world larger than Alameda. Pocatello, as a railroad town, had attracted people of many different nationalities and was a microcosm of some of the larger cities of America. There were small enclaves of Greek, Italian, Chinese, Japanese, African Americans, and other nationalities and races scattered through the town. The Shoshone and Bannock reservation at Fort Hall was only twelve miles away. In my seventh grade home room, my seat-mate was Sam Hashimoto. The next year I sat next to Dominic Lucarelli, whose parents had just come to the United States from Italy. Just down Park Avenue from our house was my friend, Ed Goins, an African American. His father was a porter for the railroad. Until I left Pocatello on my mission at nineteen, I really thought that the world at large was like my home town, composed of people of many nationalities who, from my youthful perspective, accepted one another as members of the human race and as good Americans and who never thought much of intolerance or misunderstanding among peoples of different skin color or language. Whatever the realities for the ethnic adults in Pocatello—and I'm sure they were more complex than I sensed as a youngster—my life in Pocatello is a legacy for which I shall always be grateful.

Some might think my childhood and youth were hard and limited. Although some aspects of it were hard, I have no regrets. My family was a center of stability and positive encouragement.

4.

GROWING UP
WITH CALLOUSES

The decade of the 1920s spanned an important period of my life, from age six to sixteen. It was the age of "Flaming Youth" and Frederick Lewis Allen's *Only Yesterday,* a rapid and explosive change in traditional mores and values. I, of course, did not understand any of this and only by looking back can I perceive what was happening.

In some ways, because it was on a transcontinental railroad route, Pocatello was a rather cosmopolitan little place. My parents' move to the town attracted some of their relatives from more conservative Utah. My mother's sister, Mary, and her husband Art Newland, and a brother, Chet, with his wife Hilda, came to Pocatello as did two of my father's brothers, Charley and Pearl, and Lon and his wife Leone. The two cousins with whom I had the most in common and who were my age were George (Mary's son) and Francis (Chet's son). We, therefore, had relatives in addition to friends with whom to share the delights of the 1920s. Our relationship with Chet's family came to an abrupt end, however, when at a social gathering which involved a little beer-drinking, my father, unaccustomed to the beverage, began dancing with every woman in sight, much to the horror of my aunt Hilda. But there were still Mary, Charley, and Lon.

A cousin in her early twenties, Gertrude Hanson, the daughter of Mother's sister Vilate and Charles Hanson, came from Utah to live with us for a year while she worked as a supervisor for the telephone company. She was a typical "flapper" of the day and insisted that my mother was not at all a "Modern Millie" unless she cut her beautiful long hair. One afternoon while we children were at school and my father at work, Mother gave in to temptation and allowed Gertrude to "bob" her hair. When all of us and Dad arrived home, Mother was sitting in the kitchen crying; and when we saw her hair sticking out in every direction like that of a "wild man from Borneo," as Dad put it, we all felt like crying too. She was a mess! But when she recovered from the shock, she bought some curling irons, learned to "marcel" her hair, and began to patronize the new beauty parlors which were coming into existence.

The 1920s were the era of the automobile, and Dad was able to indulge his taste for speed and power. He would have related to the story of the woman who was asked why they had a car but no bathtub and replied, "Why, you can't go to town in a bathtub." My father was obsessed with automobiles. Despite the objections of my mother, he traded off the first three-room house he had built in Alameda for a Hupmobile touring car but only after first trying it out on the special hill in Pocatello where all new cars were tested for power. I was along for the trial and remember we didn't make it all the way to the top, but Dad took the car anyway. Mother was furious because she had intended to rent the house to obtain a little extra income. From this time on, we were always in debt for a car, and the monthly payments were the bane of Mother's existence.

I started driving at about age twelve when Dad ordered me to take our old Dodge pick-up to the lumber yard for some material he needed in a hurry. I was glad to have the opportunity and have been driving ever since. There was no state law at the time about a minimum age.

The great invention of the 1920s was the radio. My first experience was a crystal set with earphones owned by the Pearson family. I remember once sitting up with Raymond and Baron Pearson until about 2:00 A.M. so that we could pick up the jazz sound of Red Nichols and His Five Pennies all the way from Denver. When Dad and Mother bought our first Atwater-Kent cabinet set, it seemed as though the portals of paradise had been opened to us. In the late 1920s you could walk down the street on a summer's evening and never miss a line of *Amos and Andy*. Nothing rivaled it in national popularity until the TV production of *M*A*S*H* in the 1970s.

Another sign of the times in the early 1920s was the appearance of the Ku Klux Klan in quiet Pocatello. The effect on our family was sudden and dramatic. Apparently, a Kleagle (salesman) received permission to speak at one of the carpenters' local meetings and convinced the members that grave danger was threatening the United States; unless all 100 percent Americans joined the Klan to ward off this danger, our very lives were at stake. Evidently, everyone joined, including my father.

I am fairly certain that he didn't know anything about the Klan and was carried along by the rhetoric of the Kleagle with the rest of his carpenter friends. The next night he bundled Mother and us children into the Hupmobile and drove to downtown Pocatello. He parked in front of the high school on Arthur Street, then disappeared. Next a parade of white-sheeted men marched south down the street past our car. After the parade came a display of fireworks on the hills west of town. I remember the American flag and Abraham Lincoln's log cabin home. It was quite late when Dad rejoined his shivering family in the open Hupmobile.

I think I was seven or eight at the time, but I'll never know because the subject was taboo in our home forever afterward. Mother later told me that Dad resigned the next day, having been a member of the KKK for only thirty-six hours. He had evidently discovered the objectives of the Klan and was truly mortified at his gullibility. He never mentioned joining it; and when I was old enough to understand the implications, I would not embarrass him by asking about it.

The "noble experiment" of Prohibition also had an impact on our family. Probably because everyone else was making home brew and because Dad liked an ice-cold drink after a hot day on the job, one evening he announced that he was going to make some beer and that, as the oldest son, I would have the privilege of helping him. (This, of course, was before he got religion.) We set up shop down in the basement, using one of the many formulas for the brew which seemed to be easy to obtain. I helped cap the bottles and, after a proper waiting period, we put a few bottles on the ice in our refrigerator.

I was allowed only a sip or two and it seemed unpleasantly bitter, so I was not enticed to try more. Dad, however, enjoyed the drink and, when it was consumed, decided to make a second batch. One awful night we were all jolted out of our beds when several of the bottles blew up, spewing their contents all over the basement ceiling. Mother would have absolutely nothing to do with the process and was quite pleased that the explosion had occurred, especially since Dad never tried a third batch.

When I was about ten, I became the direct beneficiary of Prohibition. One summer for several weeks, we boys noticed a strange and elusive sweet-sour smell which seemed to permeate the air in our section of Alameda. The conundrum was solved one afternoon when a group of federal agents swooped down on our neighbor's chicken coop directly across the alley. I watched in intense admiration as the "G Men" efficiently dismantled a beautifully-designed copper still hidden among the chickens. While our handcuffed neighbor was being hustled off, the other "revenooers" used sledge hammers to flatten all the copper pots, boilers, and pipes which had once been a moonshiner's dream. When they finished, I timidly approached the agent in charge and asked if I could have the copper, having some knowledge of the worth of the metal to scrap dealers. He agreed but warned me that if I wished to sell it, I would first have to get a permit from the local police station. Faced with this fearsome prospect and also with the necessity of having to pull my heavily-laden red wagon almost two miles to the scrap metal warehouse, I enlisted the aid of my friend, Ellis Bentley, for a 50 percent share in the profits. We made $2 each out of the transaction.

Prohibition, the KKK, radio, the change in hair and clothing styles, and fast automobiles were just a part of the tremendous social changes of the Roaring Twenties. To my parents and other adults, these changes were no doubt earth-shaking and disturbing. But to me the Roaring Twenties were a panorama of new and exciting challenges. The great stock-market crash of October 1929 brought many of the dreams to an end and introduced a somber note into our lives. I had just turned fifteen when it happened.

That Christmas Eve I found my mother crying in the kitchen because she had practically no presents for the children. Her tears really affected me. I had been hoarding a fifty-cent piece, my only cash, for some weeks, to be used in some future wild personal extravagance. Instead, without saying anything to Mother, I caught the bus and rode downtown to Reed's Riteway Hardware Store. I purchased two small pocketknives at a dime each for my brothers and two ten-cent vials of perfume for my sisters. The bus fare was a nickel each way, so I arrived home flat broke but with the spirit of Christmas writ large in my heart.

The presents helped a little to assuage Mother's despair, and I felt re-warded for my sacrifice.

Another change was that coal became too expensive for us, so we turned to wood from the mountains. From age sixteen to seventeen, I spent many an evening sawing and chopping up the firewood. When our shoe soles wore through, we glued on ten-cent rubber soles from Woolworth's.

We still ate fairly well because a dime would also buy a hundred-pound sack of Idaho No. 1 russet potatoes. Other food commodities were correspondingly cheap if you had the cash. For two weeks one summer, I raked leaves for the Village of Alameda under the New Deal's WPA program. That was the only concession my family made in search of public relief. We continued to scrounge and make our way, along with most of our neighbors. It was good to have a father who was an industrious "rustler" after every opportunity which would provide food and clothing for his family. And somehow we managed.

In the ninth grade, I met the third of the five teachers who im-pressed me. Miss Moore, with red hair and pince-nez, was a strict dis-ciplinarian. I will never forget the terrible day when Bud Wadsworth, a BMOC, in an idle moment carved his initials on his desk top. When it was discovered, all classwork came to an end, while Miss Moore stood over Bud who used sandpaper and varnish furnished by the jani-tor to erase the offending letters.

She had a favorite topic—algebra—and turned her classroom into a holy shrine for its learning. Each Friday the members of the class, one by one, were called to the front of the room to receive our weekly ex-ams, always accompanied by a scolding if we had not reached our po-tential or a word of praise if we had advanced a little. Then, at a signal from Miss Moore, we all arose and moved to the seat we had earned or lost as a result of our test scores. To sit in the front seat of the row next to the window was the throne of grace; to be in the last seat next to the interior wall was to be in hades. And yet Miss Moore was careful not to degrade those of less mental competence. She always encouraged the slightest sign of progress on the part of those whose mathematical skills were not the best.

Tenth grade required another change of schools. I attended Po-catello High School, a two-mile walk from my home that I made re-gardless of Idaho's blizzardly blasts. Going into high school was a tribulation to me because I reached puberty late. It was not until September of my junior year, near my sixteenth birthday, that my friend, Raymond Benson, was able to observe that my voice had changed into a deep bass. While the other boys had begun sprouting whiskers as early as the ninth grade and had begun outgrowing their trousers every third month, I had continued to move placidly along as a boy. In fact, I did not reach my full height of six-foot-four and weight of two hundred pounds until age twenty-one, my second year as an LDS missionary. My slow physical development meant that I could not participate in high school athletics, even if I had had the desire—which is questionable as I look back at those three years.

My years at Pocatello High School were—and still are—a kind of blur. I have little memory of favorite classes or teachers. I unhesitatingly opted for a college preparatory course of study which included full courses in geometry and trigonometry. My history and political science teacher was a bore, with little interest in or enthusiasm for her subject. I found books in the local library to be more challenging.

The only high school teacher who had a real impact on me was Miss Eulalia Schaefer who taught public speaking and drama. By the twelfth grade, I was so discouraged with myself, so lacking in self-confidence, and so backward in the social graces that I determined to force myself to learn to speak in public. I shall never forget the sleepless night I spent before I was to recite Edgar Allan Poe's poem "The Bells" in front of Miss Schaefer's class. How I ever got through the ordeal, I shall never know. But with her encouragement and understanding, I gradually gained in confidence, took another course in speech as a college freshman, and received all kinds of speaking experience as an LDS missionary. Today the bigger the crowd, the more I enjoy the art of speaking in public. As Mormon church president Heber J. Grant frequently quoted Emerson: "That which you persist in doing becomes easy to do, not that the nature of the thing has changed, but that your power to do has increased." The simple exercise of learning to face an audience and to speak with some clarity changed my life and brought out in me whatever leadership talents I may have.

Another process which helped prepare me for life was the habit I acquired as a high school student of choosing unfamiliar words from articles in the daily newspaper and committing them to memory. On my first teaching assignment in a rural school, I required my rather bewildered ninth- and tenth-grade students to memorize a list of twenty new words each week. I hope it was good for their souls.

The Great Depression was in full swing, and my job prospects looked bleak when school let out for the summer I was fifteen. Two cousins close to my age, Arlen and Blaine Miller, sons of my Aunt Lynn Madsen Miller from Riverton, appeared at our home one day in early June and announced they were on their way to central Wyoming to try and get jobs on a ranch. Did I want to go? I did.

Dad gave me permission only if we promised to hitchhike and, under no circumstances, to ride the freight trains. It seems hard to believe that Dad would let me to take off this way at fifteen, but of course, "You'll never ..." So as soon we were a safe distance from my home, we headed for the railroad yards and caught a freight for Evanston, Wyoming. We were back home a week later. The roads and railroads were swarming with unemployed men desperately seeking employment, and there were no jobs available for us.

My one week as a hobo was instructive, however. I learned to catch a freight by grasping the bars of the ladder at the front of a car, never at the rear where a lost hold could swing you between the cars for a sure death. I became acquainted with the "jungles" where the hobos and unemployed camped and how to avoid the "bulls" (police) in the yards. I chopped firewood in exchange for meals and slept in a jailhouse when a kind jailer took us in out of the Wyoming cold. (He first searched us and took our pocket-knives.) On our last night in the Ogden, Utah, "jungle" on my way home, as I shared some thin soup from a coffee can with an old "bo," he advised me to go home and give up the unprofitable life of a tramp.

We needed no urging, and my cousins left for Riverton; but I faced one other hurdle. The city officials of Pocatello had become tired of the hordes of hobos who disembarked from the regular southbound freight train each late afternoon. They had two fire engines meet the train every day, haul the hobos caught in the cars to the other side of town, and dump them there to keep them away from the citizens' houses. I was determined not to become part of this public parade down Main Street under the stares of my friends, so I jumped into some loose gravel two or three miles from town. I suffered only a few scratches, and that ended my hobo career.

Next Dad and I hired out to a local farmer for a month as hay hands. We each received $1 a day and our lunch. Then I had the great good fortune to find a job with the Continental Oil Company as an "air boy," at 25 cents an hour, working at one of the company service stations in Pocatello. My job was cleaning windshields and checking the air pressure in tires. My first day on the job, one of the other air boys challenged me to a wrestling match to determine our ranking for performing even more menial tasks. I threw him the first time. He beat me on the second try. The adult males on the staff, deciding that the honors were equal, decreed that we would split the work. I continued to work during evenings at the station during the fall and winter of that school year.

Although work was definitely more important and more plentiful than play, there was still time for relaxation. For five cents (later a dime) we could enjoy a silent movie on Saturday afternoon, usually a serial Western starring Tom Mix. The cliff-hanging ending to each episode brought us back the next week to see how our hero had foiled the villains.

My two best friends during my sophomore and junior years at high school were Raymond and Baron Pearson, two boys from a family that was well-to-do by comparison with others in our somewhat blighted community. Mr. and Mrs. Pearson were the acknowledged pinochle champions of Pocatello. It was their chief means of recreation, and Mrs. Pearson gladly taught me the intricacies of the game along with her own sons. Although I have seldom played since, I remember many pleasant evenings dealing pinochle cards at the Pearsons.

Because we lived only five or six city blocks from the mountains, it was easy to escape to them with a few close friends. Often we boys would take off and camp out for three or four days at a time, coming home only when our food ran out. There was a sled hill close to home for winter sports, and cross-country skiing was a favorite pastime, especially during my high school and college years. One winter Cassicks Johnson and I went into the business of hunting jack rabbits in the Pocatello Creek area. He loaned me his .22 while he used a shotgun. The hides brought thirty-five cents apiece which usually paid for our ammunition.

Camping was the only recreation my father favored, and I have fond memories of weekends spent with the family on Mink Creek, just below Scout Mountain. On one of our early trips, Dad wasn't sure our current Model-T Ford would make it up the last hill so he ejected the family from the car and had me run up the incline beside the car carrying a heavy rock to wedge under the tires if the car began to roll backwards. Mother was disgusted with the whole exercise.

We often went to Yellowstone Park during the summers. There were not many visitors in those days. Once we stopped at an isolated campground and spread out our picnic lunch on a park table. Just then a black bear and her two cubs showed up. Mother bundled up the food and dishes in the tablecloth and got the younger children into the safety of the car. But Dad was not about to back down, and I decided to second him. He grabbed a large stick and waved it at the bear. She immediately charged him but came to a stop about six feet away. At that point I also sprinted for the car. Dad and the bear eyed each other in silence for a few seconds until the bear suddenly turned and ambled off. Mother thought Dad had lost his senses; I don't know what Dad or the bear thought.

I never learned to play sports because my father thought they were a foolish waste of time. The only exception was his intense interest in prize-fighting. When Gene Tunney fought Jack Dempsey in the fa mous "long-count" match of 1927, Dad read every word of the punch-by-punch newspaper description. But as far as I know, Dad attended only one sporting event in his life. After I had left home, my brother Mack became an all-state tackle on the Idaho Falls High School football team. Dad never went to the games; but finally, under strong urging from my Mother and sisters, he consented to see the final and crucial game with arch rival Pocatello. He did not understand the rules of the game very well; but when the coach took Mack out for a breather in the final moments when Idaho Falls was ahead, Dad bounced down from the stands, confronted the coach, and demanded to know why he had withdrawn Mack. Mack always treasured this little manifestation of loyalty from Dad.

Because of my late entry into puberty and also because I had determined that my first objective was to get a college education, my interest in girls was minimal. During my senior year at high school, I attended a few dances at the local hangout downtown, but always went "stag." During my first two years of college, I didn't date at all.

On May 25, 1932, I graduated from Pocatello High School in the top 10 percent of my 211-member class and as a member of the Honor

Society. The Class of '32 held its fiftieth anniversary meeting in August 1982; and although I couldn't attend, it was interesting to read the short biographies of those I had come to know best. Several of my closest friends had already crossed over the bar.

There was never any question that I would go to college; but because of the Great Depression, there was only one choice—the two-year course at the Southern Branch of the University of Idaho at Pocatello, now Idaho State University. It was a small institution with about fifty faculty and 1,000 students, so I was not entirely lost. When I entered as a freshman in September 1932, I had enough money to pay the $10 semester tuition and buy my books. But by the second semester, my father signed a note so that I could borrow $10 from the school to pay my second semester's tuition. My parents, still haunted by their failed attempts at advanced schooling, were very supportive of my ambition. I lived at home; depression times did not allow for independent adventuring.

During my second year, a wonderful windfall came along—the National Youth Administration of the Roosevelt New Deal. Under the auspices of the NYA, I was hired as a foreman to supervise a crew of about ten other students in doing such odd jobs as building bulletin boards, shingling an old campus building, etc. I was chosen as foreman because I knew the difference between a hammer and a saw, and most of the others would have had to guess. The pay was excellent for the times, and I could pay my tuition and book expenses. But there was certainly not a penny to squander, and my parents had nothing to spare. When Mother and Dad attended the graduation ceremonies in May 1934, their only vehicle was an old Dodge truck, a blow for my father who loved speed and beauty in vehicles. There was not room for me inside, so I rode to the ceremonies on the running board. My parents were embarrassed because my shoes were so worn. I couldn't afford a new pair, but I was not ashamed of my well-worn shoes.

My two years at the Southern Branch, while not earthshaking, provided a glimpse into an intellectual world that had been closed to me before. My best friend during these years was Sam Garrett, whose strongly Baptist family had moved to Pocatello from southwest Virginia. Sam was the youngest of five brothers. The oldest two, Clarence and Oscar, founded the very successful Garrett Freight Lines Company in Pocatello. I absorbed Baptist tenets from Sam while attending the LDS Institute of Religion under the direction of J. Wylie Sessions, later a professor of religion at Brigham Young University.

The Great Depression ended Dad's relationship with carpenters' Local 1258. Refusing to lie around waiting for a nonexistent job and struggling desperately to find some income, in the spring of 1931 he took a labor contract to roof a machine shop. Labor contracts violated union rules. When officials warned Dad that he must give up the job or be fined a hundred dollars, his answer was that they might as well make it a thousand dollars because he was not going to let his family starve. He resigned from the union.

It was a blessing in disguise because he became a general contractor, his vocation for the rest of his life, much to his financial advantage. I never had to worry again about having a job. During my last year in high school and my two years at the Southern Branch, I worked every night and every Saturday as a carpenter. I was the only crew my father had during his first months as a contractor.

As Dad's "crew," I learned a lot about his personality. He was fair and temperate with his workmen and clients but, if pushed too far, would explode. Once he was remodeling the home of the well-to-do owner of a Pocatello movie theater, and I was given the task of building a child's playhouse in the backyard out of the scrap lumber. The owner was easy to deal with except early every morning before he had had his coffee. Dad had put up with these early-morning tantrums for about a week until one fateful morning when the owner declared that he had never seen such a sloppy job as the way I was nailing siding on the playhouse.

Dad boiled over and sarcastically exclaimed, "Well, I sure don't want you to have to look at such a poor piece of workmanship!" He then picked up a crowbar and demolished the playhouse while the owner ran into the house in fright. Dad walked off the job and never got paid for the remodeling.

In another incident a plumber who had been doing all our work began to take advantage of Dad by raising his prices. As soon as Dad figured out what was going on, he gave the next job to another plumber. One morning while my father and I were shingling a neighbor's roof, our aggrieved former plumber drove up to the job, got out (leaving his car door open and the engine running), and called Dad some very uncomplimentary names.

When my father recovered from the initial shock, which took only a few seconds, he threw his shingling hatchet into the vegetable garden, jumped off the roof, and started for the plumber, who leaped into the car and gunned the motor. He barely escaped.

At this time of Dad's career and especially during periods of stress common to anyone engaged in the frustrations of construction, my mother would often implore me in the morning before I left for work, "Don't let your dad get into trouble today"—as if I could have stopped him! Later in life he mellowed somewhat but he could flare up as of old.

Perhaps the stress of the construction site brought out Dad's aggressive side, but when he was with his family, he was much gentler. His expectations and standards were high and there was no question who was in charge, but I cannot remember a single occasion when he raised his voice to my mother or his hand to one of us children. When she said or did something that displeased him, his only reaction was a mild, "Now, Liddy." He was concerned about all of us children, kindly, and generously ready with both encouragement and an open purse—if he had any money. In fact, where his wife and children were concerned, my father was a real sentimentalist.

As the oldest son, I remember being Dad's right-hand man almost as soon as I could walk. Because the next two children were daughters, followed by two sons, this family structure of partnerships lasted all of my childhood and youth. Kept busy constantly with school and work, I did not develop as close a relationship with my siblings as they had with each other. Annie and Phyllis, in particular, were inseparable while young. Annie had some of Dad's feisty characteristics, while Phyllis was mellower. Since all of us absorbed the family values of industry and independence, we all had the satisfaction of knowing that we pleased our parents. Later, as an adult in the 1950s, when I began working with Rod and Mack in the construction business, the difference of six and nine years between us did not matter. Our partnership was not only productive but very harmonious.

While I was on my mission in late 1936, Dad became very successful in winning contracts for houses and small buildings. One evening he was invited to the home of a prominent builder in town and arrived to discover that several other builders were also there. It was a monopoly meeting. The leader indicated that Dad was becoming a menace to

My family, in 1934 before I left on my mission.
Standing left: Mack James Madsen, Brigham Dwaine Madsen,
father Brigham A. Madsen, and Charles Rodney Madsen. Front left: Annie
LaRae Madsen, mother Lydia Cushing Madsen, and Phyllis Madsen.

their cozy arrangement, which had evidently been going on for several years, of dividing up the jobs in town. They thought Pocatello was growing enough to accommodate one more builder, so they invited him to join the group and share in the profits. His answer was typically forthright. He announced disgustedly that he would not be part of their cozy business relationship and walked out. He never won another major contract. After eighteen years in Pocatello, he was forced to move in 1937 to Idaho Falls, fifty miles away, where there was no union. He soon became one of the prominent builders in town.

There is no question that Dad was the most important feature on my landscape as a youth and young man. He was a strong personality who had a great influence on me. I was fully grown before I declared my independence from him—and it says something about his confident self-image that my declaration surprised him no end.

My only extracurricular activity during these college years came when Guy Wicks, the varsity basketball coach, happened to see me industriously playing basketball in a physical education class in January 1934. He eyed my six-foot-almost-four-inch frame and asked why I hadn't tried out for the team. The tallest man on his squad was six-foot-two. After making arrangements with my father to miss a couple of weeks of evening carpentry, I began to practice with the varsity. I could probably have played center if I had gone out for the team in the fall, but January was too late. Wicks let me play with the second squad in a practice game against the Pocatello High School team.

Because the rules about eligibility were rather lax at the time, the coach urged me to come back for a third year and promised to put me on the varsity team. But by then I had committed myself to go on a mission, and that was the end of my basketball career. The persistent Wicks whispered, when I walked past him at commencement after receiving my Junior College Certificate, "Won't you change your mind about a mission and come back to school for a third year?" During my first quarter at the University of Utah after my mission, I did go out for basketball but fractured my ankle during the second practice. After a month on crutches, I never tried again.

My academic record at Southern Branch was good except for German. I have no facility for foreign languages at all and just squeezed by with "C" grades in German. Professor Paul Guyet, a tiny man with a high-flying shock of gray hair, would shake his head solemnly at me as he handed back my examination papers and would intone, "Ach, Dwaine, I am so ashamed of you."

Fortunately, I did better in history. In fact, I became enthralled with Dr. Giovanni M. D. G. Costigan, professor of history, with degrees from the University of Wisconsin and Oxford. I was fortunate indeed that his two years on the faculty coincided with my two years as a student; in 1935 he went to the University of Washington, where he had a brilliant career. I took every class he taught, listened in rapt attention to every word he uttered in his clipped British accent, and discovered, through him, what I wanted to do with my life. If I could only be the kind of college teacher he was, I thought my life would be complete. Furthermore, I discovered that history was not only intensely interesting, but rather easy for me to master. Dr. Costigan won me over completely, especially when he began to write in my blue book exams, "Very good, as usual."

Costigan first aroused my interest in historiography with his emphasis on the philosophy of Oswald Spengler. This scholar's famous work, *Decline of the West,* interpreting history as cycles of the growth and collapse of civilizations, had appeared between 1918 and 1922. His final study, *The Hour of Decision,* was published in 1934, just at the time I enrolled in Costigan's classes. Today I still find value in the Spengler thesis.

With a sense of real achievement, I received my Junior College Diploma and "Honorable Dismissal" from the institution on June 6, 1934. But my next activity was not studying. I became a Mormon missionary.

5.

MISSIONARY TO
THE MOUNTAINEERS

On April 3, 1934, Heber J. Grant, president of the Church of Jesus Christ of Latter-day Saints, sent me a memorable letter saying that I had been "recommended as worthy to fill a mission, and it gives us pleasure to call you to labor in the East Central States."

I had some hesitation about going on a mission, believing that it might be more important to finish my undergraduate college degree first. My father's emphasis on finishing my education was unchanged; but he also felt frustrated that he had never had the opportunity to serve a mission, although his two older brothers had. I sensed how keenly he wanted me to have the opportunities that he lacked. I finally said to him that if he was willing to support me financially for two years as a missionary, I would agree to go. He agreed.

He was somewhat chagrined to hear me say in my farewell speech to the Fourth Ward congregation that I could not stand up like some members and declare that I knew beyond a doubt that the gospel was true and that Joseph Smith was a true prophet of God. I continued that I might at some future date receive such a testimony but that at that time I could not. My father should have recognized in me a chip off the old block.

When I arrived in Salt Lake City in late June 1934 to enter the LDS Mission Home located on the Temple Block on State Street, for ten days of orientation before my departure for Kentucky, I was a pretty naive young man from a small town who, like most LDS missionaries of the time, had a lot to learn about the big wide world. Out of a group of fifty-six missionaries who were there to receive a cram session in the

*Elder B. Dwaine Madsen,
Tennessee, in 1934.*

principles of the Mormon gospel, five of us were destined for the East Central States Mission, which then included Kentucky, Tennessee, West Virginia, Virginia, and North Carolina. We traveled by four different railroads, stopping off for one day in Chicago to visit the Century of Progress Exposition where Ripley's Believe It or Not seemed to be the most memorable exhibit, as far as I was concerned. I was carrying Minister's Certificate No. 21725 which certified that I had been ordained a minister in the LDS church and which invited "all men to give heed to his teachings as a servant of God, and to assist him in his travels and labors, in whatsoever things he may need." We reached the mission headquarters at 927 Fourth Street, Louisville, Kentucky, on July 15, 1934, after paying twenty-five cents cab fare from the railroad station for all five of us.

Our mission president was James Mercer Kirkham, the oldest brother of LDS church authorities Oscar A. Kirkham, who would be ordained one of the Seven Presidents of the Seventy in 1941, and Francis W. Kirkham, a prominent Mormon educator and author of books on Mormon history and theology. James was born November 18, 1872, in Lehi, Utah, to James Kirkham and Martha Mercer Kirkham, one of his three wives. James M. was forced to shoulder the burden of helping raise his brothers and sisters when his father died suddenly.

Kirkham was sixty-two and had been appointed president of the East Central States Mission in 1934, just before I arrived, and served until 1937. He and his wife, Kate Woodhouse Kirkham, were the par-

Map of my mission districts: East District and West District in Tennessee, and North Carolina East and West districts.

ents of nine children, and he had made his career editing the *Deseret Farmer* (later the *Utah Farmer*) and, after it was acquired by the *Deseret News,* as that paper's assistant manager.[1] Sister Kirkham was a gifted musician, a talent that added considerably to the happy mood at the mission home. President Kirkham and I hit it off from the very first.

The next day, a Monday, one of the experienced elders at the mission headquarters decided to subject us to a baptism of fire by taking us to downtown Louisville to hold a street meeting. After we had found a spot near a busy street corner and had carefully placed our hats on top of our Bibles on the sidewalk, an elder named Backman looked the five of us over, fixed his eye on me, and announced, "The tallest one can speak first." I delivered a short sermon on the Articles of Faith, according to my diary.[2] The confidence I had gained as a public speaker

---

1. *James Mercer Kirkham: Highlights of His Successful Life* (Salt Lake City: n.p., 1961), 77 pp.

2. Brigham Dwaine Madsen, Diary, July 2, 1934–July 18, 1936, in two volumes; hereafter cited by date in the text.

in my high school and college classes really helped at that critical juncture. At least I was not in the same predicament as a frightened missionary when President Kirkham called on him at a public conference in Knoxville, Tennessee. I was a member of the audience. Grasping the pulpit to keep from falling, he quavered, "I wish I was home and that my mother was here." He then sat down.

This occasion was one of the few when being tall conferred some kind of beneficial distinction on me. Perhaps because I spent so much of my childhood miserably conscious of being shorter than most of my classmates, I tend to think of myself as being quite normal physically and hear "witticisms" like "How's the air up there?" with a twinge of surprise (as well as annoyance). My father, who was six-foot-three himself, early instructed me to rejoin, "Well, at least I don't have to stand on a stool to kick a duck in the ass." He may have used this comeback; I never have.

After I had spent five days in Louisville, Kirkham sent me to work among the hills and coves of the Cumberland Mountains of East Tennessee. Everyone in the headquarters seemed to pity me for being sent to such a godforsaken place. My own feelings at the time were mingled apprehension and anticipation, because East Tennessee District was considered the "pits" of the mission.[3] However, I knew that Kirkham was not trying to "punish" me and chose to regard it instead as a test of my mettle. In retrospect, I'm actively grateful for his decision. I not only survived but came to enjoy the mountaineer people and to appreciate their culture. My experience there with the Scotch-Irish stock of the Martins and the Coys and their fascinating traditions going unbroken back to the days when Daniel Boone pioneered the land on the other side of the Cumberland Gap strengthened my resolve to become a historian.

The modern revolution introduced by the New Deal had not yet touched the coves and hollows of the thick forest. Some of them were still living like their nineteenth-century ancestors, in log cabins with dirt floors, cooking over fireplaces, sometimes lacking even outhouses. When Mother Nature called, a stranger might be invited to visit the

---

3. Mormon missions are subdivided into districts. At the time Tennessee was split into West Tennessee and East Tennessee, while North Carolina was separated into East and West districts.

nearby cornfield, although it could be embarrassing when the chickens would follow you into the patch. One night we stayed with a miller whose grist mill dated back to the 1840s. I was astonished one day to see a yoke of oxen hitched to a cart and listened with much interest to solemn warnings that sweet potatoes should be dug only in the dark of the moon, that pigs should be killed in the last of the full moon, and that a person would surely come down with the flu if he or she should put his or her hands in newfallen snow.

Almost always the mountaineers were hospitable. If we came suddenly on a cabin in a clearing, we were invited to dine and spend the night. I learned to love persimmons, apples cooked in new molasses, and, of course, cornbread, and sweet potatoes. Within four months I had gained fifteen pounds, reaching my mature weight of two hundred pounds.

We enjoyed the common salutation, "You'ns come over and see wee'ns," with its appropriate response, "Us'ns will." The dialects were straight out of Abraham Lincoln's time with "heerd" for "heard" and "fit" for "fought." The old saw that "I raised a sight, sold a heap, and have a right smart left" would not have raised any eyebrows in Clay County.

We often got lost in the dense forest. Because of my building experience, I was particularly interested in the varieties of trees and once compiled a list of twenty-seven varieties, including eight different kinds of oak.

One of the principal reasons for missionary reluctance to serve in East Tennessee was the comparative scarcity of Mormons to whom a homesick or hungry missionary could turn for help and comfort. There were only two organized branches in the whole eastern half of the state. The Chattanooga Branch had no chapel. At Northcut's Cove a small frame chapel was tucked in a fold of the forest.

There were Saints scattered among the hills and coves, many of whom had not seen any Mormon elders for several years, but though few and far between, they were staunch and colorful. At Bristol we roomed and boarded for the winter of 1934-35 with Brother and Sister James Salley. Salley was a World War I pensioner because of permanent damage to his lungs caused by mustard gas. He and the much-younger Sister Salley had two daughters and a son, all under ten. They took good care of us; it was a fortunate arrangement for two Mormon elders.

Near Gainsboro my missionary companion, Parley Joseph Harker, and I called without warning at the cabin-and-lean-to kitchen of a home where the wife was a member. We found corn shucks and beans scattered all over the floor. A hen was laying an egg in the straw tick of the unmade bed. Two more chickens were on the table pecking at some old cornbread. The lady of the house immediately shooed us into the log cabin's front room. When we finally returned to the kitchen for lunch, everything was in order except for the disgruntled hen which flew up to the bed and began scratching around on the quilt trying to locate her usual nesting place.

Uncle Billy Sapp, a member at Speedwell, regaled us with the story of how he had caught two rattlesnakes with his bare hands and sold them to a man for twenty dollars. The following summer when a carnival came to Speedwell, Uncle Billy insisted that two of the snakes in its displays were the ones he had caught and that they knew him. The next morning, after he had come to know Harker and me better, he invited us out into the forest behind his house to see his moonshine still. It was a beautiful sight with its copper coils and tubs of mash.

The Mormons in the hills of eastern Tennessee were often under attack by people from other churches. Near Bybee on November 6, 1934, I wrote, "Went around & visited about 4 families of Saints. At Luther Talley's found a boy 21 yrs. old, just been married two days, reading & studying Book of Mormon. Found this to be case all over the community. The sectarian Ministers have been jumping on the children of the Saints. They have to study so as to defend 'Mormonism!'" Obviously, I didn't see this as all negative.

But except for these sparsely scattered members, a Mormon missionary was on his own in this no-man's land, under constant threat of being challenged by a fire-eating "Hard-Shelled" (primitive Calvinist) Baptist preacher or an even more fearsome Church of Christ or Campbellite evangelist. The Cumberland Mountains of Tennessee was the very buckle of the Bible belt. Religion was entertainment and politics as well as spiritual nourishment. The Bible was the literal word of God written by God himself in the best King James English. Preachers were expected to know the New Testament by chapter and verse, and proof-texting was the only acceptable method of religious discourse. I still have my pocket-worn New Testament with its Mormon proof-texts colored by a red pencil. I faithfully committed them to memory in preparation for combat with ministers of other faiths.

Of my nine months in the Tennessee mountains, Parley Joseph Harker was my companion for the first four months. He was from Lewisville, Idaho, just north of Idaho Falls, a hard-working farm boy of about twenty with a high-school education and a shrewd, down-to-earth approach to missionary work. Conscientious and industrious, he set me on the right track to become a successful protagonist for my faith.

About a year after his mission was over, he married Rhoda Steed of Salt Lake City, one of the lady missionaries. Her father, we heard, was an underground polygamist. They settled on the Harker farm in Lewisville, Idaho, raised a large family, and were rather prosperous citizens. In the late 1950s I heard from another former missionary that they had sold their farm and moved to Enterprise, Utah, near the Arizona border. There Parley had joined a Mormon splinter group and apparently become a polygamist. After our missions, rumors had circulated that Sister Steed was a closet polygamist, so I felt that she had converted her husband. He telephoned me a few years ago, and we had a pleasant conversation without, however, mentioning the taboo subject.

After four months as Harker's junior companion, I was made a senior companion and assigned to work with Clarence Meldrum, a college-educated Salt Lake City boy perhaps a year older than I, very likeable, and always willing to go the extra mile. We got along famously. I spent the summer and early fall of 1934 proselyting without purse or scrip in White and Clay counties in rural Tennessee with Harker and the winter with Meldrum working in Bristol, Tennessee-Virginia. The boundary between the two states ran down Bristol's main street. We spent most of our proselyting time tracting from door to door and holding evening "cottage meetings" in the homes of friendly investigators.

Old Sister Noe, a tubercular, lived just a block from us in Bristol, alone and in very unsanitary conditions. Meldrum was sure that if he kept teaching her she eventually would ask for baptism. I warned him several times to stay away from her, but the missionary urge was strong in him. While I was robust and corn-fed and suffered no more than fallen arches from the incessant walking, he became frail, fell ill often that winter of 1934–35, and was frequently racked with coughing. Within a few years of his return to Salt Lake City after his mission, he was dead of tuberculosis, a martyr, I believe, to his missionary zeal. His death will always haunt me.

To save money, we usually hitchhiked, a practice which today might seem both too indecorous and too dangerous for ministers. It was neither in the 1930s. People, for the most part, willingly gave us rides, although we were sometimes passed up five or six times for every ride. We usually stationed ourselves about a block apart, knowing that a driver would be reluctant to pick up two strangers. When the "behind" person got picked up, he would ask the driver to pick up the "before" person. If the driver refused, the stranded missionary would just have to keep trying. Once, when I was given a ride and asked the driver to pick up Harker, who was standing ahead, the man did so but later told us that "he hardly ever picked anyone up & if he did it was only one. He said he couldn't explain why he picked both of us up." We, of course, knew that the spirit of the Lord had striven with him. When you are engaged in the work of the Lord, it is easy to ascribe to him every speck of help. After all, weren't we more interesting to him than the sparrows, whose every fall, the scriptures assure us, he observes?

My journal reports that on July 26, 1934, Harker and I traversed the thirty-six miles from Chattanooga to Laager, Tennessee, by walking two miles, riding fifteen, walking three, riding five, walking three more, riding six, walking three, and riding the final eleven. This break-down adds up to forty-eight miles, not thirty-six. As a missionary, my arithmetic was faulty, but not my sense of suffering for a noble cause. On another long day of such travel, we finally broke down and hired a man for seventy cents to take us the final eight miles. Four miles later his tire blew out. We had to walk the last four miles, arriving at our destination at 2:00 A.M.

On some days the rides were not forthcoming, and we walked far more than we rode. My October 31 entry notes that we walked eleven miles carrying our "stick-grips" (small suitcases) loaded with religious tracts. "My arms nearly pulled off from carrying grips," I complained. Coming to the Powell River just above the Norris Dam, then under construction, we hired a young girl to row us across the stream in a make-shift rowboat for ten cents. On one fifty-mile trip, a man driving a coal truck let us wedge into the cab. When we noticed that he had a gun with him, he informed us that he had already been held up twice, once by the notorious Clarence Bunch gang and that, in addition, he had broken the leg of a man "who was out to get revenge." I had many interesting rides during those travels and, incidentally, found a few opportunities to preach Mormonism to my captive audience.

We spent a lot of time on the road because President Kirkham, in a conference in Knoxville on August 24, instructed all the missionaries to stop visiting the Saints so much. He outlined a plan for each set of elders to work a rural county depending on people's hospitality for food and lodging until cold weather set in. I promised myself that I would never sleep in a hayloft or in the woods, walking all night, if necessary, to avoid such undignified and tramplike behavior. And I never did, although it took a certain amount of grit to wake up some Christian in the middle of the night and ask for a bed.

On August 27, I recorded, "Asked about 10 places for nights lodging. Finally found lodging at Ernest Phifers, 1-1/2 mi. from town [of Sparta in White County] an old war veteran. Gave us fine supper & fine bed." On September 9 we "got to Ravenscraft [a coal-mining town] & tracted about 50 houses asking for place to stay. After dark finally sat down in front of gate – Mr. Clouse, who had turned us down once came & asked us to stay." On another evening a hospitable Tennessean, after an interesting evening's conversation, just pointed to the door of a bedroom and said we could sleep in there. It contained two beds with a sleeping man in each. I awakened one and asked if he would mind moving into the other bed. He was willing so Harker and I had a bed to ourselves. In a similar but more rewarding incident, our host for the evening, an Eli Mays, directed us to a room which held seven empty beds. I chose the longest one and had a very comfortable night.

Sometimes the food was not the best or most plentiful. I shall never forget a large bowl of steaming-hot white field corn, cut off the cob and boiled, which one lady placed in the center of the table. That's all there was. But there was plenty, and it was one of the best meals a lanky Mormon missionary ever had. On another occasion we ate with a family of Saints in a one-room log cabin with a lean-to kitchen, both of them dirt-floored. The cabin was clean and the floors well swept, but the meal consisted of wild raspberries and cornmeal cakes made with water. I looked at the three skinny, undernourished children and didn't have the heart to eat more than one small cake and a few berries.

Traveling without purse or scrip can be a humbling experience and good training in initiative, perseverance, and understanding human nature. I learned an old missionary song which describes being turned down for lodging. One verse offers an excuse often given by a reluctant host:

> I tell you friends we're crowded.
> My wife is sickly too—
> Yes, it's true we're crowded,
> But I'll tell you what to do.
> Go on to the next house,
> It's only a half a mile.
> The people, they are wealthy,
> And they'll greet you with a smile.

Seed ticks in the woods, bedbugs, unsanitary conditions, and dirty food were minor irritations we learned to take in stride, but a few of the elders suffered serious illness. In October 1934 I was assigned to work with Elder Max Chapple of Spanish Fork, the youngest child and only son in a family of seven. He was ill when I joined him and got steadily worse. Ten days later I called in the doctor, who diagnosed him with typhoid fever and recommended that we get him to the hospital in Louisville. By then elders Harker and Gerald Larsen had arrived in town. The three of us carried Chapple on a cot to the station, put him and the bed in the baggage car, and sent Larsen with him to the hospital. We later learned that his fever was a severe case of homesickness and that he probably would have died if we had not taken this extreme action. I never learned whether he completed his mission. I have met others like him in the army and in the construction business, in which a psychological malady becomes a life-threatening physical one. "You'll never learn any younger" can be carried too far, but so can loving protectiveness.

One real advantage to traveling without purse or scrip was the financial savings, a crucial factor given my father's financial situation. I kept a detailed record of my weekly and monthly expenses in special account books furnished by the church which reveal that my entire twenty-four-month mission cost my parents $582.75 or $24.28 a month. In September 1934, the first full month of serving without purse or scrip, I spent only $10.30: meals, $2.80; room rent, $1.40; laundry, $1.50; clothing $2.15; postage, $.55, and sundries, $1.90. (By this time, I had learned to add.) On some days, we had to take turns staying in our room all day *sans* trousers while they were being cleaned of Tennessee's red mud and pressed for ministerial service again. Most of the people with whom we dealt were as poor as we.

One night Harker and I stayed with a deputy sheriff of White County whom I described as the "raggedest officer I ever saw." While tracting in Bristol one day, I met a woman whose drunkard husband had abandoned her and a small son. I gave her fifty cents to help out. At another home in Bristol, I left twenty cents to buy some medicine for a woman who was ill. These were hard times. It is no wonder that I was amazed and disgusted to learn that one notorious missionary had been spending $60 a month in extravagant living. In self-righteous indignation, I wrote in my diary, "Some Elders seem to be out for a good time rather than missionary work."

The basic work of Mormon missionaries is usually that of "tracting" from door to door, that is, knocking at a door and offering the resident a religious tract or pamphlet which describes the general message of Mormonism. The hope, of course, is that the man or woman at the door will be interested enough in you or the tract to invite you in for a conversation. Most often such invitations are few and far between. In the country districts Harker and I usually took turns going up the long lane to the farmhouse or log cabin while the other remained seated on his upturned stick grip memorizing New Testament verses. Invitations to stop and talk were much more numerous in the rural areas than in the cities where urban life and more "sophisticated" citizens wanted little to do with the Mormons and their polygamy-tainted doctrines.

Tracting in Bristol, Tennessee-Virginia, was a hard, cold, and mostly unrewarding experience, but we drove ourselves to it for six hours a day—from 9:00 A.M. to noon and from 1:00 P.M. to 4:00 P.M. each day Monday through Friday. I did my best to submit honest weekly reports of tracting hours, refusing to pad them while staying home in a warm room as too many missionaries did. Besides, Kirkham seemed to have an uncanny way of discerning, despite his infrequent visits to each pair of missionaries, who was really working. Except for our weekly reports to the district president who sent them on to Kirkham, our other contacts were occasional mission conferences or a happenstance visit from an apostle. We were mostly on our own, a far cry from the rather rigid structure of today's missionaries.

Sometimes the reception at the door was anything but friendly. On two occasions women spat in my face, and on another a man threw some apple peelings in my face, a less obscene declaration of rejection. On another occasion Elder Meldrum and I were both invited into a home where the woman of the house assured Meldrum that he was going to hell. After more conversation she finally amended this prophesy: There might be a chance for Meldrum, but I was destined for the very depths of hell and would suffer on my bed of affliction. I don't remember being very upset; in fact, I rather enjoyed the exchange for adding interest to the monotony of tracting.

The week of February 22, 1935, in Bristol is fairly typical. We spent twenty-four hours tracting, three visiting investigators, three visiting Saints (there was only one member family in the entire city), twenty-six hours in study, and twenty-three in other missionary activity. During that week I also visited 364 homes, had twenty-eight invitations into homes, had 105 conversations (many while standing at the door), and gave away thirteen pamphlets and 399 tracts. If nothing else, we Mormons are prodigious recordkeepers! It may have something to do with the precept in a well-loved Mormon hymn which I sang frequently as a child: "Angels above us are silent notes taking / of every action." Well, I had notes of my own!

The most rewarding experiences from tracting for me, as an incipient historian, were the very interesting people I met who had little concern for my gospel message but who freely shared unusual perspectives on life and the universe. Harker and I were enthralled by old Joe Copeland who proved from the Bible that he was going to live forever and fervently believed it. Meldrum and I listened entranced as eighty-year-old B. F. Vance explained his theory of "Cellular Cosmology," that the earth is a hollow sphere in which all mankind are incarcerated. John Swenson Gannen displayed and explained his perpetual motion invention but carefully held back the key secret part which made it work.

I also filled pages of my diary with flavorful stories that various individuals told us, some of them no doubt apocryphal. For instance, an Irishman who had never been to church visited a congregation one day and heard the preacher invite the members to stand up and testify for Jesus. When no one accepted the offer, the son of Erin arose and exclaimed, "I don't know this man Jesus you're talking about, but I'll stand up for anyone who hasn't any more friends here than he has." More apropos of Tennessee's Cumberland Mountains was the missionary story of encountering bedbugs one night in a strange bed. The two elders got up twice, lit the lamp, and shook the quilts to scare the bugs away, but found that they came back again as soon as the lamp was blown out. The third time the visiting elders took a jar of molasses standing in the corner of the room and, after scaring most of the bedbugs away from the bed, poured a wide ridge of molasses all around the four-poster and went back to bed. They soon heard a strange noise and, lighting the lamp again, observed that the few remaining bedbugs in the straw mattress were carrying straws down to the floor to construct bridges across the moat of molasses so that their less courageous relatives could get back to feast on the pure-blooded Mormon missionaries.

More interesting than tracting were the open-air street meetings which we held whenever we could get permission from the small-town authorities. One Saturday afternoon Harker and I held a street-meeting in Palmer, Tennessee, a coal-mining town, and I recorded in my journal, "They were certainly a bunch of tough miners," a definite understatement.

Another Friday afternoon, while waiting for an LDS religious conference to begin, four of us were walking down the main street of Knoxville on the way to visit a family of Saints when all at once an Elder Pocock, a rather eccentric man, placed his Bible on the curb with his hat upon it and shouted at the top of his voice, "People of Knoxville, we have come to preach repentance to you." We were all involved in a street meeting before we knew it and without any permit to do so. A crowd gathered, and soon two policemen interrupted the meeting with a warning that we had better be on our way. I tried to stay away from Pocock after that. Later on Pocock was assigned to work alone in rural Virginia because he wanted it that way and because no one else would work with him anyway. He began to prose-lyte in an African-American community and eventually converted and baptized an entire congregation of about 150, including their minister. This was at the time, of course, when African-American males were not allowed to hold the Mormon priesthood, a practice which was reversed in June 1978 when the First Presidency and Quorum of the Twelve reversed the policy. I never learned what the church officials in Salt Lake City in 1935 did about their new members or Pocock.

When Harker and I were in White County, we received permission to hold a series of four street meetings in the court house square of the county seat, Sparta. The first two meetings went fairly well with a few interested listeners, but the third was a disaster. Only two people stayed around, an old man who was deaf and a boy playing mumblety-peg. The next day I recorded a real faith-promoting incident: "Yesterday, when we held the street meeting, we forgot to call on the Lord to help us before we left. ... Today we prayed for aid before holding the meeting. The benches were absolutely empty when we started, & when we got through, they were just packed & many took tracts away with them." I became so used to street meetings in Tennessee that I introduced them to the North Carolina missionaries later on, much to their embarrassment and downright fear. They had never participated in such conspicuous public exercises.

In rural areas we always tried to get permission to hold meetings in court houses and school houses. There seemed to be no constitutional questions at the time about separation of church and state. Tennesseans just naturally took for granted that almost any public building was acceptable for a religious service. During the summer and fall of 1934, Harker and I held two meetings in the Grundy County court house at Altamont. We were invited to preach twice in the schoolhouse at Dry Creek, once at the Newhope schoolhouse about two miles from Moss, and once in the Red Boiling Springs schoolhouse. At Newhope about 125 people showed up, and at Red Boiling Springs we were allowed to announce our meeting to all the children in each room. The Newhope meeting was marred when someone threw a rock through an open window and cut one of the male members of the congregation on the cheek. At once a tall man in the front row went outside and there were no more stones thrown. To the Cumberland mountaineers of the time, any kind of free diversion, especially if it were of a religious nature, brought a little interest into their lives.

Meldrum and I held no street meetings in Bristol, but we received permission to preach at a series of meetings, first at the Enterprise Car Shops and, after interest began to lag there, at the High Rock Knitting Mills. At both places we held forth every Monday noon for a half hour while the employees ate their lunches at their work benches. The second time we met at the car shops, I announced that the following Monday I would explain the Mormon doctrine of polygamy. We had a sell-out crowd that day with about 200 men crowded into the room. On our fourth visit to the knitting mills, we were told that would be our last engagement because we were keeping the 200 young women from their work. The real reason was that the superintendent had returned from a long vacation and learned that a couple of Mormons were preaching in his shop. He was opposed to such shenanigans.

At that time missionaries usually baptized the children of members. Although they were not reported as "converts," their statistics probably still helped paint a rosier picture of our efforts than otherwise. Harker, in the memorable month of August 1934 alone, baptized eleven such youngsters in Grundy County.

As a snatcher of brands from the burning, I was a complete washout. I could not bring myself to pursue an investigator aggressively until that person either threw us out or succumbed to baptism. If I were to serve under the hard-sell missionary programs of today, I should probably be sent home within a couple of months as a complete failure.[4]

I can really claim only one complete conversion in my entire mission. I met Verne Fueston, a shoemaker, on November 27, 1934, while tracting, and he shut the door in my face. Two weeks later I met Mrs. Fueston at a cottage meeting in the home of another couple, and she invited us back. From then on we were welcome visitors. On January 2 the Fuestons, since I had not extended them an invitation, asked if they could be baptized. As I reported to my diary, "My *first real*

---

4. In the Mormon missions of my day and for a century before, missionaries were very much on their own with great freedom to set their own course and to decide on how to spread the gospel message. Beginning during the 1950s and continuing to the present, missionary schedules are tightly controlled, they memorize (or at least follow in close paraphrase) a rigid plan of lessons leading to baptism, and are often assigned a monthly quota of converts. Too many missionaries can't meet these requirements, feel they are failures, and return home prematurely, traumatized by these hard-sell methods which, nevertheless, have boosted LDS membership to over ten million adherents.

converts," and, finally, my only ones. I baptized Mr. Fueston and his young son, Junior, four days later; a week later Meldrum baptized Mrs. Fueston.

I recall that we were suspicious of enthusiasm; and instead of snapping up the eighty-eight-year-old Civil War veteran who asked for baptism the second time we met him, we backed off. We were just not convinced that he knew what he was doing. On the other hand, we decided to accept seventy-three-year-old Mrs. Camper of Bristol as a member. She had been investigating the gospel for several years and finally let it be known that, if we'd buy her a dress and some shoes, she'd be baptized. Let me now quote my diary entry for December 18, 1934, to describe this unique ceremony:

> Sunny day. So decided to baptize Sis. Margaret Delilah Julina Oakley Whitaker Hill Camper, age 73 yrs. Spent 2 hrs. in morning making a dam in a creek over by car shops. Used rocks & also corn stalks which we pulled from a near-by field. Was very muddy. Elder Meldrum & I bought her a new dress, pr. shoes, & underclothes = cost $4.00. She was baptized in her *other* dress & shoes. Hired taxi & went down to creek about 2:00 P.M. Elder Meldrum performed ceremony. Water was cold & had skim of ice on top. Ordinance went all right till she hit the water. Then she threw off Elder Meldrum's hands. She was then lying flat in water, completely submerged except for her face, so Meldrum used both his hands & pushed her face under. Then he stood looking at her & finally reached down & pulled her up. She almost strangled. Elder Meldrum afterwards said that his mind was blank concerning all that happened. She was first person that he had ever baptized. However, nothing serious happened & baptism didn't hurt Sis. Camper a bit. When she came up out of the water, she said she felt as happy as could be.

I should add that I almost jumped into the stream to save our new member from drowning when Meldrum just stood looking at her submerged in the water.

However, even though I can't describe myself as a red-hot proselyter, I was definitely a zealous defender of the faith. In my second month as a missionary, I experienced a transformation on September 18, 1934. I met a man while tracting in White County who began attacking the Mormon church as untrue and especially Joseph Smith as a whoremonger and an evil man. All at once, as I recorded in my diary, I "bore my testimony to him; certainly had Spirit of Lord with me." As

I look back at that event, it is hard today to determine whether the emotion I felt was a sudden increase in faith or anger in my own defense. But from then on I cast aside all inhibitions and threw myself into the work. Occasionally, as in reporting a meeting of January 7, I "certainly felt the Spirit of the Lord tonight & bore my testimony with tears in my eyes."

Bible-bashing, or debating the scriptures with combative ministers of other faiths, matching chapter and verse, provided much of the energy of my convictions. My first contest took place in September 1934 at Doyle, Clay County, when a Nazarene woman preacher argued for a life above sin and "had me all twisted up."

But my most disastrous confrontation occurred near Moss, also in Clay County, when a driver pulled over to the side of the road, introduced himself as the Reverend Campbell of the Church of Christ, and invited Harker to share the pulpit with him next morning at the revival he was holding in Moss. He outlined the procedure. Harker would take thirty minutes, then Campbell would take thirty minutes. Harker agreed, and we tracted on to Red Boiling Springs, just over the line in Macon County, where we met Charles B. Wood who had sold a patent on a "stop-loss pocket" to ZCMI in Salt Lake City and proved very friendly. He was visibly upset when he learned that Harker had promised to speak at the revival and warned us to expect trouble.

Reverend Christian, the Church of Christ minister at Red Boiling Springs, had invited us to stay overnight with him. Like two innocent lambs, we spent the evening discussing the Bible with him while he explored our weaknesses. I was puzzled why he asked us whether we were married. I learned the reason the next morning.

Promptly at 10:00 A.M. in the Moss chapel, Harker opened up with a fine, hard-hitting sermon on the necessity for divine authority that, in my opinion, should have left the reverends Campbell and Christian speechless. When Campbell took the pulpit, he immediately asked each of us if we were married. We both said no. He then announced his text, Titus 1:5-6: "For this cause left I thee in Crete, that thou shouldest set in order the things that are wanting, and ordain elders in every city, as I had appointed thee: If any be blameless, the husband of one wife, having faithful children not accused of riot or unruly." The Reverend Campbell then explained to his delighted crowd that because we were not married, we certainly could not be elders and that henceforth he would address us as "Mr." Harker and "Mr." Madsen. We had been set up! For the next hour, conveniently forgetting the thirty-minute limit, Reverend Campbell skillfully and effectively destroyed us and our church. He was witty, satirical, obviously well-trained in the scriptures, and a master of debate. His congregation laughed at every sally and, as I glumly recorded that night, "We were never so humiliated before in our lives." We were laughed out of the community; our missionary labors ended as far as Clay County was concerned.

But our discomfiture had not ended. The next morning we hurried to Celina, the county seat, to pick up our mail before speeding away from our disaster. Reverend Campbell came in just as we were leaving the post office; and Harker, lacking the good sense to let sleeping dogs lie, at once engaged the minister in scriptural combat. It took Campbell only about fifteen minutes to effectively destroy Harker a second time, and we left amidst the jeers of the crowd who had rapidly gathered to watch our second disgrace. The whole affair was a good seasoning for our psyches. To this day I can quote Titus 1:5-6 without missing a word.

Later in Bristol I had a more successful engagement but only because the two "Holiness" preachers who challenged me did not have the polished background and training of the Reverend Campbell, although they could expound the scriptures. The affair took place at an evening cottage meeting Meldrum and I held. The reverends Curtis, who were brothers, challenged the Mormon concept that hell is not a place of literal burning. They pointed out that the rich man who had not been charitable to Lazarus prayed for Abraham to send Lazarus with a single drop of water to cool his tongue "for I am tormented in this flame." It seemed rather plain that I was denying the Bible, and I did not have an answer. The crowd enjoyed my discomfiture. In desperation I announced that I would have an answer at the next meeting scheduled a week from then. But as we left I had no idea how to meet the argument of the Holiness ministers.

The next morning I wrote a hurried letter to Apostle Joseph Fielding Smith, the acknowledged Mormon theologian, and asked if his secretary could send me a book or some literature which might help me out of a difficult predicament. Like a miracle, on the afternoon before my second confrontation with the reverends Curtis, the postman delivered James E. Talmage's *The Vitality of Mormonism,* price 75 cents. Items 16 and 17 dealt with the subjects, "Heaven and Hell" and "In the Realm of the Dead." It was an answer to prayer. Talmage, with appropriate passages of scripture, explained that there was a temporary resting place for deceased spirits in "Paradise" where sinners like the rich man could receive instruction, repent, and eventually leave the torment of the flame, to await the final judgment day when all souls would be assigned to one of three places of glory.

After my sermon of explanation, the two ministers arose and walked out in silence leaving us the freedom of the neighborhood. But it had been a close call. Oddly enough, their chief annoyance with us was that we didn't charge anything for holding our meetings. We didn't even pass the plate.

There were lesser confrontations. One minister ran two blocks to engage me in open discussion on the street. An interested crowd gathered as we sparred for an hour. My diary entry crowed, "First Preacher whom I have defeated in debate. I surprised him & he soon had to leave." About a week later, feeling my oats, I intervened in a street argument between an African American who was arguing that there were three personages in the godhead, and a Baptist minister, who held there was only one. When I asked him if Christ was praying to himself in the Garden of Gethsemane, he answered, "That's Christ's business," and hurriedly left. On March 7, 1935, in Bristol, I held forth for about an hour with two ministers who were conducting a revival with the express purpose of attacking the Mormons, and especially their doctrine of "eternal progression"—that it is possible for any man, through righteous living and engaging in ordinances performed by proper priesthood authority, to reach the status of a god accompanied by his righteous wife or wives.[5] In my diary I made a great point of explaining that only the righteousness and truthfulness of my cause

---

5. Mormons do not accept the traditional Protestant view of heaven that the righteous, now promoted to the status of angels, enjoy the presence of God in a tranquil and peaceful paradise. LDS people foresee an active work place in the hereafter where resurrected beings, still organized in families, continue to progress. The highest form of exaltation—godhood itself—is reserved for married couples who together will create and people other worlds with their spirit offspring.

allowed me, a twenty-year-old only seven months a missionary, to stand up to two well-trained and older ministers.

In one other incident, Lester Parks, a well-to-do businessman in Kingsport, Tennessee, whose wife, named Utah, was a Mormon, arranged a private debate in his home between me and his Baptist minister. To the winner would go the soul of Lester Parker. I prepared carefully for the meeting; but fortunately, the minister had more sense and canceled his appearance.

A lighter side of our missionary labors was singing. Harker had a splendid tenor voice, I sang melody, and together we sang often and late to anyone who would listen. We always carried a pocket-size *Songs of Zion,* from which we sang an opening and closing hymn at each meeting we held. I remember at a preaching service at Newhope school house in Clay County, the 125 people present did not stir after the closing prayer. After a couple of minutes of uncomfortable silence, a gentleman on the front row stood up and asked us if we would mind singing a few more hymns. We obliged by singing for a solid hour, and I believe the congregation would have stayed another hour if we had been willing to continue. We had several offers of lodging for the night from the people. Three days later and a few miles farther on down the road, a man who had attended the Newhope meeting parked his Model T, pulled from his pocket a long grocery purse, extracted two dimes, and offered us ten cents apiece if we would sing two hymns. He especially wanted to hear "Redeemer of Israel." We stood on the dirt road and gladly sang, but declined to take pay.

Two lady missionaries, Rhoda Steed and a Sister Thomas, who spent the winter of 1934–35 working in Kingsport, attended missionary meetings in Bristol one evening. We had sung several times as a mixed quartet. On Sunday evening we four visited the evening service at a nearby Presbyterian church and sat down on the back row. The minister came down and anxiously asked if we were the mixed quartet he was expecting. We weren't, but when the other singers failed to put in an appearance, we filled in with hymns, to the gratitude of the minister and the pleasure of the congregation.

I kept in touch with the family primarily through faithful letters from Mother. Dad often added a postscript but seldom penned an entire letter. My grandfather Madsen occasionally wrote, usually enclosing two dollars. I was his first grandson to serve a mission, and he seemed to take a special interest in me. Like many missionaries, I was sometimes negligent in keeping my parents informed, a lack of consideration I regret today.

My nine months in Tennessee were filled with unforgettable experiences that introduced me to a world very different from my Idaho hometown. I grew up a lot during that period, made some mistakes, learned something from them, and took on the role of a missionary with energy and commitment.

6.

"BUILDING"
THE CHURCH IN
NORTH CAROLINA

In April 1935 I was called back to Louisville and appointed president of the North Carolina East District, where I served for the next fifteen months. I was astonished at this new assignment because I had felt guilty that I was doing so little and spending so much money. Before leaving Pocatello for the wide, wide world, I had thought that everyone worked as hard as did my father. I soon learned with a shock that the Tennessee missionaries were workaholics compared to some of the indolent and easy-living elders of that district. Similarly, we met not violent opposition, but apathy and indifference from the gentiles of that state.[1]

At the same time Harker was named president for the Western Kentucky District. We both arrived in Louisville on April 16, 1935, and spent a week in conference with President Kirkham and the other district presidents, receiving instructions. In a private session Kirkham told me that the missionaries in North Carolina had fallen prey to the delightful climate and relaxed atmosphere of that "Ya'll come, heah?" country. My job was to get those ten elders and two sister missionaries on the ball and to pay close attention to the needs of the various branches and the scattered Saints.

---

1. In Mormondom all those who are not Mormons, including Jews, are called "gentiles." The term reflects Mormon beliefs that Mormons are the new "chosen people" and also that all other religions are false.

I hitchhiked four days and arrived in Goldsboro, North Carolina, on April 27 in a new world. Branches were organized in Wilmington, with a very nice frame chapel in a good neighborhood; Goldsboro, with an older but still serviceable building; two country chapels—Albertson's and Howard's—a smaller branch at Hampstead north of Wilmington, and a sizeable congregation of about 200 people on Harker's Island near Beaufort with no building. Instead of a family or two of Saints in the large cities and isolated members in the rural districts, there was a good concentration, especially in the corridor running along the highway from Goldsboro to Wilmington.

I thoroughly enjoyed the culture of the Deep South, especially in contrast with the mountaineer people of Tennessee. The language and accents were marvelous and musical. At isolated Harker's Island, the people still spoke with the accent their ancestors had brought with them from England, pronouncing "I" as "Oi" and calling their grandparents "Old Ma" and "Old Pa." The Wilmington people were especially part of the Old South tradition and culture. In a more rural area near Wilson, the Saints were less educated and "citified." In one meeting one of the youngsters spoke on the subject "Bringem Young," only to be followed by one of our western sister missionaries who discussed the destruction of "Sodium and Cumorah," the latter being the hill in which Joseph Smith said he had found the gold plates of the Book of Mormon.

One starlight night Brother J. L. Potter invited me to go fox hunting with him and several other devotees of the sport. Each man brought two or three of his best foxhounds; and when the pack was turned loose in the woods, we followed them down dirt roads as they bayed in pursuit of a fox. There was great competition among the keen-eared hunters who critically listened to the sound and identified "Old Sam" or "Belle" as leading. Another time Elder Chester Harris and I attended a "Ye Olde Tyme Fiddler's Convention" in the Topsail Schoolhouse near Hampstead, North Carolina, admission 25 cents each. My diary entry reads:

> They have a prize for the tallest man in attendance. When they called the contest, I marched up on stage. Only had two competitors, & I was easily an inch taller than the tallest one of them. The Principal was reluctant to give the prize to a 'Mormon' Elder but in front of 800

people he had to. Prize was $1.00. Came in handy because Harris & I only had $1.25 between us.

Many of the Saints were prosperous farmers with large farms. In the cities a number of the Saints were business people and belonged in the lower middle class. Hospitable to a fault, the Saints lavished invitations to visit on the young missionaries and made much of them. No wonder the missionaries had succumbed to these blandishments! I hard-heartedly broke these comfortable relationships and drove the missionaries back to work. The dedicated elders agreed with me, and so did the experienced branch presidents. These men, usually middle-aged leaders in their communities, were skilled diplomats at getting along with me as their twenty-year-old "superior," and I appreciated their ability to defuse potentially embarrassing situations while patiently waiting for me to learn temperance and a better administrative style.

Compared to the scattering of members in East Tennessee, the six well-organized branches in eastern North Carolina usually enrolled from fifty to 200 people. The congregations at Sunday meetings were only a little smaller than my Pocatello ward. Sometimes the administrative problems of the six branches stretched my skills to the limit. As district president, I was responsible for establishing and maintaining the organizations in each branch, appointing the officers, and generally keeping things running smoothly. On one of my early visits to Harker's Island, the Sunday school superintendent, a man of real leadership and the most successful fisherman on the island, asked to be released from his office because he found it difficult to give up tobacco and was tired of the undercurrent of criticism from some of the members about his "sin." As a replacement, the members favored another brother, a poor clam-digger and an absolutely orthodox and pure-living man, but a person of doubtful leadership qualities. I strongly felt that the current superintendent should have received the members' support, despite his backsliding; but I finally and reluctantly made the change. Fortunately, he remained active and continued to serve the branch with his obvious administrative skills.

A more serious problem was that of a brother at Wilmington, who, for several years, had been serving as a "mission president" for a small area of the state south of Wilmington. Although he was an enthusiastic and effective part-time missionary, several members living in the area swore that they had given him their tithing but that it was never credited to their accounts at mission headquarters. They demanded that he be put out of office. The facts in this case were not clear; but obviously some action was needed to restore stability. I recorded "a very stormy session" with this local missionary, trying to convince him that even though the charges might not be true, it would be better if he stepped down. Characteristically, I did not seek Kirkham's advice. After all, why had he named me district president if not to solve problems in my area of responsibility? This action terminated the missionary career of a fine and dedicated Saint, although he remained active in the church. I have since thought that I made a mistake and should have retained him in the position while making careful arrangements to have the scattered members send their tithing money directly to Louisville. It was a good lesson for me, and I have been more cautious in such matters since.

I also had my troubles with some of the sisters in the women's Relief Society in Wilmington and Hampstead. In one diary entry I rather plaintively recorded the dubious outcome of an attempt to resolve internal administrative difficulties in the Wilmington Relief Society: "Went over to Sis. [___] with Sis. [___] & tried to straighten out Relief Society. Now neither family will like me, but what else can I do but decide one way or the other?" When I was forced to reorganize the Relief Society at Hampstead, I recorded, "Put Sis. [___] out of a job & put in her place [___]. Another friend lost." The life of an administrator contains a fair number of no-win situations.

Because I was responsible for making out district reports, which entailed a certain amount of correspondence, especially with the missionaries, I tried to compress these duties into a couple of days each month. On March 17, 1936, I noted that I had just written eighteen letters and filed a lot of reports.

I worried a lot about my twelve missionaries. Were they working effectively? Were the companions harmonious? Were the Saints in their area satisfied and encouraged by their work? I dropped in unannounced on the twelve missionaries periodically, to see if they were getting along with each other and if they were satisfactorily diligent. One very likeable elder from Phoenix, Arizona, had difficulty in staying away from the girls, who evidently suffered from the same complaint. It seemed as though I had to move him to a new area about every three months. It was somewhat refreshing to have him write, requesting a transfer. Apparently, one mother was determined to capture him for her daughter.

When I had been district president for two months, I received word from Kirkham that he was sending an elder to me, hoping that I could persuade him to stay in the mission field. The missionary later told me that he'd gone on a mission only because his girlfriend was also serving a mission. He was filling in the time until they could be married. He had been working in West Virginia for the past nine months but had lost interest and started home, stopping at mission headquarters in Louisville on the way. Kirkham was giving him a last chance before branding him with a dishonorable release. During the month he was with me, he refused to tract or to speak at any of the meetings. He spent most of his time playing with the Saints' children or trying to take girls to the movies. I came back to our room one day after tracting alone to find him with his suitcase packed. He would have already left, he explained, but he lacked ten dollars of the railroad fare to Louisville. I loaned him the money. He never repaid it, but the expenditure was worth it. He should never have consented to go on a mission.

Another elder was disconsolate and discouraged but for another reason. Nicholas Udall of the Arizona Udall family never hit it off with Kirkham. Udall was a sophisticated city-dweller, quick-witted and ambitious. He fully expected to be appointed a district president, and, in my view, had all the qualifications. But Kirkham never granted him a higher position, and I remember spending most of one unhappy night trying to console Udall. Later he was elected mayor of Phoenix and has had a very distinguished career.

A happier circumstance was bidding farewell to Marion Henderson of Wilmington, son of a rather well-to-do family, who served a two-year mission in another area of the United States. My district also welcomed Melvin Potter from Deep Run, a rural area in North Carolina. He served a short-term mission in my district.

The sporadically scheduled conferences were dates all missionaries and Saints looked forward to. During the last of May 1935, Apostle Richard R. Lyman met with us for two days of meetings in Wilmington. In his first sermon he announced that if it weren't for Elder Madsen he could have said that he was the tallest man in the world. With such attention, I, of course, liked him very much. Kirkham held three other conferences with us in August and November of 1935 and March of 1936. Another apostle, Melvin J. Ballard, visited us on June 1, 1936, to dedicate the new chapel at Hampstead and repeated his well-known declaration that "he had seen the Saviour with his 'spiritual eyes'" in the Salt Lake temple. After listening to a conversation between him and Kirkham, I opined that Ballard was "a man of diversified interests." In October 1935 Kirkham called me in to Louisville to attend a mission-wide conference of district presidents. Meldrum was also being appointed a district president, so we hitchhiked in together, stopping in Bristol to visit the Salleys. It was a most pleasant excursion.

Although administrative chores threatened to consume most of the time, I spent as much time doing missionary work as I could. For much of the fifteen months I was district president, I had no companion. In addition to one month with the inactive missionary, I spent another month with James Simmons, a former football player from Brigham Young University; two months with Clint Adair, a cowboy and rancher from Luna, New Mexico; and four months with Chester G. Harris, a full-blooded Catawba Indian from Greenville, South Carolina. At other times I would work with a newly-arrived elder for a week or two while waiting for a good place to assign him. I very much enjoyed my labors with Simmons, Adair, and Harris.

Chester G. Harris and about 300 of the remnants of the once mighty Catawba Nation formed a branch of the LDS church at Greenville under the leadership of Harris's uncle, Chief Blue, who, according to Harris and other members of the tribe, was gradually becoming "white and delightsome" as prophesied in the Book of Mormon.[2] Harris believed this promise with all his heart and proved to be a very effective missionary and speaker for the Mormon cause. He had prac-

---

2. The Book of Mormon is, according to Mormon belief, an ancient record detailing the history of refugees from Jerusalem at the time of its destruction, translated from gold plates by Joseph Smith. Led by God to the "promised land" of the Americas, they then experienced periodic cycles of righteousness and corruption against an almost ceaseless background of warfare between two branches of the family. The religious highlight of the Book of Mormon is the visit of the resurrected Jesus Christ to these people. The history ends with the genocide of one branch of the family by the other, the Lamanites, or ancestors of the American Indians. The last prophet promised that the Indians, though they would be afflicted by the gentiles (European Americans) would become a "white and delightsome people" as they accepted the gospel.

tically no money or means of getting any; because I felt that I could keep him going financially and also because of my interest in his people, I selected him as a companion for about four months.

In September 1935 he and I undertook to proselyte without purse or scrip in Robeson County, the home of a few thousand Lumbee Indians. These people, a mixture of whites and Indians, claimed descent from Sir Walter Raleigh's lost colony of Roanoke Island and had formerly been known as Croatans. They had no official status when I knew them and did not receive recognition from the federal government until the U.S. Senate voted on May 22, 1952, to create the new Lumbee tribe for the 4,000 members then living in and around Robeson County. Harris was roly-poly, only five-foot-four in contrast to my six-foot-four. He was an ever-smiling, fun-loving, and hard-working missionary. During our work together, I usually gave a short introduction explaining the purposes of our church with a brief description of the Book of Mormon. Then Harris would take over for about fifty minutes, giving an impassioned recital of the wrongs perpetrated by white people and the U.S. government on the American Indians, the broken promises and the forgotten treaties. During his sermons, he would be transformed. His eyes would flash, and his audience would see a real Indian orator fighting for his people. We nearly always had turn-away crowds because many North Carolinians had never seen a real live American Indian. One preacher listened to our sermon to an Indian audience, then congratulated us on the truthfulness of our message.

The only time I traveled extensively without purse or scrip in North Carolina was when Harris and I were companions. One evening in Pembroke, Robeson County, we had difficulty getting lodging for the night. "The fifth place we asked to stay, they said they were going to the show & so couldn't keep us, so I said, 'Well, we'd be glad to go to the show with you.' So we did." Such gall astonishes me; in my Pocatello days I was even timid about answering the telephone. The next evening we found a place to stay with Willie Prevatt "on condition that we attend a revival with him. We went. There were only about 5 whites & about 300 Indians." The evangelist could not get the congregation stirred up and finally announced that all those who had not repented and been saved would be killed, because "God's going to kill you for not repenting." Once in September 1935 we walked nine miles asking at every farm house for lodging and finally found a place at 9:30 p.m. As I wrote, "I never heard so many excuses in all my life."

Working with Arthur Clinton Adair was just as enjoyable, but for different reasons. His ranching background had given him a quiet strength, a mirthful sense of humor, and an understanding of other two-legged creatures. He was somewhat diffident about speaking in public or pushing himself to the front at social affairs, but was very effective as a missionary one to one. We spent the two months from mid-March to mid-May of 1936 tracting and holding meetings in the small town of Kinston and had a week together without purse or scrip in Robeson County. An excerpt from my March 1936 diary brings back fond memories of Clint Adair:

> Adair decided to preach on "Word of Wisdom" [at the Albertson Chapel] which he had never attempted before. He said that some scientist allowed a "leech" to suck the blood from a person who was an habitual tobacco user. The leech was not long in dying after gorging itself on this contaminated blood. Then this man of science allowed a leech to fill itself on the blood of a person who didn't use tobacco, & it thrived. Adair said that he could prove it from his own experience for he had spent the night at a member's home up in the hills of N.C., & the next morning he was covered with bed-bug bites & he could see the "stuffed" bed-bugs crawling away. He said that the people up there use tobacco & liquor & therefore bed-bugs couldn't live off them, but when they got near these two Elders they knew that the famine was over.

Adair and I did our job and enjoyed each other's company. In September 1935, while we were traveling for a few days without purse or scrip, Adair and I went methodically from door to door for two hours in Parkton (pop. 450), "starting with the Minister" asking for a night's lodging. We finally found hospitality in the fourth to the last house; but a few days later, I recorded, "Got a place to stay at first house we asked which is unusual." It was with a certain amount of relief that I recorded returning to the home of a good Saint, Furnie Harper, in Deep Run: "First square meal I've had for a month."

When one elderly woman asked me for baptism, I agreed to perform the ceremony but, becoming slightly ill, asked if Adair could officiate. She refused. If I wouldn't baptize her, she wouldn't join the church. I acquiesced, though with some personal misgivings about the strength of her convictions.

Adair played the guitar and had a good tenor voice. In Kinston we got in the habit of taking his guitar to our cottage meetings, then singing for the congregation afterwards. We were soon attracting such large crowds that our sermons became shorter and our performances stretched out to as much as two hours. Adair's favorite music was cowboy songs, so we soon branched out from hymns, and I developed a real fondness for western music as well, including Adair's signature tune, "When It's Nighttime in Nevada." We made a lot of friends for our church. Who knows, perhaps this pleasant approach was as effective in improving the reputation of the Mormons and leading some to investigate as my public sparrings with ministers in Tennessee.

Although my administrative duties interrupted the concentrated and unrelenting tracting that was the norm in Tennessee, my well-worn record books show that, including Tennessee, my mission hours totaled: tracting, 1,409 hours; visiting investigators, 315 hours; visiting Saints, 1,330 hours; study, 1,153 hours; and other, 2,621 (which included administrative duties and carpentry on chapels), for a total of 6,818 hours. A further breakdown shows: number of homes visited, 8,393; invitations into homes, 1,264; number of visits to investigators, 152; and number of gospel conversations, 3,184. Literature distributed included: Books of Mormon loaned, 3; Books of Mormon sold, 8, pamphlets, 5,221, and tracts, 5,446. I also held 51 meetings in halls, 125 in "cottages," and 23 in the open air for a total of 199. I blessed thirteen children and baptized fourteen individuals. And finally I hitchhiked 7,525 miles. These figures should provide important data for any quantifying historians who deal in such dreadfully dull stuff.

Money was always tight. In contrast to the present, there was no great emphasis on placing or selling copies of the Book of Mormon, but at least once such a sale was a godsend. Harris and I sold one to the barber in the small town of Pembroke: "We have had 20¢ apiece for about two weeks now—no more, no less, so it (50¢) came in handy." On another occasion Adair and I got down to thirteen cents between us but were saved when he received a money order for $40. My diary records frequent disapproval of the prices charged in 1936: $12 a month for a room in Kinston, and ten cents for a large hamburger with all the trimmings. "Whew!" I wrote, shocked. Most of us missionaries had only one suit. When Adair's trousers needed mending in April 1936, he had to stay in our room all day while the tailor worked.

In North Carolina I hitchhiked more than ever because I was traveling to conferences, visiting missionaries, and supervising branches. On one trip I left Bristol, Tennessee, and reached Louisville, 306 miles away, in eight rides at a total cost of 38 cents. One of the drivers informed me that he would not have picked me up if he had known I was a Mormon missionary but politely delivered me to his destination. In contrast, another driver asked me to continue with him for ten miles beyond my destination so he could talk to me further. I did so, and then he turned around and drove me back the ten miles—a twenty-mile detour.

On the way back to North Carolina I caught a ride across the Great Smoky Mountains to Ashville with a liquor salesman who kept sampling his product all night with one hand on the wheel and one clutching a bottle. I finally gently suggested that I wouldn't mind driving if he were tired. He retorted that I had asked for the ride and would now have to put up with his driving which he maintained was the best in the nation. He let me out in Ashville in the sober light of day, commenting, "See, we made it after all." He was, technically, correct; but as I recorded in my diary, "It's a wonder my hair didn't turn snow-white the way that drunk man drove."

Holding open-air street meetings was much more difficult in North Carolina than in Tennessee where they had been part of the Bible Belt culture. In Red Springs, Robeson County, I was able to get permission from the reluctant mayor to hold a street meeting, but my triumph was short-lived. A carnival was set up just across the street from our meeting place. As Adair and I started to sing our opening hymn, the carnival calliope started up at full volume. Our meeting came to an abrupt end, and I silently paid my compliments to a very devious official. In Kinston, Adair and I were unable to get permission to hold street meetings, and the city officials merely laughed when we asked to hold a preaching service in the court house.

The ministers and evangelists of North Carolina were also different from the fire-eating kind of the Cumberland Mountains. They met us with courteous disinclination to debate the scriptures. At Parkton in Robeson County when Adair and I attended a Baptist Sunday school, the minister asked Adair to give the opening prayer and had me teach the adult class. One day Adair and I caught a ride with a man to whom, as we rode along, we explained Mormonism and that our church did not believe in a paid ministry. Only as we were getting out of the car did he politely mention that he was a Methodist minister.

The sole exception was a Lumbee Indian minister who announced at the beginning of one of our Indian meetings, "I've come to hear these preachers toot or blow their horn, & if there is a crack in the horn I'll find out about it." I hurriedly decided to change the subject of my sermon to "Divine Authority." The Mormon claim that Joseph Smith had received priesthood authority directly from Peter, James, and John and that I could, in a few steps, trace my own ordination directly to his was a sharp contrast to ordination by some cleric of uncertain priestly lineage. It worked on this occasion, and I watched the minister leave silently after the meeting ended. I just couldn't get a fight going with the preachers of the Piedmont.

This is not to say that religion in North Carolina was placid. One Southern Methodist revivalist attacked the "huggin', kissin', dirty, stinkin', nasty movies" of the time—his exact words. Simmons and I attended a Pentecostal revival at Harker's Island and watched one man dance a sort of jig down the aisle for about ten minutes; a woman soon joined the dance; another woman got the shakes; finally another man "came bounding down the aisle leaping about 3 feet in the air at every jump. Shortly after this we seized an opening & escaped with nothing lost." Later as I studied early Mormon history, I found descriptions of Mormon meetings which would rival in their emotional exhibitionism those which we saw at Harker's Island or in Tennessee.

The health of the missionaries was probably better than we could have expected, giving the traveling and living conditions. One of the elders in my district was hospitalized for malaria, and nearly all of us had stories about dirty food when we traveled without purse or scrip. I remember sitting down to a dinner of rice and sweet potatoes in a room with unscreened windows. The flies showed the same enthusiasm for the meal as I, and the rice on my plate looked as if a cup of raisins had been sprinkled on it. Following the example of my hosts, I picked up a spoonful, blew vigorously to get rid of the flies, then dexterously shoved it into my mouth. Because all of my life I have been blessed with a good appetite and a cast-iron stomach, I had little difficulty with strange or ill-prepared foods. For one week I suffered from a bad case of worms, but a vile concoction prescribed by a country doctor put an end to that complaint.

My most serious disability occurred in June 1935 and persisted for two months. I awoke one morning to discover a rash and tiny sores all over my thighs, groin, and lower abdomen. A doctor in Kinston was sure I had a venereal disease and sent a specimen to the state laboratory in Raleigh for a Wasserman test. I had a bad week while waiting in a rented room to get the results from the test which were, of course, negative. Then the doctor decided it must be ring-worm and gave me some noxious salve which didn't work. I finally went to Wilmington where I could stay in a room above the chapel where another doctor diagnosed the rash, probably correctly, as eczema. After trying eight different ointments, he found one that worked.

As ministers of the gospel, we participated in blessings, baptisms, healings, and funerals. In one incident we blessed an old lady who had suffered for some years with a hip ailment. When we placed our hands on her head to pronounce the blessing, she insisted that we place one hand on her head and the other on her hip; otherwise, she firmly believed the ordinance would be unsuccessful. We complied, but I have no way of knowing if she was correct.[3]

I directed two funerals in the swampy area along the coast and was horrified to find standing water in the open graves. I also performed two weddings in North Carolina. The first was a real church wedding in the Howard Branch chapel with flowers, music, and a proper ceremony. With the help of another little black book which gave instructions, I got through the ordinance all right. The second was a shotgun wedding which I performed about 9:00 P.M. one Sunday evening in the home of the bride. Her parents, the very reluctant groom, Harris, and I were the only participants. The ceremony was brief and quite constrained.

Only a few weeks later I had another, and even more terrible, experience with the bride's father. He was a priest in the Aaronic priesthood and asked me to ordain him an elder in the Melchizedek

---

3. Mormon priesthood holders practice the ordinance of the "laying on of hands" to heal the sick, usually in pairs. The first individual anoints the crown of the sick person with a few drops of olive oil which has been previously consecrated to that purpose and speaks a short prayer of anointing. Then two or more men who hold the Melchizedek priesthood lay their hands on the person's head and utter a blessing of no set form that will include the physical ailment but may also go beyond it in pronouncing a variety of blessings.

priesthood, which would qualify him and his wife to fulfill their life-long hope of receiving their endowments in the Salt Lake City temple and being sealed. A farmer, he had been saving toward this purpose. I said I would perform the ordination as soon as I had checked with the branch president, since everyone recognized his faithfulness as a devoted and active member of the church. When I mentioned the request to the branch president, he responded with horror and shock. He told me that the brother in question had an African-American grandparent; although he and his children certainly looked Caucasian and his wife was white, everyone knew of his black parentage. The branch president agreed with me that the man was fully worthy in every way for the ordination; but because the church then denied priesthood to blacks, he and I did not see any way to proceed. The ordination would be invalid, it would scandalize the branch, and the neighboring gentile community would condemn their LDS neighbors.

I conferred with President Kirkham who most surely also discussed the matter with church officials in Salt Lake City, but the policy was firm. I was left with the unhappy task of telling the faithful brother that we could not make him an elder. The blow almost destroyed him, and I became quite bitter about this injustice. I simply could not reconcile it with what I believed about God's desire to extend salvation to all. Throughout my adult life, I fully approved of the civil rights movement. My studies in Mormon history provided a much more plausible explanation than an unaccountable God who played favorites; and by 1978 when the policy was reversed, I had long accepted the priesthood ban as a historical aberration growing out of the church's early experience in the slave state of Missouri.

This doctrinal disillusionment coincided with a mellowing of my Tennessee-born evangelistic zeal, partially brought on by adaptation to the more relaxed culture of North Carolina. Instead of sermonizing from New Testament scriptures, I began speaking on such ethical subjects as "Happiness," "Work," and "Opportunity," sprinkling my talks with references to the Sermon on the Mount and humorous stories and inspirational poetry. This approach not only seemed more compatible with the Carolina country but increasingly reflected my own religious convictions. I worked as hard as ever, took my administrative duties very seriously, and did my job thoroughly but in a more reflective and relaxed manner.

During the last several months of my mission in North Carolina, I became involved in a rather embarrassing and disconcerting situation. A girl my own age, twenty-one, very bright, well-educated, quite beautiful, and the daughter of a prominent LDS family began to pay some attention to me, going so far as to offer to iron my shirts. She was quite discreet and very proud, and I doubt that anyone outside her family knew of her feelings.

She did not say anything direct; but one night several of the missionaries and a number of members went out to a beach to watch the moonlight on the ocean. I chose the better part of valor and stayed in my room to work on reports. When James Simmons returned, he said, "Madsen, I don't understand you. I talked to [____] tonight and discovered that she is deeply in love with you and yet you pay no attention to her." I explained that I was well aware of the situation but just did not reciprocate her feelings. I had no intention of raising false hopes, then abandoning her when I went home as I had seen other missionaries do.

I don't know if Simmons passed this message back to the girl; but she and a girlfriend came to live in Salt Lake City when I was a senior at the University of Utah. Soon I began to receive invitations to attend parties and dances where she would be in attendance. By this time I had met Betty, had fallen in love, and had made plans to marry. I decided I must not leave any possible room for misinterpretation. I invited the girl from North Carolina to attend an afternoon movie and explained that I planned to marry Betty. After that I watched the movie, and she watched me. It was a most uncomfortable afternoon, and perhaps I could have broken the news in a more tactful manner, but I have never regretted the clarity of the message. I have never seen her since and hope that she found happiness and a good life.

Perhaps my most important contribution to the church in eastern North Carolina was building two chapels. The small Hampstead Branch north of Wilmington had met in a small frame chapel for many years, but it fell into disrepair, then burned down. The members had been trying to raise funds for a new one but were not making much progress. I convinced President Kirkham that he would see a new chapel in short order if the mission would help with the financing. Kirkham agreed, and on November 6, 1935, I delivered a set of ready-made church plans to a Brother Barnhill, the only Mormon carpenter in the town. He had agreed to work for a minimum wage to help construct the building. He, Harris, and I began on November 19 and had it ready to meet in exactly two months later.

As I read my journal for this period, I can see that I was a hard taskmaster. I acted as general contractor and handled all the ordering. We worked ten and eleven hours a day. When Barnhill didn't show up, Harris and I would work alone. Once, when Harris became so ill he had to go to the hospital, I worked by myself for two days. Although Brother Barnhill was obviously not accustomed to the "high-balling" style I had learned from my father, he was usually dependable; but I was only partially successful in enlisting other members. In one diary report I wrote rather disgustedly, "Barnhill and Tobe [Shingleton] seem to be really the only two men members who are 'Saints' around here." I'm sure the other members and those from Wilmington who would come out to check on the progress occasionally, thought I was a driven man, but I saw no point in letting the project drag on for a year.

The building was in the shape of a T. The chapel formed the upright part with the speakers' stand and a flanking classroom forming the cross-bar of the T. On January 19 we held our first meeting in the new building. I proudly wrote, "Had about 50 out. Harris and I preached up a storm." Apostle Melvin J. Ballard dedicated the chapel on June 1, holding forth in an hour and a half sermon while I "enjoyed every second of it."

Even before building the Hampstead chapel, I had determined to try to provide a chapel for the 200 Saints at Harker's Island. This small island, five miles long and one mile wide, lies in the sound between the coast and outer banks just four miles east of Beaufort. About 1,200 people, who made their living as fishermen, lived there. In the late 1800s Mormon missionaries had converted a sizeable group, and the branch constructed a small chapel in 1903. Opposition of the other residents of the island was so strong that a mob burned the building. From then until I visited them in June of 1935, they had met in each other's homes for Sunday school and sacrament meetings, often holding services in the open air to accommodate their large congregation. They had saved $200 in a fund for a future chapel, were dedicated and loyal members, and sang with such power and longing in their voices that I have never heard anything quite like it. Telford Willis, who had a big boat, a big house, and a big family, was about the only one who was afflicted with

June 1936,
building the Harker's Island chapel.

prosperity, but the loyalty of the members as a group was unquestionable.

I was so touched by their warmth and faithfulness that, in some indignation, I wrote a long letter to President Kirkham informing him of the circumstances of the Harker's Islanders and asking that the church, through him, buy a lot and build a chapel. I almost demanded that it be done and offered to take the lead in getting a building constructed. Kirkham was very indulgent toward his fire-eating district president and promised to investigate the next time he visited our district. That visit came in August 1935. He agreed with me that the church owed these people a building and authorized me to buy a lot, draw up some plans, and send him an estimate of the costs. I adapted the T-shaped Hampstead plans to fit the larger congregation on the island.

The overjoyed Saints told me that they owned two lots in an unsuitable area which I might trade for a single lot in a better location. The lot they wanted was owned by Charley Davis, owner of the island's only store and the acknowledged leader of the entire community. He disliked the Mormons, but his only son, Earl, had married a Mormon and his grandchildren had been baptized into the LDS church. Alfred Willis, Telford's cousin, and I met with Charley Davis to negotiate the trade. I was completely dismayed when he took out two deeds from his safe proving that he was actually the owner of the two lots the Saints had thought they possessed. I recovered quickly, then bargained with him for the purchase of his lot. He was asking $150 and adamantly refused to lower this astronomical sum. It was only because of his Mormon daughter-in-law that he agreed to sell at all. After several weeks in meeting with Charley Davis and making numerous trips to his lawyer in Beaufort, I finally got a deed to the lot and mailed it to Kirkham. My historical interests were aroused when I noted on the abstract that the lot had the following owners' lineage: Charley Davis from Mason G. Fulford, then from Anson Barker, and James or Thomas Pollock by grant

*James Simmons,
my missionary companion at the time.*

from the King of England. I also compiled a list of needed supplies and materials, which I arranged to buy from the local lumber company in Beaufort.

Brother Barnhill of Hampstead agreed to help us construct the chapel; and with sturdy Simmons, we started construction on June 11, putting in eleven hours the first day. The Saints of the island soon realized that I meant to waste no time in getting the building up and pitched in to help in any way they could. When we got to such tasks as painting, which they as fishermen understood, I would often have a crew of ten or so people at work. With only a few interruptions, we spent eleven hours or more every day. My diary recorded the progress—brick pillars, sills, studding, rafters, German siding, ceiling lumber, exterior and interior painting, and, finally, staining the floor in the main hall. The total cost of materials came to $908.20 not including extra benches which Earl Davis donated. I worked everybody every day, including the Fourth of July, except for the sabbath. We were finished in five weeks, on July 16. My diary records that for amusement, after church services, I sometimes visited the lighthouse at Cape Lookout with Simmons and some members, and once attended the revival of a faith healer who became so super-charged that he had to stop his ministrations while he "slung the power off his hands."

Only one incident marred the construction process. Rumors began to float around the island that, as soon as the chapel was complete, it too would be burned; but some of the members told me that the rumors stopped abruptly when Charley Davis quietly passed the word to stop such nonsense. Then on the very day that we completed construction, I received a telegram from Kirkham that my family would arrive in Goldsboro the next day to take me home to Idaho. This was a complete surprise to me, and I wasted no time putting down my tools. I left Harker's Island on Telford Willis's boat that same afternoon, satisfied that the faithful Saints of the island finally had a building of their own.

I was delighted to meet my family again and, as I look back at that occasion, thankful that they put up with my obvious sense of my own importance as a district president. I believe my father was pleased with what he saw in me and rejoiced that his financial sacrifice and faith in my potential had been mostly realized. My mother commented that I seemed to have matured "a little" and still had a sense of humor. But what we mostly experienced was feeling overjoyed at being together again.

Without doubt, I was leaving the island and the mission field at a high point. My mission was a wonderful emergence into adulthood. I had gained invaluable experience in the art of administration and had learned a great deal about working with people to gain their support, respect, and willing cooperation. This early training in leadership helped me in virtually every endeavor for the rest of my life. Of all of the experiences of my life, I consider the mission adventure to be among the most valuable.

Here's just one change: To say I had overcome my diffidence was an understatement. In Goldsboro my father noticed that my shoes were completely worn out and promptly took me to a shoe store. The clerk and my father were quite embarrassed when I shucked my shoe to reveal a huge hole in my sock. Two years before I would have been mortified. Now it perturbed me not in the least.

What could be more humbling and yet more exhilarating than to knock at doors seeking hospitality and to be well received or to stand on a street corner facing a hostile crowd while expounding on an unpopular theme?

On our trip home we visited Washington, D.C., and the Big Apple, although I don't believe New York City was known by that descriptive phrase at the time. My family had never been farther from home than Yellowstone Park, so this trip was a real adventure—especially with seven packed into one medium-sized automobile. The hotel manager in New York, apparently trying to make us feel at home, put us in an apartment decorated with pictures of Western landscapes and wild horses. We thought he was patronizing us as hicks from Idaho. Perhaps it was a little of both.

My mission diary ends with the note that we reached Pocatello at 5:00 P.M. on July 24, 1936. Now it was back to school and a quieter existence for the next two years.

7.

UTAH STUDENT,
IDAHO TEACHER,
1936-38

From working eleven hours on the Harker's Island chapel to eleven hours a day in my father's Pocatello building business was an easy transition. He and I agreed that I would take no salary and that, in return, he would support me for my final two years of college. I worked only about two months that summer of 1936 before school started, so I benefitted. The following summer Dad probably had the advantage as I put in four months of labor at carpenters' wages while his financial support for my last year of college would not have equalled that amount. But he was sending money each month to my sister Ann, then serving a mission in Colorado, and I wanted to help him all that I could. It was a mutually satisfactory arrangement.

I chose the University of Utah for my junior and senior years for at least three reasons. It was a better school than the University of Idaho at Moscow; it was much closer to Pocatello; and I could have board and room with my Aunt Vilate Cushing Hanson, my mother's sister, for $20 a month. She and Uncle Charlie lived on Fifth East near Thirty-ninth South, so I had to catch the streetcar at Seventh East and Thirty-third South to get to classes. But to a well-traveled former missionary that was a minor problem. My two years with the Hansons were pleasant. I enjoyed getting to know some of my relatives and participating in the frequent get-togethers, marked by good food, good fellowship, and good singing. I also occasionally worked on Saturdays for Uncle Charlie, a carpenter, who was doing small remodeling jobs to try to make a living for his large family during the Roosevelt recession of 1937-38.

My first quarter at the University of Utah is memorable because I took beginning philosophy from Waldemar Read, a wise and provocative liberal teacher. As I sat on the front row, an obvious returned LDS missionary, he continually challenged my beliefs and directed my reading in the works of John Dewey whose pragmatic approach to life appealed to me then and still does. Read was very good in restoring a little humility and reducing some of the stuffed-shirt and superior inclinations which I brought back with me from my exalted position as a district president in North Carolina. I was still pretty confident that my convictions about religion and life were unassailable. Later, when I returned to teach in Utah, Waldemar Read and I became good friends; and when he died, I was asked to dedicate his grave.

To satisfy my science requirement, I took three classes in geology. Dr. Fredrick J. (Jerusalem) Pack was an interesting and challenging teacher who insisted that teaching students to think was more important than stuffing them with knowledge, an approach that rather appealed to me. I went on two field trips with his class and remember with some pleasure our visit to Stockton Bar and the sand dunes near Delta, Utah, and the singing on the way home, led, of course, by Dr. Pack. A Professor Schaefer probably covered more than climatology, but that's what I remember of his course in geology. Finally, I enrolled in Ray Marsell's class in petrology, the science of rocks. I found the subject boring but the teacher sprightly and colorful, especially his habit of wearing two wristwatches and also carrying a pocket watch. The grade in his class was based on performance in one midterm and a final examination. Because I was very much in love with Betty that spring, I paid little attention to the midterm. My grade, in the 30s, Marsell assured me, was the lowest in the class. He added that if I didn't get on the ball, he would most assuredly flunk me. I took his advice, earned an "A" on the final and received a "C" for the course.

I chose sociology as a minor but was totally turned off by my first professor, without doubt the most ineffective teacher I ever had in my life. I knew I couldn't sit through another class with him, so I visited Arthur L. Beeley, head of the department and acknowledged universally as a superior teacher. I told him frankly that my assigned professor was a worthless teacher and I couldn't take any more classes from him. Beeley smiled and asked if there were any other professor in the Department of Sociology whom I'd like to take a class from. I replied that

I very much wanted to take a class from *him*. He consented, and I filled my sociology requirements in his fascinating classes on criminology and aberrant human behavior.

Because I wanted to teach, I had to take several classes in the Department of Education to qualify for a teaching credential. The methods courses were just awful. In one course we all called the instructor (behind his back of course) "Old Koos and Kefauver," because they authored the text which he quoted with every other breath. I still can't remember the professor's real name. I did learn something about the psychology of learning, in spite of myself, which proved useful in the classroom.

My best education teacher was John T. Wahlquist, a sophisticated and knowledgeable professor who became chair of the department and later president of San Jose State College. He won me completely one day when he asked the class what kind of periodical literature we read. When I responded that I read the *Atlantic Monthly* and *Harper's,* he informed the class, "Now that's the sign of an educated person!" How could I not admire Professor Wahlquist?

I also have good memories of a class in educational statistics, not because of the teacher or the subject but because of another class member. More of Betty later.

My experience with Giovanni Costigan at the Southern Branch of the University of Idaho and with the mountaineers and fishermen of the South had already confirmed my determination to become a college teacher of history, but the University of Utah had a limited choice of history professors. The list grew suddenly shorter when, after only a month in colonial American history during the fall quarter of 1936, Andrew Love Neff died suddenly. He had been the mainstay of the department as the chairman and a former student of Herbert Eugene Bolton of the University of California at Berkeley. An uninspiring teacher, Neff was a competent historian whose *History of Utah* up to the coming of the railroad in 1869 is still very good for that early period. Only Harold Dalgliesh and Levi Edgar Young were left as full-time faculty members. Mrs. Betty Dalgliesh, who had an M.A. in history, was hired to finish out Neff's courses. Delightful, interesting, and pregnant, she barely finished teaching her two courses before giving birth at the end of the fall quarter. She later told me that when President George Thomas interviewed her for the teaching assignment, he kept calling her "Mrs. Doglash."

Harold Dalgliesh became my mentor at Utah, and it was upon his recommendation that I later decided to pursue a graduate degree at Berkeley. He was a highly professional scholar from the University of Pennsylvania who gave polished and well-organized but rather soporific lectures. I remember one warm spring afternoon when he was talking about the presidential election of 1932 in which the issue of the repeal of the Prohibition Amendment and "wets" versus "dries" played a part and during which the Republicans warned of catastrophe if the American people should "change horses in midstream" by voting for Franklin D. Roosevelt. I burst out that that was probably correct because the public would surely get wet if they did change horses in midstream. It was a lame attempt at humor but did wake up the class, although Dalgliesh rather stared me down. I liked and respected him; he helped me a great deal.

Levi Edgar Young, an M.A. from Harvard and one of the Seven Presidents of the Seventy in the Mormon hierarchy, was over-sensitive because he did not have a Ph.D. Because he didn't get along with the other members of the history department, the university created a special Department of Western History of which he was the chairman and sole faculty member. In the spring of 1930 Rex Skidmore, later dean of the Graduate School of Social Work at the University of Utah, and I were the only majors in Young's department. He was not very well-trained as an historian but was a great story-teller. I learned to beware of the fanciful and far-fetched facts with which he embroidered these tales. One lecture on the death of Abraham Lincoln's mother was such a tear-jerker that I later checked the record to discover that too much of what Professor Young had told us was pure fiction. Another day he spent the entire class period fulminating against an ROTC student whose blouse was unbuttoned and stressing the importance of wearing the nation's uniform properly. When Skidmore and I reported to his office in late May 1938 to take our comprehensive examinations as his only graduating seniors, he handed us questions which were so difficult and so distant from the material we had studied that we informed him we could not answer any of the questions. His reply was, "Well, it doesn't matter. You're good boys, and I'll approve your graduation anyway." We never did take a comprehensive exam. Despite his shortcomings as an historian, he was a loveable little character, and I remember him with fondness.

I had one experience that demonstrates how little most of us can predict the future. In the spring of 1937 a British statesman gave a public lecture in Kingsbury Hall after showing a thirty-minute film of one of Adolf Hitler's famous open-air extravaganzas. The British M.P. then warned all of us in the audience that a second World War was sure to come and that the United States would be drawn into the conflict. As we left the meeting, I remarked to a friend, "He is a war-monger. We will never fight in another world war. If Britain wishes to fight Nazi Germany, she will have to do so alone." Six years later I was an infantry private.

Apart from my classes and scholarly activities, I had little involvement in university affairs. My life during the two years at Utah was rather quiet compared to the frenetic pace of my mission days. Because of poverty and my less than exuberant gregariousness, my social life consisted mostly of Mill Creek Ward's Sunday services and the weeknight Mutual Improvement Association meetings. When I was asked to teach the class of M-Men (adult men over the age of about twenty), I discovered that only four or five participated because the former teacher had spent nearly every class period teaching that those who smoked would surely go to hell. I asked the four members present at my first class to pass the word that I would never mention tobacco or the Word of Wisdom[1] if they would attend class. Soon I had about thirty participants, and we all had a good time that year. It is even possible that I was able to save some souls from following the path of perdition.

In the late winter of 1936-37, I met Betty McAllister through the luck of alphabetical seating in our educational statistics class. She has said she first noticed me because my feet and those of the tall male on

---

1. Joseph Smith announced the "Word of Wisdom" in 1833 as practical advice in maintaining good health. Solidified into doctrine by my day, the Word of Wisdom asked people to eat less meat and more grain, vegetables, and fruits; but its strictures against "strong drink," tea, coffee, and tobacco constituted the enforceable and orthodox interpretation. In the early frontier days of the LDS church, conforming to these admonitions was an ideal to be sought but not an absolute requirement for entry into heaven. Brigham Young was rather tolerant of backsliding among his rough-hewn followers. It was Heber J. Grant, who became church president in 1918, who declared war on drinking and smoking. According to the latest scientific discoveries, Joseph Smith was far ahead of his time, and Mormons are recognized today for their healthful lifestyle.

Betty McAllister as a college student.

her other side were so gigantic. I first became aware of her when our midterms were handed back: I had the highest grade, she the second highest. When the final exam grades were posted, I *really* became aware of her because she had displaced me with the highest grade while I was second on the list.

Having proved, I hope, that I was first attracted to her fine mind and high intelligence, I cheerfully confess that I also admired her beauty. She was a tall, shapely brunette of extraordinary good looks, as her wedding portrait shows. I then discovered that she lived only a short distance down the street from Aunt Vilate and even attended the same ward. We had a few dates that spring to ward functions, but I was determined not to get romantically involved until I had completed my Ph.D. (It was a questionable resolution anyway.)

As I grew to know her better, it became obvious that she had a strong personality, a rich fund of common sense, impressively industrious habits—and our family standard was already very high—and an equally impressive quality that I can describe only as steadiness. Like me, she maintained an exterior reserve and emotional control that covered deep and passionate commitments. The children and I always knew that she was unequivocally on our side. These traits were immensely appealing to me, even as I sensibly told myself that I was not interested in marriage.

During the summer of 1937, I helped my father build an LDS ward house in Parker, Idaho, a small farming village just a few miles west of St. Anthony. By this time, Dad was being forced out of Pocatello, although he had taken a contract to build a chapel to replace our old

Fourth Ward building. With this start, he next won bids to construct the Parker chapel, a high school LDS seminary, and the Fifth Ward and stake center in Idaho Falls, "much to my sorrow," as he later wrote. (The church contracts proved to be financial disasters.) He and Mother moved to Idaho Falls in the winter of 1936–37 where he also began to build homes, a business which saved us from starving. I rather enjoyed my summer working in Parker. Its farmers were enjoying prosperous times with not too much effort because the irrigation wa-ter from nearby Snake River flowed in a sub-surface stream from

Betty McAllister,
University of Utah graduate in French, 1938.

the large canals to nourish the roots of their alfalfa, grain, and potatoes. It was not necessary to divert the canal water over the fields or down furrows. The water in the canals was so clear and so filled with fish from Snake River that we often spent evenings fishing in the canals.

When I returned to classes at the University of Utah in October 1937, I rediscovered Betty. I will never forget my first view of her that fall. She was walking down the street near her home, and the realization that I loved her hit me in every part of my mind and body at once. The metaphoric "ton of bricks" could not have made a more decided impact. Interestingly enough, part of the recognition was knowing that I had already loved her for a long time. As I groped to understand it, the words of a popular song came to the surface of my consciousness: "I saw you last night and got that old feeling ..."

I sensibly decided to wait until we said hello before sharing my discovery with her, and we had several dates in the next few weeks. In late October I declared my love; fortunately for me, she returned the interest. By winter we were going steady and had already decided upon marriage at some future date. "That Old Feeling" became "our" song, and it themed almost fifty-eight years of a very happy life together before her death on June 9, 1997.

It was at this time that some of my grades slipped a little, but both of us were elected to the Phi Kappa Phi honor organization, made up of the top 10 percent, or thirty-five members of the 360 graduating seniors of 1938. (Betty was a French major.) I had also been chosen as one of the eleven members of Phi Delta Kappa, the professional organization for educators. As I look at my photograph of these eleven men, it is obvious that we were all returned missionaries and rather satisfied with ourselves. My grade-point average for 107 credit hours at Utah was 3.38 based on a possible 4.00, which seems rather low given the grade-inflation pattern of today.

To complete my certification as a teacher, I had been a practice teacher at one of the Salt Lake City junior high schools and at the Stewart Training School on campus. The latter school had as students some of the bright youngsters from the university community who were a real challenge to fledgling teachers. I remember that as I stood at the door of my room the first day as the students trooped by, one little boy looked up at me and said, "Hi, Abe Lincoln." This was Walker Wallace who is now one of the city's leading citizens and businessmen. I was now prepared to enter the world of teaching but had no intention of ever teaching high school. My next goal was to earn enough money to start graduate work at Berkeley.

After commencement, I left for Idaho Falls for a year's work as a carpenter in my father's business, believing that I could save enough to get me through much of my graduate work at the University of California. After I spent two months of driving nails, however, a teachers' agency in Salt Lake City offered me the principalship of a combined grade and high school in Pingree, Idaho. This offer was a complete surprise and made me ponder what I really wanted to do in life. I finally concluded that although I would certainly make more money as a builder, if I were truly committed to teaching, I owed it to myself to get some experience in the public schools before beginning to teach college students. As I look back, I believe it was the right decision to take the job. I think that all university professors, too many of whom look with disdain on elementary and secondary school teachers, would be more understanding of students and the educational process if they spent at least one year teaching in the public schools. I feel the same way about army officers. Let them serve as privates for a year before donning their bars and stars. I must confess though that another motive for acceptance of the Pingree position was that I would be the principal and not merely a teacher.

This decision was fairly typical of my personal style: I thought about all aspects of the decision thoroughly, considered whether there were other options besides the obvious, traced the consequences as far as I could project them, analyzed whether the various options were compatible with my principles and values, then made up my mind and acted promptly on it. While the thinking process sometimes takes longer than the day or so I devoted to it in this case, I don't usually feel a need to consult other "experts," postpone making a decision, or revisit a decision once I have made it. As a result, I am usually spared drifting, dithering, and "buyer's remorse." The net result is that I have always been contented with my choices.

With the decision made, I drove down to Pingree to be interviewed. School was scheduled to start in two short weeks, putting the board under considerable pressure. I found L. S. Caldwell, chairman of the Board of District No. 40 of the County of Bingham, putting up his hay. I walked out to the stack, introduced myself, and began to explain my qualifications. He looked me over carefully and interrupted, "You can have the job." That was it. He obviously felt no need to talk to the other two members of the board; and as I learned later, my size was my chief qualification. On the opening day of school, I learned that the previous spring three of the high school boys had tried to beat up the principal. The principal had proved too much for them, but Mr. Caldwell wanted someone who looked as though he could discipline strapping eighteen-year-olds whose extracurricular activities included cowboying and riding untrained broncos. I was paid $100 a month for nine months. The other four teachers were paid $90 a month.

Pingree is a wide place in the road eighteen miles west of the county seat, Blackfoot. It was a poor farming area on the edge of the great lava field which stretches along the Snake River toward American Falls. The village was composed of a small grocery store/filling station and a small LDS chapel. The school building, only a year old, consisted of five classrooms, a principal's office, a kitchen, and a gymnasium with a stage at one end. I made arrangements to sleep in the office as well, and shared these quarters with Boyd Earl from Paul, Idaho, who had a new teaching certificate and two years of college. Earl taught fifth and sixth grades. A Mrs. Larsen and another married woman, whose name I have completely forgotten, were to teach the first and second grades and the third and fourth, respectively. They had taught at the Pingree School for several years, and without them I would have been lost. A Miss Jones, fresh out of college, taught the seventh and eighth grades. I had twenty students in my ninth- and tenth-grade classes. There were 125 students altogether. This was before the consolidation process had begun in earnest in Idaho, and I had many titles: superintendent of District 40, principal of the high school, principal of the junior high school, and principal of the grade school. There was one school bus—a sheep wagon with benches along each side, straw on the floor, a small stove in the center, and a team of horses in front driven by one of the high school boys.

With the ninth grade seated in two rows on my left and the tenth grade in two rows on my right, I organized the two classes so that they alternated in their recitations and in presenting their assignments. I taught English, world history, business methods, public speaking, algebra, and geometry. My worst class was world history which I probably knew too much about.

My best classes were algebra and geometry, although I had had no training in mathematics since high school. Because of my multitude of duties, I often did not have the time to work the problems myself before assigning them to the class and so had to solve them in front of the class if no student had come up with the answer. Then one day it happened. A problem in geometry came along which no class member could solve, and I discovered that I couldn't either. The students were ecstatic. "Old Madsen" (I was all of twenty-three) was stumped. I immediately challenged them to take the problem home to work on and invited them to involve their parents and friends in the contest if they wished. For three days the community tested wits with their school principal and the other four teachers but no solution came. At 3:00

I am standing to the left of the fifteen students in my ninth- and tenth-grade classes at Pingree School in 1938-39. Kinya Mikami is on the right, front.

A.M. on the fourth day, the light dawned on me, and I hurriedly got out of bed and wrote the answer down before it left me. The honor of the University of Utah was saved, and I had triumphed after all.

In the early spring we teachers had to prepare our grade school, junior high, and high school students to pass the state proficiency tests. It was a period of tension for all concerned; but we did well and, since then, I have come to believe that such regular exams are quite worth-while.

One particular state regulation would be unconstitutional today. Each morning I was obliged to read a verse of scripture from the King James Version of the Bible. The specific verses were listed in a special directive sent to all schools from the state superintendent's office. I have often wondered who made the selections and on what basis.

My twenty high school students ranged from dull to very bright and from apathetic to highly motivated. I lost my first three tenth-graders when a young man named Junior, ringleader in the attack on the previous principal, refused my attempts to interest him in school.

One sunny fall day he asked permission to go to the restroom. A minute or two after he returned, in came Miss Jones in tears, soaking wet from head to foot. Junior had filled a paper bag with water and tossed it through the open door of the seventh- and eighth-grade classroom. I had been very patient with Junior, but now I exploded. I called him out into the hall and told him in no uncertain terms to get his cowboy hat and to get out of the building before I threw him out. He was a six-footer as were his two friends who I expected would now join him with unfortunate results for "Old Madsen." Instead, Junior meekly retrieved his hat and left. His two buddies remained seated but failed to show up the next day or thereafter.

I saw Mr. Caldwell that evening, explained what had happened, and asked if he and the board were going to back me up. He assured me that he would. I would not allow Junior to enter the building again until he gave Miss Jones a public apology. Because it was the only place for any social activity in the village and, I suspect, because he may have secretly regretted his impulsive action, he showed up one day and apologized in front of Miss Jones's class. Later that winter he and I played on the town basketball team and became good friends.

My remaining seventeen students endured that winter, but another boy flatly refused to stay in school when spring came and left with his father's blessing (and mine) to plow and plant. It was what he really wanted to do. When a sixteen-year-old girl failed to show up one Monday, I learned that she had been married over the weekend. The other students seemed surprised that I was surprised. There were several Japanese-American boys and girls in the two classes. As I had come to expect, they were among the neatest, best-mannered, and most industrious students. Kinya Mikami, a tenth-grader, was very bright especially in science and math. I gave him extra attention and encouraged him to go to college.[2]

As principal, I had a lot to learn and marvel today that I had the te-

---

2. In 1995, while grocery shopping, I purchased a five-pound sack of potatoes bearing the company name, "Mikami Brothers," from a town in eastern Oregon. Impulsively, I wrote, asking if they were related to Kinya Mikami and could supply any information about him. I received a nice letter giving me Kinya's address in Massachusetts. He responded to my letter sending photographs of himself and his grandchildren. After military service during World War II, he had earned a Ph.D. in physics and had been employed by NASA. It was delightful news.

merity to take the job when I had had no experience as a school man at all. The two experienced teachers helped me over the rough spots. I had made arrangements to eat lunch at a widow's place just a block from the school, but in January my two experienced teachers demanded that I eat a brown-bag lunch at my desk so that my room could serve as detention for the unruly. Their logic was irrefutable, and from then on I became the warden to frightened little boys and girls sentenced to my room at lunch time. One of the larger high school boys offered to supervise some boxing matches in the gym to use up the boys' excess energy. I innocently agreed until I noticed that the lunch hour had turned into general mayhem. I terminated that particular activity.

Because school was the only setting for community socials, the teachers and I felt obligated to try to provide some kind of entertainment. We put on some talent shows with the help of the PTA which included, in one performance, my singing a bass solo. That fact alone should provide ample evidence of how desperate the social situation was. I also officiated as bouncer at the community Saturday night dances in the gym. One spring evening I was forced to evict three slightly drunk young men, one of whom was a drop-out friend of Junior's. As I prepared to reenter the building after escorting him outside, he yelled into the night air, "S—on Old Madsen!" an instruction which I, along with the universe, loftily chose to ignore.

Two outstanding events of the year were the appearance of the Glen Taylor actors from Pocatello. One of my students at Utah State University, F. Ross Peterson, who later wrote a first-rate biography of U.S. senator Glen Taylor and who has since been on the faculty there and served as chair of the Department of History, once asked me for any information I could give him about Taylor. I wrote:

> Your request for information about Glen Taylor takes me back a few years. My first recollection of him was as a radio presence over station KSEI in Pocatello. As I remember, he had a daily program of about half an hour composed of light chatter and cowboy music. One of his favorite expressions was, "Dora, she's my wife." He also used to introduce his small son as "Arod—that's Dora spelled backwards."
>
> In the fall of 1938, I took the job of principal of the combined grade school and high school at Pingree, Idaho. There was very little opportunity for social life in the community, and the school served as the only

outlet for such occasions. Early in the fall, I received a letter from Glen Taylor asking if I would be interested in having his troupe perform at Pingree. The older teachers said he had come the year before and had put on two successful performances. They advised me to sign him up, which I did.

The first performance was a sell-out. First, the troupe presented a comedy with Glen Taylor as the leading character and comedian. He was a consummate actor and knew how to appeal to the crowd assembled in the rural schoolhouse. After the play, his cowboy band then played for a dance. Similar performances were given all over southern Idaho and he used his radio program to help advertise the events.

I then contracted with him for a second performance at Pingree for three or four months later. Again, he was the leading comedian in the play and also led the band afterwards. After the crowd left that night, I met in my office with Glen and Dora Taylor to settle our financial account and soon became involved in a political discussion with them. The rest of the troupe had already left and the three of us sat and talked until quite late.

Glen Taylor told me the following story of how he had become involved in the Glen Taylor Players (you will have to check my memory of this incident against other sources). When the Great Depression reached its low ebb, Glen and Dora were living in Chicago where Glen was employed as an actor. He had a savings account of $18,000 which he had accumulated from some successful performances in various plays. The bank in which he held his account closed its doors, and he and Dora lost their life savings. This event had a tremendous effect on him. He had never been interested in politics before; but now he suddenly became aware that history has a way of making dramatic, and sometimes traumatic, changes in a person's life.

With the little money he had left, he bought a trailer house and for two years devoted his time to reading political tomes, philosophy, and history. Dora worked during this period to help support them. After two years of such study, he adopted a plan of action. He decided to move to Idaho where he would organize a cowboy band and a company of play actors. He wanted to make himself well-known to the people of Idaho and well-known as a man of the people who understood the problems of the common man and who could speak their language. He concluded his story by saying that he was preparing himself to run for the United States Senate and intended to do so at the appropriate time. I was so impressed with his political skill, his audacity, and his well-conceived plan that I said at the time, "I believe you'll make it."

That is the last time I saw Glen Taylor. I left Idaho to pursue graduate studies in California and never lived in Idaho again. My only information about him from then on came from news stories. He struck me as being very sincere and far from the charlatan or demagogue which some have accused him of being. His later radical espousal of Henry Wallace's cause is quite understandable to me when I remember that night in the Pingree schoolhouse and the fervor with which he spoke about the rights of the little people of the nation.

In addition to my other duties, I was expected to coach the high school basketball team, the junior high basketball team, the baseball team, and the track squad. Fortunately, there were not enough boys to make up a football team. Boyd Earl, who knew less about basketball than I did, became the coach of the high school basketball squad on nights when I was busy with the junior high boys. One memorable night at Rockland, he barely quelled a riot when our pugnacious boys challenged the whole town of Rockland. The high school team usually played the "B" team of the larger neighboring towns and one evening enjoyed a tremendous victory over Idaho Falls. We were not so successful at American Falls when the coach of that team, dis-gruntled that our boys were winning, began running in some of his varsity players to ensure a victory. I almost had a riot on my hands that night and finally just walked off the floor with my team. The crowd, who did not know the dastardly tactics their coach was employing, jeered.

The real interest was in the junior high basketball league of Bingham County. The eighteen towns in the league had been involved in a very heated competition for a number of years, and Pingree had never even come close to winning the annual tournament against such metropolises as Blackfoot, Shelley, and Firth. But things were different in 1938. My predecessor was apparently a very competent and knowledgeable basketball technician and over a period of about three years had formed a fine team. Furthermore, the boys had played so much together they knew instinctively what each player would do. I knew most about man-to-man defense but soon gave up any attempts to change their zone defense which they had perfected to the nth degree. The team was composed of Bud Bedwell, the center and best player; Kenneth Ropp, guard and floor general; a steady second guard surnamed Cammack; "Lefty" Caldwell at forward; and little Tommy Summers at forward. In reserve I had Williams, a forward, and the solidly built Willard Bales, who couldn't shoot worth anything but was tremendous at guard.

My championship basketball team,
a first for Pingree, in 1938. The names of some have eluded me but I still
remember, back left: Bud Bedwell, Kenneth Ropp, Cammack, Williams,
and Willard Bales. Front left: Tommy Summers and, with
trophy, "Lefty" Caldwell.

During the playing season, we won every game but one. The Fort Hall Reservation team beat us by a few points when I was forced to bench Tommy Summers for playing hookey. We even beat Springfield (Grandview), which all knowledgeable people knew was almost as good as Pingree. The scores in these games were rather small in this day when the rules demanded a center jump after each basket. In our game in Wilson's cracker-box gym, the floor space was so tiny that we won in a hard-fought battle, 6-4.

The week before the start of the double-elimination tournament in Blackfoot, my whole team came down with the flu. As a result, our weakened team lost to Springfield by two points when one of the

Springfield guards made a last-minute desperation long basket. After we defeated Springfield in a second game, the tournament officials were forced to schedule the championship game between Pingree and Springfield for Monday night. I was feeling rather confident by Sunday because the boys were over the flu and determined to beat rival Springfield. Then disaster struck. Late Sunday evening Bud's mother came to tell me that our star player had smallpox. It looked as though our dreams of capturing the county championship for the first time were evaporating. Also rumors had already spread that some Pingree partisans had invested large sums, for them, on a sure victory. My only recourse was to put poor-shot Willard in to defend our basket.

By the end of the first half, the score was 8 to 3 in favor of Springfield because Willard saw a chance for glory and continued to try to make points, leaving our basket undefended. During the half break I warned him that if he took a single step across the center line towards our opponent's basket, I would take him out of the game forever. It worked. He was a bulldog on defense, and our team came through to win 14-8. The people of Pingree were so proud that I believe I could have signed a life contract as principal the day after our victory. If it seems that I have devoted too much time to a description of our basketball victory, I am only acknowledging what is most important in American education. The picture of my team holding the winner's trophy is no doubt still much treasured by those boys, now old men.

My year at Pingree was a fine experience. I was the first Mormon principal in a community badly divided along religious lines. When the bishop asked me to speak early in the year, I was careful to dispense words of wisdom on "education," rather than a religious topic. The non-Mormons of the village were reassured, and I got along well with both factions. As an educator, I learned a lot!

But my heart was elsewhere. My busy schedule at Pingree, supplemented by Saturdays working in Idaho Falls with Dad, was interrupted as often as I could to see Betty. She was teaching first grade at Roosevelt Elementary School near her parents' home during the 1938-39 year. I bought a used Plymouth two-door sedan which made many trips to Salt Lake City that year. Often I would get back to the schoolhouse after an all-night drive from Utah just in time to ring the bell. My students were quite understanding on those long, sleepy Mondays and probably got away with murder in their assignments.

Betty's parents, Ethel Carpenter McAllister and Delos R. McAllister.

At Christmastime Betty and I became engaged and planned to marry in August just before leaving for Berkeley and graduate school. The thought of teaching during the school year and attending summer school to piece out a higher degree had no appeal to me. I was determined to make whatever sacrifices were necessary to drive straight through to the Ph.D.; and Betty agreed with me that if we did not seize the opportunity determinedly, we might never have another opportunity.

In this, as in other values, we were well matched. Her parents, Delos R. McAllister and Ethel Carpenter McAllister, had spent their early lives in the harsh but beautiful country of Kanab in southern Utah. Betty's mother was a woman of much common sense, a strong mind, a great love for her three children, and an abiding interest in education. She had attended Brigham Young Academy as a young woman and intended that all three of her children graduate. They did. Her approach to Mormonism, also highly practical, is captured in a favorite family story. While Betty was preparing for her temple endowment and our sealing, she was quite taken aback when some elderly women in her ward solemnly told her that she was about to assume terrible responsibilities. Her mother's advice briskly punctured any exaggerated assumptions: "Well for hell's sake, Betty, don't laugh when you go through the ceremony."

Delos McAllister had been a cowboy on the Kaibab Plateau during his youth, then had attended a small college in the east for training in business and accounting. He later served as Kane County clerk and had other responsibilities in Kanab before taking a job with U.S. Fidel-ity and Guaranty Company in Salt Lake City where the family moved when Betty was nine. He and I got along famously, and I always con-sidered him a model father-in-law: never criticizing, never interfering with our decision, always encouraging, and generously offering his help during times of stress.

A famous family story concerns his father, a polygamist, who as Kanab Ward choir leader began courting a choir member as a possible plural wife. He had developed the habit of bringing her by his house after choir practice and continuing the courtship by snuggling in the large rocking chair in the parlor and conversing in low tones. Betty's grandmother, listening from the next room, could hear the gentle squeak of the rocker as it moved back and forth. Although it was the only decent piece of furniture she owned, one morning after such a tender rendezvous, she took it out to the woodpile and chopped it into firewood. This story tells something not only of the grandmother's personality but also of the emotional toll exacted by polygamy. (The grandfather, incidentally, married the choir member anyway.)

8.

GRADUATE SCHOOL
AT BERKELEY AND THE
SHIPYARDS OF WORLD
WAR II, 1939-43

Betty and I were married on August 11, 1939, in the Salt Lake temple and held our wedding reception in the Old Jensen Home at 2700 South and Highland Drive with all of our family on hand to help us celebrate. Our two families meshed very well. The previous winter, while I was teaching at Pingree, Betty had accepted an invitation to spend a weekend with my folks and left with mutual satisfaction on all sides. Dad and Delos became congenial friends almost at once, recognizing the same driving type of personality in each other.

Betty and I left the next day by train for Berkeley. I had sold the Plymouth to Boyd Earl to help supplement our joint savings. In Berkeley we rented a walk-up flat at 2525 Dwight Way which has since been razed to make room for the famous "Peoples Park" which dissident University of California students promoted during the confrontation days of the 1960s.

This "first home" was better than some of the places I'd lived in as a missionary, but it was a new experience for Betty. We had little except for each other, but that was enough. Betty was incredibly willing to put up with next to nothing in the way of furnishings. I suppose all newlyweds have their "adjustment" stories. Ours was a cheese soufflé, an experiment for her. (She wanted to cook well but not out of any intrinsic desire to be a great chef.) The soufflé was a success and I praised it lavishly. Well, we had cheese soufflés for the next few weeks until I finally inquired, "Is this all you can make?" We haven't had a soufflé since, and I've learned to exercise considerably more tact in my comments.

An odd sort of recreation was observing life in this university town, and I captured some of these observations in limericks, a form I had never experimented with before. I still have about eighty of these slightly obtuse efforts in my records but hide them for reasons which will become obvious from the single example I am willing to share:

> A convivial gent from Ukiah
> Threw some gasoline on to a fiah.
> Then he shouted with glee
> For, you see, it was he
> Made the fiah go hiah and hiah.

This collection of limericks was prompted, in almost every case, by current affairs which were being discussed by everyone. The campus communists of the time were easily recognizable by their uniforms of sandals and berets and by the noon meetings which they held every Friday just outside Sather Gate. Here the principal speaker would play a recording of a satiric song: "I hate war and so does Eleanor," attack President Franklin D. Roosevelt as a

Betty (at right) and me (opposite)
in our wedding finery,
married August 11, 1939,
in Salt Lake City.

war monger, and launch into a harangue of severe criticism. I suppose that Berkeley has always been on the cutting edge of radicalism and social change.

Financially, we were on a short tether. Betty and I were both realistic about our financial constraints. There were few fellowships and scholarships in those days even if my scholastic record had been superior; there were no federal student loans; and our parents were not in a position to help us. Betty self-sacrificingly postponed her own professional ambitions and took a number of jobs, some of them considerably beneath her qualifications, to support us while I supplemented with part-time work and considerably more than full-time credit hours. It was a hard-scrabble existence, but we did not feel sorry for ourselves. Most of our friends were in the same position.

Nor did we feel that Betty's ambitions and capabilities were less

than mine. We were simply facing the fact that a graduate degree for me would probably yield higher economic returns for me than for her. But I think the most important reason is that we saw ourselves as a team working for a common goal with each of us contributing absolutely everything possible to it. Because each of us was making a 100-percent contribution and recognized the contribution of the other as 100 percent as well, the fact that the contributions were different mattered less.

Later I felt rather guilty that Betty with her fine mind had not been able to do graduate work; and when she expressed an interest in linguistics after the children

Betty and I outside our walk-up apartment on Fulton Street in Berkeley, California, in 1940.

were in school, I enthusiastically encouraged her as she completed her M.A. at the University of Utah. But in Berkeley she took a number of full-time jobs. Her first job was as a secretary at Montgomery Ward's in Oakland. Then for several months she was a clerk-typist for the University Graduate Division and finally got a job with the Department of Political Science typing bibliography cards, a most boring and unchallenging occupation.

I did gardening for about a month, then we got a rent-free basement walk-in apartment on Euclid Avenue in return for my tending the furnace and picking up the garbage every morning for the thirty tenants. One night, quite late, a drunken man walked in through our unlocked door, stood at the foot of our bed for a few seconds, and then left, only to return immediately to say, "I apologize for disturbing you." He left a second time and didn't come back, but we started locking our door after that.

For three months I worked twenty hours a week as the hat-check man in the basement of the university library. My next part-time job was as a supply clerk at the university hospital. Then I was able to get a job as the weekend night watchman at Hale Brothers Department Store in downtown Oakland near the waterfront. I worked eighteen hours a week, from 12:00 P.M. on Saturday to 6:00 P.M. on Sunday. The pay was fairly good for those days; and as my regular rounds in the four-story building took only about twenty minutes, I had the remainder of each hour for study. I held the job for the next two years and learned a great deal about the seamy side of life on the Oakland waterfront. This income permitted us to rent a walk-up flat at 2605 Fulton Street, our home from the spring of 1940 until I went into the army in July 1943.

During our second Christmas in Berkeley, Betty sold toys at H. C. Capwell's Department Store while I did the same at Hale Brothers. We certainly didn't have any excess money but found that our friends, who were also graduate students, were in the same boat. We very much enjoyed these years in Berkeley.

At the Department of History, I soon became acquainted with the departmental secretary, Mildred Radke, who was every graduate student's friend and certainly mine. She advised me to work with Lawrence Kinnaird, a former World War I aviator and oil-field equipment salesman, who had earned a Ph.D. under Herbert E. Bolton and, by this time, had taken over Bolton's work. I followed this excellent advice, and it was a most fortunate choice. I took his seminar each semester I was there; Kinnaird was patient and understanding with me; and without his guidance, I probably would never have completed my graduate work. He lived into his nineties and enjoyed his retirement in Carmel, California.

In my letter of application to Dean Charles B. Lipman of the Graduate Division at Berkeley, I requested a waiver of out-of-state tuition because of my election to Phi Kappa Phi but was turned down because "your scholarship at the University of Utah cannot be considered as distinguished." I'm happy to say that, after one semester at the University of California, my scholarship was considered "distinguished" enough that I got the waiver. Furthermore, after a year, I qualified as a resident. The graduate school also informed me that I would have to take an additional fourteen hours of upper division history credit to meet the department's requirements. This was quite a blow, since I was determined to complete my degree in a year. So I buckled down and took these courses while also carrying eight hours of graduate course work required for a master's degree.

My classwork kept me very busy. I began to absorb the philosophy of "Greater America" which Bolton had introduced into the discipline. To him and his many students, historians of U.S. history who were oriented toward New England and England had overlooked the contribution of Spain and Latin America to the development of the Americas. Bolton spent a vigorous professional lifetime trying to rectify that omission. His special interest was in the Southwest borderlands area, and he wrote such influential books as *The Rim of Christendom,* a biography of Catholic Father Kino, and the story of Coronado. He and such scholars as Herbert Ingram Priestley and Charles Edward Chapman had developed Bancroft Library into the premier repository for Latin American and American Western history materials. My desk, back in the stacks, was next to that assigned to Meredith Wilson, a Utah Mormon, future dean at the University of Utah, and future president of both Oregon State University and the University of Minnesota. It was my first year and his last as a Ph.D. student.

Two of my most memorable classes were Priestley's course on the history of Mexico and a two-semester course in Latin American history from Chapman. The latter was an extraordinary ham as a lecturer and most of us used to leave his classes with sore stomach muscles from laughing at his antics. In one remarkable performance he would describe Spanish social customs, ending by donning the complete costume of a matador. Then one of his graduate students, adorned with a papier-mâché bull's head, would dart out from beneath the lecture desk where he had been hiding for the entire lecture hour, and Chapman would graphically enact a bull fight. It had to be seen to be believed!

To get training from instructors of the traditional English-oriented history, I took a class in the history of the American frontier from Frederick Logan Paxson, on whose shoulders had fallen the mantle of his mentor, Frederick Jackson Turner. He, Bolton, and James Westfall Thompson of the Berkeley faculty were all past presidents of the American Historical Association which gives some indication of the department's prestige.

Laurence Harper's seminar in English colonial history was an ulcer-producing exercise. I felt fortunate to earn a "B" in the class because he was so demanding and critical.

To satisfy the requirements for exposure to non-U.S. history, I took a two-semester seminar in French history from Franklin C. Palm. He allowed me to research and write on "Western American Newspaper Opinion of the Formation of the Third French Republic." The title was long, but the research was very interesting and introduced me to the gold mine of information available in such western publications as the *Gold Hill News* of Nevada and other sprightly and dogmatic western journals. Palm was a delightful and unorthodox bachelor who liked to party occasionally.

I concluded my first year at Berkeley with six "A"s and three "B"s in a history department as demanding as any around. Those nine courses included eight hours in graduate studies and all fourteen hours of make-up work. Under Kinnaird's careful scrutiny I completed, by August 1940, a master's thesis on "The Early History of the Upper Snake River Valley." It was a very immature production which I wish I could now burn so that no one will ever see it again; but at the time I was pleased and proud to receive my M.A. for it.

In the fall of 1940, I entered my Ph.D. program. I knew that the Ph.D. regimen was much more rigorous and had already seen the toll it took on some friends who were more advanced than I. Spencer Taggart, a very bright and able scholar but of a very sensitive and artistic nature, walked out of his preliminary written Ph.D. exams two different times and never did complete his degree but later went into the State Department where he had a distinguished career. The Ph.D. oral exam was even more demanding. While I was working at the university hospital, a Ph.D. candidate in history, whom I didn't know, came in for advice from a physician because his heavy beard was falling out on one side of his face, while the other remained unaffected. The doctor advised him to complete his oral exam, saying that the beard would grow back in. His diagnosis was accurate.

As a sign of my exalted status, I was also invited to join Phi Alpha Theta, the history honor fraternity, on October 18, 1940. It was a wonderful opportunity to meet various faculty members in informal socials. Because spouses weren't invited, the virtually all-male configuration of graduate education meant that these gatherings were basically for men only. The first party I attended was held at a brewery in Oakland where Palm was the invited guest. When I left the function after a couple of hours, he and three graduate students were trying to harmonize "Auld Lang Syne." Most of the meetings were much more decorous, depending on the personality of the faculty member invited for that particular night.

The first obstacle was the German language exam for the second time. My two years of elementary German at Pocatello had prepared me fairly well for the M.A. exam in German, and, perhaps too confident, I approached the Ph.D. exam in the language with little apprehension. Professor Paul Schaefer, who administered the language translation exams for the department, exclaimed, "My God, Madsen, what happened on this second exam?" He passed me, nevertheless, for which I was very grateful. Because Betty had majored in French at the University of Utah, I felt that I should be able to pass that exam with her tutoring. However, my lessons came to an abrupt end because she wanted to teach me French while I wished only to pass the exam. So I just memorized vocabulary for three months and, luckily, was directed by Professor Schaefer to translate a couple of pages concerned with the history of the administration of Thomas Jefferson, a subject which I knew rather well.

With the language exams out of the way, I spent the spring, summer, and fall of 1941 preparing for my Ph.D. preliminary written exams while simultaneously doing coursework. My major field was colonial America; my two minors were U.S. and English history; and my outside field was geography. When I compare those requirements with the minimum three fields which we ask of our graduate students at Utah, I am convinced that the University of California was no bed of roses for history Ph.D. candidates.

On December 7, 1941, I had just finished making my rounds at Hale Brothers Department Store when the radio in my little office blurted out the news of the Japanese attack on Pearl Harbor. And all at once, along with millions of other Americans, my life was changed. The next day some of my graduate student friends attempted to enlist, assuming that defeating the Japanese would take only a few months. One, a fellow named Carboni, spent most of Monday at a recruiting office in San Francisco without getting to the head of the line. On Tuesday he told me that he had thought better of enlisting. About a month later a friend, Bryant S. Knowlton, and I visited the Naval Recruiting Office in San Francisco on a Friday and inquired about commissions in the Chaplain Corps or any other branch of the navy. We were told that there were no opportunities to become chaplains at the time but that, if we would return the following Monday, they would take our applications for other commissions in the navy because the navy desperately needed instructors. On Sunday the *San Francisco Chronicle* reported that the officer in charge of navy recruiting had been selling commissions and the whole office was under investigation. I never returned and missed a chance at a naval career.

Lawrence Kinnaird accepted a position as cultural attaché in Chile, and Bolton came out of retirement to take over his classes. Kinnaird recommended me to Bolton as a reader for his upper division class, at least partly because Bolton had a strong preference for big men as assistants, as I found out later when Bolton told me that that was one reason he had chosen Kinnaird, who was six-foot-two himself, as his replacement at Berkeley. In any case, working with Bolton was an opportunity I did not want to miss.

Without much of a qualm, I postponed my patriotic plans for enlisting in the military that semester. Still, it was obvious that sooner or later I would either have to be in the military or in some kind of defense work, and I anticipated that moment. It never occurred to me to try to get out of it. After all, I was young and healthy and felt I owed it to my country to help defeat the Nazis and the Japanese military. Perhaps more important, I had strong patriotic feelings. I felt protective of America. I *wanted* to do my part. I had no doubt that it was a contest to the death—us or them, and that the Nazis and Japanese were determined to enslave the rest of humankind by taking away the precious individual rights which we as Americans held dear. There was never any question in my mind that we were fighting for survival and for our free way of life.

These feelings were nothing unusual. The entire nation was galvanized by a desire to do our duty. My patriotic feelings were a simple and uncomplicated set of feelings. I felt such love and devotion and identification with my nation that I'd be hard put to find words to describe the strength of my feelings. I still feel a thrill and an emotional charge when Old Glory passes in review. I don't understand any citizen of this country not feeling an immense obligation to it. People hunger everywhere for the freedoms that America gives its citizens liberally.

Furthermore, I was strengthened by knowing that Betty was behind me completely when I made the decisions that put me in the army. She understood that her role was to cope with the hardships that the war and my military involvement created for the family. And she did. Her standard for herself was to cope—and not just to cope but to do it without making a fuss or striking heroic poses. She must have been afraid but she kept it to herself. She would have been disgusted with herself if she had allowed herself to indulge in self-pity, and she would have been affronted if anyone else pitied her. This was her standard in dealing with our many moves and career changes, the worries and demands of parenthood, and especially the protracted illnesses of her last years.

Meanwhile, I threw myself into my classes. Bolton was not a great lecturer, but his material was so new and challenging that students flocked to his classes. A chain-smoker, he took perverse delight in offering me a cigarette—knowing that I was an abstaining Mormon. During the semester he asked several times how a certain student was doing. Only at the end, when I informed Bolton that the student had earned a "B," did he tell me that the fellow was his grandson.

Two more anecdotes may help give insight into the man. He gleefully told me about one of his Mormon Ph.D. students, Thomas Romney, who wrote his dissertation on "The State of Deseret." At the time Bolton was having some difficulty with Frederick Teggart, chair of the Department of History, who despised all Mormons. When Teggart arrived a little late for Romney's oral defense, he immediately demanded, "How can you, being a Mormon, write an impartial history of the State of Deseret?" Romney asked, "Professor Teggart, are you a Mormon?" "No!" exploded the chairman. Romney continued, "Do you think that, as a non-Mormon, you could write an impartial history of the State of Deseret?" Teggart became so angry that he stalked out of the room. Romney's dissertation was approved. As Bolton told me this story, he ended with, "I've always liked Tom Romney." Romney taught in the LDS Institute of Religion at Utah State University during the 1920s and 1930s.

In the other incident Bolton was obsessed with geography and insisted that an historian should be completely familiar with the geography of any area he was studying. He had hired a number of cartographers to prepare large and rather simple maps of Middle America and the American Southwest. It was my daily task to hang the maps for that day's lecture—usually covering almost three walls. Once I could not locate a certain map, which some negligent teaching assistant—not I!—had apparently not returned to the map room. Bolton was quite put out and, during the lecture, kept saying to the class, "Now, if Mr. Madsen had been able to find my map, I would point out certain locations on it which you should know." It did not happen again because I let the other readers know they hadn't better tamper with Bolton's maps. Getting to know Bolton was an interesting and important part of my historical training.

During the first five months of 1942, I worked double shifts as a night watchman because of the store's fear that the Japanese might land troops in the Bay Area or that Japanese submarines might enter the Bay and shell nearby buildings. It was a time of fear and apprehension. With the end of spring semester, I left school along with many others and obtained a full-time job as a weld-checker in the Kaiser Shipyards in Richmond. Each day I was assigned about forty welders whose number of feet of welding I was to measure and record to ensure they were working and not just sleeping on the job. The usual footage I measured for a day's output ran from 150 to about 220 feet for each welder. Another history graduate student, Andy Anderson, had started early in the business and was, by this time, a foreman. He not only gave me a job but also provided for several other history graduates and even hired Professor John Van Nostrand from the history department, whose seminar in historical methods most of us had taken.

I had to join the International Brotherhood of Boiler Makers, Iron Ship Builders and Helpers of America, as Helper No. 614204. The monthly dues were $15.00, and the officials who conducted the initiation ceremony at the union office on the Oakland waterfront exuded such belligerence and toughness that I promised myself I would never attend another meeting.

I worked only during the months of May and June as a weld-checker but learned a great deal about Victory ships and how they were constructed. I escaped being sent to look for the key to the chain locker which many neophyte shipyard workers fell for. I learned about bulwarks, hawser pipes, degaussing systems, masts, booms, roller chocks, king posts, the bilge keel, and, of course, the difference between port and starboard. After one month I had the opportunity to transfer to operating an automatic welding machine which was used for the large seams on the decks. It would have meant a draft-deferred job throughout the war. Most of my friends leaped at such an opportunity, but I chose to take my chances in what was the greatest adventure of my generation—military service in World War II.

I made this decision not only because I was drawn to the adventure but also because my father's construction business had collapsed in Idaho Falls. Materials were simply not available. I wrote suggesting that he come to the Bay Area where there was a great demand for construction workers. When he arrived in June, he stayed with us until we both secured jobs as carpenters working on the construction of a large machine shop in the Kaiser Shipyards. The welding job was draft-deferred but the carpenter's position was not. My draft board warned me that I would surely be drafted, but I didn't hesitate a moment. It was my way of volunteering by way of the back door. Betty may have secretly hoped I would take the welding job, but not a syllable of complaint crossed her lips.

Mother arrived in a few days, and they rented a house. My father didn't want us to look green in our first day on the job, so he insisted that I purchase used tools from a second-hand shop. When I could not find an old beat-up square, he very carefully placed my shiny new square on the lawn and sprinkled it so that it would be nice and rusty the next morning. These precautions were wholly unnecessary, as we immediately discovered. We were almost the only ones in our twenty-man crew with any experience at all. In fact, Dad and I were the only ones who would venture out on the steel roof beams to bolt on the purlins which were to receive the wooden sheathing. The other men had had no experience working at heights.

Our work on the machine shop ended rather abruptly when, after three weeks, one of the crew came by during the lunch hour to inform us that we were building office partitions too fast and that, if we didn't slow down, all of us would soon be out of work. Dad and I were outraged. We worked like demons all afternoon, built as many partitions as all the rest of the crew combined, and quit that evening.

The next morning we applied to the Oliver M. Rousseau Company for jobs. This San Francisco firm had a contract to build about 300 eight-unit apartment houses for shipyard workers in Richmond. Dad was hired as a foreman. Two years later Rousseau made him superintendent of all the company's construction. Dad worked for the firm until late 1944 when he and Mother "retired" and moved to Salt Lake City.

Both of us had to join the Oakland Carpenter's Union, Local No. 36. The examining board took one look at Dad and didn't ask him any questions at all. I was asked two: What was a purlin? and How long would I make the legs of a saw-horse? I responded to the first satisfactorily and indicated 27" as the proper length for saw-horse legs. The initiation fee was $50, and the date was July 10, 1942. When I went into the service, the union continued me as a member so that when we returned to Berkeley in August 1946 I was able to go right to work as a fully paid-up member of the local. After a few months as a member of Dad's gang, I was made the foreman of a finish crew of twenty men.

There was a great deal of rivalry among the many crews of almost 300 carpenters working on the project. Mine was the fastest, mostly because of my lead man, a Norwegian immigrant named Stephenson who just would not be beaten by anyone. One day during lunch hour the men began betting about who was the fastest nailer in the West—Stephenson, or a big, burly man named Gomez, the older brother of the fa-

My parents, Brig and Lydia Madsen,
in Berkeley in 1944 when Dad and I were a
carpentry team again.

mous baseball pitcher, Lefty Gomez of the New York Yankees. Stephenson used a small hammer and drove his nails in staccato machine-gun fashion with quick strokes. Gomez, on the other hand, used a heavy twenty-four-ounce hammer and drove the nails in with two or three blows. To settle the argument, we squared out equal surfaces of siding on the wall of one of the buildings and let them go at it for fifteen minutes. Stephenson won, much to my gratification and to the direct benefit of my wallet.

We worked ten hours a day, seven days a week, and with such

good salaries that I was able to purchase an automobile and minimum luxuries unknown to us as graduate students. This was an interesting and busy time.

I would have been drafted much sooner if Betty's pregnancy had not made me eligible for a six-month deferment. We had wanted a baby much earlier, and Betty and I had gone through a lot of sorrow because she could not become pregnant. We sought the advice of a specialist, and finally, in the late summer of 1942, we were overjoyed when she became pregnant. We would probably have had a much larger family, but the problems related to Betty's difficulties with conception produced a sort of natural spacing of about four years. Our four have turned out to be the very best children any parents could ask for.

The birth of Karen on May 12, 1943, was memorable in many ways. When we arrived at Alta Bates Hospital in Berkeley about 8:00 A.M. after a night of increasingly interesting contractions, the head nurse, on learning that I was a carpenter, asked if I would build some shelves in their delivery room. The materials had been lying in a hallway for about three months, but they hadn't been able to find a carpenter. I promptly refused. After all, this was my first child, and I was understandably preoccupied with the blessed event.

Two hours later I had changed my mind. I wasn't sure I could take any more of watching Betty's labor, so I ducked out by telling the head nurse that if she would find me some tools, I would start to work at once. She did and I did. I would build a few shelves, then leave while a baby was being delivered. I'd check on Betty, then go back to work on the shelves. In the early afternoon Betty was wheeled in; and after Karen's birth I was allowed to see her as the nurse took her into an adjoining room to be cleaned and dressed. I will never forget the strength of my feelings when I first saw her—the awesome sense of responsibility that descended on me to take care of her.

After Betty was taken back to her room, still unconscious, I returned to my labors in the delivery room. When Betty awoke from the anesthetic about 4:30 P.M., she asked the nurse who had just come on shift to tell her husband who was building shelves in the delivery room that she was now awake and would like to see him. At first, the nurse thought that Betty might be hallucinating. I worked a couple of extra evenings but I finished the shelves. As an epilogue, it is interesting that

Karen has worked as a hospital administrator at Alta Bates in Berkeley and proudly displayed her birth certificate, signed by Alta Bates, on the wall of her office.

Karen was born breech and had obviously been in the position before delivery as well. Her legs remained cramped up around her ears, and we were quite concerned about whether there would be permanent damage or whether the hip joints had not formed properly. Betty spent a lot of time for the first month gently massaging Karen's legs; we were so thankful when they relaxed into a normal position.

The proud parents, Betty and I, with six-month-old Karen in 1943.

When my draft notice came in August 1943, giving me ten days to report to the induction center at the Pre-sidio of Monterey, I moved Betty and baby back to Salt Lake City so she could stay with her folks. We both felt so sad to be parted. For Betty it was worse since she was giving up the independence of being in a house of her own. Betty's parents made her and Karen more than welcome, but it was a wrenching change.

I returned to Berkeley where Mother and Dad escorted me to the Oakland bus station. Shortly afterward Rod would enter the air force. Mack had enlisted in the air force the year before Pearl Harbor, hoping to become a pilot, but it turned out that he lacked proper depth perception, so he became crew chief on a general's personal plane with the rank of staff sergeant. He served in this position or something similar for over five years. All three of us were fortunate not to see combat, but none of us knew what the future held—or how long that future would be—as I headed for Monterey in September 1943.

9.

INFANTRY RIFLEMAN,
1943-45

On September 15, 1943, with about 200 other inductees, I arrived at the Presidio of Monterey to begin whatever the army had in store for me. My first army meal was a revelation—turkey and dressing, with most of the dressing consisting of part of a string mop. The second adjustment was my name. After being "Dwaine" for almost twenty-nine years, with two more formal years in the mission field as Elder B. Dwaine Madsen, I was suddenly "Brigham," a name that almost at once was shortened to "Brig." Since "the brig" is naval slang for military jail, the easily amused soldiers enjoyed my nickname. Although my family still calls me "Dwaine," I'm used to "Brig" and prefer it. In the Intermountain West particularly, I shall never know whether it has hurt or helped my progress in life because it is so "Mormonish."

We arrived on a Saturday. The following Monday everybody but me was shipped out to various training centers. When I asked the classification people why I was being retained at Monterey, I was informed that because of my scholastic qualifications, I would be assigned to a clerk's job as soon as they could rearrange the army red tape. For six weeks I sat around Barracks 345 as a "barracks guard" under the watchful eye of a corporal, while six more groups of soldiers came and went. After inquiring three or four times when I was to be assigned, in some disgust, on a Saturday morning I informed the Classification Section that, if I was not assigned to a unit by the next Monday, I was going to see the commanding officer of the Presidio. The magic worked. The vengeful classification clerks took care of me

*Infantry private
Brigham D. Madsen, 1943,
at Camp Roberts, California.*

by assigning me to an infantry outfit at Camp Roberts, California. It was a fortunate assignment. Not only was this the real army but I had the opportunity to do something besides shuffle papers in a clerk's office.

From October 25 to 29 I was in the 89th Infantry Training Battalion, a heavy weapons company. But as fate would have it, I was then sent to the 77th Infantry Training Battalion, 2nd Platoon, a rifle company. We fifty-two trainees started our seventeen weeks of basic training on November 1. On November 7 I started keeping a diary which, because of my rigorous schedule and lack of interest, contains only one entry, until, two years later, I made the other entries in November 1945, en route to Europe and when I arrived in Bamberg, Germany:

So far, the Army has been good to me; I've been placed on K.P. only twice. However, the list has crept slowly down the alphabet to the G's & next week sometime will probably catch up with me.

Last week I was taught the rudiments of the manual of arms, gas mask procedure, bayonet tactics, & of course marching. On Tuesday & Thursday nights our Company took a 10-mile march into the surrounding hills. About 10 or 12 boys were eliminated because of foot trouble. Two of them had the flattest feet I've ever seen.

Last week, also, a few interesting incidents took place. One of the fellows in the Company was no doubt as confused as the rest of us by the new regimen of army life. One day in the ranks the Captain approached & asked his name. "Klemme, Sir," answered the Private. "'General' or merely 'Captain Klemme,'" asked the Captain sarcastically. "August

Klemme, sir," answered our Private. Somewhat tired, the Captain yelled, "*What* August Klemme?" "*Mister* August Klemme, sir," answered our friend. That is how August acquired the nickname of "General Klemme."

Last Friday I was taking notes during one of the lectures as is my habit when the 2nd Lt. in charge yelled, "Hey, you, lift your head up & pay attention to me." I answered, "I'm taking notes, sir." Whereupon he informed me in no uncertain tones that I was to stop taking notes, that I could get more out of the field manual, that I was to pay attention to him alone, etc., etc. Of course, I ceased scribbling immediately, although I had really been complimenting him by tak-

Private Brigham D. Madsen and Betty, at Berkeley, California, 1943.

ing notes on his lecture. However, Lt. doesn't seem to understand the purpose of note-taking; his is the "grasp-the-bull-by-the-horns-and-throw-him-over-the-fence" method. That night our own Lt. Holt, incidentally the best all-around officer I've yet met in the army, held a bull-session with us in the barracks. During his remarks he suggested that we take notes. I told him of the above incident, whereupon he immediately colored in anger at the mere mention of such stupidity & informed me that I had his permission & that of the Company Commander to take notes at *all* of the lectures. The next morning all the boys arranged for me to sit in the front ranks, & I waved my notebook in front of the Lt. for a whole hour hoping he would say something. But he was too smart & smelled a rat, because he carefully ignored me. Now that everything is up to date, the record can be a daily report if I don't become too dilatory.

Camp Roberts was a 50,000-acre training base situated on the main north-south highway and rail line about halfway between San

Francisco and Los Angeles and halfway between the village of San Miguel and the town of Paso Robles and quite fittingly, for me, was one of the few camps in the United States named for an enlisted man, Harold W. Roberts, a hero of World War I. The lieutenant, a man named Holt who saw some value in note-taking, was my platoon officer, the son of a wealthy family involved in the manufacture of farm machinery and a very good army officer. Our sergeant, a man named Johnson, was the technical sergeant who ran the platoon. He was aided and abetted by two corporals only one of whom I remember, a man named Seyler from Montana.

Not all officers were so competent. After a month of training, our company received a new commanding officer, an air force captain who had been redeployed as an infantry officer. He was obviously unsure of himself and tried to cover up his insecurities by being a hard-nosed disciplinarian. At the slightest infraction of any rules, he would order the company assembled in formation, then give all of us a tongue-lashing. The noncommissioned officers, with the willing aid of the fourth platoon, decided to get rid of him. On a dark night march, we were to execute a U-turn at the end of our outward-bound journey and return to camp, but our noncom just continued leading his men out into the great beyond. The next morning the "lost" platoon returned to camp, and the captain was reassigned.

Another officer, a first lieutenant who was well-trained as an infantryman, wanted to go overseas and to escape the tedium of Camp Roberts. He was granted his wish when the battalion commander one day observed him order us, "Prepare to march." This was a command newly-created by the lieutenant and meant that we were to lift our left feet into the air before he gave the next command of "Forward march!" I'm sure it was a comical sight; we in the ranks enjoyed the whole spectacle.

My two best buddies turned out to be Douglas E. Johnson from Missouri and Chesterman C. Linley, an attorney from Kansas City. Linley would have made a good officer but unfortunately was so heavy that he barely made it through basic training. I still have the letters I received from these two after their assignments when basic training was over—Johnson from Hawaii and Linley from England. Our platoon was also favored with eight former members of a federal stockade who were being given one final chance to become good soldiers. Technically, they were superb riflemen but had difficulty staying out of bar-room fights or from going AWOL. I came to know and like two of them very well. They continued to get in a fight somewhere every weekend; but about midnight one Saturday I came upon them in our barracks latrine where they were pummeling each other because they hadn't found any worthwhile opponents in the nearby bars. They all made it through basic training. I hope they got their wish to battle either the Germans or the Japanese.

Basic training for infantrymen probably hasn't changed too much since the Roman legions established drilling and forced marches as essential to soldiery. For some reason, probably because I was the biggest soldier in the platoon, I usually ended up on the marches carrying either the 30-caliber machine gun or the mortar barrel. And nearly always I was the guidon bearer in our various maneuvers on the parade ground, again because I was tall and could keep in step, a skill which some of the privates just could not master. But my size wasn't an undiluted benefit. When we dug foxholes under a time limit, the inspecting officer stopped at my spot to remark that I had to dig faster and deeper than any of the shorter soldiers in the company. My pup tent was too small for me to pull my feet in; and on one bivouac, the foot of snow that fell during the night covered both of mine. My buddies seemed to derive unnecessary glee from these small disadvantages.

In looking back at these four months of winter training, it is much pleasanter to remember the amusing incidents rather than our shock when a soldier in our company was killed when one of the training cadre shot him as he ran a course under live fire. This was just a few minutes after I had traversed the same course and had cursed one of the cadre who fired so close to me that I was showered with gravel from the stream bed.

There could have been a second tragedy very easily just a few weeks later. We were again scheduled to run a squad exercise with live ammunition. The "enemy" had two machine guns spraying the field of attack with live ammunition. Our twelve-man squad was to attack with our M-1 rifles and one BAR (Browning Automatic Rifle). An eighteen-year-old, who had already demonstrated a serious lack of brains, volunteered to carry the BAR but was denied the opportunity when the rest of us explained his mental condition to the training cadre. The noncom in charge then explained very carefully to him how he was to run to a certain tree and stay there. Instead, when the exercise was over, we discovered that he had crossed in front of the fire of our entire squad and that of both "enemy" machine guns. It was an absolute miracle that he escaped being killed. He was soon discharged under a Section 8 (mental incompetence) ruling.

A retrospective diary entry summarizes this period:

> In February of 1944 I completed my basic training at Camp Roberts, California. During the cycle I had applied for OCS (Officer Candidate School) along with 11 other men from my company, at a time when the quota from the whole camp was 1 man every 6 wks. After appearing before a Regt'l Board I was the only man selected to meet with the Camp Board. During the first Board Meeting a hypothetical situation was presented to me; it was interesting at the time & I shall never forget it. (I was successful in giving the proper orders to execute a very complex maneuver.)
>
> About a month before the cycle ended, I was asked if I wanted to be one of four men kept in the company as cadre. I declined because I wanted to go with the men I knew and had trained with. Finally, I was the only man of the company kept as cadre, probably because I was listed as a potential Officer Candidate.

Lieutenant Holt was amazed at my decision in turning down a "safe" assignment at Camp Roberts in return for a chance to "get shot" in combat. Most of my company went to England for further training after which I understand that many of them were in the "D-Day" invasion of France, an opportunity which I missed.

For about three months, I served as a corporal in the training cadre of my old company at Camp Roberts, an experience which was very valuable and gave me an advantage over other officer candidates later in my training in OCS at Fort Benning, Georgia. During my basic training cycle at Roberts, Betty and Karen moved back to Berkeley to live with my parents. I could see them occasionally on weekends. I would catch the train at noon on Saturday to travel to San Francisco and had to be back in camp by midnight Sunday. The cars were always crowded, and a few times I had to sit on the floor. When I was assigned "permanently" as a trainer at Camp Roberts, Betty moved back into our old apartment on Fulton Street which my Uncle Charley and Aunt Pearl Madsen had been occupying for several months. Charley had come from Idaho to work as a carpenter with Dad.

I got one weekend trip to the Bay Area by being sent to pick up a prisoner who had gone AWOL. He turned out to be a five-foot-four-inch, eighteen-year-old kid. I felt definitely foolish as I handcuffed this "dangerous" prisoner to me with my M-1 rifle slung over my shoulder.

My three months as a corporal meant going through a basic training cycle again, interspersed with guard duty and other onerous tasks. One Saturday night while on guard, I was called into the nearby post exchange where a drunk-crazed Hispanic-American soldier was fending everyone off with a wicked-looking knife. The guards did not carry live ammunition so I fixed my bayonet to the M-1 and advanced toward him, hoping he wouldn't force me to use it. Fortunately, the bayonet convinced him to surrender.

In June I received a furlough and Betty and I spent a week together in the redwood country of northern California. On our return I was stopped for speeding through the town of Willets. The policeman didn't give me a ticket because I was a member of the armed services. It was June 6, D-Day, and news had just come of the Allied invasion of Europe. When we got back to Berkeley, I had a telegram telling me to return to Roberts: I had orders to go to Fort Benning as an officer candidate. This was a bad time for Betty who, for a second time, had to pack up and move back to her folks in Salt Lake City. It was an even more stressful move than our first move the year before.

I had applied for OCS partly to get away from the tedium at Camp Roberts but mostly because I was ambitious to get ahead in the army. When I appeared before the camp board, I was ranked second among the candidates approved. I left Roberts in mid-June with three other officer candidates, traveling by the Southern Pacific Railroad for Fort Benning in Columbus, Georgia. We stopped for a few hours in New Orleans where one of the men tried to move in on a girl at a hotel lunch counter, ignoring her sailor escort. Just in the nick of time, we were able to get him out of the hotel before a brawl ensued. But he began drinking, and the train started to pull out without him. We saw him running down the track, desperately trying to catch the train. We exhorted him to greater effort but the train was faster.

Fort Benning is the sprawling Infantry School which covers a large area of mountainous and forested terrain, with plenty of area for field training. I was assigned to the Third Platoon, Fourth Company, Student Training Regiments in the Harmony Church section of the camp

*Lieutenant Brigham D. Madsen, towering over the rest of the First Training
Platoon at Fort Benning, Georgia, 1945.*

along with sixty-two other would-be lieutenants in the platoon.

The very first Saturday morning, our company was assembled on
a parade ground and a member of the First Platoon was called out of
ranks to drill the company. He succeeded in marching all of us into a
fence. A second soldier from one of the other platoons then took over
and marched us to the brink of a ditch. A candidate from the third platoon then took command but was so confused that we ended up scattered all over the field. Then I was called out and, in one of the better
moments of my military career, looked over the field very carefully,
planned my moves, gave a series of marching orders, and delivered the
company in correct formation to the officer in charge. My training as
a corporal helped a great deal, but it was mostly a matter of common
sense (none too abundant that day) and, I suppose, stability under pressure. This demonstration brought honor to my platoon and to Lieutenant Glenn W. Porter, our tactical training officer.

I was already in his good graces because, as my diary notes, "I made an immediate hit with him because I was the only member of the platoon to make a perfect score on the TIS [IQ] test." However, my diary fails to note that just before induction, I'd purchased several books with instructions about how to prepare for the military IQ test, complete with sample tests. As a result of careful cramming, I achieved a score of 149. Ever since, I have had little respect for these tests and consider them to be really achievement tests based on a person's education and training. My parade ground performance and my test scores did, however, pave the way in giving me some prominence in the training company.

My next "performance" came in about a month when I was ordered to direct the platoon in building a bridge across a stream. Again my construction experience as a carpenter foreman gave us the edge, and we easily beat the other three platoons engaged in the same exercise.

In a third field maneuver just about two weeks before the end of the four-month training cycle, I was called out of ranks at daybreak one morning, put in command of the company, and told to take a mountain top which was being held by some "Japanese troops." This "final exam" for us as officer candidates was a full-scale, all-day exercise with a number of "enemy" machine-gun emplacements, cannon, etc., hidden in the forest and underbrush on the mountainside. I asked the officers in charge to describe our "location." When I learned that we were on a Pacific island, I called on the nearby navy ships to bombard the Japanese positions for an hour before we began our attack. The officers said later that, although they had run the exercise a number of times, I was the first candidate commander to call for naval support.

I planned the attack carefully with the four assigned platoon leaders but soon discovered that one of them lacked the gumption and leadership necessary to move his men forward at a critical moment in the charge up the mountainside. I ran over and chewed him out in some colorful construction language, ordering him forward on pain of being relieved of his command. That galvanized him, and we were able to take the mountain. I was told that I received a high rating for my performance that day.

My chief contribution to our training program was the class I held almost every evening in our barracks to help some of the slow learners get prepared for our weekly exam. They were really tough. Officer Candidate School was no picnic, either physically, mentally, or psychologically. As the news got around that I was instructing our platoon, men from other platoons began to crowd in. I kept this up throughout the entire training period.

The physical demands were as great as the intellectual. By the end of training, I was down to a "lean and mean" 185 pounds and could traverse the obstacle course with the best of the company. I was particularly adept at flying over the eight-foot wall encumbered with a full pack and an M-1 rifle. I missed by two points becoming an "Expert" rifleman.

Even more than at Roberts, we were trained in how to kill other human beings. That was the objective. I became expert in wielding the bayonet with the thrust, the upper-cut, and the butt stroke; I learned over and over again the principles of hand-to-hand combat; and, of course, gained the skills of multiple mayhem in large groups of infantrymen equipped with the latest technology of machine guns, mortars, hand grenades, automatic rifles, bazookas, flame-throwers, and anti-tank guns. I learned all these techniques well and also served my time in teaching them to others.

Although I was a good soldier and learned my lessons, since leaving the army I have never had any desire to relive these experiences and, today, have an ingrained reluctance to watch war movies or even to talk about soldiering. If I had had combat experience, I believe that feeling would be even more powerful.

I don't remember much leisure at Benning. On field maneuvers we sang such traditional favorites as "On Moonlight Bay," "I've Been Working on the Railroad," and "Harvest Moon." There was no accompaniment, not even a harmonica, but enough people knew the harmony that we thought we sounded pretty good. Such evenings added to the feeling of camaraderie and brought back memories of home and loved ones. We also listened to a stand-up comic from the second platoon mimic an officer who had instructed us about the malarial dangers of the anopheles mosquito, and watched another expert each payday clean out anyone who dared shoot craps with him. Hardly anyone took a weekend pass to nearby Columbus. There was too much to do, and the prospect of being washed out was too threatening. Sundays were devoted to personal projects and letter-writing.

Betty and I corresponded faithfully during these years. She kept nearly all of my letters, but hers to me did not survive my many moves. I also tried to write my parents regularly.

About twenty of the candidates in my company were washed out and sent to OCRU (Officer Candidate Replacement Unit). The rest of us were commissioned on October 24, 1944, as second lieutenants. I was selected as the Honor Man of the company. This was a signal honor, since I was selected not only by the officers but also by my fellow candidates as the number one man in the company to represent them all. I marched the group over to the ceremony, and had my bars pinned on my shoulders by the commanding general of Fort Benning.

At this point my diary reads, "A week before graduation 12 of us appeared before the Board. After some preliminary questioning, the Col. asked me how I'd like to be a Tactical Officer [a training officer assigned to oversee and help train the candidates, usually in one platoon]. I candidly replied that 'I can think of a lot of other jobs in the army that are more pleasant.' Nevertheless, I was appointed a TO." Only one other graduate was retained as part of the "permanent" cadre at Harmony Church, a part of the Fort Benning infantry complex.

I then received my reward—in the quaint language of the military, "a delay of ten days ... being considered in interest public sv." In other words, I had ten days' leave coming. I had made arrangements to fly from Atlanta to Salt Lake City to drive Betty and Karen back to Columbus where I hoped we could find some housing. As I was about to climb the stairs leading to the plane, a senior officer gently informed me that he had to "bump" me because he had an important package to deliver as a courier. To say I was disappointed is an understatement.

I spent the ten days locating three rented rooms in the rear of a rather run-down house while Betty prepared to drive our car across country with another army wife, also accompanied by a child, who was meeting her husband in New Orleans. The regimental adjutant, Captain Dewey Campbell, who was a good friend at Fort Benning and later in Germany, cut some special orders so I could meet Betty and Karen in Jackson, Mississippi, and drive them to Columbus. This was the weekend of November 18, 1944. Betty had her own adventures crossing the continent, but we were united once again, this time for almost a year, until October 1945. After two months in the rear three rooms, we were fortunate to get a very nice apartment in Benning

Betty, Karen, and I
at Fort Benning, Georgia, in 1945.

Park, a housing development constructed for the officers stationed at Fort Benning.

My first assignment at Fort Benning was as a tactical officer, Third Platoon, First Company, and Third Student Training Regiment. Captain Ansel E. Jackson was company commander, a New Englander who had decided to adopt the accent of the South. Therefore, we platoon leaders called him "Cap'n" Jackson. He was a good officer, and we all liked him. First Lieutenant Herbert L. ("Pink") Hodgetts was First Platoon leader; Second Lieutenant David Westwater Jasper was in charge of the Second Platoon; and Second Lieutenant Thomas J. Dwyer headed the Fourth Platoon. Jasper was from a wealthy industrialist family in Chicago, had had a very liberal college education at Kenyon College, and became my best friend. I think he was rather interested in me as a Utah Mormon. Dwyer also came from a wealthy family that was involved in the automobile business in Detroit. "Pink" and "Cap'n" Jackson, and I were the poor folks in the company.

"Cap'n" Jackson gave me very high ratings for my performance in his company with one exception—a slightly less-than-perfect rating for "physical efficiency." I knew that this rating was not through any deficiency on my part. Immediately after sending in the ratings of his four officers, he announced one evening that all of us would run the obstacle course. I beat all of them, including "Muscles" Dwyer, by several yards; in some embarrassment, Jackson afterwards explained that he could not give me a perfect rating and had to find some deficiency in my record.

The one quality which the Infantry School emphasized above all others was "leadership," a quality that is very hard to define but whose absence or presence can be perceived almost at once under stressful conditions. My infantry training and experience at Benning has so ingrained the importance of this quality in me that I almost subconsciously measure whatever man I meet according to his leadership capacity and expect that he is doing the same for me. As we tactical officers followed our trainees around with our little notebooks, we were trying to determine whether they were leaders and fit to be commissioned as second lieutenants. Later, when the Battle of the Bulge took place in Germany in December 1944, word came to us from higher headquarters that there was a desperate need for lieutenant platoon leaders and that, if we could find men in our companies who "had the guts to lead a group of men forward fifty yards in the face of enemy fire," we were to recommend them for commissions. That is about as blunt a definition of leadership as I've ever heard.

Special board meetings were held three times during each training cycle in which each tactical officer was expected to provide written analyses of candidates from his platoon about whom he had misgivings as officer material. For each man under scrutiny, the tactical officer prepared a brief "Character and Personality" sketch (the evidence) and a "Summary" (the recommendation of whether the candidate should be "returned back to repeat the course" or "relieved from further duty as an Officer Candidate"). The colonel commanding the first board at which I presented candidates announced that my written characterizations and summaries were the best he had ever read as a presiding officer. He was probably wrong, but his remarks gave me a lift and did not hurt my standing in the battalion. Here is a sample that illustrates what we were looking for in candidates:

> Although Candidate has demonstrated great improvement during the course as a result of hard work and a sincere desire to succeed, he lacked so many of the qualities of leadership to begin with that he does not at all measure up to the standards of the school. He was rated 21 out of 25 by his section and 49 out of 51 by his platoon leader [with 1 being the highest rating]. An academic record which begins with 3 D's and

then becomes slightly above average indicates the slowness with which he picks up new ideas. Physically, he is above normal; he has great strength and is quite agile for a man of his size. While working with weapons he is at ease and shows an average aptitude in handling them and understanding their function. His instructional performance has been very weak, a vacillating manner and a too-deliberate way of speaking detracting from his presentations. In field work, he has displayed an inability to think correctly under the pressure of responsibility and ever-changing situations and has evidenced impotency in his attempts to maintain forceful control of a group of men. It is therefore recommended that he be relieved from further duty as an Officer Candidate.

My Fort Benning experience convinced me that the United States Army provides excellent training in the Officer Candidate Schools focused on the psychology of learning and the necessity for practical results—qualities, I might add, that schools of education in our universities should emulate.

I remember two candidates from my first training platoon who showed their grasp of leadership principles. One eighteen-year-old from Tennessee seemed to lack the education, sophistication, and forcefulness needed for combat leadership, and I was thinking of him as a questionable candidate until our first field exercise. He took command of the platoon like a veteran, gave orders quietly but with strength, and planned his strategy with intelligence and good judgment. You can't fool the customers and the platoon knew they had a leader in him.

The second was Herbert Y. Miyasaki, a Japanese American who had already had some combat experience, probably in Italy. One morning I called him out of ranks to take command of the company. He took the position and moved his eyes slowly down the ranks from the First Platoon to the Fourth, looking sternly at each man in the front row. When he had completed this unhurried visual survey and gave his first order, there was no doubt in any candidate's mind that he was in full command. Sometimes leadership can be instantaneous; in other men it takes a crisis to bring it out.

After my first platoon graduated on January 13, 1945, there was a change of officers. Captain Fred L. Stickels took command of the company with the following platoon leaders: Lieutenant Alastair Nixon, David W. Jasper, Charles C. Burke, and me. Stickels was an urbane, intelligent, and competent officer. He and I were the "poor relations" this time because both Nixon and Burke were from high society in the East. They were all capable officers. I did have one run-in with Burke who was something of a fuss-budget, always reminding the rest of us not to forget to do something. After I had had enough of this, one day I blew up and used some language on him that, as a highly cultured person, I doubt he had ever heard before. We got along well after that.

In the June 12, 1945, graduation booklet of my second platoon, they commented, "We only wish we could pin something on Lt. Madsen. However, come what may—we'll always be 'his boys.'" They gave me a silver chain bracelet with my officer number on it—a nice gesture which I appreciated.

About three weeks before the end of the second training cycle, I was appointed battalion adjutant of the First Battalion and promoted four days later to first lieutenant. The battalion commander was Earle M. Shine, a Florida shrimp-boat captain and a National Guard officer before World War II. Though not well-educated, he was a shrewd and common-sense officer who knew the army and how to get things done. We meshed very well. For the next three months as adjutant, I had such assignments as payroll officer for the entire battalion which meant handling sums of about $200,000 with any losses or errors coming out of my wallet; serving on four different court martial boards including, in one case, acting as defense counsel for a poor private who had gone AWOL; serving on a board to conduct tests for expert infantry badges; and for a few weeks acting as commanding (additional duty) officer of the Second Company while the captain was ill. At one formal party for the battalion officers and their wives, I was the official keeper of the liquor. I also lectured the battalion cadre on "America's War Aims." Such were my duties as adjutant.

In mid-August 1945 I was sent to the 29th Company as a tactical officer, slated to go overseas in about two months. I came into the company just before the first board meeting and had the responsibility of recommending candidates for dismissal or to repeat their training. My men called me both the "grim reaper" and also a "regular guy."

During the training period with the 29th, I had a ringside seat for a display of complete lack of leadership in the 29th Company. We were scheduled to move to another part of the Harmony Church area and had all the men assembled in the company area with their barracks bags, waiting to board about a dozen buses. There was no captain in sight. I found him cleaning out the garbage cans. I told him we were awaiting his orders to move, but he insisted that he had to personally clean the cans, a very bizarre decision. I gave up on him, took over as the senior first lieutenant, and moved the company. This captain was soon relieved of his command.

After only six weeks when the company was entirely through the training cycle, I was granted an eighteen-day leave on September 27, 1945. My orders were cut to send me to Germany.

These ten months at Fort Benning were good for us as a family, despite my rather arduous duties that often consumed weekends. It was an opportunity to become better acquainted with Karen who was about eighteen months old when she and Betty arrived in Georgia. Karen was a bubbly, enthusiastic, and delightful little girl who would run across the field every evening to welcome me home. Her favorite nursery story was "Goldilocks and the Three Bears." She always asked for it, but I stopped reading it to her after a few weeks because she would burst into tears when Little Bear discovered that his rocking chair was broken. By the time we started back to Salt Lake City and the McAllister homestead, Betty was five months pregnant with David. It was another sad time for both of us, but at least the war was over. I would serve with the U.S. occupation army in Germany, not in a combat unit.

On October 15, as ordered, I was back at Fort Benning, preparing for a transfer to Germany.

10.

THIRD ARMY
HISTORIAN IN GERMANY,
1945-46

After another twelve days' leave which I spent in the BOQ (Bachelor Officers' Quarters) at Fort Benning, I left on November 7, 1945, for Camp Pickett, Virginia, and then to Newport News on November 17 where I boarded the USS *West Point* (formerly the passenger liner *America*) with 8,000 other troops. Twelve of us junior officers were wedged into a small compartment. I remember best Fitzhugh Mayo, an aristocrat from Virginia; George Anderson, a banker from South Dakota; and a college student named Peyton who later played basketball for the University of Wyoming while I was at Brigham Young University. Peyton was seasick the entire trip. In fact, the November storms on the Atlantic were so violent that the enlisted men in the lower decks were almost all seasick. Even if someone wasn't particularly queasy because of the pitching and heaving of the ship, the heaving of his fellows over the edge of their hammocks usually did him in. As an Idaho landlubber, I remained miraculously immune and enjoyed a lot of solitary meals in the mess hall.

Mayo, Anderson, a fellow whose name I've forgotten, and I formed a quartet and whiled away the ten-day passage by singing such songs as "It's Harder for Me to be a Bad Boy than It Is for Most Boys to Be Good," a rather innocuous ditty but with good harmony.

The ship dropped anchor at Le Havre, France, on November 25, and we immediately moved by truck to Camp Pall Mall at the small seaside resort of Etretat where I was introduced to cigarette currency by exchanging two of them for some shoe repairs.

Two days later I was named a train commander to transport a

trainload of GIs and officers to the replacement center in Bamberg, Germany. The boxcars were old "40 hommes + 8 cheveaux" affairs (forty men and eight horses), and most of them had been used to haul coal. At the first stop the enlisted men detrained, black with coal dust, shivering in the bitter cold, and swearing at everything.

I commented on conditions in this part of Germany:

> Chow at Chaulnes. Little kids 4 to 12 getting scraps & leavings ... thru Germany. Buildings & countryside drab, esp. in Saar, Saarbrucken, Bad Munster & Schweinfurt pretty well smashed. Evidence of fierce fighting already covered by nature. Shell holes & bombed buildings exceptions. Train & track system all torn & bombed—bridges down.

When we arrived at Bamberg on November 30, Mayo, Anderson, and the others were shipped on to the First Division at Kitzengen, leaving me alone without an assignment. After two boring weeks of sitting around the barracks with new officers coming and going, I finally got my orders and drove by jeep on December 13 to the headquarters of the 3rd Army at Bad Tolz, forty kilometers south of Munich. At Munich I wrote my shocked impressions: "Really leveled—worse even than Nuremberg—I have a deep respect for the Air Force—block after block after block of gutted buildings—walls alone usually remaining standing." Bad Tolz was a beautiful winter resort town at the foot of the Bavarian Alps, and Third Army Headquarters were housed in a huge *Kaserne* (barracks), the former Nazi SS West Point. I was interviewed by a major of the Adjutant General's Section, who "two different times took a newly purchased revolver out of his desk drawer & flourished it around, all the while snapping the trigger!" My misgivings about my colleagues extended to the job: "It appears to me that the staff is creating a job for me so that I can do some of the work; I'm not sure."

The next day I was introduced to full Colonel Thomas Robinson, head of AG; a Lieutenant Colonel Hamlin, the executive officer; Captain Earl Batchelor; and First Lieutenant Robert Knecht, with all of whom I would be working for the next three and a half months. I was quartered at the Kaiserhof Hotel in Bad Tolz.

My work in the AG Section consisted of writing circular directives for the troops, indexing circulars and correspondence, writing recommendations for decorations for various enlisted men and officers, and similar office duties. There was plenty of work and extra duty. As I wrote in my diary one day, "It's a good thing I like my work because this AG Section does nothing else but." I was duty officer for New Year's Day when I seemed to be running Third Army all by myself as the other officers from the lieutenant general on down just celebrated. It was my reward for being a nondrinker.

Duty at AG, however, was boring, and I was toying with an alternate plan. In Munich I had explored the possibility of trying to get a job with Military Government, the civilian arm of the occupation force. This introduction to United States Military Government at Munich while en route to Bad Tolz opened up the possibility of transferring into a history-oriented job with M.G. which would also give me experience in another aspect of the American occupation of Germany. On my first day at Bad Tolz, I had met a Major Fetzer from Salt Lake City who was stationed at USFET (United States Forces European Theater) in Frankfurt and who gave me the name of a Major Robert H. Slover, head of the M.G. Historical Section at USFET. I wrote Slover on New Year's Eve, asking if there was any possibility of getting a historian's job in one of the provincial offices in the American Zone. On January 11 I received a telephone call from a Captain Langland, the M.G. Historian for Bavaria, who was officed in Munich. He was going home in three weeks, needed a replacement, and asked if I could get released to take the position. My diary then tells the story:

> Immediately saw Col. Hamlin who said he would "put in a plug" for me to Col. Robinson. Robinson said "No" so I went in to see him myself. When I asked him the reason behind his refusal to release me, he said "In the first place, I have no use for Military Government or any of the people associated with it." I don't remember any of the other reasons because they were just added, anyway. If he had given other reasons, of which there are a few, I probably would have been disappointed & resigned to my fate. But the excuse he gave not only stunned me (bald as it was) but also raised grave doubts in my mind as to whether our occupation of Germany will ever be successful if our high-ranking army officers hold that attitude toward the occupation gov't. I called Capt. Langland & told him & he took some information about me and said he'd do what he could for me. But that is a forlorn hope.
>
> January 12, 1946. Had a busy day. Learned from Col. Hamlin about 1400 that Col. Hamilton had called from Mil. Gov't requesting my release. Robinson turned him down. About 1630 I took some work into

Hamlin. Gifford was there too. Robinson walked in & said, "Are you still mad at me? Some day you'll thank me for keeping you out of Mil. Gov't. I'll tell you what I'll do. I'll let you write a history of the AG Section." With that he laughed & walked out. That needling really hurt and it was a good hour before I calmed down enough to be human again. If he represents the R.A. [regular army], then I'll certainly have ammunition for future lectures about same.

13 Jan. 1946. Slept late. Reached Kaserne about 11:30. Duty officer until 2200. Hamlin told me not to give up hope. He was still trying to get a replacement. The real encouragement came from a letter from Maj. Slover who told me to call him if I didn't get Capt. Langland's place because there are to be several Civilian jobs open soon & he wants me to have one. They need trained historians. Robinson will never release me unless some higher pressure is put on, however.

Lieutenant Colonel Hamlin did the best he could for me by finding a replacement for my AG job, but Robinson turned me down again, finally and absolutely, on January 19. When I recall what I said to him, in some anger, it's a good thing it was in the privacy of his office or he would have court-martialed me. However, my relations with the colonel improved so much that by February 9, 1946, I had the temerity to write him a formal request asking for reassignment to M.G. in Bavaria. My diary reports:

Feb. 13, 1946, Wednesday. Since the last entry my application for Mil. Gov't has been approved and I am to leave in about 10 days—if something else doesn't happen. One Major and all my other army friends advise me not to go—they have no use for the "parasites" of Mil. Gov't. That's my main reason for wanting to go. I want to look at occupation from both Army & Mil. Gov't points of view. I'm sure I'd be happier here but I'm going to Mil. Gov't for other reasons. It has long been the practice in Army to shunt off to Mil. Gov't all second-rate and no-good officers. I am to be congratulated that Col. Robinson refused to let me go the first time—i.e., I must be a fairly good officer.

Feb. 25, 1947, Monday. Last week followed about the same pattern with one notable exception. Last Friday a cable (TWX) came from US-FET requesting that I be put on TDY [detached duty] to travel to Frankfurt for 3 days of interviews for a historical job. Of course, I did a little operating to bring about that desired result. I expect to leave Wednesday evening by train for Frankfurt. Captain Lusk still wants me to take over G-3 historical section of Third Army but for several reasons I'd rather get into M.G. work. (1) I'm getting a little tired of the Army system. My personality clashes with too many of its phases (2) I can be a more impartial reporter of occupation if I see it from both sides—of the occupying forces—Army & M.G. (3) There will be more opportunity, I hope, to gather material for a thesis in M.A. work.

In Frankfurt I met two historians named Berlin and Robbins who were just packing up to move to Berlin to head the historical section there. They asked me which job I would prefer—the Bremen Enclave or Wurttemburg-Baden—and I indicated the latter. They promised to let me know within three days. On March 4, I was in Stuttgart, Wurttemburg-Baden, talking to a captain at that Historical Section. My diary gives the first installment in my soap-operetta attempt to become an M.G. historian:

> The next day I was interviewed by a Lt. Col. who temporized in the best traditions of Mil. Gov't and finally said he hoped he could give me a definite answer in 10 days. After two different TDY trips and two months of flirting with M.G. that was the straw that broke my camel's back.
>
> The only man I've met in all of Mil. Gov't who would make a decision was a Major in Munich and then he was wrong. Even though I still have a chance to get the $7,000 a year civilian job I'm too disgusted to go through the process and have no desire to work for these people. Most of them are opportunists. They're usually very intelligent in a theoretical paper-sense manner but quite inept at accomplishing anything practical. They are the epitome of the thought that Americans don't practice what they preach [allied with the thought that the Russians don't preach what they practice].
>
> At any rate at the conclusion of my interview I had definitely decided that my patience was exhausted and that if the Third Army historical job were still open—that's for me.
>
> 12 March 1946, Tuesday. Captain Lusk said O.K.; I saw Col. Robinson, told him my views on Mil. Gov't which pleased him no end [he even apologized for being so selfish about the Bavarian M.G. job] and we parted on best of terms with a 5.5 rating on my 66-1 when a month ago I would have been fortunate to get a 1.8; was interviewed by G-3; and took over the Historical Section of Third Army. Capt. Lusk took off for a 5-day trip to Prague for a swimming meet.

On March 14 I was formally transferred from the AG Section to G-3 and began a four-month tour of duty which was perhaps the most interesting part of my military career. Colonel Robinson's reversal, allowing me to apply for an M.G. position, came as a result of what was happening in Salt Lake City with Betty. My diary is filled with expressions of homesickness and loneliness for her. On December 9, I wrote, "It makes me realize how much Betty means to me. A real helpmeet, self-sacrificing, encouraging, wanting me to make a success of the things I've always aimed for. My chief hope is that I may always make her happy—no matter what life brings." But I hadn't heard from her since leaving Camp Pickett. Then on January 16, I received twelve letters in one batch—a red-letter day. And, of course, our baby was due the last of January.

No other letters came until I received a cablegram on February 8. I had gone to bed with a headache, but about 9:00 P.M. Bob Knecht came to my room with a message from Betty, "Born okay January 31—David Brigham." I went downstairs to offer cigars to everyone in the bar from the box I had been saving from my tobacco ration and drinks from my liquor ration. I should have known this would not be enough; I had to buy another $20 worth of drinks before being allowed to depart.

I was so pleased and proud of our new offspring that I couldn't be angry with anyone, including my nemesis, Colonel Robinson. So I marched into his office the next morning, announced the birth of a son, and offered him a cigar. In this way our cold war came to an end—which was just as well because a lieutenant could never win against a colonel, and a bird colonel at that.

Although I worked seven days a week and long hours, there were a few moments of relaxation at Bad Tolz. The village was in a beautiful setting and covered with about five feet of snow at this time of the year. Everyone seemed to be on skis. I noted one day, "I saw a fat woman of about 250 lbs. who was as adept as any of the rest and traveled downhill considerably faster than most. There was even one fellow with a broken arm in a cast. He seemed unperturbed and took the corners with everyone else." I rented some skis and joined in the fun. In late March, Dewey Campbell, Bill Blyler, and I were able to spend two days at Garmisch-Partenkirchen and Oberammergau. In the evenings around the hotel bar, I joined in the singing, confining my drinks to Cokes while most of the other officers imbibed stronger drinks. On January 8 I wrote, "In the evening we had a song-fest in the bar, and later on it developed into a meeting which finally produced a club with a constitution and officers. I was elected door-man and had the job of seeing that every officer took off his tie before he entered the dining room."

My eight months' duty with the occupation army in Germany gave me an object lesson in the old truism: to the victors belong the spoils. In the various cities of West Germany, the army took over the best hotels, gathered together the best entertainment for very little financial output, and, in a word, lived it up. Many of the officers—a lot of whom were married—"shacked up" with German women, although a few were like a captain who confided to me, "To hell with the bitches. Last year this time they were throwing rocks at us from their bedroom windows." I sought out friends like Dewey Campbell and William Blyler who also wanted nothing to do with this fast life. On Christmas Eve Third Army Headquarters threw a gigantic party at the Kaserne with an hour-and-a-half floor show and thirteen different performances. It was a command attendance and rather subdued because the Commanding Officer, Lieutenant General Lucien Truscott, was in attendance.

At Frankfurt living conditions for some officers were mighty convenient. I entered this observation in my diary: "Officers may bring their German girlfriends to spend the night with them as long as the girls sign in at the MP gate before 2230 each night & out before 0800 next morning. According to Jake [Lieutenant Jacob Nagode, an old OCS buddy] a great number avail themselves of the opportunity."

This fraternization came to an abrupt halt after an unsavory incident in which a German woman committed suicide by throwing herself to the street from an officer's window. This incident occurred in Frankfurt, but General Truscott, probably because of pressure from above, called a general meeting of all the officers in his headquarters and laid down the law. He also announced that officers' wives could join them in Germany by about June 1, which he thought would straighten everyone out if nothing else would. Shortly after the Truscott speech, the general of our section held a meeting with his staff to plan a last farewell party. The dumb major in charge of office administration asked why we didn't wait until the wives arrived. The general asked the major why the hell he thought we were having the party anyway. I put in a brief appearance at the party; and after the wives began arriving in June, things became as sedate as an ice cream social.

HEADQUARTERS
SQUIRREL CAGE COMMAND
G-3 OFFICERS' PARTY

19 April 1946

1. Pursuant to verbal authority, G-3, this headquarters, 17 April 1946 and Staff Memo #6, this headquarters, subject: "Recreation," the following unit is organized effective 27 April 1946 with station as shown: Unit G-3 Get-Acquainted Detachment Station.

SCHLOSS GUTHRIE (R-7189)

2. a. Male personnel will be obtained thru normal G-3 channels; Allied female personnel will be obtained by organic male personnel on the basis of one each, per officer.

b. A report of personnel to be present will be submitted to this headquarters, attention: Lt Newlin (3rd Army 5141) by Wednesday, 24 April 1946.

3. a. Equipment necessary will be requisitioned in the normal manner.

b. Report required in paragraph 2b, above, is mandatory for the requisitioning of class I & VI supplies.

4. Administrative details:

a. Time: 1900, Saturday 27 April—class VI supply point opens at 1900, 27 April 1946. Class I supply point opens at 2000, 27 April 1946.

b. Place: SCHLOSS GUTHRIE—follow route past Schloss Hotel 2 Kms; turn right on Wolfbrunneweg and quarters will be on left—probably all "lit" up.

c. Uniform: Blouse with trousers or skirt as the case may be—those so blessed would honor us were they to appear in evening dresses.

d. Visitors park on sidewalk of main road—MP guard will establish perimeter defense.

e. Finance: Approximately 5000 Yen will be collected from Field Grade Officers and 3500 Yen from the pick and shovel gang of G-3. Exchange rate for those who yen to know is 1000 yens per dollar.

FOR THE BIG WHEEL OF THE BAND WAGON:
Chief, Small Spoke Section

OFFICIAL:

The Big Hub.

Acting Cheese of Staff

By March 22 I learned that all officers who would have completed two years of service as of August 31, 1946, would be immediately available for deployment home to the United States. I wrote wistfully in my diary, "The best hope for me is that I'll leave in July for home. That's just right." In the evenings to the tune of "Lili Marlene," all of us who could look forward to the end of army service in the very near future joined in singing a three-verse song which included this stanza:

> Please, Mr. Truman
> Please may we go home?
> We've conquered Paris,
> And we have conquered Rome.
> We have subdued the Master Race.
> Don't tell us there's no shipping space.
> Oh, please may we go home?
> We care no more to roam.

Sections of the other two verses were less printable, but the message was clear. As I look back, it is obvious that under such pressures, the American government allowed for the too-early dissolution of the magnificent army which had helped to conquer the Nazis and the Japanese military. The history of the world and our relationship with Russia might have been different if we had kept our guard up more forcefully in these months of 1946 and 1947 when the Cold War began shaping up. Hindsight is one of an historian's best talents.

My new job was a real pleasure as my diary entry of March 22, 1946, records: "As Chief of the Historical Section for 3d Army I'm enjoying myself very much. Work is no longer drudgery. Now I begrudge the clock its announcement of 5:00 PM quitting time." I now was privileged to sit in on the weekly G-3 staff meetings although, as a first lieutenant among colonels and a brigadier general, I was expected to sit in the corner, take my history notes, and keep still. Only once did I have the temerity to speak up on a subject under discussion. Even though I was the most knowledgeable person in the staff room on the topic, the cold silence and colder stares I received checked any further attempts to enter their privileged circle. The topics discussed were usually top secret, and I had to be careful about making any diary notes about them.

While still in the AG Section, I was not under such close obligation and did jot down some observations concerning material which
came across my desk. On December 19, 1945, I noted an incident
about a Jugo-Slav lieutenant "who had had his epaulets torn off by an
American officer. The Jugo-Slav challenged the Am. Off. to a duel
and said further that the only person who could take his epaulets away
from him was the king of Jugo Slavia." In a more serious vein were
some comments about Jewish emigration on January 7, 1946:

> Work! Am very interested in the movement of Polish Jews into the
> American Zone, apparently financed by a well-organized group. They
> are beginning to tax the facilities and more are being provided. These
> people have suffered so many times during their stay in Central Europe
> that the last & worst of their persecutions [by Nazis] has given them a
> driving desire to leave forever. Palestine seems to be the favored spot,
> perhaps because no one else wants them. Biblical prophecies seem about
> to come true.

On January 28, 1946, I added:

> The Jewish migration from Poland seems to be following two
> routes—one thru Czechoslovakia and one thru Germany. Munich is the
> goal and the Jews seem content to wait there for the opportunity to get
> to the promised land—Palestine. They are well-fed & well-clothed &
> well-financed. They seem to distrust the Polish Gov't and State & want
> to leave Europe entirely.

And finally a few observations from my March 14, 1946, entry:

> Spent entire day doing research for a paper on "Fraternization."
> Source materials provide a "field day" for a historian. Start writing study
> tomorrow and I get *paid* to do it!
> Interesting how Lithuanians protest they did not join SS or allow
> themselves to be conscripted for military purposes by Nazis. Only they
> & the Poles!!
> World situation looks bad. Seems inevitable that U.S. & Russia will
> meet in world conflict. How long postponement of hostilities will last,
> no one knows. R. armies reaching into Iran remind one of Hitler's
> march to Saar, Rhineland, Austria, etc.
> If F. D. R. had lived, do not think present situation would be nearly
> so bad. Truman is a weak, vacillating President without stature required
> of our leader at present time. "War monger" Churchill strikes proper
> key-note. Atlee is a true partner for Truman.

Like many other Americans, my judgment of Harry S. Truman was premature. I now rank him as a near-great president.

In addition to my formal research project on Jewish emigration, I used my diary as a sort of field notebook to record observations. Here are my notes on an American officer, two Russian officers, and a German sergeant:

27 Dec. 1945. Spent about 2½ hrs. this evening with a Lieutenant [_____] AG Personnel, of Washington D.C., 22 yrs. of age, only son of wealthy parents—father a lawyer. Brilliant, rapid-fire mind. Has a Civil Service job waiting for him if he wishes it. Spent 2 yrs. in Infantry as Sgt. Won a battlefield promotion, Bronze Star, Purple Heart, Croix de Guerre. Took me to his room to see some of his war "loot." Must have about $10,000 worth of stuff besides what he's sent home. The members of his platoon always tried to get cameras or revolvers when they hit a town but he hit for the jewelry shops—knocked out the window with the butt of his gun & helped himself. He has sent home a priceless set of China, a 132-piece silverware set, paintings. Has on hand about 12 watches—one of them the most beautiful piece I've ever seen —worth at least $400, 10 or 12 rings he has had made here out of precious stones he picked up. Admitted to me that the Army had been a wonderful and needed experience. Had taught him to rely on himself instead of his family and friends.

January 7, 1946. The Russians are also meeting a problem that they probably didn't foresee during the war years—the discontent of their peoples (soldiers in the main) who have seen the high standard of living obtained by people allowed to compete individually for their livelihood. Many of them are being sent back to Russia by force and a high-powered propaganda program is attempting to destroy the "lies" that other Europeans are passing on to the Russians.

January 28, 1946. During lunch two Russian officers (man & woman) with an Am. Major interpreter. They were very clumsy with the eating utensils and watched every thing the Major did and then followed his actions closely. About half-way through the meal the man discovered his napkin & spread it out full length over his front. I imagine, however, they've killed a number of Germans apiece.

March 22, 1946. The night before last a young West Point captain and I stayed up until 0200 talking to [_____] the bartender—35 yrs. of age & a radar Sgt. for 6 yrs. in German Army. He knew Germany prior to Hitler, draws some interesting comparisons. His first experience with the American Army in off-duty hours came last September. During his first night behind the bar he saw an M.P. private come in, lean over

& tap a Major on the shoulder & tell him he was wanted on the phone. He had barely got over his amazement at this incident when 2 full Colonels picked up their empty glasses, walked to the bar, & placing them on the bar, said "Thanks" to the bartender who thought they were "making a joke" & asked the barmaid if it were a joke. He says Allies should have stopped Hitler in 1933-34 when his SS men killed leaders of all other political parties leaving poor German people helpless. War guilt of German people therefore not justified. Russia = only 2 questions: Shall Allies fight Russia now or later? 98% of all German women who fraternize with Americans also frat. with SS men & would frat with Russians if given chance. This bartender is so sharp, that he can't be trusted in political affairs. He intends to learn Russian & is now a true *internationalist*. He cares nothing for any country but only of himself & would serve any nation (except Russia) if that served his purpose.

As chief of the Historical Division, I asked permission for Sergeant Charles Hatch of my section and me to visit the War Crimes Trials in Nuremberg. We were only allowed one day—ironically, April 1. We drove a jeep, leaving quite early and returning quite late so we could have a whole day at the trial. We were required to sit through an hour of movies of the liberation of the various death camps. The room where the trial was held was like a small private theater with the eight judges, two from each of the four Allied nations, the International Military Tribunal's General Secretary seated just below, the prosecution attorneys next, then the audience equipped with headphones and simultaneous translation, and, finally, the twenty-two prisoners present seated in a sort of jury box just to the right of the justices. There were several American M.P.s standing guard, shoulder to shoulder, behind the prisoners' station.

Admiral Karl Doenitz was on the witness stand during the entire day we were there. The American prosecutor asked him several questions concerning the movements of the German fleet near the Russian base of Murmansk during the period when Germany and Russia were allies, before Hitler's invasion of Russia. The implication of the line of questioning was that the Germans would not have attempted to establish a base in Murmansk, from which to invade Norway, without Russian permission. The Russian counsel objected strenuously to the questions and demanded the subject be dropped. Throughout the whole tiring procedure, Doenitz insisted that his only participation lay in obeying orders from his superiors and therefore he shouldn't be tried at all. He had just been a good naval officer. Whenever he was asked rather unimportant questions, he answered immediately, but several times when he received rather tough questions, he would look at Hermann Goering, seated in the front of and in the left corner of the prisoner box, who would nod yes or violently shake his head negatively for yea or nay answers. If Goering indicated a no, Doenitz would refuse to answer the question. It was obvious that Goering was still in command and seemed rather arrogant about the whole proceeding.

At one point the British prosecutor apologized for being at fault on a case of procedure whereupon Goering laughed out loud. At another time one of the American M.P.s tapped him on the shoulder and told him to wake up Rudolf Hess, sitting next to him. Goering responded rather sullenly but shook the sleeping Hess by the shoulder until he was awake. Of course, Goering escaped execution after all by committing suicide after sentence was imposed. For a would-be historian, the day at Nuremberg was a memorable one.

On March 1 we began preparations to move Third Army Headquarters from Bad Tolz to Heidelberg which had been the headquarters of Seventh Army, now being deployed back to the United States, leaving Third Army in sole control of the American Zone of Occupation. While Seventh Army troops had reverted to peace-time duty with weekends off from Saturday noon to Monday morning and accompanying reductions in uniform requirements, Patton's Third Army was still working seven days a week clad in helmet liners and combat boots. When Sergeant Hatch and I drove into Heidelberg in our jeep in early April along with all the rest of Third Army Headquarters personnel, there were no German citizens on the street, and it was a couple of days before the people of Heidelberg ventured out of doors, so great was the fearsome reputation of Patton and his army.

Heidelberg was untouched except for the bridges across the Neckar River blown up by the retreating German army. I found comfortable quarters in one of the better hotels taken over by the U.S. military command and enjoyed my three months' stay in the city.

During my almost four months of duty as chief historian for Third Army, I wrote the 109-page quarterly report for January-March of 1946 and prepared the materials for the second quarterly report. The first quarter's report was organized under eleven headings: (1) Quarter in Review, (2) Administration and Personnel, (3) Security, (4) Operations, (5) Army Operational Services, (6) Medical Affairs, (7) Law and Order, (8) Army Welfare, (9) People, (10) Military Government, and (11) Happenings of Significant Note. The most interesting and important subjects were concerned with political activity, denazification and demilitarization, war crimes, relationship with Allied and friendly armies and states, inspections and investigations, black market activities, displaced persons, prisoners of war, civilian internees, and military government.

I was so pleased with the report that I asked permission of my general to deliver it in person to the chief historical officer of USFET in Frankfurt. The general granted my wish, and I flew up to Frankfurt in an artillery observation plane. The whole incident proved embarrassing. I had expected a chance to "talk shop" with a well-trained and senior professional historian; but the colonel in charge of USEF's historical section quite obviously knew nothing about the discipline of history, having received his office as a sinecure, a comfortable niche into which he could retire with few demands. We both recognized how ludicrous the meeting was, and I left his office as soon as possible. His staff, of course, did all the work, a very different arrangement from mine. Although I had about six noncoms who helped me with the research, I wrote the official reports, as spelled out in my job description.

I seized the opportunity of being in Heidelberg to enroll in an art history class taught by a Professor-Doctor Hoffenrichter. He was well prepared and an interesting lecturer but so poor during this period of famine in Germany that I and other American soldier members of his class gave him cigarettes to use as currency to buy food. He very gratefully gave me a copy of one of his lectures, "Art in Crete and Greece." I still have the Certificate of Achievement for six hours of instruction in that course.

Dr. Hoffenrichter was not the only German suffering from want during this terrible winter of 1945–46. Cigarette currency was in great demand; other GIs and I regularly gave our candy rations away to little children on the streets. One lieutenant from Texas A&M became an embarrassment to all of us when his habit of overeating made him so obscenely fat that no one wanted to be with him where the emaciated German civilians could see us.

At Bad Tolz I had become very friendly with the pilot and copilot of General Truscott's private two-engine aircraft. Because the general did not like to fly and because it was necessary for the two fliers to maintain their skills, they usually made weekend flights to various parts of the Continent. On two occasions some others and I were invited along for the ride. Thirty-one of the headquarters personnel spent the weekend of April 5, 1946, in Paris on one of these trips, including my good friends Bill Blyler and Bob Knecht. The whole thing was rather irregular, barely qualifying as "official" because a captain of the A.G. Section and the keeper of the Great Seal of Third Army was willing to stick his neck out and write orders authorizing the trip "for the purpose of carrying out instructions of the Commanding General." The "instructions," of course, were to enjoy ourselves, visit the Follies Bergère, and eat at the finest restaurants of Paris. The following weekend thirteen of us visited Brussels with the A.G. officer writing out the orders while we were airborne.

In another, more regular trip, I spent a twelve-day leave in England and Scotland. I wanted to get to Inverness to check out Betty's McAllister clan but learned from a knowledgeable Scot that most of the McAllisters had been wiped out at the Battle of Culloden on April 16, 1746. It was an enjoyable trip, my first to England and Scotland. I shall never forget the forlorn little Scottish boy near Loch Ness who asked me for a stick of gum and then rather matter-of-factly stated, "Americans are lucky." The truth is he was right but most of us don't realize how fortunate we are.

On the night train from Edinburgh to London, I was in a compartment with an elderly English couple, two British naval officers, and a Scottish lady. I had hoped to get some sleep but was kept awake for the first two hours by the Scottish lady, who harangued us about the necessity of Scottish independence from England, declaring that the crowned head of that terrible country should be thrown into the Firth of Forth. After she wound down, the two British naval officers attacked me as a representative of "Uncle Shylock" who had stolen portions of various British possessions in the western hemisphere in 1941 in return for fifty worn-out World War I destroyers or "tin cans" in the famous "destroyer deal" Franklin D. Roosevelt made with Winston Churchill. One of the officers, who was especially belligerent, later revealed he was from Jamaica which had had to grant a base to the United States as a result of the deal. I hope that I defended the United States with proper decorum but, nevertheless, with spirit.

My military service in Germany was finally terminated with orders to report to Bremerhaven on June 22, 1946, to be sent home by a Victory cargo ship, along with 3,000 other GIs. On July 11, I was named currency exchange officer which meant that I had the responsibility of checking the official currency books of all the men assigned to my ship and taking in their occupation currency. I held office in an aircraft hangar in Bremerhaven to ensure that each individual GI and officer had not exceeded the amount of occupation money he was supposed to have, as listed on his official currency book. Of course, nearly everyone had dealt on the black market and usually had many times the amount of occupation money he should have had. It would have been very easy to fudge on some of the cards and on my own card and to make an illegal haul of money for myself. Perhaps the officers in charge chose me for the assignment because my first name was Brigham. I shall never know. Only one man, a full colonel, attempted to get me to sign off on many thousands of dollars more than he should have had. I refused. The process of examining the cards took all day. Later, three days out into the Atlantic to ensure that no one could cheat, I held office a second time to disburse over $500,000 in American currency to the men aboard. This was a hair-raising assignment because I would have to make up any discrepancies out of my own pocket. I came out $2.50 in the red at the end of that day and gladly paid the difference.

The voyage was serene, the sea calm. I reached New York harbor only to discover that I had been assigned as the commander of a trainload of soldiers and officers to be transported to Fort Sheridan near Chicago for discharge. I endured this final responsibility. I was separated from the service at Fort Sheridan on July 30, 1946, one of only a few of the approximately 250 officers discharged at that time who did not sign up for the Reserves. In fact, when I responded negatively to the officer's question about the Reserves, he could not believe his ears. Startled, he repeated the question. Unhesitatingly, I repeated, "No."

I think I had had a successful career in the Army as attested by the evaluations of my superiors, but I wanted no more of the military. My nature was just too independent to want ever again to be placed in the position of not being able to speak my mind and to act as I wished whenever the spirit moved. I was proud to serve my country and would have done so again if a national emergency had arisen, but I was not willing to subject myself to a peacetime army, the allurements of a reserve commission and retirement pay notwithstanding.

I reached home in early August to rejoin Betty, hug three-year-old Karen, and see my seven-month-old son for the first time. It was a wonderful reunion, one we could enjoy with extra gratitude since we knew we would face no more long separations. Karen was as delightful as ever, and David was an unfailing source of joy and pride to both of us. Betty's folks had generously made their home hers during the eight months I was away, and we were anxious to establish our own home for our little family. Nothing we ever experienced in our marriage would equal the unhappiness of being separated during my three years in the army. Betty's letters to me revealed her loneliness. I, in turn, strove to deal with my own loneliness by painting word pictures of our future happiness and pledging my determination to make her life easier and happier. Thus it was with genuine joy that we optimistically left for Berkeley and a second try at my Ph.D.

II.

PH.D. AND
NEW PROFESSOR

Berkeley and Brigham Young University, 1946-51

Moving Betty and the children to Berkeley in August of 1946 was a pleasure, especially for Betty, who naturally felt that her life had been on hold while I was in the army. Finding housing was a problem, but, again, my carpentry skills helped me when we were able to rent an old apartment at 2337 Grant Street, a former stable which had long before been converted into student living quarters. Of the many applicants for the place, the landlord chose me because I agreed to restore the front porch, repair the bathroom floor, lay linoleum in the kitchen, and do some general painting. We have always joked about this "back house" where we lived for one year until moving into the larger and more commodious "front" house in 1947-48. The bathroom floor had sunk away from the walls so that blackberry bushes were growing into the room, coiling above the pull-chain toilet. But it was liveable and was within walking distance of the university campus.

During our two years at Berkeley, it was a real satisfaction watching Karen and David develop into personalities of their own. Karen started kindergarten only two blocks away during my last year in graduate school. One somber note was the trouble Betty began to have with her lower back, a condition which became worse, finally required a painful operation, and was an unceasing concern for the rest of her life.

Another difficult part was the very real work that post-war adjustment took. It took some time for me to shed three years of being steeped in the military mentality to a peace-time one and, I hope, a more tolerant and easy-going disposition. The process required considerable patience and understanding on Betty's part, I shall always be grateful that she could weather my transformation from lieutenant to private citizen. I had inherited my full share of Carl Madsen's temper, though I confined its manifestations to occasional outbursts, which Betty dampened by the simple expedient of listening patiently. She could occasionally be caustic, usually as a result of a careless or unfortunate remark from me. These flashes from her always brought me up short, and then it was my turn to be patient.

As for money, our income was much better than it had been before World War II. Since Betty was caring for two children and could not work, I probably could not have stayed in school otherwise. The GI Bill paid us $90 a month under an entitlement good for two years, ten months, and nineteen days. I was immediately accepted as a teaching assistant in the survey course in U.S. history, a position I retained for my last two years of graduate work. And, finally, a building contractor in our LDS Ward, Elmer Harker, hired me to work part time as a carpenter. It was a nice arrangement for me because Elmer needed another finish carpenter and allowed me to work whenever I could. During preparation for my Ph.D. exams, I would hardly lift a hammer; but after passing a set of exams, I would don carpenter overalls and work almost full time for a while. With income from the three sources, we got along so well that, when we left Berkeley to accept a teaching position at Brigham Young University, I took a cut in pay. Elmer Harker thought I was making a mistake and offered me a very good proposition to remain as an employee of his construction firm. But I have always considered the challenge of the job first. Income is a secondary consideration as long as there is enough money to pay the utilities.

Professor Kinnaird was able to place me as one of the teaching assistants for John D. Hicks, the historian of populism, who had come from the University of Wisconsin during the war years to become dean of the Graduate School at Berkeley. I was also one of two readers for Hicks in his large (500 students) course on social history of the United States. He was easy to get along with, but I had brought a chip-on-the-shoulder attitude back from my military service, an independent won't-take-anything-from-anybody feeling typical of many ex-GIs. Although I meant nothing personal by it, I managed to alienate Hicks; and after one semester, he exiled me to Outer Slobovia with another graduate student, Robert Gilmore, to become TAs at the Davis campus of the University of California. Gilmore and I would take the train every Thursday morning and spend the day teaching four sections of United States history apiece. It was good experience and so successful that the head of Davis's history department offered me a job at the conclusion of my Ph.D. program. I chose not to take it because, among other reasons, *he* was a bear-cat to get along with.

Even though I worked only one semester with Hicks, he has had a great influence on my style of teaching. Aside from Professor Costigan at Idaho State University, Hicks was probably the best history lecturer I have ever heard. He followed the unit method, organizing each lecture as a separate entity. He used notes which had been carefully constructed over the years and were always changing as he discovered new information or ideas. Any success I have had as a lecturer has been greatly influenced by his example.

I was more successful in cultivating Laurence A. Harper who taught constitutional and New England colonial history. Most graduate students tried to avoid him because, as an ex-lawyer and a rigorous teacher, he expected more than many students were willing to give. During my first quarter back, I took two hours in readings from him to prepare for the English colonial part of my exams. In an off-hand way, he instructed me to write a short paper on the causes of the American Revolution. His manner made me determined to win his approval, so I spent about three months in exhaustive research and produced a sixty-five-page paper. He was amazed, confessed that he had expected only a five- or six-page affair, and gave me an "A." I had caught his attention; and from then on I had a solid supporter in Professor Harper. In fact, when the time came for me to select the chairman for my oral qualifying exam, I chose Harper even though Kinnaird thought I had lost my mind and suggested Hicks as the better choice. I did not explain my relationships with the two men and insisted on Harper, who did a wonderful job and supported me during the exam. I think he was so pleased to finally be chosen as chairman of an exam committee that everything turned out peaches and cream for me.

As the regular chairman of my supervisory committee, Lawrence Kinnaird was very kind, patient, and understanding in his dealings with me. My first two papers for his seminar drew on my experience as historian for Third Army: "Security Conditions in Bavaria—VE Day to 1 April 1946" and "Fraternization in Germany, 1945." As a veteran of World War I, he understood the group of ex-GIs at Berkeley in 1946-48 perhaps better than any of the other faculty members. Later, he wrote to me, "My Utah graduate students ... were unusually able and, perhaps more important, the kind of men I liked. They were endowed with practical common sense which many academicians seem to lack." His three other Utah Ph.D. candidates were Everett L. Cooley, who had a long and illustrious career at the University of Utah; S. George Ellsworth, who had an equally long and illustrious career at Utah State University; and the late Dello G. Dayton, who served as academic vice president at Weber State College.

After refreshing my memory of the classes I'd taken before the war and doing some additional boning up, I took my Ph.D. written examination in late March 1947 in U.S. history and modern England. Professor George Guttridge fashioned the questions for English history which were concerned with the Elizabethan and Victorian ages as periods of greatness; the constitutional relationships in 1485 between England, Wales, Scotland, and Ireland; and the development of British seapower. Of the three questions given us concerning U.S. history, one asked for a summary of our relations with Russia; a second wanted an account of the relative positions of the three branches of government from 1789 to the present; and the third proposed, "Discuss the cotton plantation aristocracy—the Old South, including other origins than political and economic position in the Old South, their attitude during the Civil War, and their fate during Reconstruction." I never learned who asked the first two questions, but the last one was so ambiguous that we soon learned a new professor, Kenneth Stampp, had originated it. He was rather embarrassed since all four of us taking the exam manfully tackled that question about social conditions in the South. He passed all of us. I sat across the exam table from Richard D. Poll with whom I became close friends during this graduate period and with whom I finally went to Brigham Young University. Dick and I both cleared the written exams and began preparing for the more horrendous oral qualifying exam. The committee members who would examine me on the subjects of colonial America and geography were Laurence Harper in English colonial America, George Hammond in

Spanish colonial America, Lawrence Kinnaird in French colonial America, Engel Sluiter in Dutch colonial America, and Carl Sauer in geography. These were five difficult fields; and when I consider the mere two fields that the University of Utah's history department requires its students to master for the oral exam, it is little wonder that a Berkeley Ph.D. counts for something in the discipline.

Hammond was a very generous spirit, and I had taken so many Latin America courses from Bolton and the other experts in the field that I felt fairly confident about him as I did with Kinnaird and Harper. Sluiter was another matter. He had asked me to read Gilberto Freyre's *Masters and Slaves,* describing slavery in Brazil. He thought the book was almost perfect in its analysis, but I was somewhat critical of certain aspects, and let my views be known in the interview we had about it. I was not at all wise in challenging him, but I was more than ready to take on anyone with whose views I disagreed. His attitude toward me in the exam would be problematical to say the least.

But the dean of the committee was Carl Sauer, internationally famous for his work on Middle America and the most feared faculty member in the field of the Western Hemisphere. I knew that, if I could satisfy him, there was a good chance I could pass the exam. Therefore, I audited all of his courses, read everything he had in print, and virtually committed it to memory.

The exam was held on Thursday, December 18, 1947, at 3:00 p.m. in 430 Bancroft Library. Sauer was the first questioner as the others deferred to him. Kinnaird later recalled, "I recall the fact that you took your Ph.D. oral examination when you had the flu. I remember that Professor Sauer asked some very minute and difficult questions and, when you knew all the answers, he stopped questioning by saying, 'I see that the candidate has read all my works.' I think that you have always known most of the correct answers in life." Sluiter next probed my nonexistent knowledge of early explorations at the headwaters of the Amazon River. I was becoming disheartened when Sauer intervened with the observation, "Professor Sluiter, you are asking the candidate questions about a subject of which only you have any knowledge." It was true because Sluiter had never published anything on this matter and, in fact, never did write anything of consequence. The rebuke from Sauer ended Sluiter's questions, and the rest of the exam was a piece of cake, as the saying goes.

Brigham D. Madsen, Ph.D.
from Berkeley, and new faculty appointee at
Brigham Young University, 1948.

When I was asked to leave the room while the committee deliberated my fate, I loitered just outside the door long enough to hear Sauer say through the open transom, "He not only has a good memory but he uses his head." I wasn't supposed to hear that but was glad I did. It was one of the finest compliments I've ever received and compensated for the months of preparation I had put in. The news of my successful performance before the noted geographer spread quickly through graduate student ranks, and I was a one-day wonder.

As president of Phi Alpha Theta for 1947-48, I had the opportunity of becoming acquainted with a great number of graduate students and also quite a few of the faculty. An outstanding occasion was a reception which Phi Alpha Theta sponsored for the noted Harvard historian, Samuel Eliot Morison, who came to the Christmas meeting of the American Historical Association at Berkeley in 1947. After we stood beside each other in a receiving line for an hour or so, he reached into his pocket and gave me a pamphlet of his lecture, "History as a Literary Art: An Appeal to Young Historians."

I still treasure it, not only because he was kind enough to give it to me, but also because I believe that what he wrote about history as literature is so important. Too many historians seem to believe that a work is not truly professional unless an author omits all human interest, that narrative history is somehow disreputable, and that statistics rather than people should be emphasized. It is little wonder that the general reader must turn to a journalist like Bruce Catton, or a writer like Catherine Drinker Bowen, or a professor of English like Wallace Stegner, to get any life out of history.

These last years at Berkeley were not all taken up with academics. Betty and I shared our experiences as graduate students with other couples also engaged in the scholarly process. We belonged to a couple of groups which met for monthly socials and which also were interested in the intellectual aspects of Mormonism. Le Roy and LaReal Eyring were special friends. He was the youngest brother of the famous Henry Eyring, who was a chemist on the Princeton faculty and later dean of the University of Utah's graduate school. Le Roy was also a chemist but much less orthodox in his religious faith. In addition to the group, we occasionally participated in events at the LDS institute next to the campus, directed by George Boyd who has become a lifelong friend. George has always been a liberal thinker and a down-to-earth person of much humanity and common sense. He was a great help to me as I struggled with my religious convictions.

During my army service, and especially while overseas, I had shied away from any involvement in church activities. My historical studies had included no very flattering account of religion's role in generating power politics and the indiscriminate slaughter of thousands who had the misfortune to be classified as "unbelievers." It had bred a considerable cynicism in my mind about the claims of all religions, including my own, especially Mormonism's claim to be the only true church. Furthermore, my friendship with men of different faiths, or no faith at all, but who would lay down their lives for you and give you the shirts off their backs, led me to question whether they should be consigned to hell or to a lesser degree of glory in any next life. There seemed to be no justice in such a scheme. In our Sunday school classes, I began to raise questions—sometimes rather blunt ones—about the plan of salvation as preached by the Mormon church until the more orthodox class members began to gang up on me. There was often such a feeling of hostility in these discussions that I stopped participating and attended as a mostly silent observer. I felt quite alone, as though I was the only one around with such heretical ideas. This was not true, of course. Betty's unorthodoxy was, in some ways, more profound than my own; but she was emphatic about the need to remain participants in our faith community. For both of us, it was essential that our children grow up with strong moral values and attachments to their Mormon heritage. In retrospect, this approach was a wise one. It kept us from throwing the baby out with the bathwater many times.

With no one else to talk to, I wrote a short treatise for myself in January 1948 that expresses my solid appreciation of both the doctrine of Mormonism and the social achievement of the institutional church but remains silent about such problems as the Joseph Smith story:

What My Religion Means to Me

Religion is fundamentally concerned with ethics, and the Church of Jesus Christ of Latter-day Saints especially emphasizes the importance of maintaining a high moral tone among its members. In this day of quick marriage and quicker divorce, of increasing juvenile delinquency, and of a general lowering of long-established social standards, the Word of Wisdom and the Thirteenth Article of Faith gain new meaning. Mormonism provides a culture in which youth can be nurtured and trained towards a future of accomplishment and well-being.

But the gospel as taught by Joseph Smith is more than just a guide for this life; it encompasses time and space. The questions of every intelligent being about the reason for life, the nature of the Creator, and the prospect of future existence after death—all become understandable as the searching light of the Priesthood traces the eternal plan of salvation through the pages of scripture.

Within the organization of the Church, moreover, there is unceasing opportunity for growth and development. The principles of service to others and of participation in the ordinances of the Gospel both stem from the basic philosophy of "eternal progression," God's glory is intelligence, and the boundless opportunity of new worlds to conquer presents a never-ending challenge to His children.

At this juncture, in the spring of 1948, George Boyd invited us to the institute one evening to meet a friend of his, Sterling M. McMurrin, then a professor of philosophy at the University of Southern California. The two had taught in the church's seminary system, and George apparently discerned that it might help me to meet McMurrin. It was not only helpful but a revelation to me to meet someone else who not only had the strange ideas I had but who was even more questioning and bolder in expressing his views. That spring began a lifelong friendship with Sterling whose mental ability, very retentive memory, humanity, and moral courage I have come to admire above those of perhaps any other individual I have known. I no longer felt so alone as I came to know him and George Boyd. I could never again be so accepting of the theology and practices of the LDS church. My regard for my Mormon heritage was as strong as ever, and so was my reverence for the Mormon virtues of family, physical well-being, and the old values of honesty, hard work, and integrity. There simply was no room within the traditional boundaries, however, for my questions.

Most of the time I chose to avoid any confrontations with other church members about my unorthodoxy, but I did have a run-in with Thomas Ferguson, an attorney originally from Salt Lake City but a longtime resident of Southern California. We both found ourselves at an evening meeting at the institute. He and Milton R. Hunter, one of the Seven Presidents of the Seventy, had spent some years attempting to prove the authenticity of the Book of Mormon by studying the remains of the ancient civilizations found in Central America. They had finally produced a book, which would be published a few years later under the title of *Ancient America and the Book of Mormon* (Oakland, California, 1950).

That evening Ferguson was extolling Hunter's virtues as a historian. He had studied with Bolton and had asked Bolton to write a preface to *Brigham Young, the Colonizer,* which had been Hunter's Ph.D. dissertation. Bolton told me that he had discovered over 400 errors in the manuscript and agreed to write the preface only after Hunter had gone to great expense to make the necessary corrections. I grew exasperated with Ferguson's efforts to wrap his Book of Mormon project in the reflected glory of Hunter's church status and supposed prowess as a historian. I could not refrain from telling him of Bolton's less than admiring opinion of his former student. Ferguson became so angry he advanced as though he was going to take a punch at me. He might have if George Boyd had not intervened. Interestingly, several years later Ferguson became disenchanted with Hunter and external proofs of the Book of Mormon. He remained in the LDS church but came to doubt the authenticity of the Book of Mormon.

As my last semester at the University of California neared an end in the spring of 1948, I had to make a decision about a teaching job. GIs thronged the nation's colleges and universities, most of which were looking hard for faculty. The Department of History, with Kinnaird's energetic support, encouraged me to apply at Rutgers and Michigan State University, but eastern schools had little appeal for me. There was an opening at Humboldt State College in northern California which seemed attractive to Betty but not to me. It seemed too far away from the centers of intellectual activity. Another opportunity appeared at the new Sacramento State College which would have meant half-time teaching and half-time in administration, but I wanted no part of a job in academic management. As I look back, this last position would have been a great opportunity, and I probably should have taken it. But my heart was in the Rocky Mountains where the University of Utah had just hired David E. Miller.

Brigham Young University was also advertising for two historians to teach U.S. history. Richard Poll and I decided to apply for the BYU jobs and were interviewed by Apostle Albert E. Bowen while he was attending the Oakland Stake conference. Because of my unorthodoxy, I was uncertain about whether to go through with an application to BYU and decided to postpone a decision until after I had seen how Elder Bowen conducted the interview.[1] Betty preferred the climate and culture of California and saw some real advantages to being a little farther away from Mormonism's core area, so her misgivings added to my own. In other words, if he pressed me too closely and began asking rather personal questions about my beliefs, I was determined to look elsewhere for a job. To my surprise and relief, he turned out to be a very temperate and common-sense individual. I did not expound on my religious reservations, but I candidly expressed my concerns about my independent nature and whether I would be well accepted at BYU. He merely pointed out the obvious—that there were a lot of positions available and that if I felt I could not be comfortable at a church university, I should not consider BYU at all. With such general authorities in charge of the school, I could see nothing but a pleasant and profitable career at the Provo campus.

Dick Poll had no reservations at all and was supremely happy to be offered a job at BYU. We both accepted when President Howard S. McDonald offered us positions as assistant professors at a salary of

---

1. At Brigham Young University, each teaching applicant is interviewed by an LDS General Authority to ensure that his or her religious views are in line with Mormon theology. I deplore the idea that BYU students cannot handle disrupting and dangerous ideas from unorthodox teachers, e.g., evidence which disproves the historicity of the Book of Mormon or the facts of Darwinian evolution. So much for untrammelled academic inquiry!

$3,500 a year. As an epilogue, we were both amused when we heard McDonald declare in a sermon before the Berkeley LDS Ward that although BYU had just lost the famous and accomplished composer LeRoy E. Robertson to the University of Utah, he had made up this loss by hiring professors Madsen and Poll for his faculty.

With a job secured, of course there was still the little matter of completing my dissertation. I had decided to write on "The Bannock Indians in Northwest History, 1805-1900," although Kinnaird had pointed out that not much significance was assigned to Indian history at the time and that I might have difficulty landing a job. But I was interested in the topic and determined to do it anyway. It is interesting that, since the social revolution of the 1960s and the great emphasis on ethnic and minority history, Indian history is a field trampled by scholars competing to write on every conceivable aspect of the subject. That was not so in 1946; I was one of a few graduate student pioneers willing to tackle such an arcane field. At least my dissertation was later published as a book, which cannot be said of many Ph.D. theses.

The research on the topic was complete by June 1948 and I had no intention of dragging out the process by teaching full time and trying to write on odd weekends. Therefore, for six weeks in June and July, I took my notes, plenty of pencils and paper, and two lunches, found a desk in the basement loneliness of the university library, and wrote from 8:00 A.M. until closing time at 10:00 P.M., six days a week. I stuck at the work so rigorously that I developed a partial paralysis (fortunately it was temporary) in my left hip from sitting continuously on a hard library chair. By the last of July the manuscript was complete and was approved by my three-member dissertation committee composed of Kinnaird, Hammond, and Robert F. Heizer, a young anthropologist on the Berkeley staff. I was able to go to BYU with my Ph.D. in hand.

I have little comprehension of or patience with scholars who temporize, postpone, and sometimes never get their theses or "books" written either because of laziness, attempts to gain perfection, or an inability to organize their material effectively. I have discovered that the only way to write is to sit down, glue yourself to the chair, and write a sentence at a time until, glory be, a manuscript appears. Betty and I put our few spare possessions in the car and, with Karen and David, started off on what we hoped would be a permanent residence in Provo, Utah, and a lifelong tenure as a faculty member at Brigham

Young University. We felt that "preparation" was over and that the work of "real life" had finally begun.

It was also a new stage of family life for us, since all of my siblings were launched on similar adult activities. In 1945 my parents had moved to Salt Lake City, intending to spend their remaining years closer to their ancestral roots. Dad had purchased an old apartment house at about 450 South 400 East and remodeled it from four into seven apartments. He continued a pattern of building a home, living in it for a short while, selling it, and building another. This pattern of repeated moves tried my mother's patience, but the profits were good.

My sister Annie, after her mission to Colorado, had married Eldon Carter of Ammon, Idaho, in June 1940. During the war Eldon worked as a pipe-fitter in the shipyards at Richmond, California, and their daughter Kathleen was born. They also moved to Salt Lake City in 1945 where Eldon started a successful career as a builder and where Robert, James, Peggy, and Denise were born. In 1956 Annie contracted Parkinson's disease, which she combatted with courage and great patience until her death in 1993. Eldon died of prostate cancer in 1995.

Phyllis also served a mission in Colorado, moved to Salt Lake City with our parents, and began working for the Internal Revenue Service. In 1949 she married Kelly Eldredge, whose first wife had died of cancer, leaving two children, Timothy and Christine. They moved to Sacramento where Kelly became a professor of biological science at Sacramento State and where Kathryn and Diane were born. Kelly died of a heart ailment in March 1998.

After five and a half years in the air force, Mack joined Rod and Dad in construction, marrying Lee Self in 1948. They are the parents of six children: Michael, Brent, Cindy, Maleia, Danny (killed in a car accident), and Paul. Except for eleven years in Garden City, Idaho, they lived all their married lives in Salt Lake City where Mack died of Parkinson's disease in December 1992.

Rod served a mission to Denmark (1948-50), learning the language with remarkable fluency. In 1950 he married Heidi Stäuble, a Swiss convert who had immigrated to the United States in 1949. They have no children, but their beautiful Mill Creek home is an example of Rod's excellent carpentry.

Betty's only sister Jaclyn graduated from Utah State University in home economics and taught elementary school in Salt Lake City most of her life. In 1943 she married Stephen Cornwall, a navy veteran and successful contractor. Together they have raised six children: Kenneth, Marie, Bruce, Michelle, Stewart, and Janet.

Betty's brother, Delos, served in the U.S. Navy, graduated with a B.A. in engineering from the University of Utah and an M.A. from Stanford, and had a highly successful career with Hughes Aircraft Company in California. In 1947 he married Geniel Pratt, who graduated with a degree in chemistry, her career after raising their five children: Diane, Marcia, Lloyd, Neil, and Karl.

Housing was still in short supply at Provo as elsewhere; but again, my carpentry skills proved an advantage when we were able to rent an unfinished basement apartment with the understanding that I would hang the doors and complete the finish work. It wasn't the best quarters, but it was a home for a year and within walking distance of the university campus. It says something about Betty's saintly qualities that she was willing to keep house and raise children in one construction zone after another. In the summer of 1949 we succeeded in getting an apartment in one of the World War II structures reserved for married student families in Wymount Village adjacent to the campus. The university administration agreed to designate one of these temporary buildings for young faculty members. We spent our second year and a half at BYU in Wymount Village waiting to buy a lot so I could build a home for us. Dick and his wife Imogene ("Gene") Poll also acquired an apartment here.

Before becoming president of BYU in July 1945, McDonald had been deputy superintendent of schools in San Francisco and superintendent for the Salt Lake City School District, which position he left to come to BYU. During his four years as head of the university, his most important contribution was to convince the Board of Trustees, consisting of apostles of the LDS church, to continue the Y as a church university. Some of the authorities, like J. Reuben Clark, had considered selling the school to the state or withdrawing from it in some other way, allowing the institute system to take care of the religious education of the church's youth.

McDonald added a number of new and young faculty members to take care of the burgeoning student population and continued the very humane, enlightened, and academically-free spirit which had been representative of the school during the 1920s, 1930s, and 1940s. But he never quite meshed with his trustees, who expected to be involved in day-to-day decisions but refused to support decent faculty salaries and efficient operations. McDonald also seemed unable to shift gears from being a public school man to becoming the president of a university. His speeches to the students and faculty were sometimes on such a high-school level that all of us felt embarrassed both for him and ourselves. Nevertheless, he allowed his faculty great freedom to teach, and we liked this about him.

Dick Poll and I shared an office in one of the World War II buildings on campus and looked forward to our first year of teaching. Poll and I were part of a combined Department of History and Political Science. The senior member, Christen Jensen, had been a dean and, for a few months, acting president of the university. His field was political science, his teaching was competent but dry, and he had never published anything of consequence. Stewart Grow, a recent addition in political science, had just started work on a Ph.D. at the University of Utah. He was a most congenial colleague and a good teacher. The other political science man was William Carr, whom Betty and I had come to know at Berkeley where he was working on his Ph.D. Carr was an unimpressive teacher, too caught up in minutia to see the grand picture, but an amiable and friendly person. Russel Swensen, a Ph.D. in history from the University of Chicago, was chairman of the department, a man of very liberal tendencies and consummate good humor. He was an effective teacher in European history and a good administrator. Dick Poll and I were to handle the classes in U.S. history.

The teaching load for each of us was four classes per quarter, a stupendous assignment for a first-year instructor who had to make preparations for classes he had never taught before. I was forced to get up at 3:00 A.M. each morning, repair to my office, and write feverishly to prepare the day's lectures which often left me stranded after only thirty to forty minutes of a fifty-minute period. But the students were understanding and joined in a discussion at the end of the hour to use up the time. For my first three years at BYU and until a few new faculty members were appointed, I also taught a two-quarter survey course in English history, a third quarter of English constitutional history; a two-quarter survey course in Latin American history with a third quarter devoted to the history of Mexico; a two-quarter survey course in U.S. history plus courses in the history of the American West, American historians, and a graduate seminar. It was not until fall quarter of 1949 that I could stop to take a breath.

Dick Poll and I were recognized as good teachers and soon attracted a following among the students. I enjoyed teaching then and always have; I looked forward to my classes every Monday morning and marvelled that the administration was willing to pay me for doing something that was so much fun and that I would have gladly done for nothing if the little matter of making a living for a family had not been a factor. There were about 4,000 students at BYU in the fall of 1948, many of them ex-GIs. They and I were members of a special fraternity of war veterans, and I welcomed them in my classes.

The older faculty members were pleased to see the eager young teachers being added to their roster at BYU in the years after World War II and welcomed us to their mostly liberal and enlightened ranks. P. A. Christensen of the Department of English was the recognized intellectual leader of the campus, supported by other outstanding scholars like geologist George Hansen, biologist Thomas Martin, English scholar Karl Young, and the old gadfly John C. Swenson. They became special friends as they seemed to recognize a kindred spirit in me. There was also a good cadre of graduate students in these first years who went on to some prominence in their respective fields after completing doctoral degrees elsewhere. I remember especially Kent Fielding who earned an M.A. with me, Irene Briggs, Carolyn Stucki, and three men who later joined the BYU faculty—Paul Hyer in Far Eastern history, DeLaMar Jensen in medieval history, and George Addy in Latin America, among many other bright and inquiring minds.

The chief liability to what was otherwise very pleasant circumstances at BYU was the low salaries, a problem McDonald was unable to rectify because of his declining influence with his conservative Board of Trustees. In the spring of 1949, when I discovered that Bill Carr was receiving $4,000—$500 more than I—while he lacked a Ph.D. and was not a very dynamic teacher, I headed for the president's office in high dudgeon, confronted him with the disparity, and demanded at least equal pay. McDonald assented and was also forced to raise Poll's salary when I told Dick of my experience.

Throughout my six years at BYU, I struggled constantly to meet my family's financial needs. In practical terms, it meant that I was forced to moonlight as a carpenter instead of spending my spare time in research and writing. I was soon involved in evening and weekend work for other faculty who were struggling to build homes for themselves as economically as possible.

In the summer of 1949, I was able to get a temporary permit from the Carpenter's Local Union in Provo, so that I could take a job at Garfield, Utah, helping to build the new copper smelter underway there. My brother, Mack, who was also employed there, helped get me the job. We worked together for two months, all the time looking for an opportunity to strike out on our own. Dad's success with his remodeling project interested him in trying to build two four-plexes. He finally mortgaged his apartment building for $2,100, added some cash from his savings, got a loan of $3,200 from Prudential Insurance Company with my help, and got $500 from me. The three of us purchased two lots at 1750 South 600 East. Mack and I quit our jobs at the smelter and started the four-plexes about August 1, 1949. It took eight months to complete, with Dad and Mack doing most of the work, although I put in about six weeks in August and September and every weekend from then on. We poured the concrete, did all the carpenter work and painting, and struggled to complete the buildings within the small construction budget we had. We held them six months to enjoy the capital gains provision of the tax laws, then sold them at a good profit. We shared our proceeds with my younger brother, Rod, who was on a mission in Denmark.

The following year, joined by Rod, we four built a four-plex and a duplex near 700 East and 1500 South, again holding them for six months before selling at a profit. This was the beginning of a successful business for us, successful only because we were all willing to pitch in and work hard with a minimum of resources and not much more than strong backs and willing hands to devote to our projects.

In the spring of 1951 we razed a hundred-year-old pioneer adobe home next to Dad's apartment and cleared the lot so that we could build a six-unit apartment on it. Dad very generously made his three sons co-owners of the lot, a gesture which I could only repay by trying to help my children in similar fashion. After completing the rough construction on the six-unit building, we asked, Why not add six more apartments on an upper story? When Dad and I approached our loan agency with this proposal, the manager thought we had lost our minds but finally was persuaded by our enthusiastic assurances. By late fall the twelve-plex was completed; and after the usual six months wait, we sold the building to a lawyer from Price, Utah, and realized an excellent profit, divided equally among the four of us.

With my share of the proceeds, I bought a new Buick and a lot in a new area just a few blocks east of the campus in what had been a cherry orchard. Charles Redd, the millionaire cattleman from LaSal, San Juan County, in southern Utah, had already been dickering to buy a lot in the orchard but was willing to join with eleven faculty members from the Y to develop the plat into a subdivision. As the "BYU Homeseekers," we purchased the land, subdivided it, and drew lots with the understanding that Charley Redd would have his choice. I drew a corner lot on Cherry Lane which was eminently satisfactory to Betty and me and accepted my father's offer to draw plans for a house. I was able to get a low-interest Veterans Administration loan of $13,000 and started construction in July 1950. We moved into the partially completed home by the spring of 1951. Betty did much of the painting while I worked every spare minute completing the carpentry. Occasionally Mack and Rod would spend a Saturday helping me raise the walls and put on the roof. It was a labor of love for Betty and me. We had waited a long time to get a home.

An outstanding scholarly event for me in the fall of 1949 was the invitation to represent BYU at the First Congress of Historians of Mexico and the United States held in Monterrey, Nuevo Leon, Mexico, September 4-9. The school paid my expenses, and I was able to associate with 125 very prominent university historians from both countries for an entire week of wining and dining as well as interesting papers. I roomed with John Higham, a young, able historian from UCLA who was on the program. The first three days went as merrily as a wedding-bell; but on Thursday and Friday, the Mexican professors reading papers blasted the "Colossus of the North" whose ancestors had stolen the great Southwest from Mexico during the war of 1846. We American historians listened in pained silence to the tongue-lashing; and, as far as I know, there has never been a second "Congress." The meeting was a memorable one for us and, I suspect, for all of the other North Americans present.

I returned home just in time for the birth of our second daughter, Linda, on September 15, 1949, after Betty had gone into labor while helping other women from our ward can fruit for the Mormon Welfare Program. Linda, who is concerned about others and sensitive to their needs, has been a real joy to us. She has artistic gifts and is always involved in painting and writing.

One of the pleasurable and satisfying aspects of our six years in Provo was the relationship we developed with the Saturday Night Chowder and Marching Club, a group of like-minded friends who met monthly. In the group were Monroe Paxman, juvenile judge of the Provo District, and his wife Shirley; Merrill Bushnell, manager of a large pipe mill in Utah County, and his wife, Lucille; Richard Taylor, an attorney in Spanish Fork, and his wife, Lucille; Ray Canning, professor of sociology at BYU, and his wife, Lois; Maynard Dixon Stewart, professor of art at BYU, and his wife, Helen; and Gaylon Caldwell, professor of political science at BYU, and his wife, Vickie. There were others, but these were the ones we came to know the best and still see occasionally. Some of the wives enrolled at BYU to finish their college degrees after working to help their husbands get started in professional careers. We discussed subjects of general interest but usually ended the evenings in a freewheeling discussion of current events at BYU, church politics, and Mormon theology.

Although unorthodox in some respects, as I have described, Betty and I were still committed Mormons when we moved to Provo, attended meetings faithfully, and regularly participated in our ward. Working at BYU did not, however, have a strengthening effect on my faith. One disturbing incident occurred in the spring of 1949 when the student body officers asked permission of the administration to hire the black orchestra leader Dizzy Gillespie for the annual prom. The answer was no, because blacks were not allowed to hold the Mormon priesthood. If there were other reasons, I never learned what they were. Several of the younger faculty were outraged by what we discerned as a racist and discriminatory policy. Two other faculty members and I descended on Wesley P. Lloyd, dean of students, demanding that the administration reverse its decision. Lloyd was sympathetic and understanding, but the policy was the Board of Trustees' and there was nothing he could do. I was never more upset at such blatant racial intolerance.

Another incident was even more dismaying. During the spring of 1950, the three-year-old son of a religion faculty member, whose family lived in one of the apartments of our Wymount Village building, wandered away from a negligent babysitter, passed through a gate in disrepair, and drowned in a nearby canal. The whole community was shocked by the tragedy, but at least a few of us were also angered and disconcerted to hear another religion faculty member explain in his funeral sermon that the child's death was probably a good thing because now he would not have to face the temptations of life and would be forever in the arms of Jesus, destined for the highest degree of glory. To make matters worse, the following day as I was repairing the broken gate, the deceased boy's father happened along and told me I was wasting my time. If the Lord had determined to "call someone home," any efforts at intervention were a waste of time and energy. I, of course, subscribed strongly to the position that the Lord helps those who help themselves and fixed the gate anyway. This same member of the religion department later displayed his anti–intellectualism by assuring me that all that was necessary for a higher education was to study the four standard works of the church; one need not read any other literature. Attitudes and beliefs of people like this man were too common among some BYU faculty and seemed to belie a university's responsibility to provide higher education.

In June 1949 I first met the man who would take McDonald's place as president of BYU and build it into a giant complex which at least has the outward appearance of a university. The school planned to honor the long career of Christen Jensen by giving him a testimonial dinner. Stewart Grow and I were co-chairs of the arrangements committee. He and I decided to invite as the speaker Ernest L. Wilkinson, an attorney who had recently won a $32 million judgment for Ute Indian land claims against the government and was the most prominent of Jensen's former students. At the banquet J. Reuben Clark of the First Presidency was seated at the head table with Christen Jensen, Howard McDonald, Stewart Grow, and me. In his hour-long speech, Wilkinson spent about five minutes extolling Jensen's virtues, then launched into a well-prepared exposition directed at Clark of what BYU should concentrate on: theology and history. He insisted that BYU would become the greatest educational institution in this world if it so trains its students that they will have the desire and the knowledge to take the revealed Gospel of Jesus Christ to all the ends of the earth. Those of us who think of our revealed religion as something separate and apart from our education miss the whole point of this school. He emphasized that there was no point in continuing the school unless it added truth to the gospel message to benefit humankind.

But it was his declaration on the importance of teaching history that caught Clark's attention. Wilkinson asserted that every student at BYU should be required to study U.S. history and government because of the Mormon belief in the Constitution, the LDS concept of government, and the Mormon explanation of the rise and fall of governments. It was obvious to all present that Clark was absolutely delighted with the speech. Later some of our liberal friends blamed us for Wilkinson's selection as BYU president. Grow and I were convinced that this speech basically made Wilkinson president of BYU and could only plead guilty.

In my conversation with Wilkinson that evening, I told him of my interest in his Indian case and explained that I had written my dissertation on the history of the Bannock of Idaho. He was immediately alert because his firm was then negotiating with the Shoshoni and Bannock at Fort Hall to become their tribal attorneys in a land claims suit against the government. The following spring he invited me to spend a whole day, May 31, 1950, with him and his partner, John Boyden, in a meeting at the Hotel Utah with about fifty Shoshoni chiefs and subchiefs from Fort Hall and the Great Basin where the two lawyers hoped to nail down a contract with the tribes. Wilkinson wanted me there as a special consultant to aid in the process, and I was asked to answer questions about some supposed Bannock who lived in eastern Oregon. A few weeks later he asked to borrow a copy of my dissertation. I sent it to him but had a difficult time getting it back after it had been in his office in Washington, D.C., for two years. It came back to me well thumbed and obviously well used.

Wilkinson also arranged through me to hire Kent Fielding, one of my M.A. candidates, for a summer to research the valuation of western tribal lands in the mid-nineteenth century. Fielding earned his degree out of the project with a thesis of only about a dozen pages but with some invaluable tables of land values. It is the shortest thesis I have ever approved but one of the best.

In early October 1949 Howard McDonald decided to walk away from his deteriorating relationship with the Board of Trustees by accepting a position as the president of Los Angeles State University. The board accepted his resignation with alacrity, asked Christen Jensen to become acting president while a search was made for a new leader, and started the process, although it soon became obvious that Wilkinson was the choice. He was named to the position on July 27, 1950, and took over in February 1951 after the successful conclusion of his Ute case.

All of us waited to see how this human buzz-saw would change affairs at our Provo school. I remember that I admired his energy and determination. From my contacts with him, I expected a strong-handed and hard-nosed approach toward management and administration, but I did not expect the ruthlessness he exhibited and his frank willingness to let the end justify the means.

12.

MY YEARS AT
WILKINSON'S BYU,
1951-54

The takeover of Brigham Young University by Ernest L. Wilkinson in February 1951 introduced immediate and dramatic changes to what had been a rather somnolent campus. He insisted to his Board of Trustees that all school matters must go through him—no more end-runs with faculty members taking complaints to their favorite apostles. He also expected that "correct" economic doctrines—i.e., free enter-prise—would be taught and practiced at BYU; that the university would continue to function as a marriage broker for Mormon students; and that the new administrative arrangements which made the president of the church the president of the Board of Trustees as well would assure Wilkinson direct access to the top hierarchy in the church.

With these concepts set, the new president plunged into a vigor-ous campaign to get more money for faculty salaries, for student hous-ing, and for classroom and office buildings to provide for what the board thought would be a grand university of about 10,000 students. They didn't realize that their diminutive and vigorous administrator had grander ideas of expanding the school to the nearly 30,000 stu-dents it presently has (1998). As two historians of BYU have put it, every Wilkinson conference with the Board of Trustees was like a day in court, complete with dozens of charts, volumes of statistical infor-mation, and a totally overwhelming demonstration of his command of the programs he was presenting for approval.[1]

---

1. For an analysis of Wilkinson's working style, including his relations with the board of trustees, see Gary James Bergera and Ronald Priddis, *Brigham Young University: A House of Faith* (Salt Lake City: Signature Books, 1985), 24-25.

He was ruthless and indefatigable in gathering information to support his cases. In one instance, upon learning that I was engaged in writing the annual article on "Utah" for the *Encyclopedia Britannica* and that I had certain classified information about the population figures of another state college, he asked to see the statistics and then, without my permission, incorporated the facts in a presentation. I never allowed myself to be used by him again in this fashion.

With such tactics and disregard of the means as long as he achieved his ends, it is little wonder that he and the older and more liberal faculty members clashed from the beginning. The confrontation started when P. A. Christensen was asked to preside as master of ceremonies at the faculty banquet in honor of the new president in February 1951. Christensen introduced Wilkinson by saying that the Washington, D.C., lawyer was really faculty member John C. Swenson's second choice for president; and when someone asked who Swenson's first choice was, Swenson had said, "Almost anyone." Wilkinson laughed at the sally but not too heartily.

The role he saw for the faculty in helping to establish policies for the university became apparent quite early when he unilaterally announced that instead of one campus-wide devotional assembly held traditionally at 11:00 A.M. each Monday, there would now be three such meetings—on Monday, Wednesday, and Friday at 11:00 A.M. The faculty protested that this arrangement would cut too much into class time, but their pleas were ignored. Therefore, someone started a petition to Wilkinson which was signed by over a hundred faculty, including me, making a formal protest of his action. One of his spies, while the petition was circulating, delivered it to him. Wilkinson called a special faculty meeting, rushed into Maeser Hall flushed with anger, and denounced the petition signers as cowards who signed papers behind his back. Hugh Nibley, a former paratrooper, and I were the first on our feet to challenge him, but Hugh beat me to it by exploding back at Wilkinson.

Then when I had a turn, I asked what part the faculty would have in formulating policies for the school.

He answered bluntly, "None whatever."

I said, "Thanks. Now we know where we stand."

We faculty had not known before that the Board of Trustees had already agreed with their new president that we would not be allowed to be involved in administrative matters in any manner. As a footnote to this meeting, the faculty now determined to stay away from all faculty meetings as long as our voice was not to be heard anyway. At once Wilkinson directed that henceforth he would take the roll at the meetings and absent faculty would be punished. At the very next meeting, with a fairly full house, when the roll we were to sign reached P. A. Christensen, he crumpled it up and put it in his pocket. Wilkinson lost that skirmish, but few others.

A basic part of the Wilkinson program to win churchwide support for BYU and to make it a great university was his plan to send thirty or so selected faculty to stake conferences in the western United States with various apostles. The church president agreed that each faculty member would have fifteen minutes in which to extol the virtues of BYU and to urge church members to send their sons and daughters to the Provo school. In the first phase of this campaign, from April 1951 to May 1952, faculty dutifully visited 179 stake conferences. Opposition developed at once, especially from Mormon faculty and students' parents at the University of Utah, Utah State University, Weber State College, and the various Utah junior colleges about church influence being used to steal students from their institutions. A modified program was allowed for the next year during which the visiting BYU faculty were admonished to talk only in general terms about the value of a higher education. After these two years, the campaign was terminated, but it had achieved Wilkinson's objective: the student population at BYU increased from 5,492 in 1950 to 10,542 by 1956.

As one of the speakers, I had some interesting experiences with several of the apostles and seventies. I went on two stake visits with Joseph L. Wirthlin, the Presiding Bishop, one to Oakley, Idaho, and one to a stake in Los Angeles. At Oakley, in the Saturday evening priesthood meeting, one suntanned farmer told Wirthlin in no uncertain terms that he and the other members of the ward were not going to follow certain recent directives from church headquarters about their MIA (young people's program), because the instructions were designed for an urban population and not a rural community like Oakley. Wirthlin agreed with the man. If he had not, there would have been open rebellion in the small Mormon town. I saw this drama repeated several times in other plain-spoken Mormon stakes in the outlying districts. The independent pioneer spirit was still alive and functioning in the 1950s. On the way to our Los Angeles rendezvous by train, as the conversation lagged, I innocently asked Joseph Wirthlin what he thought of Franklin D. Roosevelt and the New Deal whereupon the good bishop stood up in front of his seat and got so purple in the face I was afraid he was about to have a stroke of apoplexy. I hurriedly got him a cup of water; the crisis passed; and I never mentioned politics and the Democrats again. Bishop Wirthlin was a devoted right-wing Republican, a political predilection shared by nearly all general authorities even today.

In other visits I had a delightful time at the Boise, Idaho, stake with Oscar A. Kirkham of the Council of Seventy who turned out to be as generous and friendly as his older brother, my mission president, James M. Kirkham.

I traveled to Rigby, Idaho, with a member of the General Welfare Committee who told amusing stories about the various general authorities he had come to know. Evidently, all of them enjoyed stories at the expense of each other. One of them contrasted the personalities of the gregarious and open Apostle LeGrand Richards and the more precise and formal Stephen L Richards; LeGrand, visiting a stake conference in the Uintah Basin, stayed at the home of the new stake president, whose wife wanted to ensure that everything was perfect for the comfort of her first apostle visitor. Unfortunately, the bed he occupied fell down during the night and the stake president had to help put the springs back in place. As the apostle came down the stairs the next morning, he said to the discomfited lady of the house, "What did you think last night when you heard the bed fall down?" She answered, "I got out of bed, fell to my knees, and thanked the Lord that it was LeGrand R. and not Stephen L."

At Rigby, just a few miles from LDS Ricks College at Rexburg, Apostle Joseph L. Merrill warned me to be careful in my speech never to mention BYU but rather to talk about the glories of higher education. I rather liked Joseph Merrill.

In a trip to one of the stakes in Idaho Falls, I drove with the visiting apostle, Henry D. Moyle, a man of large ego who spent the entire journey to Idaho Falls telling me the story of his life accentuated by all of his successes. One I recall was that, as a missionary in Germany, he was asked to translate Apostle Rudger Clawson's address to the congregation. Clawson evidently made some remarks that would have created enormous political problems for Mormons, so, as Moyle put it, "Apostle Clawson gave one speech, and I gave another." Moyle was particularly upset by the implications of David O. McKay's action as church president in demoting J. Reuben Clark from first counselor in the First Presidency to second counselor. As a strong Clark supporter, Moyle told me with some satisfaction that at the previous Thursday council meeting of all the apostles, McKay had asked Clark to take care of some important financial matter. As Moyle put it, "J. Reuben Clark is still in charge."

At Idaho Falls Moyle strongly rebuked the Saints because they had not supported a Mormon candidate for mayor, thus allowing a free-wheeling gentile to become the city leader. Afterwards the stake president rebuked Moyle, predicting that his speech would cause the Mormons all kinds of difficulty. My final observation about Moyle was that he had driven his new Cadillac at speeds up to 100 miles an hour, so when he asked me to drive on the return trip, I set what I thought was a moderate pace of 80 miles an hour. He said rather gently, "Please don't go over 70." I guess it depends whose foot is on the accelerator—both in a car and in life.

I enjoyed two trips with Apostle Marion G. Romney and his wife, Ida, appreciating their down-to-earth approach. We went to Malad, Idaho, and to Betty's home town of Kanab, where Romney was so taken with my speech that he asked for my address and phone number, saying he intended to write a letter of commendation to Wilkinson.

I visited Malta, Idaho, with Apostle Spencer W. Kimball and his wife, Camilla. They were both very gracious with me, but Elder Kimball was somewhat critical of my speech. The day was a hot one in the Snake River plains. There was no air-conditioning, and Kimball put a lot of people to sleep in the morning session of conference. In the afternoon meeting, I told the well-known story about Karl G. Maeser, BYU's first president, who because of his manifold administrative duties, was often late to the one class he taught. When he was tardy one day, he discovered that the students had tied a jackass to his desk. He immediately said, "I see that you have chosen one of your number to take my place during my absence." The congregation thought it was mildly amusing and listened to my talk. In the meeting with stake and priesthood leaders immediately after the afternoon session, Apostle Kimball looked sternly at me and said, "There is no room for levity in the chapels of the Lord." He received more graciously my comment on the way home that my great-grandfather, Hosea Cushing, was an adopted son of his grandfather, Heber C. Kimball. He made note of that fact for his family record.

In a final stake meeting, Apostle Joseph Fielding Smith, later president of the church, rode up with me to Richmond, Cache County, Utah. It was a delightful weekend for me; I found him to be a pleasant companion, a real gentleman, a puritan of strong conservative religious convictions but somewhat uninformed about matters outside his own field. At the morning session, he angered the congregation by announcing that he wanted them to go home and read a certain passage in the Bible but added, "You probably never read your Bibles." Then he referred to a section of the Book of Mormon with the observation, "A lot of you probably don't even own a copy of the book." Finally, he said, "I see you have a baseball diamond just across the street from this chapel; and if I weren't here, most of you would be over there watching a ball game instead of being in church." After the meeting the crowd just turned their backs on him and walked out. Only the stake presidency congratulated him on his sermon. I had the impression that he felt it was his mission to call the Saints to repentance, but the fact that he sermonized like Cotton Mather did not endear him to many people. Nevertheless, he was most gracious to me and everyone when away from the pulpit.

During the grand dinner served us at the home of the stake president in Lewisville, Smith suddenly looked sternly at me directly across the table and demanded, "What's the matter with BYU?" When I asked what he meant, he explained that the Friday before, his daughter and granddaughter had gone to Provo to arrange for the girl's housing so she could attend BYU, but there was none available. I rather startled the local people around the table by saying, "As I remember, you are a member of the Board of Trustees of BYU." After he had acknowledged that obvious fact, I told him that we would be happy to build sufficient student housing to avoid such problems as he had encountered with his granddaughter if his board would grant us the money for that purpose. He smiled at me and said no more about the subject. I hope my plain talking helped President Wilkinson in his search for building funds.

In one final incident, on the trip home as the conversation faltered,

I asked him what he thought of Juanita Brooks's book on the Mountain Meadows Massacre which had just been published. He exploded, "Very bad, very bad!" That ended that conversation![2]

President Wilkinson's successful campaign to preach BYU demanded an increased faculty to match the growing student body. Under the new regime, recruiting new teachers did not involve the faculty members of a department at all. The dean of the college concerned would offer a preliminary list of candidates, and Wilkinson would make the final choice by himself. For example, one April day in 1954 when I was acting chairman of the Department of History and Political Science, a man walked into my office, told me his name was Dr. Albert Fisher, and announced that he was a new member of the department. None of us had ever heard of him or knew that the administration was even contemplating adding a new person to our ranks. He reminded me some time later that my response was, "The hell you say." Fisher thought we knew all about his appointment, and both he and I were embarrassed by the situation. He turned out to be a very competent teacher and scholar in his field of geography. He later joined the faculty of the University of Utah.

The faculty sensed Wilkinson's scorn for most of them as nondoers who probably couldn't earn a living in the "real world" that he knew. His attitude was sharply revealed to me one day at the conclusion of a meeting I had with him in his office. He said to his secretary, "Show

---

2. The "Utah War" was a very traumatic event for the Mormon people. Reports of the approaching federal army set the stage in southern Utah for a Mormon-Piute attack on a group of emigrants. The Fancher train, passing through Utah on their way to California, was "holed up" against hostile Indians at Mountain Meadows, about thirty-five miles southwest of Cedar City in the fall of 1857. In the massacre that followed, about 120 emigrants were killed; the only survivors, about eighteen very young children, were taken temporarily into Mormon homes. The local leaders had sent a message to Brigham Young asking for advice, but his counsel to do nothing had reached them too late. John D. Lee, the Mormon Indian agent in southern Utah, one of the Mormon leaders in the massacre and Brigham Young's adopted son, was later excommunicated from the church and executed by federal authorities for his part in the event. Many, including Juanita Brooks, felt that he was a scapegoat. The topic had been taboo in Mormondom for almost a century, with Indians receiving the blame. Brooks, a loyal Mormon and fine historian, wrote *The Mountain Meadows Massacre* (Norman: University of Oklahoma Press, 1962), an excellent book that is still the definitive analysis of the event. Smith, obviously, had still not accepted that a thorough airing of the subject was the best way to put the massacre to rest.

in—oh, I've forgotten his name. You know, that anthropologist." It was Wells Jakeman, waiting in the outer office. The contempt in Wilkinson's voice was apparent to everyone in the room. A few of the faculty challenged him to his face, perhaps most noteworthily Professor Golden Taylor of the English department. Golden was a good friend with whom I worked for about two months one summer building a house for one of the university librarians. He was a man of practical skills and a fierce supporter of the kind of liberty his favorite American character, Henry David Thoreau, had taught and practiced. Golden was extreme in his views, having coursed from being a ward bishop in the church to outright disbelief. He had a consuming dislike for Wilkinson's dictatorial tendencies, decided to resign from the faculty, and did so with a violent denunciation, delivered in person, of Wilkinson and the Mormon church.

I had my own confrontation with Wilkinson, but in a different context. My salary was so low that, when I was offered an opportunity to spend spring quarter working at much higher wages with my father and brothers in their construction business in Salt Lake City, I made arrangements for other faculty to take over my teaching assignments and asked Wilkinson for a quarter's leave of absence. He refused and did so in such peremptory fashion that I fumed all day. By that evening and the annual faculty dance, the news was all over campus that I had been turned down but was not going to accept it. At the dance William F. Edwards, the poor Rigby, Idaho, farmboy who had made his million dollars as a stockbroker in New York and was now financial vice president at BYU, took me to one side and pleaded with me to accept Wilkinson's decision because my determination not to would just worsen relations between the president and the faculty. My answer was no! The next morning I was in Wilkinson's office to tell him that if I didn't get the leave I was going to resign. He granted me the leave, and I was able to make enough extra money to buy a few items of furniture and help pay some hospital bills. Standing up to him was the only way to gain his respect. He was hardnosed and ruthless.

Throughout my three and a half years of service with him, he continued to give me practical assignments as one of the few faculty members who, in his judgment, had any pragmatic sense. One spring he asked me to direct the campus-wide Y Day activities during which the students and faculty cleaned up the campus and made it presentable. The same quarter when high water caused flooding along the Provo River, school was canceled for a day while I directed the students and faculty in sandbagging the river banks in low-lying areas of the city.

But the most illuminating incident, both in revealing his perception of me and in emphasizing his combative nature, was when he asked me, during my last year at BYU, to chair the Scholarships Committee which not only made financial grants to scholars but also to all the athletes. He had already received the approval of the Board of Trustees for a policy that athletes were not to receive preference over other students. In his conference with me, he indicated that, while he had been a poor student at BYU, he had watched with some dismay and anger while athletes had received such comfortable jobs as distributing pillows at games at high pay while he and other students had to scramble for a living and tuition. He was not going to allow similar sinecures in his administration and said rather bluntly that I was the only faculty member with guts enough to deny athletes scholarships they didn't deserve. Ordinarily, athletics and other school expenses are handled separately for the athletic department; but in this instance athletic and academic scholarships were to be awarded by the same board.

I took the responsibility with deep reservations, knowing that he was attempting to fly in the face of American sports tradition and just could not win in his attempts to destroy intercollegiate athletics at BYU. Although I have always done my best to be loyal to my boss, in this instance I was not and, in fact, refused to follow his instructions in what I considered to be the best interests of the school. I met with Athletic Director Eddie Kimball, told him what was going on, and made arrangements to help the athletes all I could by granting them almost the same numbers of scholarships they had previously received. After I left BYU the next spring, I heard that Apostle Stephen L Richards became aware that Wilkinson was trying to destroy the athletic program and put a stop to it. Wilkinson then decided that if you can't fight them you'd better join them and supported athletics from then on in his usual whirlwind fashion. The fact that BYU was selected as the No. 1 football team of the nation in 1984 may be one of the results of this turnaround.

Not all my attention was focused on Ernest Wilkinson. I had a number of opportunities to represent BYU as a speaker at high school commencements and baccalaureates. Two which come to mind were at Park City where the principal warned me that this was a mostly Catholic community and at Parowan where the principal apologized to me because three or four of the male graduates reeled down the aisle, having started their celebration a few hours too soon. It had long been a "macho" tradition to come to graduation drunk—one which he had been unable to change completely.

A more memorable speech was one I gave at the San Juan County Annual Livestock Growers Association banquet held in the Monticello High School gymnasium. Charley Redd, my neighbor and a good friend, was the president of the organization that year and asked me to speak. When I inquired about a subject, he replied that he thought I was a man of good sense who would choose an appropriate topic. He may have had reason to question this judgment in light of my performance. At the time Senator Joseph McCarthy was hunting for "Communists" in the State Department and elsewhere. Outraged by these irresponsible character assassinations, I decided to use my appearance before the cattlemen and sheep-raisers of San Juan County to attack him. What I didn't realize was that this was perhaps the most politically conservative county in the state whose people admired McCarthy as a defender of the true Republican faith. As my speech progressed, the atmosphere in the gym became colder and colder. At the end there was no applause at all. To a man, everyone glared at me. I have always thought it was one of the best speeches of my life but delivered to the wrong crowd, or perhaps to the right audience after all. Charley joked that he had better get me out of the county before they lynched me.

During the banquet before my speech, I listened to some enjoyable western stories as each one of the stockmen told a tale on the neighbor sitting next to him. Apparently, it was a long-established custom at these annual get-togethers, and each rancher saved an especially interesting yarn to tell on one of his friends. One I remember is that Bill had been out on the spring round-up, rubbing shoulders with other cowhands in the rough give-and-take of campfire conversation, and was not yet prepared to settle down to civilized life when he rode into Monticello on his way home. He stopped, astride his horse, at the fence of the leading society matron in town who was pruning and spraying her flowers. During the conversation, in which Bill was having difficulty holding up his end, the lady suddenly asked, "Bill, have you ever had any aphids in your delphinium?" Taken aback, Bill answered, "I don't rightly believe so, but I once had a wood tick in my navel." This story gives the flavor of the other western stories of the evening.

Charley Redd chose me as the most likely conveyer of the free-enterprise doctrine in BYU's Department of History and decreed that his eldest child, Katherine, should take her American history from me, since I would be most likely to teach her correct economic principles. Kathy was very bright and easily earned an "A" in the class. One summer Betty and I were invited to spend a weekend at his ranch at LaSal, Utah, along with a few other faculty couples. Charley Redd was a man of substance, character, intelligence, and culture, and a real cowman. It was a privilege to know him.

Teaching remained my most enjoyable occupation at BYU. There were no awards at the time for outstanding teaching, but I believe I was recognized as one of the better instructors by both my peers and students. Because of the heavy teaching load and my extracurricular building activities, there was little time for research and writing. Furthermore, the academic climate at BYU was not conducive to publication. Faculty members spent most of their spare time gossiping about Wilkinson's latest outrage or rumors about what the apostles were saying.

At Betty's urging, in 1952 I sent a copy of my dissertation to Caxton Printers, Ltd., of Caldwell, Idaho, and asked if they would be interested in publishing it. To my amazement they answered that, with a few revisions, they would. Betty then undertook the task of retyping the whole manuscript for their consideration, and I hired a former BYU graduate student then living in Washington, D.C., to do some extra research for me at the National Archives. To make this long story short, Caxton finally published the work as *The Bannock of Idaho* in 1958, when I was a full-time builder. I was gratified that the reviews were quite favorable. In the late 1980s the book was out of print and selling for $40 if a copy could be found. The University of Idaho Press printed a paperback edition in 1996 with a new foreword.

In the spring of 1952 Betty was finally forced to have a back operation in which Dr. Nephi Kezerian, a wonderful surgeon, was able to fuse the two lower vertebrae, leaving her back quite stiff and unbendable but relieving her of the terrible pain which had been getting worse since our last year at Berkeley. Betty's father died near that time. He was only sixty-three and his death was a terribly sad time for Betty, who loved and admired her father with deep devotion. Her mother lived another twenty years and died on October 28, 1972, the same year my own mother died.

Our three children were developing into very bright youngsters. Karen and David were both doing well in elementary school, and Linda was just learning to walk when we moved into our Cherry Lane home. Betty became pregnant after her back was healed. We looked forward to a fourth child, but, to our sorrow, Betty suffered a miscarriage. She experienced the usual difficulties becoming pregnant again; and when Steven was born on August 29, 1955, he was six years younger than Linda, not what we would have liked for him or ourselves but the way fate arranged the schedule.

Betty and I continued our congenial relationship with our friends in the monthly Chowder Club, although by 1953 an unlovely incident marred its existence. By this time Ernest and Maurine Wilkins had joined the group. He was professor of Spanish at BYU, and she was the daughter of Apostle Harold B. Lee. One evening, for some reason, she and Ray Canning became involved in a heated discussion of the merits and liabilities of Sterling McMurrin. I joined in on Ray's side, defending Sterling. Maurine closed her argument by quoting her father to the effect that McMurrin was dangerous and perhaps even evil. The Wilkinses quit the club, leaving a rather bad taste for everyone. Maurine died only a couple of years later at a tragically young age.

I continued my friendship with Sterling by becoming a member of the "Swearing Elders," an informal organization of about forty academics that he and Dr. William Mulder organized at the University of Utah where both of them were faculty members. The group's purpose was to meet monthly to listen to speakers who had something of interest to say about Mormonism or the Mormon church. Several other BYU faculty also participated, and we drove up together each month to the University of Utah campus. The liberal sociologist Lowry Nelson gave the group its jocular title.

In one outstanding meeting, historian Whitney Cross, author of *The Burned-Over District,* addressed us about his research specialty, which was the religious revivals which swept upper New York State in the early 1800s when Joseph Smith was producing the Book of Mormon. It was interesting that while a few in the audience were attacking Joseph Smith as a false prophet, Cross, although a non-Mormon, defended him as a man of ability.

A second memorable get-together hosted a sort of debate between Melvin Cook, a chemist, who defended a rather thinly supported thesis that the earth was only 6,000 years old, with the support of Bruce R. McConkie, Joseph Fielding Smith's son-in-law and, even though he was only in his thirties, already a general authority. Opposing this view of a young earth was Jennings Olsen, a philosopher from Weber State. The meeting degenerated into a heated argument.

Church authorities were afraid of what was going on in the "Swearing Elders" and, partly because of his leadership of the group plus some other accusations against him of church disloyalty, tried to excommunicate McMurrin. President David O. McKay, who admired McMurrin's intellectual power and integrity, stopped the action. I, and other longtime friends of Sterling, were especially gratified by President McKay's action. We knew of McMurrin's genuine commitment to his church, despite his critical judgments about some of its theology and process. As he often said, "I am for the church, not against it."

There was a small group of faculty at the BYU who had, for years, been investigating historical aspects of the church, especially the origin of the Book of Mormon. We were discreet to the point of being underground, for obvious reasons. Foremost among this group was Wilford Poulson, a psychology professor who had spent numerous summers over about a thirty-year period traveling through the areas of Vermont and upper New York where Joseph Smith had lived, collecting books which he might have owned or used, and in other ways checking his history. As I began to question my own beliefs more and more, I decided to ask Poulson to share his discoveries with me. During my last year at BYU (1953-54), I went to school with Poulson for an hour each week when both of us should have been attending a devotional assembly.

He shared with me his belief that Joseph Smith had written the Book of Mormon himself using as a guide an 1823 book, *View of the Hebrews,* written by the Reverend Ethan Smith and published in Vermont near Joseph Smith's boyhood home. Poulson had a well-annotated copy of *View of the Hebrews* with numerous similarities to the Book of Mormon carefully marked. Ethan Smith's book has a theme similar to that of the Book of Mormon: that the American Indians were of Israelite descent (perhaps from the Ten Lost Tribes in Ethan Smith's opinion), and he found supporting evidence in his examination of Indian beliefs, traditions, customs, and especially ancient American ruins. Poulson was convinced that there were no visions, no angels, and no gold plates. Rather Joseph Smith had used his fertile imagination to write the Book of Mormon and had then organized his church. Poulson's arguments were very persuasive to me as a professional historian who had been trained to examine evidence critically.

I have to describe my experience with Poulson as rather traumatic. At first, he was hesitant about sharing his most important discoveries with me until I exploded, "I'm not one of your graduate students, Wilf! I'm your colleague, and I've got some concerns about my religious beliefs." He then showed me his comparison of the Book of Mormon and *View of the Hebrews*. It was a defining moment and swept away the remnants of my belief in the Book of Mormon, a belief that had been slowly crumbling over several years, especially during my years at BYU.

Another program which helped transform me into the agnostic I became at BYU was Wilkinson's insistence that, beginning in 1953–54, history faculty would teach a class in church history in addition to their other classes, using Joseph Fielding Smith's *Essentials of Church History* as a text. Since it was perhaps the most juvenile and inappropriate survey of the history of the church ever written, I began to read B. H. Roberts's six-volume *Comprehensive History of the Church of Jesus Christ of Latter-day Saints* as a basis for my lectures instead. I had never read Roberts before, and his approach to and honest narration of the facts of church history were a revelation to me. As I was sitting in the office I shared with Dick Poll one day, I came to Roberts's account of the "first miracle of the church," the story of the "levitation" of Newell Knight who found himself floating above his sick bed, hovering near the ceiling of his room. I had not been aware of this so-called spiritual event before. I slammed the book shut, turned to Dick, told him what I had just read, and announced, "This whole thing is a lot of baloney."

In short, during those years at BYU, I stopped being orthodox in my beliefs although, as I have already mentioned, I saw great value in orthodox behavior in its benefits for our family and in remaining attached to the Mormon community. As I examined the plausibility of Mormonism's historical claims, my inquiry broadened to those of Christianity. My good friend Russel Swensen recommended Albert Schweitzer's *The Quest of the Historical Jesus* (1906; London: P. Black, 1954), which I found a devastating analysis of the inaccurate history and myth built upon myth that formed the foundational claims of Jesus' godhood. Reading it had the same defining effect as reading *View of the Hebrews*. I could no longer accept uncritically the truth claims of any organized religion.

Although excruciating and exhausting, this intellectual process also brought welcome clarity and relief. Naturally, I did not reach it overnight, and thirty years of experience and thought since that point have refined the results of that paradigm-shifting year; but perhaps this is an appropriate point to discuss my personal intersection of faith and reason. I think such discussions are urgently needed. In the 1990s I have seen the rise of anti-intellectualism within Mormonism, including but not limited to BYU, to a degree that I would not have believed possible thirty years earlier. Perhaps those earlier beliefs that all truth was essentially harmonious were naive, but I see the new anti-intellectualism as driven by a fear of losing adherents that seems to be a revelation of profound uneasiness on the part of Mormon leaders. I make this point because I think some people today would simply say that I was "over-educated" or that I "intellectualized" myself out of the church. On the contrary, I invested considerable time, money, and effort in continuing to contribute to the church. I was not seeking to leave the church, nor have I to this day. Furthermore, as my father's experience in reading Genesis shows, a man characterized by considerable tough-minded practicality but virtually no education also found himself unable to uncritically accept the unreasonable and the illogical just because it was a matter of "faith."

As a young missionary, I quite honestly said during my farewell that I could not bear an unqualified testimony about the truthfulness of the gospel. I consider both my honesty and my hope for more conviction to be honorable. My missionary diary, from the second month on, documents what I think most members would call spiritual experiences, answered prayers, and confirmations. I certainly considered them such at the time, all of them reinforcing my commitment to be a hard-working missionary and zealous defender of my faith. At BYU, looking back on those experiences with twenty years of perspective, I considered that they said less about Mormonism than they did about one particular Mormon—me. I saw in my younger self a high sense of duty and commitment. I saw these traits as praiseworthy, and so was my determination to defend both my church and myself. The question of whether Mormonism was objectively "true" was less important to me than the fact that that young missionary had been "true" to his sense of integrity and commitment.

And now, looking back both on that young missionary and that BYU faculty member with an even longer perspective, I would say that reason tells me that my work, especially in the hills and hollows of Tennessee, followed a pattern of accepting twenty years of indoctrination by trusted authority figures who had, in turn, accepted a similar set of beliefs and values from their own authority figures. I now accept with tolerance and sympathy the human need for security in a world full of chaos and uncertainty. Religion fills that need and promises a better life in a next world when this life deals too much in suffering and sorrow. Although in 1954 I was angry neither at the church nor at BYU for teaching me a faith that, in my opinion, my reason could not sustain, I was primarily disappointed in myself. I thought that coming to BYU had been a mistake, a bad decision, the unmaking of which was going to disrupt my family and remove us from a society which included some genial and valued friends. I now see those years as valuable. I'm glad for them and their lessons.

Some people are able to compartmentalize logic and reason from supernatural and spiritual beliefs. I do not have that facility. I do not criticize the compartmentalizers. Many of them are highly intelligent and, in other respects, have high criteria for truth; I, however, found illogical and unreal assertions that a heavenly and eternal existence awaits us in some ethereal place where a benign God watches over all. I cannot surrender my independence and rationality to such a process but must follow the road where reason and evidence take me. I have only my mind and its tools to reveal reality to me. To deny what they show me is to undercut that reality and to leave me with no way of appraising the new "reality" that unsupported faith claims to produce. I cannot deny myself the opportunity of venturing into the unknown where there may be a God with "body, parts, and passions" or, more likely, nothing but this temporal life where all of us should be helping each other in the "pursuit of happiness" toward a good life in the present.

Sharpening the edge on these ponderings during my last year at BYU was a great debate among faculty and students over evolution. The scientific evidence of progression from a single cell to the very complex body of today's human being was so comprehensive and compelling, even at that stage, that I found it impossible to accept the simplistic Adam-and-Eve story as an adequate explanation of life on our planet. The facts of evolution raised many unanswered questions, most of them leading to logical absurdities, during that year-long debate. Did a heavenly creator supervise the development of the first single cell, then let nature continue the process? At what point did the creator decide that an individual was a human being capable of receiving a soul while his or her parents were still members of the animal kingdom? I am reminded of my Danish grandfather's query, "Is it reasonable to believe that God is the actually or reall[y] Father of the Billions of spirits that has lived on this Earth?" He would have been a vigorous participant in those BYU debates.

My feelings of uneasiness with the shaky defense of "faith" in these debates extended to the stories of the cosmic creation. I was not acquainted with astronomer Carl Sagan at that point, but he later phrased my feelings with precision. First noting that there are 100 trillion stars in 100 millionth of the sky and that earth is a mere pale blue dot in the universe, he continued:

> Stare at the dot for any length of time and then try to convince yourself that God created the whole Universe for one of the 10 million or so species of life that inhabits that speck of dust. Now, take it a step further: imagine that everything was made just for a single shade of that species, or gender, or ethnic or religious subdivision. If this doesn't strike you as unlikely, pick another dot. Imagine *it* to be inhabited by a different form of intelligent life. They, too, cherish the notion of a God who has created everything for their benefit. How seriously do you take *their* claim?[3]

---

3. Carl Sagan, *Pale Blue Dot* (New York: Random House, 1994), 11, 25.

In this context Kolob and God seem quite ephemeral. There may be such a creator, but the chance seems so remote that agnosticism seems not only the only internally consistent position but also the most appropriately humble one. I disdain the zealous certainties of both the atheist who proclaims godlessness with absolute surety and also the Sunday Mormon who knows "without the shadow of a doubt" that God not only lives but takes a particular personal interest in him and his doings.

Finally, I have struggled in vain to reconcile a conception of God as just with the manifold misery and inequality present in his creation (the earth) and among his children (human beings). As a historian, I must conclude that the narrative of recorded human suffering lends itself better to a "survival of the fittest" hypothesis than to one of a loving father.

Although I express these opinions with considerable conviction, mine is not a militant agnosticism. I respect other people's religious beliefs and make no attempts to dismantle their belief structures or even to advocate for my own. As an agnostic, I remain skeptical about my own skepticism as a matter of personal honesty. Perhaps my position is best captured by an incident in the early 1980s when I was teaching history at the University of Utah. Sterling McMurrin, who was teaching in the same department, was officed near me in Carlson Hall. Usually we had brown-bag working lunches; but one exquisite day in late spring, we decided to wander down to University Avenue for a hamburger. The sky was blue, the grass a vivid emerald. A border of scarlet tulips and bright daffodils flamed along the south side of the building. In a mood of appreciation so deep that it did not require conversation, we two amiable agnostics ambled along in silence. All at once Sterling stopped, looked up at the sky, and asked in a tone of genuine inquiry, "Brig, what if we're wrong?" He spoke for me. My reservations about my disbelief may be small, but I have them.

Do I believe in anything? Of course, I do. Along with Albert Schweitzer and many others, I have a deep "reverence for life." Long ago I quietly gave up hunting, even though I recognize that human beings raise, kill, and eat animals for food. It is not death itself that is wrong, in my opinion, but exploitation and waste.

Second, I have faith in the innate goodness of people and their desire to help others. With practically no possibility of an eternal "reward" in my system of belief, I strongly feel that each of us should help each other in the struggle for existence and for equality of opportunity in this, the only life we presently know. It is one reason why I became a teacher, and I hope I have helped some of the thousands of students I have taught to become better citizens, more responsible family members, and more productive human beings. Life is full of uncertainties; if we can help each other face that uncertainty with courage and kindness, we shall all be better off. We are still our brothers' and sisters' keepers.

Needless to say, as these ideas evolved, I felt more and more uncomfortable and guilty that I was accepting tithing money for my salary while holding basic beliefs which were in opposition to traditional Mormon doctrine. In addition, I became convinced then—and still hold the conviction—that Brigham Young University is not, and never has been, and cannot be a true university since it rejects the need for proper academic freedom to teach students in the various disciplines and promote the free thought necessary to the educational process. Academic freedom can be measured, not by the lectures that are given but by those that are not given, and not by the books that are written but by the books that are not written. At BYU there are too many lectures not given and too many books not written. There is a subtle and sometimes not so subtle pressure to conform to the beliefs of the "true gospel," definitions of which seem to shift in exact accordance with internal church politics. If a faculty member steps over the line, doesn't attend church or pay his tithing, or in any other way indicates that he is not completely orthodox and perhaps even engages in "bootleg" teaching of students in the privacy of his office, then he comes under close scrutiny, may not receive salary raises or promotions, and finally is given the word that he is no longer wanted. In my own field of history, perhaps the worst sin is that of omitting historical incidents which might embarrass the church or bring its doctrine into question and which then results in "faithful" or apologetic history with the result that outsiders—and members, too, for that matter!—do not know whether to trust the histories written by those scholars who are on the church payroll.

My chief concern with the rigid control of scholarship and teaching at BYU is that the students are being short-changed. They are led to believe they are getting a university education, when they are not.

For most of them, higher education is the one time in their lives when they can be intellectually challenged and exposed to new ideas which may clash with their traditional beliefs. That is what a university education is all about. The LDS church would like to see BYU students graduate with religious faith intact having escaped the perils of fundamental questions that other students expect to grapple with at real universities. I have met too many BYU graduates who, exposed later to new ideas, feel that they were betrayed as undergraduates. Many retain their membership in the LDS church but with deep-seated convictions that they missed out on an important part of their educational experience while at BYU.

My troubles with my conscience and with the absence of freedom to teach as I pleased with no fear of the consequences finally came to a head in May 1954, about a week before the end of school. There was no precipitating event, just the realization that I could no longer remain at BYU as a disbeliever in Mormonism and as a teacher who demanded and would not accept anything less than the academic freedom granted faculty in real universities. I just sat down, wrote a brief letter of resignation to Wilkinson, and returned home to talk it over with Betty. My decision was not exactly a surprise to her, but she fully appreciated the difficulties that awaited us, giving up the friendships and place we had made for ourselves in Provo because I had "lost my faith," or whatever was left of it. Both of us knew there was only one place to go to make a living and that was with my family's construction business in Salt Lake City. Although I hadn't consulted my father and brothers, I was fairly certain that they would welcome me to their partnership. (They did.) But if not, I had no question that there would be other opportunities for a skilled carpenter. Betty and I decided it would be best to move to Salt Lake City to be nearer work, but we planned to make the move in a year to ease the adjustment for our children and especially for Betty.

I did not give up the idea of returning to a university and maintained a sort of low-level search for the next seven years; but, psychologically, it was a relief to make a clean break from BYU. I must admit that the pressures of running a construction business left little time for a concentrated job search.

My friends on the faculty were astonished at my decision to leave. When I talked to P. A. Christensen, he urged me to reconsider, saying that my departure would precipitate a hemorrhage of other young and liberal faculty. (He was right, because over the next two or three years, a number of the most able left to escape the tightening controls imposed by Wilkinson and the church authorities, which resulted in even less academic freedom.) Christensen finally said at the end of our conversation, "By damn, if I were as young as you, I'd leave, too."

My best friend, Dick Poll, was so upset that he accused me of "taking out intellectual bankruptcy" by giving up the degree I had worked so hard for to go into the materialistic world of business. He argued that I should remain with him and others to fight the "creeping dictatorship" from within BYU. My answer was that it was a no-win situation and that I would not be on a faculty where I did not have the freedom to teach as I pleased. Further, I argued that he, too, would eventually be forced out, as he was, some years later. It is interesting to contrast his convictions about "intellectual bankruptcy" with the point of view of an attorney that a builder friend and I had to consult about a legal problem just two years after I left BYU. When the other builder introduced me as a former college professor now in the construction business, the lawyer ran around his desk, grabbed me by the hand, and exclaimed, "I'd like to shake hands with a man who has had the guts to leave teaching and to venture out into the real world." Perhaps town and gown will never understand one another. I have learned to live in both worlds and have come to appreciate the values of each.

In my short note of resignation, I had given no reason for leaving. After school was out and when I had already begun driving daily to Salt Lake City for my carpentry, Wilkinson wrote me a letter demanding that I come to his office and give him an explanation for my sudden decision to leave. I threw it in the wastebasket. Two weeks later I received a second and more conciliatory note asking me to see him at my convenience. It joined the first.

The only other time I saw Wilkinson was in a Washington, D.C., hotel in 1963 on my first evening there just before I went to work for the Peace Corps. We saw each other in the dining room and had dinner together. It was not an experience I either sought or avoided, but I had no desire to repeat it. He spent the meal denouncing Kennedy's Peace Corps while I defended the idea of voluntary service for America. He wrote me a couple of letters later in Salt Lake City disagreeing with some ideas which I had expressed in interviews with newspaper reporters.

There is no question that I disagreed with most of Wilkinson's goals, objected to nearly all of his methods, and had no liking for him as a man; but I could never hate him as some faculty at BYU did. In fact, I don't find it in my nature to hate anyone. Perhaps my experiences with a rough element in construction and the military gave me a better understanding of the man and his methods. I believe impartial thinkers must acknowledge his tremendous contribution to BYU in building a great physical plant, in raising the student population to its present level, and in committing the church to try to make BYU into a great institution. If controls over the faculty and teaching have tightened, as they have, it is a natural, though regrettable, consequence of the church wanting a firmer grip on an institution into which it is pouring a lot of money and attention.

When I severed my connections with BYU, I wasted no time looking back. I directed my total energy into the building business, which occupied my time for the next seven years.

13.

THE SMELL OF SAWDUST,
1954-61

After a year we were ready to move to Salt Lake City. We had listed our house on Cherry Lane a few months after my resignation, but the sale was delayed because it caught fire just as our good friend, Merrill Bushnell, was sitting in the living room with Betty and me, completing the listing. I had foolishly left a basket of "cold" fireplace ashes in the garage. They ignited the open studding, and the fire spread quickly into the attic. Fortunately, I had used fire-resistant asbestos shingles, which contained the blaze. A neighbor and I had most of the fire out before the fire department arrived, and there was no smoke or water damage. But it took me three or four months to repair and strengthen the rafters and ceiling joists, and I also covered the garage walls with sheet-rock. I have been especially conscious of fire hazards and suspicious of smoke ever since.

We finally sold the house in the early summer of 1955 and, with Betty seven months pregnant, packed and moved into a smaller but new residence at 1506 East 4160 South in Salt Lake City.

For a while we drove to Provo for monthly meetings with the Chowder Club, but it was taxing. Fortunately, Angus and Grace Woodbury invited us to join another study group in Salt Lake City that also met monthly to discuss subjects of mutual interest, including an exchange of views about the church. Angus was professor of zoology at the University of Utah, while Grace was a delightful and witty individual who attracted friends very easily. Other members were Allan Crockett of the Utah Supreme Court and his wife, Eulalia; LaMar Peterson, a music teacher, and his wife, Fae; Horace Christensen, a

The Madsens in 1959 in Salt Lake City.
Clockwise from upper left: Karen, Linda, David, and Steven.

Social Security employee, and his wife, LaVonda; our good friends Ray and Lois Canning; Gordon Howard, a dentist, and his wife, Alta; and later John and Mary Fitzgerald, who were members of our ward. John was later excommunicated for opposing the Mormon policy forbidding priesthood to black men. This group thrived for about ten years until the tragic deaths of the Woodburys in an automobile accident led to its gradual demise.

I immediately bought a lot at 2571 Olympus Drive (4200 South) so that eventually we could build a larger home that would fit our specifications. Eventually, I built a total of three more homes for us. I have often joked that Betty was always willing to pull up stakes and move again as long as I promised to let her design a new house each time. Our youngest son, Steven McAllister, was born August 29, 1955, just a couple of months after we moved to Salt Lake City. When we left for the hospital, nine-year-old David instructed his mother in no uncertain terms that she was to bring back a baby brother. We were not sure if we could have more children (we were right), so we were delighted with the symmetry Steven added. All of our children have been a joy and a pleasure to us as parents and, as they matured, as friends.

By the summer of 1956 we sold our "temporary" home and gladly moved into our more spacious new dwelling on Olympus Drive. We didn't intend to stay there very long as, like most builders, I wanted to build a "dream" home for us. We found a large lot to our liking at 2181 Lincoln Lane, complete with apple, plum, and peach trees and bordered on the back by bushes and shrubs, and I started to build a 2,600-square-foot house with five bedrooms, three baths, and other amenities, which Betty designed. In the fall of 1959 we moved in. This was the home about which we had the most permanent feeling, the place where the children did most of their growing up, from which they left for college and marriage, and to which they returned as "the homestead." Betty and I lived there until May 1997, though not continuously—and actually, we bought it twice, but I'll explain how that happened later.

During these years Betty and I continued to take our children to Sunday school and sacrament meetings except for the monthly testimony meetings.[1] They also attended MIA as teenagers, and both boys played ward basketball and were members of the Boy Scout troop sponsored by our ward. Linda, very independent like all of the children, had an argument at age fifteen with her seminary teacher. She found it implausible that the Jaredites, one of the Book of Mormon peoples, had sailed from the Middle East in a submersible and fully-enclosed boat that could turn over in midvoyage. How was that possible, she demanded, without killing the animals and passengers? Her teacher's unsatisfactory response and lack of respect for her quite valid question started a process of disaffiliation for her.

---

1. When we were raising our children, Sunday school was held in the morning and sacrament meeting in the evening. The evening meeting was a preaching service with two or three speakers during the last three weeks of the month, but the first week was a testimony meeting, open to any member who wanted to rise and express his or her feelings about the truthfulness of the "restored gospel." Most such utterances are rather prosaic and commonplace, some were intense and meaningful, but others were rather maudlin accounts of intimate personal experiences that, in my opinion, should have remained private. Since 1980 this double-meeting schedule has given way to the "block" plan, in which members meet for three hours of back-to-back meetings.

One may well ask how a confirmed agnostic could continue attending religious services, at least for several more years. I saw many positive values in Mormonism: the emphasis on family relationships, the Word of Wisdom which teaches proper care of the body, and the old Puritan virtues of honesty, industry, and frugality, among others. Betty and I wanted our children to learn these precepts, and we wanted them to have the social acceptance which came with our church activity. We never imposed our liberal religious thought on our children, but allowed them to develop their own concepts. Later on we watched as all four decided independently to withdraw from the church altogether. They probably inherited some heresy from us through osmosis, but finally they made up their own minds.

I will always consider myself to be a Mormon. My heritage is Mormon, my sympathies are Mormon, and my culture is Mormon-oriented. Any legal or technical separation from the church will not change my Mormon nature. After all, my first name is Brigham!

When we moved to our home on Olympus Drive, the bishop of the Olympus Fifth Ward, "Bud" Curtis, who also became the children's orthodontist, asked me to teach the Gospel Doctrine class where John Fitzgerald was disrupting the sessions with his provocative questions. Curtis thought I might be able to control him and to improve the instruction. I told Curtis that I wouldn't teach the Book of Mormon, the Doctrine and Covenants, or the Bible but that I'd be happy to take the assignment if he could discover any other subject I could use. He informed me that the prescribed text was David O. McKay's *Gospel Ideals,* a wonderful exposition on ethics and morality. I took the job, was able to control Fitzgerald, who became a good friend, built the class up to about eighty participants, and taught it for two years. I never tried to undermine anyone's faith in the institutional church, concentrating instead on teaching ethical conduct. But the opening and closing class prayers by the members so frequently included gratitude for my faithfulness and testimony that I felt very guilty and finally resigned.

Curtis was quite upset with my resignation. Casting about for something that he hoped would be appealing, he said he'd see that I was ordained a high priest (the highest ranking in the Melchizedek priesthood) if I would only pay a little tithing. When I rather flippantly asked, "How much will I have to pay?," he dropped his attempts, and we remained good friends.

Our children grew up rapidly during these years. Karen worked one summer at an ice cream and hamburger fast-food establishment, became the editor of the student newspaper at Olympus High School, and in her senior year (1960-61) was named the number one National Merit Scholar, the first girl to win that distinction at Olympus. As a result, she was offered a tuition and cash scholarship for the freshman year at Stanford University and enrolled there in the fall of 1961.

David was busy with Little League baseball and began his working career at age eleven with Engh Floral Company as a repotting boy. He recently confessed that he was fired after the first fifteen minutes when Hank Engh found him busily repotting petunias upside down. David didn't dare return home and face what he called my "glare," so he simply waited until Engh had left, slipped back into the shed, worked for the rest of the day, and reinstalled himself in Engh's good graces. That job introduced him to his enduring love for plants.

In babyhood he had had difficulty in swallowing. After a couple of unsatisfactory consultations, Betty, whose tiger-mother instincts were aroused, marched into our doctor's office and announced that she was not leaving until he found out what was wrong. She got action then! When David was eleven, he developed some growths on his vocal chords which the physician we consulted insisted were cancerous and had to be removed. After the operation the doctor insisted that David should remain silent for some days. This inactivity unfortunately allowed the vocal chords to grow together; and to disguise his incompetence, the surgeon insisted that David could not talk because he had a psychological problem. The psychiatrist was soon convinced that it was a physical problem, but the physician was evading us at every turn. We took David to a throat specialist in Denver and to two others in Los Angeles, deliberately seeking a range of expert opinions. All three made the same recommendation: that the vocal chords had to be cut apart and a metal plate inserted between them while they healed. The operation was successfully performed at the UCLA Medical Center, and David regained so much of his speaking voice that most people do not detect anything out of the ordinary. David adjusted in a remarkable manner to this condition, but Betty and I were always heartsick over it. We never forgave the original doctor for his cowardice; if the same thing had happened today, we probably would have sued him. Since then we have routinely insisted on second opinions for medical problems.

I remember one day when Betty unexpectedly drove out to the construction site, got out of the car, and, in tears, informed me that "my" son David had just been expelled from his fifth grade class, and what was I going to do about it? I went straight to the school where I found "my" son incarcerated in the principal's office. In the conference with his teacher, the principal, and David, we agreed that David would be reinstated but under very strict supervision from his father. I expressed my sincere appreciation to the teacher for not putting up with David's disruptive behavior. It was obvious that he was somewhat bored and not challenged, but that was no reason for his misplaced behavior. David never again got in trouble in school.

Linda was ten when we moved into our home on Lincoln Lane, and Steve was four. He was already manifesting his life-long passion for dogs (his family today includes three), and we bought a border collie puppy for him when he was about five. He and Tip, who survived to the ripe old age of fourteen, grew up together.

We encouraged all of our children to find part-time employment beginning about age twelve to fourteen so that they would learn what hard work was all about and learn to be independent. They might say that I did more than "encourage" them; I insisted on work as a necessary part of their education.

As soon as Steve entered kindergarten, Betty returned to teaching which gave her an interest outside the home but, more importantly, provided some financial stability during the roller-coaster years of the construction business. Betty enjoyed teaching in the school where John Fitzgerald was principal, particularly since he allowed his teachers a lot of independence to set their own course.

Dad was going on sixty-three and often ill from a heart condition when I joined the Madsen construction team. Within two years he retired completely and died in 1959. Mother's health was better, and we had her with us until February 1, 1972. Thus, almost from the beginning, the business was in the hands of the three brothers. To say I was busy during these seven "sawdust" years is an understatement. In addition to running a successful and demanding construction business, I always had work on our homes to occupy my evenings and weekends. At the time I entered construction full time in Salt Lake City, Dad,

Mack, and Rod were subcontracting the rough and finish carpentry on a number of tract homes in Granger. They had already completed forty homes in Bountiful for the partnership of George Daley and Richard Prows, a project on which I had worked on Saturdays while still teaching at BYU.

I have always liked and admired Dick Prows. The Bountiful project, his first, taught him the basics of building. I remember one day when we told him we could not put on the subfloor until he procured some wooden bridging for us. He tried to tell us to go ahead with the subfloor and nail the bridging in later. Since this plan was literally impossible, we had a good laugh, and he dropped the suggestion. But he learned so well and so fast that he has become one of the outstanding land developers and builders of the intermountain area as one of the two principals in the Prowswood firm. Later, when I was director of libraries at the University of Utah, he asked me to get involved in a vocational training project with him during which, for about five months, I taught two classes of carpenter foremen in weekly sessions in the Granite School District's night school; and because of my background, I hit it off immediately with these foremen. We covered how to deal with minority workers, home buyers, real estate salesmen, and subcontractors. It was a course in how to improve interpersonal relationships on the job.

The Granger project eventually involved over 200 homes which we built for the firm of Whitey Nielsen and Brig Scott. When my father and brothers first approached the two developers seeking a contract, Scott warned them that two subcontractors had already built a house apiece but had lost money when they accepted the amount offered for the subcontract. The Madsens not only made good wages but cleared about $250 on their first house and never lacked for work with Nielsen and Scott thereafter. We were used to hard work, insisted on "getting the damn thing done" as fast as possible, and saw to it that the workmanship was of the best. With proper organization, skilled craftsmen, and attention to detail or "tending to business," speed and a good product can be fruitful partners.

The family business was an informal partnership, and right from the start, Mack, Rod, and I developed a division of labor which we followed as long as we were in business together. I laid out the houses and ran a crew which poured the foundations and built the subfloors.

My brother Mack framed the houses, while Rod took care of the finish carpentry.

As our reputation and professional ego grew, we incorporated in 1957 as Madsen Brothers Construction, Inc. Legally, I suppose, the corporation protected us from the risks involved in our business, although we always seemed able to work out any problems we had with suppliers, crews, and buyers. I enjoyed the novelty of signing my name as president, meeting with a board of directors which consisted of Mack and his wife, and placing the Great Seal of the Corporation on legal documents.

As a corporation, our working relationship remained the same. I continued to provide foundations and subfloors but also negotiated the construction loans with a bank, dealt with city councils and Federal Home Administration (FHA) and Veterans Administration (VA) inspectors, oversaw the subcontractors, worked with the real estate firms to sell our houses, took care of problems with homeowners, and supervised the accounting and bookkeeping. We usually had a crew of about twenty carpenters and laborers.

To the amazement of all the people with whom we dealt, we got along extremely well, never had a single serious disagreement, and made money. We loved the competition, never found another firm that could build as fast or as well as we, and took great pride in that accomplishment. In the world of building, there are so many problems, and construction workers are so independent and ever-ready to take offense that the irritations endemic in construction can easily lead to explosions and feuds. My brothers had rather short fuses while I have always been slow to anger and usually maintained equanimity in the face of irritating and often seemingly impossible situations. But sometimes the pressure would build up, and I might blow off a little steam much to my brothers' amusement.[2]

2. I suppose some of our experiences might be considered colorful. A few months after leaving the construction business in 1961, I wrote an article, "The Autobiography of an Ex-Builder," and sent it to the editor of the magazine published by the National Home Builders' Association in Washington, D.C. He sent it back with the note that he and all of his staff had read it with some interest and even some amusement but that he was afraid of a libel suit even though I had left out or disguised the names of the people mentioned in the article. Much of the information, which seems much tamer with the passage of time, makes a new appearance in this chapter.

Starting with the Granger project in 1954, we first built a group of five houses, then thirteen, twenty-one more, then four more groups of twelve, ten, sixty, and thirty respectively in Granger, Salt Lake City, and Murray. In 1959 Mack and I contracted with a new company to supervise the construction of tract homes in Idaho Falls and Ogden. We were interested by the company's far-reaching and imaginative plans and saw an opportunity to make a good profit. Rod, who has always been more conservative, dropped out of our firm to pursue a building career on his own. Mack moved his family to Idaho Falls to complete the construction of seventy-two houses already underway with full responsibility for another 130 to be started. He and I were to receive a good return per unit, or one-half of the net profit on the home, whichever was greater. I engaged to do the same for a project of 117 homes in Ogden. It was a good contract, and if the houses had sold, we would have made money. But the houses did not sell; and after a year and a half, there was no money to pay us. We had no liability as a result of the failure—I had seen to that—but we never recovered all that was coming to us. Mack moved back to Salt Lake City, and we returned to our own construction work.

We agreed to take over twenty-one lots in Washington Terrace, a small community on the south edge of Ogden, as partial payment. That is all we ever recovered from the disaster, but it was a start again. Conditions slowly improved, and our homes began to sell. These cycles occur all the time, and smart builders have to be prepared financially to ride the roller-coaster.

The building process is a complicated one with potential pitfalls at every turn. The first step is to shop around for construction money. Most lending institutions in our area charged 2.5 percent for servicing a construction loan.

Then there was the discount fee of 3 or 4 percent that the builder pays the bank to encourage it to accept the mortgage. (This fee could be as low as 1.5 percent under Congressional special assistance to housing and as high as 10 percent for a VA loan). Usually, we had a signed agreement with our financial agency covering a number of proposed building starts, which placed a maximum discount rate on those particular loans. Some builders "shopped around" for better discount agreements, but cut-rate outfits often were unrelenting if the builder got into financial difficulties. We preferred to stay with a larger and more stable institution whose sympathy was a little deeper in times of stress (which always describes construction). On a typical $15,000 house, then, complete finance charges might rise as high as $1,700 for the contractor, and successful mortgage lending institutions seemed to increase their capital in almost geometric proportions.

The construction loan to the builder was usually 80 percent of the Federal Housing Administration's commitment of a guaranteed loan to the buyer. Supposedly, the builder got this entire amount for construction costs but actually $700 to $800 was earmarked for "loan costs." Then, with the aid of your bookkeeper, you would set up accounts to pay the balance for materials and labor. But often, as the house neared completion, the bank would retain another $500 to $600 for "expected interest" or some other expected expense, so that the contractor never knew exactly how much he'd have for bills. During the halcyon days after World War II, one enterprising promoter in our area was able to purchase his land so economically that he found a balance of $200 in his construction loan account after all bills had been paid on the house. This situation no longer existed and the small builder was faced with unpaid bills of from $1,000 to $1,500 on each speculative house. He spent most of his time assuring suppliers and subcontractors that they need not place liens on the house—that as soon as the house sold, there would be sufficient money to pay all accounts.

"Free enterprise" supposedly directs the management of low-cost building, particularly in establishing a sales price for the house being offered. But the FHA or VA (sometimes both) considered the plans and specifications submitted by the contractor, decided on a loan guaranty amount, and left the "enterpriser" one "freedom of choice"— either accept this sales price or submit new plans and hope for better luck next time. It was possible to appeal, and sometimes the two agencies would raise the price if sufficient evidence showed that costs had risen. Appraising houses is a very tricky business, and often FHA, VA, loaning institutions, and builders could be far apart in their evaluations.

Before leaving finance, I should note that mortgage investment banks were changing rapidly from the old system of disbursing cash out of the construction loan upon completion of a certain percentage of house construction. Too many builders used the money to invest in other property, buy new pick-up trucks, or (in rare cases) take a long weekend in Las Vegas, leaving subcontractors and suppliers holding the proverbial bag. Instead, the bank began to issue books of vouchers to all builders, who, in turn, would write a voucher for the proper amount to the supplier. The supplier thus received his money directly from the bank.

Another aspect of finance involved the purchase of land or lots. Sometimes a builder was able to pay the entire cost of the lot out of his construction loan, but this procedure left some other creditor waiting for his money. The usual procedure was to pay cash for half the cost of the lot and ask the subdivider to wait until the sale of the home for the remainder. But if the builder were also the subdivider, there were at least two possibilities: (1) Invest enough personal cash to make a down payment on the ground, or (2) Get a land mortgage through your loaning institution. This ruinous option left the bank the chief gainer, collecting monthly and monotonously a high rate of interest. Land contracts were always too short, from the subdivider's point of view. Interest charges mounted as local and federal bureaucracy took their red-tape time in approving the project.

The engineers hired to survey and plot the land did not materially speed the process. The developer usually hired them on the basis of their reputation to squeeze the greatest possible number of lots into a given area. We bought some sites in one project where the lots were so misshapen and tiny that we found it impossible to place a house on one. Municipal codes provided some regulation—usually an average of 3 to 3½ lots per acre.

Above all, the builder must beware of low ground since it may be waterlogged. An enthusiastic realtor almost sold me a fifty-acre tract as a joint venture with two other developers. Its outstanding feature was a beautiful brook meandering through a meadow. At the last moment I hired a drainage expert to dig some test holes for me. He estimated that it would cost $30,000 to drain the area, and even then could not guarantee dry basements. We three developers withdrew and watched with a cynical eye as the salesman found some new believers in "Duck Acres." They had a disastrous time trying to develop the property be-yond a few "model homes."

In our area of Murray and, later, South Ogden, my rule of thumb was to buy land in July or August when irrigation was at its height. Many a parcel of January "dry" could be a July bog. I once sold a house to a buyer who moved boxes of valuable books into the basement.

The next morning he discovered a small canal flowing through a basement window from the alfalfa field across the street. His books were doing a Venetian tour around the room. A lawsuit against the farmer produced only attorney fees. More than once I would start the working day by renting a pump and extracting the evening's deluge from the basement of a house under construction.

Second only to water is the problem of dirt. Experience eventually taught me how many yards of fill dirt it would take to bring homes up to street level, but the key word is "eventually." I once bought twelve lots, six on each side of a street. The east side proved no problem; but on the west side where the land fell sharply away, my six houses were soon standing like Sherman's sentinels above the surrounding terrain. After much telephoning, I located an excavation company that was lowering the level of a city street. It willingly hauled the necessary dirt and fill—and it only cost me my profit on the six houses.

Subdividing also entailed interminable delays interspersed with meetings of city councils and FHA officials. The local city council sees the subdivider as an economic royalist who is out to make more royalties. Because the city has only so many acres available for subdividing, it seeks every conceivable means of profiting. One council insisted I put in the main water line (which is normal), then charged me a high fee per house for the privilege of hooking my houses onto my own water line (which is exorbitantly abnormal). Cities also charge inspection fees on the installation of curb, gutter, sidewalks, and streets.

Next the builder is faced with designing the houses. Architects came in all prices, from $1,000 to $150 for low-cost tract housing. We found that AIA (American Institute of Architects) men were too steeped in their superior knowledge both pricewise and in dealing with FHA officials and buyers. We turned to the $150-per-plan designers hired by local lumber dealers to help customers. It is true they weren't as imaginative, but they were proficient draftsmen, and we usually stayed with the tried-and-true split-level, rambler, picture-window type of housing. Most builders agreed with this rule by a contractor friend of mine: "When a home is selling, don't change even the size of a window. Build it until you have exhausted [possibly he meant literally] every prospective customer."

Of course, house design and construction techniques had altered since World War II. The pre-Depression Era house used a single form for the basement wall, and the concrete was poured against the dirt. The floor joists were set in the concrete. One-by-twelve sheathing was used as a subfloor and, in horizontal fashion, as sheathing for the outside walls. Rafters were hardly ever larger than two-by-fours. The roof was covered with cedar shingles, and the interior was finished with lath and plaster. This was the house that America had been building for many years. But after World War II, doubleforming insured a concrete wall of uniform thickness; subfloors and roof sheathing were made of plywood stapled to the joist; walls were built in component sections in a mill and assembled on the job; trusses supported the roof and allowed partitions to be moved at will in the interior; built-up roofs gave economy and long-lasting quality to a house; interior walls were covered with dry-wall, which prevented cracking and checking; and pre-finished cabinets added beauty. More recent developments had such efficiencies as premolded, one-piece plastic bathrooms installed in one operation and interior and exterior walls of pre-finished metal and plastic sections that a carpenter can install with a pot of glue and a screwdriver.

Many of these improved methods could be attributed to the Federal Housing Administration, and we found that FHA architectural and engineering inspectors were nearly always practical and experienced. Usually they exhibited very good judgment unless constrained by a foolish order from higher up. On inspection days we watched to see whether our inspector was the soil expert, the paint expert, the drawer expert (one man never missed checking every drawer in the house), or the framing expert. I shall never forget one inspector who arrived, nattily dressed in a suit and tie, to examine footings which could be reached only through an access hole in the foundation wall. I assured him that the footings were placed properly and that he wouldn't have to crawl under the floor to see them. My assurance must have aroused his suspicion because without hesitation he fell to his knees in the mud and slithered under the floor. He emerged plastered with mud, but he passed our footings.

The risk of injury on the job is a real one in construction. One carpenter was so accident prone that everyone avoided him because they didn't trust him. He once failed to nail securely the barge rafter on an overhanging roof. His partner stepped on it and fell about twenty feet to the ground. No one would work with him after that, and ultimately

I fired him. One day when laying sheathing on a roof along with two other men, I was cutting with a hand-power saw when I brushed the still-rotating blade across the left lower pocket of my carpenter overalls and cut a three-inch gash in my thigh. Fortunately, the blade did not sever any major veins or arteries, but I still carry the scar.

Perhaps my greatest frustration was getting proper performance from our subcontractors. The pattern never varies. In the winter building slows to a crawl; in desperation they tour the projects, bidding on everyone's houses. Then to their surprise, they get more work than they can handle and by summer they're swamped. Large tract contractors are usually assessed daily fines for all no-shows. Furthermore, subcontractors prefer tract housing because each house is the same and they can build up assembly-line speed. But the small contractor or private home-builder often spends evenings and early mornings coaxing, cajoling, and sometimes cursing the subcontractor who had promised to be on the job yesterday or last week.

We once contracted with a masonry contractor to lay the brick on thirteen homes. We paid him regularly as the project developed; but shortly after the last home was completed, the company that supplied the brick presented us with a bill for $1,500 which the mason had failed to pay. Although an elder in his church and a family man with children, he had absconded with his remaining capital to take up residence with another lady, we knew not where. We naturally told the brick company official that we had paid the $1,500 once and did not intend to pay it again. He naturally pointed out that we had just ordered brick for ten more homes and that if we didn't pay the $1,500 we would get no more brick. We paid the money—but we don't like the brick company to this day. After that we made all checks jointly to subcontractor and supplier.

We also discovered that experienced carpenter-mechanics were fast disappearing; apprentices learned a single specialty and never advanced beyond it. I once worked with a carpenter who had done nothing for seven years but lay out two-by-four plates with a tape, a square, and a pencil. He was very good at this specialty but could do nothing else. With the new component building and nearly everything being built on jigs in a factory, the modern carpenter spends most of his time just with a hammer and a nail gun, little else.

Perhaps the most important phase of a small builder's work is proper bookkeeping. Many a contractor has sailed on a sea of imagined prosperity, daily totalling up profits on a nearby piece of 1 x 8 "d" pine. He is amazed at the year's end to find only a bomb crater where his high hopes once stood. We ran through two or three mediocre bookkeepers until, by lucky chance, we were introduced to Mrs. Winifred Manwaring, a very cultured and refined woman who had taken up accounting after her husband's death. She knew nothing of the construction business at first; but within two months she had informed our lumber dealer that he had misfigured his board feet and overcharged us about $500. After that our suppliers checked our statements very carefully before mailing them. She once caught our bank in a mistake of interest, resulting in a nice little refund and some $4,500 altogether to the rest of the builders serviced by this particular loaning institution. Reciprocally, she kept *us* on our toes with her demand for exact costs and procedures.

Then there's the real estate salesman, the builder's enemy in an undeclared war. The builder deals with cold, misery, mud, and all the other problems tied to building a house; the well-dressed realtor drives up in a new Cadillac, escorts the buyer into the house, and collects as much in commission as the builder has made over a period of several months. Don't misunderstand me, we needed the salesman and without his efforts we would have been out of business. It just didn't seem fair! We once decided to sell our own houses; but after spending several hundred dollars on advertising and two weeks of evening and weekend efforts, we gave up. I could get a prospective buyer right up to the dotted line, and then I didn't have the nerve to force a sale on a couple who (I thought) couldn't afford our house.

I ran afoul of the Salt Lake Real Estate Board when we built twelve houses just off 33rd South near the city's eastern foothills. The board had a firm rule that if the occupants of the homes on either side of the one listed for sale objected to a prospective buyer, the real estate firm should discourage the buyer. One day when our broker was away, I sold one of the houses to a Japanese woman moving from Idaho Falls with her husband, an attorney. I was very much opposed to the board rule; furthermore, it didn't apply because the houses on either side were unsold. When I delivered the earnest money agreement to our real estate broker that evening, he saw the Japanese name on the contract and protested that it would be difficult to sell the other homes because people wouldn't want to live near a Japanese couple. I lost my temper, told him that I as the builder would take my chances with such an unlikely prospect, and instructed him to proceed with the sale. Instead, after we left work, he visited the residents next to our project, asked if they wanted to live next to a Japanese family, and then told the Japanese couple that their neighbors objected to them. The attorney and his wife withdrew from their purchase agreement. I told off the real estate man in no uncertain terms and never had anything more to do with him. Several years later, as a member of the faculty of the University of Utah, I had the satisfaction of working with one of our law professors to help make that rule illegal.

In one of our early projects when my father was still somewhat active, we had contracted with a subdivider to buy our lots and had also given him the exclusive right to sell the homes. He turned out to be a smooth-talking, rather devious, and quite obnoxious character who finally got to my father. One Monday morning, after stewing about this man over the weekend, Dad met him and announced, "You're not such a bad guy; I just wish I'd never met you."

Some of our buyers have been eccentric indeed. One man, for example, stopped each morning at 8:00 o'clock on his way to the office to say hello to his builder and crew. Within half an hour, a telegram would arrive with detailed instructions about the day's operations. After the third telegram on the third day of this charade, he and the contractor came to a sudden and mutual understanding in the unfinished living room of the house. One buyer conscientiously instructed us in the intricacies of construction, laying out the stairs on the wall three or four times with different colored pencils. Another insisted on having long heavy bolts made to suspend the kitchen cabinets from the ceiling when a few eight-penny nails would do the trick. Another left notes all over the house with instructions to "move the guest closet from the living room to the hall" or "change the pitch of the roof from 2 1/2 and 12 to 4 and 12" or "tear down the north wall of bricks and do it over because the mortar is not the right shade of gray."

The do-it-yourself buyer also usually had a relative who could lay linoleum or bricks, and we had to work this new subcontractor into the setup and satisfy an FHA inspector simultaneously. We learned to spell out in meticulous detail the costs in time and money for each of the "little changes" a buyer wanted.

When the buyer moved in, then our phone kept on ringing. One enterprising contractor put his phone under his wife's name; others had unlisted numbers; but I always believed that we should at least try to have satisfied buyers. The common complaints were caused by wood shrinkage and earth settling. A floor joist 7.5 inches wide might shrink anywhere from 1/2" to 5/8", resulting in cracks in the drywall or plaster, loosened grout between the bottom row of tile and the bathtub, and a gap between baseboard and oak floor. All of these reactions were quite normal and could be rectified; but it was difficult to persuade yourself and your subcontractor that such little jobs were important when you had other houses under construction.

Normally I was patient and tolerant about fixing these minor post-building problems; but I really hit the ceiling once. In 1958, our best year, we built sixty homes, fifty of them in a subdivision in Murray, Utah. The developers got involved in financial difficulties, and the loaning institution, Prudential Federal Savings & Loan, took over the project. Its vice-president, H. M. Calvert, invited us and two other builders, the Crus Brothers and John Carter, to build in the tract because he knew and trusted the work of all three. We worked with Mooney Real Estate, built a show of five model homes, and by early summer had sold nearly all the homes on selected lots before we had even started construction on most of them. Furthermore, the Veterans Administration reduced its discount rate so that we almost doubled our profits on each house.

That was the good news. The bad news was the pressure on me as we tried to complete the dwellings in time for the start of school in September. I supervised a crew to get subfloors ready for the rough construction, worked with the bank, dealt with the subcontractors, and tried to satisfy the new home-buyers. My patience finally wore thin one day late in August when I was going through a house with the prospective buyer in a final inspection before he moved his family. He complained about poor workmanship throughout, but I patiently explained everything until we reached the bathroom. He noticed the crack between the wall tile and the tub and declared that was the final straw; I was a crooked builder who cheapened all my houses, etc., etc. At that point I exploded and ordered him out of the house. My brothers were highly amused.

Here are some unusual complaints I catalogued: One man complained that microscopic worms were eating holes in his oak floor and leaving piles of sawdust by each hole. We hired an exterminator. Another fellow pointed out that we had hung an interior door so that it swung over the basement stairs. His mother-in-law, hurrying to the bathroom, had chosen the wrong door and tumbled downstairs. We immediately rehung the door. A woman reported that her steel cabinets were electrified and she couldn't wash the dishes without getting a shock. We responded quickly to that call. Another man complained that his garage was too short by three feet to accommodate his Chevrolet and that, adding insult to injury, our foreman had suggested he get a Volkswagen. Finally, one distraught gentleman reported his discomfort and amazement on discovering that the toilet was connected to the hot water pipes.

Then there is the central figure in this confused tableau, the builder himself. Most of those I knew were conscientious, careful businessmen trying to make a fair profit on a quality-built home. One read the surveyor's stakes wrong and got a home partially built in the middle of an intersection. Another forgot that a trapezoid has two sides that are parallel, but not necessarily sides equal in length. His house was seven inches narrower on one end than the other (and still is). Dick Carruthers (a pseudonym) was locally called "One Nail" Carruthers because he supposedly put only one nail in each board. When kidded about this, he replied, "Not so. I have that nickname because I put one more nail in a board than any other builder." As a way of life, speculative house-building is interesting and stimulating to say the least, and risky to say the most. There is money to be made and money just as easily to be lost. A builder needs the courage of a mountain lion, the skin of a rhinoceros, the tenacity of a bull dog, and the pure gall of a magpie. At least, that's my judgment as I look back on my seven sawdust years.

Although these years were challenging, interesting, and financially remunerative (for the most part), they were years of intellectual famine. I kept alert for doors opening back into the university work. At the end of 1955, Lawrence Kinnaird said the California State Historical Society was looking for a director; he and other Berkeley faculty would recommend me if I wanted the job. I turned it down, knowing that a large part of my job would be fund-raising but that I would never fit into the tea-drinking and cocktail society of San Francisco.

When Gregory Crampton, a history professor at the University of Utah, took a year's leave in 1955-56, Leland Creer, head of the department, asked me to teach Crampton's survey course in U.S. history. I met that class each morning at 8:00, then went to concrete and two-by-fours at the construction site. Creer was impressed with me and tried to get me approved for a full-time tenure-track position. He failed, chiefly because he told his faculty that Sterling M. McMurrin, then dean of the college, approved of the appointment. The faculty members, offended that the dean was apparently trying to force me down their throats, voted against my appointment. In reality, McMurrin knew better than to use such tactics. Creer had blundered in his approach. I was disappointed but was making so much more as a builder than as a university teacher that I did not stew very much over the missed opportunity.

My reentry into the university finally came as a result of David's second surgery. While the metal plate was still between his vocal chords, I returned home from work one night to discover that his throat was swollen and dangerously infected. Betty and I immediately put him in the car, called his doctor, and drove straight through to the UCLA Medical Center. As soon as the doctor examined him, he had him taken to the operating room. During the surgery that followed, David choked, but a tracheotomy saved his life. He will always bear that scar on his throat.

During the three days we spent at UCLA while he was recovering sufficiently to be taken home, I went to the university bookstore and stocked up. I had not had such a concentrated period of time for reading for years, and I lost myself in the first book, Catherine Drinker Bowen's *John Adams and the American Revolution*. It was written so well and with such feeling that I underwent a genuine emotional experience. My seven years as a builder disappeared in a flash and my love for history and teaching rekindled. I decided that it was impossible to remain separated any longer from my deepest passion. I determined that I would move heaven and earth to find a university position, despite the probable financial sacrifice involved. Betty enthusiastically shared my dream. She knew it would make me happy, and she also loved academic life.

As fate would have it, I immediately learned that there was an opening at Utah State University because my friend of graduate school days, Everett L. Cooley, was leaving Logan to become director of the Utah State Historical Society. The USU job was exactly in my field and would mean taking over the teaching and graduate responsibilities long performed by Dr. Joel Ricks, whom Cooley had succeeded for a single year. The hiring process was very simple compared to the formalities of today's search committees, affirmative action advertisements, vitae and resumes, site-visit lectures, and multiple interviews. I had a single meeting with my Berkeley friend, S. George Ellsworth, Dr. Ricks, and Academic Vice-President Milton R. Merrill. They knew me and my record at BYU and were satisfied I would give them what they needed. I was employed at a salary of $7,000 as associate professor and was scheduled to start work that fall of 1961.

I made arrangements with Mack to complete the houses we had underway in Ogden, although I spent nearly every Saturday for the next several months working with him. Then Mack returned to Salt Lake City to build on his own. He did not try to persuade me otherwise; he could see how much teaching meant to me.

Betty was not overjoyed at having once again to sell out and move to a small Utah town but approved of my decision to get back into academic life and anticipated the new home in Logan, which I promised she could design. We bought an older house in Logan, 138 West 500 North, as temporary living space until I could construct our new home, and I "batched" there during the fall quarter of 1960-61, driving back to Salt Lake City on weekends. We sold our home on Lincoln Lane to Arthur Brown, coordinator of Higher Education for the State of Utah, and moved to Logan by January 1, 1961. Karen had begun her first year at Stanford that fall. David was fifteen, a tough age to be uprooted. He did not welcome the move from urban Olympus High School to the more rural Logan High School. Perhaps to his surprise, he discovered that the intellectual competition was just as challenging at Logan because many of his classmates were the children of university faculty members. Twelve-year-old Linda continued her interest in art without a break, and six-year-old Steven began first grade in our neighborhood school of Crestview, but transferred in the middle of the year when we moved to Logan.

As for me, I was almost forty-seven. I had found the smell of sawdust sweet for seven years, but now I was ready for the smell of chalk dust once more.

14.

UTAH STATE UNIVERSITY AND THE PEACE CORPS, 1961-65

Returning to academic life after an absence of several years was an easy transition, made easier by the congenial atmosphere in the Department of History. It was enjoyable to work with George Ellsworth and pick up the threads of our graduate school friendship. Although Leonard Arrington was a member of the economics department, I came to know him well and appreciated his industry, his enthusiasm for economic history, and his careful scholarship.

But my closest faculty associate was Stan Cazier, later president of Utah State University. He had an office next to mine in the old, decrepit Forestry Building next to the heating plant. We were isolated from our colleagues, who were officed in Old Main, and formed a close friendship as a result. Stan was a delightfully witty person, a man of liberal tendencies and great humanity, and a splendid teacher. The students flocked to his classes and liked to recount how one day, in the midst of a lecture, the table on which Cazier was sitting collapsed suddenly. It did not disconcert him at all. He continued his animated lecture without missing a syllable. During one quarter he was gravely ill, and I took over his basic courses. I have always liked and admired Stan; he was an excellent university president.

The real support of the department was Academic Vice President Milton R. Merrill, one of the world's fine human beings. He was a political scientist and, therefore, had a special interest in our discipline. He always treated me with great courtesy and friendliness; and if I had decided to return to Utah State after my Peace Corps experiences, he would have been the chief reason.

To prepare for my return to the classroom, I spent my evenings and weekends during the summer of 1961 making major revisions of my lectures for the survey course in American history. I was so eager to teach again that it seemed the summer would never pass. In addition to the survey course, I also was assigned to teach the Constitutional history of the United States, a new subject for me but one which I soon came to enjoy and appreciate second only to basic American history. I plunged into teaching with great enthusiasm and soon had a reputation as one of the better teachers on the faculty. One morning President Daryl Chase dropped in to listen to my lecture on Constitutional history, the only time I ever had a classroom visit by a university president.

In my third and last year at Utah State, I was nominated by my students and a faculty committee as one of five finalists for the Robbins' Award for Professor of the Year and placed second behind Professor Moyle Q. Rice of the English department who had been a member of the university faculty for about twenty years. To be granted distinction as an outstanding teacher is, in my opinion, worth more than any other kind of award that I might achieve. I can contemplate few satisfactions greater than those which come from challenging and interesting students in their history and heritage as Americans. My three years at Logan as a teacher, without the distractions of administrative duties, were some of the best in my entire university career.

By the time the first school year ended in May 1962, we had purchased a lot at 1439 East 1100 North, and I was ready to begin our new home. Meanwhile Betty, although she had majored in French, had never visited France. She enthusiastically agreed when I proposed that she join a USU group touring Europe for six weeks under Twain Tippetts of the art department. She had a wonderful experience.

Karen returned from Stanford. Her grade point average had not remained high enough to maintain her scholarship, and we could not afford to support her at Stanford without it. I never talked to her specifically about the slump in her grades. I suspected that one problem was that she had to work (she waited on tables in one of the dining halls) because we could not send her any surplus funds. My lower income as a faculty member left us without money. I also speculated that Karen, who had worked so hard in high school that she hadn't had much social life, may have spent less time on books and more time on socializing during her freshman year. If so, I would be the last to criticize. She deserved a year away from the grind of always being number one or close to it. And during the writing of this chapter when I queried her about it, she informed me that this is exactly what she did. Through a relative, Karen got a summer job as a waitress at Jacob's Lake, near the Grand Canyon. She made good tips, rather enjoyed the job, I believe, and transferred to USU in the fall.

David, on his own, began working at the Forest Service nursery, made some money, and was such a dedicated green-thumber that he kept working there part time when school started. Linda, almost thirteen, stepped into her mother's household responsibilities, cleaned, watched seven-year-old Steven, helped me with the construction, fed Tip, and cooked meals. Only a couple of times she got carried away listening to Peter, Paul, and Mary sing her favorite, "Lemon Tree," and forgot to start dinner. Steve took time off to play with the neighborhood boys but was always ready to help. During the first year in our new home, I'll never forget how he rounded up two other boys to build a doghouse for Tip. He was a superintendent of construction even then. David also pitched in on weekends and evenings when I needed another strong back and a sharp eye. By the time Betty and Karen returned, the house was roofed. I did the interior that fall, and we moved in just at Christmas time 1962.

Our home was one of just a few in a new subdivision on the south edge of an old airport. One day we were startled when a small plane passed rather low over our home and landed on the airstrip. The last year we lived there, a snow-cat manufacturer used the airport to test his machines, running them twenty-four hours a day for several days at a time.

Otherwise, the two years we spent in our new home on 1100 North were very pleasant. All of the children lived at home; Betty taught at one of the elementary schools; and we were all busy at work and play. We attended our neighborhood ward but never got involved too deeply. I reserved much of my free time to finish our house and landscape the yard, but I was also growing increasingly committed to the Peace Corps.

Utah State had accepted a contract to train about forty volunteers to be chicken farmers in Iran, and I was assigned to teach the "American institutions" segment of the course during the summer of 1962. I not only lacked the slightest knowledge of this new John F.

Kennedy idea, but I was initially irritated not to spend full time in building our home. The irritation dissolved under the enthusiasm of the volunteers, mostly liberal arts graduates of eastern colleges, idealistic but determined to learn practical skills so they could really help the poor people of Iran. The Peace Corps program was so inspirational and challenging that I would have enlisted myself if the rules had permitted it. By this time my idealism found little room for exercise in my church, and I wholeheartedly welcomed the Peace Corps as an outlet. The concept of American young people willingly spending two years of their lives in service to less fortunate people really appealed to me. And when I came to know these youngsters as individuals, I was even more impressed.

The training officer assigned to the program from the central office in Washington, D.C., outlined the basic facts about this new government agency. Applicants took a placement test and provided several letters of reference. Those chosen received a living allowance during their foreign service plus a termination pay of $75 for each month served. The term of duty was two years. Developing nations that wanted volunteers asked first for teachers and then for individuals with agricultural and farm backgrounds, but any kind of practical skill was welcome—carpenters, social workers, physical education instructors, etc. The Peace Corps had three goals: (1) to help people of emerging nations meet their needs for trained manpower, (2) to help promote a better understanding of Americans among those served, and (3) to promote a better understanding of others among Americans. By mid-1963, its second year, the program boasted 5,000 volunteers in the field selected from 40,000 applicants. During the three-month training period, special emphasis was placed on teaching the volunteers to speak the target language by up to six hours a day with native speakers. The volunteers didn't even get grammar textbooks until the sixth week. This method was so successful that it has influenced many American colleges and probably the LDS church's language training for its missionaries as well.

The campus director of the Iran project considerately scheduled my hour of teaching first thing so that I could spend the rest of the day on my house. I have never had such eager and intelligent students as those would-be chicken farmers. We became very close, and I responded fully to the spirit of the Peace Corps. At the end of the training period, two of the volunteers, one with an M.A. in history from Harvard, wrote to the national training director in Washington, urging him to recruit me as a training officer. I had no idea they had done such a thing, of course, and was surprised when a member of the director's staff appeared in Logan to interview me. My enthusiasm for the program was sincere; and I finally agreed to spend the summer of 1963 as a training officer in the Washington office. I didn't relish being separated from my family for three months, but the extra pay would come in handy.

In early June 1963 when I arrived at the Peace Corps Headquarters located across from Lafayette Square and just a block from the White House, I was assigned, with Mayland Parker, a Mormon from Arizona State University, to work under Gregory Newton, an African-American educator from Maryland State College. Greg was delightful and very competent; it was a shattering loss when he died the following year of a disease contracted while serving as a Peace Corps field representative in Central America. He sent me to Springfield College in Massachusetts to supervise thirty-nine volunteers being trained as physical education instructors for Ecuador and Venezuela. Jack Frost, a former Minnesotan and dean of the college, had been named director of the training program at Springfield. He had good common sense and a congenial personality, and we formed a good working team. Springfield College had been chosen for this particular group because it was the premier institution in teaching scientific aspects of physical education. It is a small college but one with an international reputation in its field.

That summer was busy and enjoyable. I soon came to be the father confessor and chief supporter of the volunteers as they dealt with the red tape inevitable in a major government agency. I had to make inspection visits to other training programs occasionally and managed to wangle one trip back to Logan where I "inspected" a second group of volunteers for Iran, undergoing training at Utah State. Betty also flew back to Washington and we spent two or three days at Springfield and visiting some of the historic places around Boston and Concord.

Glen Ferguson, one of the top officials from the national headquarters, spoke at the graduation exercises in early September. When I was introduced as the project's training officer, all the volunteers stood and applauded me, a tribute which I prized as a teacher. Ferguson was apparently so impressed that, in 1965 when he became the first Director of the Volunteers in Service to America (VISTA), the so-called Domestic Peace Corps, he named me its first director of training. I'm getting ahead of my story, but the explanation of why Ferguson became interested in me is part of the summer of 1963. The Springfield volunteers were a wonderful group. A couple of weeks after they departed for their assignments in Ecuador and Venezuela, I received through the mail a handsome plaque with all of their names engraved on a brass plate and a special salute to my "kindness during the training period." It has been hanging on my office wall ever since.

To give the flavor of the Peace Corps, I am including copies of three letters. The first letter is to a volunteer who was washed out, not for lack of expertise or weakness of character but for a strength which, on assignment, might prove to be a weakness.

October 25, 1963

Dear _____,

It was with much regret that those of us who know you best reluctantly but affirmatively agreed with the decision of the board. Self-confidence is certainly an essential ingredient for success in any venture but if such a trait is over-emphasized, there is a tendency to arouse resentment in others.

My feeling is that in our own culture you will go far—you have the leadership, certainly the brains, and also the initiative requisite for success. Among the hyper-sensitive Latins, it was felt that you might have a little difficulty, and the judgment of the board was that there was thus too much risk involved.

Throughout my life I have rarely been accused of being too modest and operating a free-wheeling building business has certainly not lessened my assurance; so, I have a certain sympathy for you in this situation. The people who have really changed history have had their conspicuous share of self-confidence, in fact, have been mavericks of a sort.

And mavericks have always gotten great sympathy from me inasmuch as I have frequently been accused of being one.

This is a rather difficult letter for me to write, because I know you are disappointed, as anyone would be who had committed himself to the completion of a certain objective. In almost any other situation, you would not only be approved but placed near the top. It is perhaps only natural that a person with the mental astuteness which you possess sometimes finds it difficult to accept less competence in others.

I don't know what your ambitions are right now but, sincerely, I do believe you would make a great academician. The American University is so in need of thoughtful people who can inspire through vigorous teaching and effective writing. Whatever you undertake to do now, I wish you every success. I'd like to hear from you about your plans.

My association with your group has been one of the fine experiences of my life, and the plaque which you had inscribed nearly overwhelmed me. Please let me hear from you.

Sincerely yours,
Brigham D. Madsen

The second letter went to the leader of the Springfield volunteer group, Larry McDonough, after his departure for Ecuador:

October 24, 1963

Dear Larry,

It was very good to hear from you and learn of your interesting training in Puerto Rico. Someday, I'm going to have to get down there and observe it.

Your plaque just about overwhelmed me. I shall always treasure it; it hangs on the wall just over my desk for one and all visitors to see. My experience with your group last summer was one of the finest of my life, and I haven't given up the hope that I might possibly see all of you in Venezuela and Ecuador.

You have, no doubt, heard by now that the Final Selection Board "selected out" [_____]. It's unfortunate for him, but the board was of the opinion that it was a wise decision from the point of view of the Peace Corps. On the other hand, Les Young, about whom we were concerned, came through with flying colors and is probably the center of attention of all of his Latin-American friends wherever he is stationed.

The Peace Corps has been very kind to me, and I am still working part-time as a Training Officer. Before I left to come back to teaching, I negotiated a contract with the University of Arizona at Tucson to train 35 Volunteers in Physical Education for Colombia. Springfield College didn't get the contract for some reason. We are hoping that Janet Driscoll is among the volunteers. They enter training next weekend, and I shall be there on November 1, 2, and 3 and nearly every weekend thereafter.

I am just a little homesick for the Peace Corps. Señor Petisco just wrote me; he is apparently doing very well at Springfield College. He teaches the basic Spanish courses and is taking a full load towards a Masters degree as well. I am certainly happy for him. He's been kicked around all his life and this looked like the best opportunity for him to prepare himself for teaching. He is such a superlative teacher of Spanish that it would be a tragedy if he didn't spend the rest of his life doing just that.

You made a very good record with your training program and were the acknowledged leader of the group. This speaks very well for your abilities, and everyone concerned with the training expects a great deal from you, not only in the Peace Corps, but in whatever profession you enter after your service in Ecuador. Say "hello" to Clancy, Hinkle, Larsen, Mucha, Richwine, Roble, Sidlosky, Stock, Sykes, and last but not least, Les Young. They are a great bunch!

Sincerely yours,
Brigham D. Madsen

The third letter is from Marty Richwine, one of the volunteers who went to Ecuador. Dick Clancy, whom he mentions, was a big lovable Irishman. Though a superb basketball player, he just couldn't learn Spanish. As one of his peers put it, Clancy could only speak sixteen words in Spanish, and no one could understand those. The review board wanted to dismiss him during the training program, but I argued successfully to retain him and send him to Ecuador where I was sure his body-language would overcome his lack of expertise. Richwine's letter vindicated my judgment:

Sunday, Dec. 23, 1963

Dear Dr. Madsen:

I thought you might like to hear how the Ecuador group is getting along, so, just a few lines to put you up to date. We have now been in Ecuador and at work for some two months, and all of us are liking it and getting along well. Of course, we have just started and haven't accomplished a great deal, but we hope to remedy that with time. Judy Mucha, Doug Hinkle, Dan Roble, and Les Young are stationed in Quayaquil. Dick Clancy is in Cuenca, Larry McDonough is in Porto Viejo, and Dave Sykes is in Bo-bahoyo. Clem Sidlosky, Bernie Stock, and I are living together and working in Quito. Gary Larson was in Quito, but has since been transferred to Ambato. We are all coaching in our respective sports, and also working in such activities as recreational centers, schools, and Y.M.C.A.'s. I am coaching the Quito wrestling team, that is, whenever they happen to show up for practice. Clem and I are also working in the Y here in Quito. Because of the lack of equipment and experienced co-workers, we are still trying to get things started as far as programs are concerned. We have got one foot in the door, but it sure is tough getting that second one in there too.

Our Spanish is coming along, but we still have a long way to go before really mastering the language. We try to study a little each night and speak it whenever possible. Clem and I are making a good team together as our abilities complement each other. He can understand Spanish, but has trouble speaking. I have trouble understanding, but can speak fairly well. So, when together, he does all the listening and I do most of the talking.

I guess Bernie, Clem, and I have it the easiest of any in our group. Living in Quito is a far cry from the idea people back home have of the typical volunteer's life. Although we don't have heat or hot water, our apartment is more than sufficient and located in a nice neighborhood. We eat most of our meals downtown and in most cases the food is good. However, it is expensive living in Quito and we have to watch ourselves to keep from spending all of our money before the end of the month.

I have not heard of any of our group being sick. There has been the usual number of colds etc., of course, but nothing serious. One common problem of us all has been the loss of weight. But for some of us, this has been a blessing since we were just a little bit overweight when we left the States.

Dr. Monroe, the Peace Corps doctor, when returning to Quito from making his rounds, tells of the other volunteers' progress, health, etc. Everyone seems to have plenty of work to do, and apparently, have been well accepted in their respective communities. Within two days after arrival, Larry organized an "Old-Timers" basketball game in Porto Viejo to raise money for his team. Dick [Clancy] played for his team in Cuenca soon after arrival, scoring twenty-one points, the team beating one of their big rivals by one point. From what I understand, he is just about considered a king now, almost with divine rights. Dan and Les have had their pictures in the papers several times and are very popular in the area.

I will try to keep you posted of our progress from time to time. Thank you again for all that you did for us while we were in training. We all appreciated the interest and time you gave to us and our project. I hope that you and your family have had an enjoyable Christmas.

Sincerely yours,
Marty Richwine

Richwine's comments depicted some of the difficulties the Peace Corps volunteers faced in trying to change the deeply-ingrained and long-held habits and customs of other peoples. Many of the volunteers were involved in community development projects to train local leaders to take over when the volunteers left. One example of a project that failed because it violated community mores was the attempt of two volunteers in Costa Rica to persuade mountain villagers to use outhouses, "chic sales," instead of the cornfields. After the village leader built a chic sale, the idea became fasionable and every family improved its status with an outhouse, though nobody used them, as the frustrated volunteers soon noticed. When asked why, the natives answered, "If we don't leave something in the cornfields for the chickens, what will they live on?" Of all the Peace Corps stories, this one expresses best, for me, the extreme difficulty involved in trying to help people of another culture to improve their lives. It cannot always be done by imposing American standards and customs on them.

Probably the highlight of my summer's work in Washington, D.C., was my participation in the now-famous "March on Washington" on August 28, 1963. When the news came that Martin Luther King, Jr., would address the civil rights marchers in front of the Lincoln Memorial, I heard fears about serious riots and perhaps bloodshed. Bill Moyers, assistant director of the Peace Corps under Sargent Shriver, asked the staff whether volunteers should be allowed to march in the demonstration carrying Peace Corps banners. I sent him a memo, addressed formally to Mr. William Moyers, recommending that volunteers be allowed to participate but without placards because of possible political fallout. Moyers responded in writing, first gently pointing out that his name was just plain Bill, and inviting me to a discussion meeting. My recommendation, which was also the consensus of the group, was adopted, and I had a chance to meet Moyers.

While most of the Peace Corps headquarters staff went home on the day of the march, joined by most of the other government workers in Washington, all of whom feared trouble, Carsten Lien of Seattle, another training officer, and I joined the crowd at about 11:00 A.M., as they proceeded toward the Lincoln Memorial. I linked hands with Carsten on one side and a gray-haired African-American grandmother on the other. We secured a spot on the concrete plaza in front of the temporary speaker's stand and stood there from 1:30 to 4:30 under a blazing sun as speaker after speaker, singers, choral groups, and other participants held forth. When Martin Luther King finally stepped forward to address the 250,000 gathered there, I remarked to Carsten Lien that I didn't see how he could hold the attention of this great multitude who, by this time, were hot, frustrated, and just plain tired out. I was wrong.

King's speech was only twelve minutes long, but it electrified the crowd. It was probably the greatest speech I have ever heard. He asked the American people to make each person in the nation sacred and punctuated each plea with the famous statement, "I have a dream." Using the words of the anthem, "America," he implored, "Let freedom ring" from every corner of the nation. Finally, he ended his oration with a quotation from the Negro spiritual, "Free at last, Free at last! / Great God Almighty, We're free at last." I have never witnessed such an emotional response as that elicited from his audience, and his call to freedom has become one of the great dramatic moments in the history of America. I was glad to be a part of it.

That fall, in addition to a busy course load teaching U.S. history, U.S. Constitutional history, and the history of the American frontier, I kept up my Peace Corps "mission." For three months, from November through January, I flew from Salt Lake City every Friday afternoon to Tucson, flying back late Sunday afternoon. In supervising the thirty-five volunteers destined for a physical education program in Colombia, my most demanding challenge came on the Friday when President John F. Kennedy was assassinated. Shattered and distraught, they came to me in a body to say there was no purpose in what they were doing—that the death of their idolized president meant the end of any meaningful service for humankind. I fully shared their grief and spent all weekend convincing them that life must go on and that they should continue with their program. Sam Brill, associate director of the Division of Continuing Education at the University of Arizona and local Peace Corps supervisor, was very helpful in getting the volunteers to refocus on turning their anguish and anger into a commitment to serve.

The program was successful but did produce one frustration. I had convinced the Training Division in Washington to include four hours of instruction in how to teach English as a second language (TESL). No matter where they went or for what purpose, the local people asked volunteers to teach them English. Unfortunately, the University of Arizona teacher spent the entire four hours lecturing on the *theory* of how to teach English as a second language. What the volunteers and I wanted to know was what words we should teach first and other very practical approaches. It was just another example of why universities have difficulty in translating theory into practical application. The next year Peace Corps leaders were able to make a respectable twelve-hour TESL component part of all training programs.

In February 1964 after my stint at Tucson, the Training Division in Washington asked me to spend a week in Puerto Rico teaching Latin American history to the volunteers undergoing their mandatory two-week "Outward Bound" training at one of the two camps in that commonwealth. Utah State gave me a week off, and I flew to San Juan, took a taxi to Arecibo, and then went by Peace Corps truck several miles to the camp in the mountains. Sargent Shriver, who had married John Kennedy's sister Eunice and had entered heartily into the clan's touch-football culture, was sold on the idea that rappelling down cliffs, floating in water with tied hands and feet, and living off the country during a three-day solo hike through the rugged tropical rain forest would produce valuable psychological benefits. These new and unique activities injected some starch into the spinal columns of some of the well-protected volunteers. I thoroughly enjoyed the week at the camp and began to consider possible full-time employment with the Peace Corps.

The need to make a decision came with an offer to join the agency full time beginning the first of June 1964. Utah State University granted me a two-year leave of absence, and I accepted. We found renters for our new home, stored our furniture in the basement, and left for Washington, D.C., with nine-year-old Steven and fifteen-year old Linda. Karen had been accepted as one of two or three women students at the University of Utah Medical School in Salt Lake City and was living with Betty's widowed mother in her home at 1000 East and 3900 South. We were able to buy a used car for her. David, just out of high school, was doing experimental work for the summer with a forester in the juniper forests of eastern Nevada. This experience further deepened his interest in channeling his professional interests into environmental work. In the fall he attended the University of Utah, living in one of the men's dormitories.

We settled down in half of a furnished duplex at Jasper Place in Alexandria, Virginia, a fifty-minute bus ride to Peace Corps Headquarters at Lafayette Square. We began attending the Alexandria Ward where I was asked to teach the Gospel Doctrine class, then studying the Old Testament. I felt I could handle it because it was ancient history and not Mormon theology. I had already started research on the manuscript about freighting and stagecoach travel between Salt Lake City and western Montana before the completion of the railroad branches in the 1870s, eventually pub-

As assistant director of training for the Peace Corps, Washington, D.C., 1964.

lished as *North to Montana*. Betty has a keen interest in history, although it is not her first love, and I asked her to coauthor it with me. She agreed and began spending a lot of time in the Library of Congress and the National Archives. I usually joined her on Saturdays, and we managed to complete most of the needed research. Linda was a dutiful and affectionate babysitter for Steve; but they were lonesome for the wide open spaces of Utah. In late August Karen and David came by train to Washington and spent ten days with us. We all piled in the car and drove to New York City to visit the World's Fair. It was an enjoyable experience for all of us. That fall Steve adjusted well to his new school; Linda had a more difficult time but gained a new experience in a different school system. We had spent many weekends visiting historic places in and around the nation's capital and had a good year learning about the early history of the nation.

At the Peace Corps I was almost one of the old-timers. As a new government agency, it saw a lot of staff coming and going. The new director of training was Bascomb Storey, a former American International Development (AID) official, and one of Lyndon B. Johnson's Texas crowd. He was very competent, an experienced and tough-minded bureaucrat. I liked him; we got along well. Just one month after my arrival, he reorganized his division and named me assistant director of training for Latin America. I had a staff of about six training officers and two secretaries. Carsten Lien and Olin Robinson, another bright and able Texan with a Ph.D. in history from Oxford University, became my best friends. Olin was a personal friend of Bill Moyers, then White House press secretary. They and their wives used to go out to dinner almost every Friday evening, but, according to Olin, President Johnson nearly always interrupted with a phone call part way through the evening, directing Moyers to take care of some "urgent" business at the White House that just couldn't wait. After their Peace Corps experience, Lien became the executive of a western sportswear company in Seattle and Robinson became, first, provost of Wesleyan University and then president of Middlebury College. One of the other training officers was an older man named Yarborough, another competent Texan.

I soon became very busy. My responsibilities included getting approval for training contracts with universities and social service agencies all over the nation for the many volunteer groups going to Central and South America, writing letters for Shriver's signature to answer Congressional critics of the Peace Corps, supervising the activities of the training officers who usually had four or five volunteer groups to look after and who spent most of their time traveling to the training projects, and defusing any political time bombs which seemed to occur almost every day. I also had to travel occasionally to work out special problems concerned with new contracts, although the training officers normally negotiated the agreements. My job was to get them through the Peace Corps Budget Office.

I also decided to supervise one training program myself to keep tabs on what was going on away from Washington. Marquette University in Milwaukee had accepted a contract to train a group for Brazil with a Catholic brother, Leo Ryan, as the director. I became well acquainted with Leo, one of the best administrators I've ever known, and kept up a correspondence with him for several years after the Peace Corps. In the fall of 1964 I supervised a second group headed for Brazil, this time at the University of Wisconsin at Milwaukee. I came to look forward to my trips to that city; it is one of my favorites in the United States.

Another major responsibility was to supervise the two "Outward Bound" training camps in Puerto Rico. When I first assumed this task, there was such a personnel blow-up at the main camp that I had to visit it immediately to see if it could be straightened out. Storey was very pessimistic about the chances for a turn-around. I knew I was on the spot and vowed to do my best to solve the problem. Betty flew down with me, and we had a good time in San Juan at the camp and, later, on a one-day trip to St. Thomas in the Virgin Islands. I spent three days in meetings with the entire staff and in talking to them individually and was so successful in settling things down that upon my return to Washington Storey and other people in the Peace Corps looked upon me as a miracle worker. It helped my image.

Not everything turned out so successfully. Storey once directed a problem to me because I was a Mormon. A volunteer who had once served a mission for the LDS church was now working for the Peace Corps in Chile. However, he was so difficult to get along with that he had to work by himself. Worse, he spent more time proselyting than he did as a Peace Corps volunteer. I tried to straighten him out by correspondence, but to no avail. He continued to preach Mormonism along with his development project and finally had to be sent home. Perhaps if I'd been able to meet with him face to face I could have been more persuasive.

Working as a bureaucratic official in Washington, D.C., can be like a brisk walk through a land-mine field. I had been there only a couple of weeks in June 1963 when one of Shriver's "inspectors" wrote a lengthy attack on my "inattention to duty" and "overall incompetence" in directing my division. This was Richard Ottinger, a young and wealthy New Yorker, who had been a Peace Corp volunteer, then was elected U.S. Congressman from his district. I knew that I had to act fast and forcefully. I sat up half of that night drafting a lengthy defense which I hand-delivered to Ottinger the very next morning. I convinced him that his facts were in error, and we actually became good friends. It was typical of what can happen in Washington.

A more serious incident occurred with Sargent Shriver. Olin Robinson and I had successfully negotiated a training contract with Southwest Texas State Teachers College, Lyndon B. Johnson's alma mater. I knew that Shriver would like to make some brownie points with the president by giving him the news so that LBJ could call the college administration with the announcement. I asked Shriver's young smart-ass administrative assistant for an appointment and told him the reason. Without telling me, he got the president of the college on the phone and called me in to talk to him. That's when I made my mistake. I should have walked out and let the assistant extricate himself. Instead, I gave the college president the news that he had a training contract and left, feeling that there would be a fallout. I was right.

The next morning while I was at Dulles airport waiting for a flight to Texas Tech in Lubbock where I was to negotiate a contract, I was paged over the airport telephone. A very angry Shriver was on the phone and proceeded to chew me out to a fare-thee-well. He would not listen to my explanation concerning his know-it-all administrative assistant. Shriver, himself, must have been told off by LBJ when the news of the college contract reached the White House. This chain reaction of people being told off by the highest official right down to the poor clerk is commonplace in Washington. My only consolation was in knowing that my political instincts were right; my mistake was in allowing the assistant to get away with putting me on the spot.

After seven months of very active duty, long hours at the office, and many days away from home, I was rewarded, in a way, by being recommended for the presidency of Idaho State University, my alma mater in Pocatello. I have never learned who was responsible. Elvon Hampton, the president of the trustees, invited me to apply, and I did. Several friends, including Lawrence Kinnaird and Sterling McMurrin, wrote letters of reference for me. I would have been the first native son and former student of the school to become the president, factors which normally would have favored my candidacy. It was a nice compliment, but I must have been dropped rather early in the selection process.

In the early spring of 1965, the fast pace and many responsibilities of my job must have gotten to me. One Sunday I noticed that my right arm had gone numb. When it stayed numb, Betty insisted I go to a doctor. He informed me that I had had a mild heart attack and put me in the hospital for ten days. He then released me under a regimen of various pills and medication including blood thinner and nitroglycerine and with the admonition to slow down. I was fifty. The diagnosis of a heart condition was quite correct because ever since then I have suffered angina pains in my chest if I over-exert. I have learned to live with the knowledge that I have a heart disease and might have additional trouble at any time, including a sudden attack which might totally incapacitate me. This realization has made the years since then more precious to me, but I decided to live my life fully nevertheless. Living as a recluse or at only half-speed is not for me.

There was no hesitation on my part, therefore, in early March when Glen Ferguson asked for my release from the Peace Corps so that I could become the first director of training for the Volunteers in Service to America (VISTA). I was appointed March 26, 1965, and began the arduous job of recruiting a staff, negotiating twenty contracts, and getting the first thousand volunteers into training programs. Our headquarters was in a building on M Street. According to the local newspaper reports about my appointment, I was "responsible for selecting institutions and agencies which train VISTA volunteers for assignments with local antipoverty efforts, establishing curriculum guidelines and evaluating the effectiveness of training methods." The volunteers would be assigned to city ghettos, Indian reservations, Appalachia, and migrant work camps. The service was for one year with only six weeks allotted for training.

From the first, I was determined to steer clear of ivory-towered universities and to sign training contracts with social service agencies who knew what poverty was all about. For example, I asked the director of Hull House in Chicago how he would train volunteers if he should get a contract. His reply was that the minute the new volunteers arrived he would assign each of them to live with a ghetto family throughout the entire training period—no nice quarters in a university dormitory. If they could adapt to these poverty conditions, then they might have the makings of a real volunteer. I signed a contract with Hull House at once. Their volunteers were competent and effective.

I recruited five or six training officers who had a practical orientation. One, a Ph.D. in history who had grown up on a farm in the Midwest, knew what hard work was and had the common touch. I gave him the toughest assignment, working with Indians and Inuits in Alaska. All of the training officers were exceptional. I took a program for myself among some very poor Hispanic-Americans in Colorado. The University of Colorado ran the project, not on the campus, but at the poverty-stricken village of Rodeo, on the outskirts of Monte Vista, in southwestern Colorado. These two projects, in Chicago and at Monte Vista, were typical. My immediate superior, a young yuppie by today's standards, was Padraic (Pat) Kennedy, who gave me a free hand to run the training division.

My worst problem during my eight months in VISTA resulted from the trainees' over-enthusiasm and idealism. We had one group at Temple University in the heart of Pittsburgh's ghetto. As instructor the university hired a left-wing urban "rabble rouser" from Chicago who had organized rent strikes against slum landlords and promptly launched the same effort in Pittsburgh. He was certainly successful, but his picketing trainees aroused so much opposition from local officials that we had to replace him with a more tactful instructor.

The University of Utah applied for a contract to train volunteers at the Ute Reservation in Uintah County for service to Indian groups. I visited with Edward Moe, a sociologist connected to the U's Division of Continuing Education who would direct the program if it were awarded. He turned out to be very competent and practical, and I signed a contract. While I was at the campus, I visited with Karen and David. David was doing as well as most college freshmen but Karen was being dropped as a student by the College of Medicine. Other interests had intruded upon her studies, and her grades had suffered as a result. She was more than a little disconsolate, so I suggested that she might be interested in the Peace Corps before tackling the last year of her undergraduate degree. She was interested, and I helped her get into a training program at Ohio University with a group headed for India. She did very well in her three months of preparation and was assigned to a public health project in the village of Baswa, Rajasthan, southwest of New Delhi. She was a splendid Peace Corps volunteer as I knew she would be.

During my campus visit, I also spent some time with my friends Sterling McMurrin and Jack Adamson, who was then academic vice president. They both urged me to apply for the position of dean of the Division of Continuing Education. When I expressed interest, they offered me the position, together with a faculty slot in the history department, and I accepted. The whole process in those innocent days took just a couple of hours. We agreed that I would start on January 1, 1966.

Betty was overjoyed at the prospect of being back in Salt Lake City and of being affiliated with the University of Utah. We decided to move back to Salt Lake City so Linda and Steve could start school there in September. We sold our Logan house, I rented an apartment for my last four months with VISTA service, and we bought a house at 3745 S. Twinbrook in Salt Lake City in August. It had no basement because Betty's back operation kept her from negotiating stairs easily. Our plan was that I would rejoin the family at Christmas and start work at the university on January 1, 1966.

After signing the earnest money agreement, Betty suggested we drive by our old house on Lincoln Lane for a last look at the home in which we had invested so much of our hearts. To our utter amazement, we saw a "For Sale by Owner" sign on the front lawn. Betty burst into tears. It was clear that we had to repurchase the house. We pulled up in front of the house, rang the doorbell, and went in. Art Brown greeted us with amazement. They were moving to the East, and he had put up the sign just a few minutes before we drove by. Art sold it to us for exactly the same price we had sold it to him. He was willing to do so because he saved a real estate commission in the deal. Betty and I were ecstatic at the miracle which had delivered our old home back to us, and it remained our home for the next thirty-two years.

There was, of course, the problem of the house on Twinbrook. When I tried to get out of the purchase, the owner sued us for violation of the earnest money contract. So we were forced to keep the house vacant over the winter and sold it at a $5,000 loss the next spring. But getting our home back was worth it, and David moved back in as well.

I returned to Washington to complete my work at VISTA, but the autumn was not a good one. The constant action and the never-ending responsibilities of my position triggered another mild heart attack in late October. One evening, as I was preparing a meal for myself in my bachelor apartment, I experienced some severe chest pains. The manager of the apartment house called an ambulance; and I had a wild ride through Washington to the hospital in Alexandria where I was to stay for the next ten days under the care of the same physician who had treated me after the first heart episode.

Betty flew back to be with me; when I was released from the hospital, I resigned from VISTA and returned to Salt Lake City. The University of Utah was glad to have me start my new position on November 15, and I hoped that the reduced pressures at the university would help alleviate my heart ailment. In fact, as long as I curtailed strenuous exercise, I had no problem—even though my new responsibilities were anything but "stress free."

15.

AT THE
UNIVERSITY OF UTAH

Dean and Deputy Academic Vice President,

1965-67

When I arrived at the University of Utah on November 15, 1965, as dean of the Division of Continuing Education, I had already gained some knowledge of this academic step-child through Peace Corps and VISTA contracts with various universities throughout the nation. While Continuing Education may have "college" status at some universities, it is usually the experimental part of a university set-up, a place where new programs can be tried without disturbing the equanimity of the traditionally staid departments. It may be a truism that a university can change everything but itself. If new programs are introduced, they are usually sponsored by Continuing Education.

I was replacing Harold Bentley, a creative and imaginative man but one who had difficulty in following through, especially in budget control. The university had hired Grant Holt, an accounting professor from the College of Business, as associate dean to straighten out the division's fiscal affairs. During the nine months I was dean, I came to appreciate very much Grant Holt's attention to duty, his wisdom, and his very congenial disposition. He was a tremendous help as I tried to instill some spirit into the staff, most of whom had settled into a routine of just doing their jobs.

The division was housed in the east wing of the Annex Building, a World War II frame structure which had served as the administrative headquarters for Fort Douglas. Little had been done to improve the facility except to paint over the old wallboard and wax the GI-brown li-noleum on the floors. I decided that extensive remodeling was a visible way to dramatize that a new administration meant a new course, new energy, and new enthusiasm. The Physical Plant architects provided the plans and an estimate of $16,000 for the work, a sum which just about floored Holt when I insisted that we find it in our budget. To his credit, Holt succeeded. We tore out walls, opened up the spaces, es-tablished a reception area for students and visitors, carpeted the floors, bought new furnishings, and even included a conference room. The effect on the staff was almost electric. They began to drop by my office with long-incubated ideas and even their faces showed new pride in our quarters. It is astounding what a little improvement in physical quarters can do for an organization.

When I took over, the division had numerous programs, some of which existed only on paper but which looked promising given the right directors and the necessary funds. The main section, of course, was devoted to class instruction for afternoons, evenings, and Satur-days. Don Harper and his aides handled the fees and finance, while ad-visors helped students choose courses and enroll. Alton Hadlock served competently as director of Adult Education. Norinne Tempest ran the Home Study section and administered about 200 correspondence courses so efficiently that I never had to be concerned about her opera-tion. John R. Barnett, very genial and relaxed, coordinated the Insti-tute for Technological Training in computer science, electronics, and mechanical and industrial technology. This rather high-falutin' de-scription meant, in lay terms, technology training given through Utah Technical College. W. Donald Brumbaugh directed the university-wide Audiovisual Bureau which dispersed films, projection equip-ment, operators, and audiovisual instruction. He ran a very efficient and independent organization. L. Kent Kimball, one of the sharpest ad-ministrators I have ever known, ran Institutes and Conferences and, simultaneously, was working on a Ph.D. in political science.

Edward Moe, sociologist, administered the Bureau of Commu-nity Development which was the vehicle for university involvement in state-wide projects. In one noteworthy program, Moe and his assis-tant, Jack McDonald, completed a half-hour documentary film on San Pete County that persuasively demonstrated to the skeptical county commissioners the rapidly deteriorating conditions in their area. I hired S. Lyman Tyler, BYU's director of libraries, to head our Bureau of Indian Services. Lyman had been restive for some time with the lack of academic freedom at BYU. He later served as dean of international education and for several years as director of the American West Center at the University of Utah. I was fortunate to obtain his services.

The university catalog also listed such divisions as Artists Series, Audubon Screen Tour Series, University Travel Club, University Dinner Club, Institute of Industrial Relations, Intermountain Laboratory in Group Development, and Institute for Urban Studies and Services. Some were quite active, like the Travel Club, which presented "top travel films for armchair travelers," while others lay dormant.

I inaugurated several changes to create a tighter organization, the most important being a weekly staff meeting with department heads, always held at 9:00 A.M. each Tuesday. They needed a forum for complaints and new ideas; the collegial interchange provided cohesion and momentum. I chose Tuesday so that Monday could be a preparation day. I also started a monthly newsletter, not only to keep our staff informed, but also to publicize to the university community that there was a Division of Continuing Education which was an integral part of the campus.

As an administrator, my operating assumption has always been: "See what needs to be done, then do it." One of my first innovations was to try to get administrative approval of a "university degree," a bachelor's degree offered by the Division of Continuing Education with no specific major but recognition that a student had completed four years of college work and was prepared to enter a number of fields. I hired James Traver, then administrative employee of a local oil company, as my assistant to help construct the program. He entered a doctoral program with the "university degree" as his dissertation topic. The University of Oklahoma and other schools already had such a program in operation, BYU was considering it, and I was convinced the University of Utah should not be left behind. Candidates for the degree would be granted some credit for years spent in business, professions, and trades. The program would offer them an inducement to complete a college degree part time while holding down full-time jobs.

I received the "silent treatment" from my academic colleagues who assumed that their traditional degrees in traditional disciplines would be tainted by a general university degree. We still don't have such a program, which I am convinced is not only an error but also evidence that universities are really not very interested in community involvement and in helping people in nontraditional circumstances get a college education. A good example of the type of student who was interested in obtaining a "university degree" was Lavor Chaffin, education editor of the *Deseret News,* who had only a high school diploma but who, over the years, had become better educated than many college graduates. He lacked only the "union card."

Because some people in Salt Lake Valley failed to sign up for evening study with our division, either through trepidation at entering our august halls of learning "on the hill" or because of the inconvenience of having to travel so far, I started a series of courses at Granger High School. We advertised the new program well, but the reception was less hearty than I expected. As I look back, I was too impatient. I expected instantaneous results without letting the idea settle in or let word-of-mouth publicity help. We also started a similar program in the Farmington area. Both were still underway when I relinquished my position as dean.

I was also frustrated in my attempts to begin a series of credit courses over KUED-TV, the university educational channel. All of us involved, including the station staff, failed to find an effective system, and I finally threw up my hands. As I examine credit courses offered by TV today, it is obvious that we expected too much from our efforts. Too many TV credit courses are still not very popular as teaching tools.

We did have one smashing success with a class designed to help nontraditional women students, including homemakers returning to the classroom for degrees or just to take some courses that interested them. We hired Esther Landa, a prominent local woman, as first director of our women's programs with Fae Dix, a widow who had gone back to school under traumatic circumstances, as the day-to-day administrator. Instead of the twenty or so women we hoped for, about 200 applied for the first course. Betty, ever the advocate of equal rights for women but taking the role of devil's advocate, astutely asked why I didn't establish a "men's program," and I suppose she had a point. But Landa and Dix opened up new opportunities for women at the university and helped ease their fears about starting school again.

Although these objectives met with mixed success, my chief goal—to help integrate university and community—was an utter failure. My other career as a carpenter and builder has, I believe, given me a broader perspective of the role of a university than that held by too many ivory-tower professors who have had little or no experience away from the classroom. Specifically, I hoped to establish a close working relationship with Utah Technical College, knowing that some of the failing students we received in Continuing Education were under family pressure to earn a college degree or just didn't realize the possibilities for technical training which might assure them of a job and a successful career. The Mormon church's emphasis on the importance of higher education, in many instances, made some non-academic LDS students feel that they were not "living the gospel" if they opted for positions as mechanics or beauticians. As a carpenter, I knew many laboring men of high intelligence, and I've always resented the superiority of some professors toward those who work at the manual trades.

A graphic illustration of the problem occurred during the first few weeks of my service as dean. A prominent Salt Lake physician brought his nineteen-year-old son to consult me. The boy had failed most of his university classes and was now in the process of failing my division's remedial classes. The doctor, an aggressive and self-confident man, explained that both his father and grandfather had been physicians, and his son would also be a medical doctor come hell or high water. The son just sat silently while the father delivered this harangue. I asked to talk to the young man alone and soon learned that he really wanted to be a diesel mechanic. Not only did he have an aptitude for the trade, but he was absolutely determined *not* to become a doctor. I called the father back in, told him of this discovery, and suggested how we could help the son meet this quite commendable goal. The father greeted my information with stony silence and quickly withdrew, taking his son with him. I never learned the outcome. To me, being a good diesel mechanic is an honorable and productive way to contribute to society while making a living. I'm not sure society needs an unwilling doctor with no aptitude or liking for his profession, even if he were able to drag himself through the course work.

To get the plan underway, I met with Jay Nelson, the competent president of Utah Technical College, and received his enthusiastic support to exchange counselors at registration time. Some of our Continuing Education people sat at tables at Utah Technical College, while several from the Redwood Road campus occupied seats in our division. In addition, I took a busload of our counselors on a tour of the Utah Tech campus which, to their surprise, turned out to be quite large, nicely landscaped, and well-housed in very modern buildings. This was a good start, but I needed university approval to exchange credit between the two institutions. Students from Utah Tech whose introduction to university classes convinced them they would prefer to seek a traditional bachelor's degree could do so and receive credit for selected courses taken at the college. Conversely, the hundreds of students who should never have enrolled at the university could now easily shift to a program at the college where they had a better chance at success, taking university credits with them to shorten their training period for a technical job.

To push my credit-exchange program with Utah Technical College, I scheduled a meeting with President James C. Fletcher and other administrators, using a flip chart to make my various points. Fletcher, newly appointed from the business world, gave me his full support. At the meeting's end, the administrators asked me to win the endorsement of the Liberal Education Committee.

It was the kiss of death. The committee of seven faculty was headed by Sidney Angleman, dean of the Undergraduate Division. A graduate of Amherst, he was determined to keep the university pure from the corruption of my proposed indecent connection with Utah Technical College. He was persuasive and probably already represented the sympathies of his fellow committee members. The committee voted unanimously against the program. Both Fletcher and I were disappointed and considered that vote a serious mistake as we looked at the long-range prospects of the university and, even worse, as we contemplated the many students who would fail at the university with little way of helping them start anew at Utah Tech. Today the technical school has been transformed into a real community college with an easy credit-transfer program. It should have started a long time ago under the Fletcher-Madsen plan.

The exercise was not completely wasted, however. Fletcher had been impressed by me. In the summer of 1966, he and Academic Vice President Alfred Emery asked me to become Emery's acting deputy in addition to my duties as dean of Continuing Education. I accepted and filled in for Charles Monson while he recuperated from back surgery. When Monson returned to duty in February 1967, I was relieved of my responsibilities as dean and named second deputy academic vice president, a position in which I served until September 1967, when I was named administrative vice president.

During my year in the academic vice president's office, I was closely involved in the affairs of the various colleges. I asked Emery if I could be responsible for specific colleges under his direction, thus allowing me independent action. He agreed; and when Monson returned to duty, the two of us divided the colleges between us and Emery sent a letter to each of the deans explaining the new arrangements. In a typical letter, this to my old Division of Continuing Education, Emery wrote:

> I have divided the colleges and activities reporting to this office into two groups and have asked each of the Deputy Vice Presidents to concern himself with one of these groups. I should point out that I view the dean of a college as reporting to this office and not to a particular person in the office, however, we can facilitate the operation if in the matters concerning your college you would work with Deputy Vice President Brigham Madsen. Dr. Madsen will act on behalf of this department on all such matters with the same authority and finality of decision that would be the case had I handled the matter personally in the past. I have every confidence in Dr. Madsen's ability and objectivity.

I suggested that, because *deputy* connoted assistant, our replacements be named associate academic vice presidents. Emery agreed and made the change when Boyer Jarvis took my place.

As in most administrative jobs, and especially in a university setting, there is a lot of minutiae to take care of, including smoothing the ruffled feathers of hypersensitive deans, chairs, and faculty. Occasionally, Emery would ask me to appear with him when he needed support in a particularly difficult confrontation. In one instance a group of students asked for a meeting after demanding that the newly-appointed editor of the student newspaper be replaced by someone they liked better. Emery handled the matter superbly, pointing out that if he should interfere with the selection process, the students would be acknowledging that he could step in at other times and so restrict the freedom of the press which the students expected.

In a second memorable problem, Emery and I held an extraordinary Saturday morning meeting with the Department of Political Science whose members had been at each other's throats for years. I have never witnessed such ill feeling or heard such blunt accusations among faculty as in that meeting. We accomplished little more than deciding to hire a new chair from outside the university in an attempt to improve conditions. The new appointee, Jack Wann, was a gifted administrator who managed to talk the political science faculty into a modicum of collegiality.

In a more rewarding activity, I helped Sterling McMurrin, then provost, to negotiate a $370,000 grant from the Rockefeller Foundation to establish a modern dance repertory company which has since gained international recognition. The foundation was interested in the project because of Virginia Tanner's longstanding reputation for directing successful dance programs, especially children's dance. As dean of Continuing Education, I administered the grant and conducted the annual negotiations with the Rockefeller people.

A more difficult assignment which fortunately turned out well concerned the Middle East Center. Dr. Aziz Atiya had founded the center under former president A. Ray Olpin, using his international reputation as a historian and scholar and his expertise in collecting books to build one of the best Middle East collections anywhere in the United States. After some years as the center's first director, he wanted to step down, and I was asked to chair the search committee. The university administration was pleased that Atiya wanted to relinquish the post because, although successful in every other way, he lacked administrative skill and was not adept at fund-raising with likely federal agencies. The committee and I chose Khosrow Mostofi, a Ph.D. in political science and a student of Atiya's, for the job. We thought Atiya would be pleased, but he disagreed and, in an angry confrontation with me, demanded that I withdraw the appointment. I stuck to my guns. Atiya then went directly to Fletcher. Fletcher had already decided to recommend Atiya as Distinguished Professor and had me give Atiya the news. He was so pleased with the honor that he dropped his opposition. Once again I admired Fletcher's skill in personnel management.

Most major American universities were increasing their programs in international affairs at the time, a situation encouraged by the availability of federal funds. The University of Utah already had thirteen different programs concerned with international education and was planning eleven new ones. The president and his advisors decided to establish a Division of International Education. I was the first dean, responsible for heading a search committee to hire an assistant dean who would take over after one year. Upon my recommendation, our committee chose S. Lyman Tyler, then director of the Bureau of Indian Services. After three good years federal funds dried up, interest lagged, and the division was finally scrapped.

One of my major contributions to the university as deputy academic vice president was instituting a regular review of college deans. Some young turks in the College of Business focused my attention on the problem by demanding that their dean of almost twenty years be replaced by someone conversant with the changes sweeping through university business colleges. The dean was determined to continue in his position. I read the faculty regulations and learned that there were rules already on the books that department chairs should be reviewed every three years and deans every five years; chairs were routinely evaluated but no dean ever had been. When I proposed to Emery that we do so, he was reluctant to stir up trouble. But I persisted; during a break at one of the quarterly retreats which Fletcher regularly held with his deans and vice presidents in Park City, I tackled Emery again and he gave me the go ahead. When the retreat reconvened, I explained the situation to those present and recommended that we begin reviewing the deans at once. Fletcher immediately asked, "Brig, which dean do you want to start with?" I said I planned to start with the dean who had been in office longest and proceed down the list. Fletcher approved, while the deans looked on in deathly silence.

I acted individually in making these evaluations, drawing on my OCS experience. My procedure was to interview each faculty member of the department, asking for both positive and negative comments about the chair's performance. I then prepared a written report which I discussed, first with Alfred Emery and then with Fletcher.

The dean of pharmacy came first. I interviewed each faculty member individually. While some were dissatisfied with his administration, they were reluctant to ask that he be replaced because he was only a year away from retirement and had done a good job for most of his tenure. The second dean was Mildred Quinn of the College of Nursing, one of the best administrators I have known. Her faculty gave her unanimous support. The College of Business was next. While I was setting up faculty interviews, the dean resigned, realizing that he would be forced out in an unpleasant confrontation with the members of his college. Shortly after this, I left the academic vice president's office. Vice presidents are, of course, reviewed every day by the president with whom they interact and, periodically, as they deal with the Board of Trustees, or, now, the Institutional Council.

My year as deputy academic vice president was interesting and led directly to my appointment as administrative vice president under Fletcher to supervise the $60-million building program and campus expansion just getting underway. Apparently, as a former builder and, by now, a somewhat experienced university administrator, I was the logical choice. The next four years gave new meaning to the word *challenge*.

16.

ADMINISTRATIVE
VICE PRESIDENT,
1967-71

The new position of administrative vice president came, like my previous three appointments, as a surprise, but unlike my previous experiences, I was not eager to take it on. I had been deputy academic vice president for a year when President James C. Fletcher unexpectedly called me into his office and offered me the position of administrative vice president, a job just created to handle the rapid expansion of the physical campus. I explained that I did not want to be an administrator. I wanted to teach and write; and after years as a builder and government servant, I was ready for the life of a professor. I had, at my insistence, taught a history class each quarter, usually first thing in the morning, and tried to maintain contact with my academic department. However, these conditions were not ideal and I was anxious to devote more priority to the classroom.

After a night's thought, I realized that I felt both a responsibility to the university and a stirring of curiosity about the challenges of the position. Could I measure up to its demands? The upshot was that I told Fletcher the next morning that I'd take the job for a few months, a period which eventually lengthened into four years.

Many new buildings were being planned. Under a fortuitous combination of a recently passed state bonding program and available federal matching money, the university was in a position to construct some badly needed structures for its rapidly expanding student population. Unfortunately, Fletcher and the longtime business vice president, Paul W. Hodson, had different ideas about how to operate in such a new financial environment. Hodson had been very successful under the previous president, A. Ray Olpin, who had allowed him to run the financial, construction, and legislative portions of the university pretty well on his own. But Fletcher insisted on being his own money man and had the corporate experience and know-how to do so.

The differences between the two came to a head when Hodson presented to the University Board of Regents a bid for a new physical education complex that exceeded the architect's and university's estimate by $292,000. Fletcher and the board were very concerned at this increase, and Fletcher was further dismayed when Hodson suggested, "If we use the interest earned on the student building fee bond, we have more than enough" to make up the deficit.[1] Fletcher was embarrassed by this disclosure which seemed to indicate that he was not in control of university finances. He gave Hodson a new job as vice president for special projects, a job with some important duties but away from business administration. When Hodson failed to get a teaching position with the College of Business, he left the university to start a home-building business which eventually was quite successful. His experience confirmed that I had done the right thing in insisting on a faculty position with the history department. Within another year the department granted me tenure which ensured that I would have a teaching position no matter what happened in the uncertain world of administration.

Another factor working against Hodson was that he had too many responsibilities: lobbying the legislature, handling university finances, and then trying to deal with a huge building program. Fletcher could see that it was necessary to divide the increasing workload among more administrators and so established an organizational structure built on vice presidents—an academic vice president with an associate vice president, an executive vice president with an administrative vice president and a finance vice president under him, and two other vice presidents, one over medical affairs and one in charge of development. For a time also he had a provost, Tom King, a physician, but finally

---

1. Before making this proposal, Hodson remembered, "I hesitated just a second, reflecting on my relationship with my boss," surely a relevant premonition. Paul W. Hodson, *Crisis on Campus: The Exciting Years of Campus Development at the University of Utah* (Salt Lake City: Keeban Corporation, 1987), 234.

abandoned what had become a superfluous position.

My relationship with Jim Fletcher during my four years as administrative vice president was also very good. Often, when he didn't have a business luncheon, he would call me, and we would walk down to a local hamburger stand for a pizza or a sandwich. He was shy and often seemed ill at ease in large groups. He could be brusque and sometimes alienated people, especially those who were his equal or superior in power. Recognizing this failing, at one time he appointed a man named Martin Erickson as his personal advisor to help him in social situations. The appointment came to an end when Erickson advised him to enroll in one of the "sensitizing" sessions popular at the time in which a group of individuals sat around for a week baring their souls and criticizing each other's failings. Fletcher read a book during the first two days and left the group when they began attacking him for refusing to participate.

Very much a "city boy," he always brought a special pair of shoes to change into when he and I took our annual "walking tour" of the campus so that he could inspect the progress of construction. I shall never forget when long haired and fantastically attired Charlie Brown, Berkeley resident and minister of the "Temple of the Rainbow Path," left his psychedelic van to take possession of Fletcher's office by sitting down in the center of the carpet. Fletcher immediately went home while the rest of us took care of Charlie Brown by having him arrested. Jim Fletcher was a superb administrator in matters financial and came at the right time to guide the university through a significant physical growth period. He, like Neal Maxwell, let me run my own affairs and backed me up when I needed support.

Neal A. Maxwell was given the post of executive vice president and really became the chief executive officer of Fletcher's administration. Ted Davis, the financial vice president, and I had weekly meetings with Maxwell, mostly to keep him informed about what we were doing. Maxwell delegated well, so I was quite independent and usually reported directly to Fletcher. Maxwell was good to work with, and we had a very congenial relationship. I admired his "clean desk" approach to administration; he took care of things with promptness and decision. When he left the university to become LDS Commissioner of Education in July 1970 after three years as executive vice president, he wrote me a note: "Your calmness under pressure and your good will towards others have been a source of strength to both me and the institution." He is now an apostle in the Mormon church.

Maxwell and I agreed that he would handle legislative relations, public relations, the alumni, and athletics, while I took over physical plant operations, personnel, university security, campus planning, construction, parking, and traffic. Now to examine each of these responsibilities, one at a time.

I knew from experience the problems that emerged when a bid exceeded the architect's estimate for a building. I had learned through years of building experience that the best architects were artists at heart, concerned with function and beauty, and only secondarily interested in assuring that construction costs were within the prescribed budget. I decided to keep our architects grounded in reality by hiring an outside estimator to check the figures. The architects objected strenuously to this novel idea, and eventually I had to involve the Utah State Building Board to get my way. The Building Board is responsible for supervising the letting of bids, conducting inspections, and constructing all state edifices. The university and other state agencies are the board's clients, although they are naturally very actively engaged in the process. During my tenure as vice president, Glen Swenson was director of the board, a good man to work with. Throughout a long tenure, he had supervised millions of dollars in state building without a whisper of scandal concerning his handling. We got along well, and he supported my proposal to hire an engineering firm to check the architect's cost estimates. The process was quite successful; in over twenty major projects during my four years of service, not a single building exceeded the engineer's estimates.

The closest I came to missing that standard was with the two Medical Towers Student Housing buildings which came in only $3,000 under the estimate. The rest were well under the estimates and let us fund a number of alternates for each building.

The first building to which I applied the process of another cost estimate was the Behavioral Sciences Building which the engineering firm estimated would exceed our budget by $750,000. In a knock-down-and-drag-out session with the architects, I insisted we would not go to bid until they had cut $750,000 out of the building. There was much weeping and gnashing of teeth, but I was firm. A month later the architects came back with new plans that eliminated $500,000

and insisted they could cut no further. I then suggested the simple expedient of cutting the two top floors off the building. They spent another month and squeezed out another $250,000 to meet the
engineer's estimate. The result was a bare-bones tower, the worst eye-
sore on the campus. It doesn't fit the design of the other buildings and
rapidly acquired two nicknames: Fletcher's Folly or the Grain Elevator. Stung by these epithets, Fletcher asked me to provide an estimate
for brick siding. It would have cost $120,000, but he finally decided
that was too much for a facelift. Because it was a project that was already underway when I took over the office, I usually have no hesitation in disavowing any but the most perfunctory responsibility for it.

The interior had virtually nothing but four walls, a floor and a ceiling for each office and classroom. I was confident that an enterprising
faculty would find the means over the years to make the building liv-
able, and they have lived up to my expectations. Because the difference between the bid and the engineers' estimate was $120,000, I
proposed to Fletcher that we build one of the alternates, an auditorium
at the south end of the building. He refused, although I argued that we
should build as many auditoriums as possible to meet the demands for
classroom space as students were bound to crowd into the university.
My meeting with him was on a Friday, and the next morning he called
me at home to say he had been thinking about my arguments, that I
was right, and that we would build the Behavioral Science auditorium.

By October 1967, shortly after I took over as administrative vice
president, we had $61 million in construction projects underway.
They included the Marriott Library; the Biology, Chemistry, Mines,
Behavioral Science, Nursing, and Pharmacy buildings; the Special
Events Center; two Physical Education structures; three buildings for
Art and Architecture; the last building of the business complex; an addition to the Union Building; a remodeling of Orson Spencer Hall; a
new road north of the stadium; the twin Medical Student Housing
towers; the Eccles Medical Library; and a heating plant addition. Still
to come was a $7-million married student housing project. Major
landscaping projects were yet to come. To say I was busy is to under-
state the case.

Fortunately, I had an excellent staff. First, there was Mark Money,
deputy administrative vice president, who was thoroughly experienced in financing. He worked with federal agencies to get matching

money and with the state finance officials, in addition to supervising the financial aspects of our office. He was simultaneously working on a Ph.D. in business, and, after three good years together, he completed his degree and became director of the University Research Park in the fall of 1969.

I hired Blain Bradford to replace him with the new title of Operations Manager. Bradford, also a highly competent administrator, was a great help to me. Gordon Boss was my administrative assistant and later became a very efficient assistant director of campus planning. He kept me out of a lot of trouble by his concern for detail and his congenial manner. One of his duties was to keep updated organizational charts for each subdivision of the university. Annually, he and I would meet with Fletcher to go over the organizational changes mirrored on these charts. Fletcher would sometimes explode in anger and frustration when he discovered what some of his very independent subordinates were doing. He would interrupt our meeting, get on the phone, and demand explanations about who had authorized new positions. These meetings were something of an annual drama which I took seriously but also rather enjoyed.

JoAnn Johnson was a superb secretary. The directors of the other divisions under my supervision I shall mention when I get to a description of their activities. I held a regular staff meeting every Tuesday morning at which we went over our preparations to make proposals to Fletcher and the Board of Regents and identified action items.

Much of the work in preparation to construct the new buildings was razing, moving, or getting rid of all of the numerous World War II "temporary" structures that had been used for married student housing and academic purposes. Office space was so scarce that many campus interests clamored to keep the dilapidated frame structures, but the university architects and I were determined to dismantle all of these eyesores. I succeeded in razing all of the barracks being used for married student housing and nearly all the structures on the present enlarged campus. A few can still be seen hidden in between the new buildings, tokens that we were not always successful. We did move six of the ramshackle affairs to the foothills east of the Medical Center where some doctors are still using them as laboratory space. Wilhelm Kolff started his artificial organs project in one of these buildings.

At the request of the LDS church, we removed most of the old structures from the "Church Triangle," the property south of Hempstead Road and west of the road leading into Fort Douglas from the south. Evans & Sutherland began their thriving computer business in one of them. Finally, we razed the old heating plant north of the Park Building and used the space for parking. Space is always at a premium on a growing university campus, and it is a truism that how the president and his staff assign office or laboratory space indicates which departments are the favored ones and are the most successful.

While most of our attention had to be concerned with the many new buildings going up all around us, the campus planning staff and I had also to monitor the many remodeling projects which are part of university life, along with complaints from the temporarily inconvenienced, which are also part of university life. When we undertook major renovations of Orson Spencer Hall, I moved seventy of the English and language faculty to small carrels in Marriott Library for one year, much to their disgruntlement. On another occasion a biology professor protested loudly when we moved him and his experimental turtles from the Annex Building to the basement of the Thomas Building. I think the turtles made the move more gracefully than their keeper.

I decided to close Carlson Hall, a women's dormitory, because it was too far from the other residence halls and had no facilities for food preparation. The space was reapportioned to the Law School with the history department being assigned the third floor. Dean Samuel Thurman of the Law School, our architects, and I met in the old dining room one day to work out the details of the change. As we were concluding our meeting, the door opened suddenly and in marched about a dozen of the women residents in single file, dressed in flowing robes in classical Greek style, each bearing a lighted candle. The last two women carried Mrs. Carlson's portrait draped in black. They did not say a word as their ghostly procession circled around us, and neither did we. We hurriedly gathered up our things and left.

I received a more welcome reception when we agreed to find housing for the ROTC in the remodeled old fieldhouse, a big step up from the old horse stables where they had been meeting. I consider as a triumph our agreement with the State Building Board to handle small remodeling jobs, not to exceed $16,000, by employing our physical plant department's construction crew. This agreement freed us from seeking bids from outside contractors. In a few instances, university departments tried to break up a job into two or three segments of $16,000 each. Jesse Jennings of the Department of Anthropology almost singlehandedly built the Utah Museum of Natural History by his extraordinary efforts to scrounge money for the necessary remodeling in the Thomas Building. I helped him in every possible way; and when I was able to squeeze another $4,200 out of a tight budget in July 1969 for him, he wrote me, "With friends like you, I really need enemies."

My main support throughout all the new construction activity on campus was Bruce Jensen, probably the best university architect in the entire nation and recognized by his peers as such. Bruce and I worked very closely together as he proposed and I disposed of the many, many decisions that had to be made on almost a daily basis. He was determined to build a campus of outstanding beauty, and I supported him in every way, particularly when it came to landscaping. We were committed to construction for the ages and agreed not to give in to temporary expedients. The results of our joint efforts can be seen today; and where we failed, it was not because we didn't try.

One project Bruce and I fought for successfully was to provide a decent building for our physical plant operations. When I took over, a General Service Center was not even on the list of priorities; but as an old carpenter, I was determined that the craftsmen deserved quarters as convenient and comfortable as those for the intellectuals. Fletcher recognized the justice of my cause, and we made a service center the number one priority in our 1969-71 building request, advancing it above all others. It stands today just west of the Huntsman Center, a tribute to the firmness of our intention. Jensen and I also fought hard for a dance building constructed on a site east of Merrill Engineering, but lost out. With considerable pleasure twenty years after the fact, I note the construction of a fine building to house the dance department south of the bookstore.

One project we spent a lot of time on but which never reached fruition was a 1970 plan to build twenty-three fraternity and sorority houses at the north edge of the golf course to relieve the pressure on the residential neighborhood north of the university. The anti-establishment furor of the early 1970s, during which fraternities were labeled as elitist and, consequently, became less popular, probably contributed to the defeat of this project.

Ever the environmentalists, Bruce and I opposed alumni plans to spend $20,000 to repave and light the block "U" on the hill overlooking the campus. We believed that letting it disappear without a trace would be a contribution to natural beauty; but standing in the way of sports-minded old grads is like resisting a steamroller. Today the "U" lights blaze forth for every varsity game.

An integral part of all the new construction was landscaping designed to create a unified setting for the new buildings. Before I arrived on the scene, Bruce Jensen and the university administration had hired John Lyon Reid and his associates of San Francisco as architectural consultants to plan the entire campus.

With a very few exceptions, they successfully created a beautiful campus, an endeavor in which they had my fullest support. The two major east-west and north-south malls provide wide walkways with accompanying flower beds and grassy and tree-lined connecting smaller walks. The chief defect here is that the Behavioral Science Building blocks a view of Salt Lake Valley from the east-west mall. The berms create a more interesting landscape by providing small knolls and elevations.

The Tanner cascading fountain east of the Marriott Library, the jet fountain at the south end of the mall, and the round fountain at the mall's north end have to be turned off for most of the school year, of course, but add sparkle and pleasure during the warmer weather. We also added six tennis courts north of the residence halls, landscaped so that they fit into the rest of the greenery while Fred Emery and others threatened me with bodily harm if I ever attempted to take over any of the nine-hole golf course set in the very midst of the campus. The last touch to our plans for landscaping was to provide some unique and functional directional signs. The Board of Regents and the later Institutional Council, whose members thought we were already spending too much money on landscaping projects when mere grass-planting would do, objected rather strenuously when we hired a consulting firm from California to design our signs, but Fletcher let us have our way here.

The many buildings under construction, the necessary trenches for utilities, and the landscaping projects combined to present a campus which, for four years, seemed to be nothing but dirt, rocks, and mud. Those who don't understand that construction means dirt, rocks, and mud—especially some sheltered faculty members—were in high dudgeon throughout the entire period. Often I would receive a delegation of upset faculty complaining loudly about why such a trench were necessary or why trucks had to cross their favorite pathways. I would listen patiently and then announce, "If you think present conditions are bad, just wait. It will be worse before it gets better." They didn't get much sympathy from me. Bruce Jensen used to send complainers to me knowing that I would help him out with such unconsoling declarations.

Throughout all the organized chaos which accompanies construction, I also had to provide parking spaces and a traffic plan for the faculty, staff, and students of the university who were nearly all commuters. Clayton Kimball, university engineer when I entered office, was named traffic engineer until his untimely death from a heart attack in 1969. Then I hired Emmett Quinn, a big, friendly Irishman and experienced engineer who, just a few years ago, served as grand marshal of the St. Patrick's Day parade in Salt Lake City. Emmett began taking classes in traffic planning to better fit him for the position and turned out to be a very competent and congenial traffic engineer. We had already hired Wilbur Smith & Associates of San Francisco as consultants on traffic and parking. Paul Bay of that company made a survey which disclosed that an average of 1.2 persons rode in the automobiles which entered the campus each day. Working with John Lyon Reid, the Wilbur Smith company convinced us that a peripheral road system was the best way to avoid conflict between pedestrians and vehicles within the campus. We closed 1500 East, which had for years bisected the campus between east and west. Since it had allowed drivers easy access to all buildings, there was a great outcry but the Associated Student officers supported us, and the deed was done.

The next step was to replace the eighteen different parking stickers with only two—an "A" for faculty and staff, and a "B" sticker for students. The response to this move was visceral and emotional as students cried discrimination; but this time Noel de Nevers of the engineering department, who headed the faculty student Traffic Committee, gave us encouragement and unwavering support. In fact, without the wisdom and backbone of de Nevers we could not have made some of the changes in traffic and parking that I deemed most desirable. I developed a thick skin as some members of the campus community took out their frustrations on me personally. On December 15, 1970, Robert Bliss, chair of the Department of Architecture, sent me a booklet in which he thought I'd be interested accompanied by a short note: "Sorry to have yelled at you the other morning." I've forgotten what he was upset about, and today we're very good friends.

Another example of how emotional parking can be happened one day shortly after the "A" and "B" rule went into effect. I parked my "A" stickered car in a "B" parking space because an "A" space was not available. When I went to my car at the end of the day, I found a large piece of butcher paper under my windshield wipers with the words, "You inconsiderate bastard! Why don't you park in your privileged parking stall?"

I brush aside student and faculty objections to the "high" price of parking stickers even today. Our survey at the time of the change to the "A" and "B" system showed that while we were charging $7.50 and $15.00 for parking privileges, such campuses as UCLA were charging up to $200 per person for some parking spaces, while the director of parking at Wayne State University in the heart of Detroit's ghetto told me, "We have a fine university, a competent faculty, and we open our doors every morning to any students who can get to our classes." In other words, Wayne State had practically no parking places at all for students; they had to get to classes the best way they could.

I have little sympathy for University of Utah personnel who may have to walk two or three blocks to get to classes or offices. After we completed our parking lot system, we had about 500 empty spaces at the peak period of parking (10:00 A.M. on Wednesday morning), most of them north of the Merrill Engineering Building, just a few minutes away from the center of campus. By April 1971, we had 11,700 parking stalls available for the 23,900 students, faculty, and staff who made thousands of vehicle trips for each school day into the campus. Emmett Quinn and I endured other protests when we installed parking meters on the lower campus circle and at other strategic points around campus. Because of the great number of parking violations, I set Leslie Courtland up in the Park Building as Traffic Appeals Officer to handle students, staff, and faculty complaints. He did a remarkably patient job.

To try to quiet complaints about not enough parking stalls during heavy construction, I opened a temporary dirt lot southwest of Marriott Library only to be attacked for providing a sea of mud for patrons. During the crisis time caused by the Vietnam War and just prior to an announced moratorium in October 1969, I hurriedly announced that

700 new parking spaces were available in the annex parking lot, south of Fifth East. It didn't help much to diffuse student anger. Of course, there were those on the other side of the parking controversy who objected to turning green and grassy areas into blacktop for parking lots. One law professor threatened to lie down in front of the caterpillar tractor which was lifting the sod from a playing field for a parking lot east of the Law Building.

Toward the end of my career as vice president, Fletcher and I had developed plans for two parking structures to meet the demand for more and more convenient parking—a four-story building at the northwest corner of the Union Building and a large two- or three-story structure which would have covered the entire large parking lot south of the business and education buildings. They still need to be built.

The amount of space devoted to construction and parking indicates the importance of these subjects in most minds, but I had other responsibilities including the supervision of physical plant operations. The university amounted to a city of about 25,000 and required a large maintenance staff of carpenters, plumbers, electricians, landscapers, gardeners, janitors, and food handlers. I developed an excellent rapport with the staff when they learned that I had been a carpenter-builder much of my life. I spoke their language, understood their problems, and was sensitive to any hint on the part of our faculty or administration that they were anything but first-class citizens.

I well remember the "silent insubordination" I got from the landscape staff who just refused to water Walter Cottam's botany experiment in growing oaks along the hillside above the campus. It took some doing to find a few men who were willing to trudge up the slopes to handle the irrigation project, which they thought was rather foolish.

The janitors and custodians especially needed moral support. Some of them were students, including my own son, David, while the rest came from the lowest ranks of society and received the lowest pay of any of the physical plant personnel. I supported them in every way possible to give them a living wage and, at the same time, to ensure clean buildings and tidy landscaping. About a year after I took over as vice president, some union organizers tried to organize the physical plant employees. I certainly was not opposed to a union but believed that the university could offer the same benefits without demanding monthly dues. I asked Fletcher to raise the workers' wages; and in an open meeting at which I presented this decision, with the backing of Ernest Poulson, personnel director, the staff dropped its plans for a union because the raise was what they wanted anyway. Poulson handled another prospective strike and unionization of the hospital staff on his own, convincing the employees that they could get what they wanted without a union. I had a good relationship with the state officials of the A.F. of L., and had to deal with them several times to end strikes of the glaziers, carpet layers, and other trades who periodically held up the completion of buildings. We understood one another.

Bud Cross was the efficient director of the physical plant. He had the support and cooperation of his people and mine as well. He fought for them, was particularly pleased, along with the staff, when I was able to get approval of a new Service Center Building for the physical plant, and made his presence felt at our weekly construction meetings. His principal concern, and rightly so, was to make sure that all of the new buildings and landscaping worked efficiently or he and his employees would be faced with horrendous maintenance problems. He and his construction people became such meticulous inspectors of the construction projects around campus that I received complaints from the State Building Board inspectors and had to work out a compromise between the two groups. Cross was especially interested in establishing a motor pool to replace the old junkers that his staff had been forced to use. The plan was to buy a new fleet of vehicles and then replace them after only a few years of service. I was not altogether sold on his idea about the ideal number of trucks. He argued that the campus was so large that it was cheaper to provide each crew with a truck than pay for the time they wasted waiting for transportation. Fletcher had the same reservations; but after three of Cross's presentations, Fletcher finally gave in; and a fleet of gleaming white service trucks moved in. I am still not sure if there is a real economic benefit, but Cross and his employees were pleased at the convenience and status.

As the cost of electricity went sky high, Fletcher undertook a hard-nosed campaign to force reduced rates from Utah Power & Light Company. We sent Mark Money on a fact-finding trip to a Texas university that had built its own coal-fired plant and was generating electricity far below the cost of buying power from the local utility. Fletcher was enthused by the report; and when Utah Power &

Light glimpsed the engineering drawings and cost estimates that Mark Money and I had put together, their officials called for a meeting. Fletcher and I met with the president and vice president of UP&L for about two hours and left with an agreement for a reduction in rates.

Ernest Poulson took care of the personnel department so well that, even though I was his supervisor, we rarely met to discuss what he was doing, and I got involved only when he needed my support for program approval from Fletcher or the Board of Regents. Ernest is one of the very best administrators I have ever known. He initiated needed changes on his own; he inspired his staff to such efforts with his high demands and made his relationships with them so rewarding through his graciousness that they were quite disconsolate when he left in 1970 to become assistant director of University Research Park with Mark Money. Like Money, Poulson also completed a Ph.D. while working full time as head of personnel. Two of his enduring contributions were a fine group life insurance program and a disability insurance plan. In the last year of his administration, he successfully coordinated the university's compliance with the affirmative action and equal opportunity regulations inaugurated by the Johnson administration. He was able to start the university off in the right direction with the various federal officials concerned in this area.

A major responsibility was supervising University Security. Just as I began my service as vice president, the Utah State Attorney General ruled that the University of Utah must establish its own security force, rather than drawing on the Salt Lake City police. By 1968 another ruling added that the Salt Lake City police were not to get involved in campus security unless our own officers called them in. In light of the wave of anti-Vietnam unrest about to break over America's campuses, these directives were fortunate in allowing us to get prepared.

Among the many applicants for the new post of director of security, Mark Money and I recommended Elroy Jones, a former FBI agent who was then a regional representative of the national heart association. He was tired of traveling and wanted to return to his first love—police work. He was a fortunate choice in many ways. He was well trained and thoroughly professional, had a friendly yet firm way, and was an especially good organizer and administrator. His one failing was that his letter-of-the-law approach to security matters came just at the time when students were demanding greater freedom and more say in how the university was run.

Jones eventually hired twenty-five officers. We both agreed on giving preference to college-trained candidates, since we were convinced that recent college graduates would understand campus conditions and do a better job with students. Fletcher allowed me to offer tuition waivers to all officers as a way of encouraging them to acquire further training. Fletcher also supported my position that we had to offer substantial salaries to attract good men, and we finally had the highest-paid police force in the entire state. Unfortunately, that is no longer true.

With officers like Wayne Shepherd and Dan Waters, excellent officers with extensive police experience, University Security rapidly established an excellent reputation as one of the best police outfits in the state. They dealt with serious crimes like rape, assault, theft, and drug dealing, but their most numerous cases were controlling drinking at games and enforcing parking regulations. All of these problems, normal enough on campus, were exacerbated by the new anti-establishment trend of calling police officers "pigs" and intentionally breaking rules.

Jones's strict approach to law-breakers sometimes involved me in delicate situations. When Apostle Richard L. Evans and Reed Brinton, an insurance executive, of our Board of Regents received parking tickets while they were attending the annual faculty breakfast, Neal Maxwell asked me to "talk" to Jones. In contrast, Ed Clyde, chair of our Institutional Council, was ticketed for parking in a restricted slot while he presided over a council meeting and uncomplainingly paid the ticket. I was asked more than once to "talk" to Jones, and sometimes I did; but I must say that I defended Jones more often than I "talked" to him, believing that the law should not discriminate and admiring his devotion to duty. On February 17, 1971, Jones brought his entire force of twenty-five on a surprise visit to my office to express appreciation for my support. They presented me with a brand-new 38-caliber Smith & Wesson pistol and honorary police badge #40 which made me a "duly sworn police officer of the State of Utah" with the power to make arrests, etc. I immediately put the pistol out of sight on a shelf at home.

Jones was the right security director for the time and did a good job in organizing the campus police and guiding their actions during the student riots in the spring of 1970. Shortly after I left, the administration advised Jones to look for another position, and he moved to the state security organization. His successor, Wayne Shepherd, was equally dedicated but had a more laid-back philosophy and has been a splendid director of security since 1971. A few years ago I presented the Smith & Wesson to him. He recently retired.

The nationwide student protests of the late 1960s were fueled to a high pitch by the Vietnam War and the unpopular draft laws. Although Salt Lake City is a conservative community, the University of Utah was affected by the protest movement. In the fall of 1968, a Coalition for Student Rights was organized; and on November 26, 1968, the ASUU approved the formation for one year of a chapter of the radical Students for a Democratic Society. Elroy Jones advised against permitting the group to organize and began, at once, to monitor the meetings with the group's full knowledge. The ingenious proposal of the SDS in February 1969 was to try to disrupt a Challenge Lecture (a prestigious annual lecture given by individuals selected by a student committee) by Ronald Reagan, then governor of California, and simultaneously hold a Reagan Film Festival to show how bad an actor he was. In December 1969 President Fletcher and Governor Calvin Rampton received bags of marijuana through the mail with the message, "Merry Christmas." We assumed the SDS was behind this "gift," although we never found out for sure. On another occasion, at a performance of the San Francisco Mime Troop, four young men suddenly stood up in the front row, each with a large letter stenciled on the backs of their T-shirts that spelled out an improper four-letter word. Some SDS plans were neither so benign nor so foolish, and the SDS was not the only organization to demonstrate, although it was probably the most feared.

In October 1969 the students organized a moratorium march against the war and several thousand paraded from the campus along South Temple Street to the Federal Building on State Street, where a rally was held. I participated in the march, since I was as much opposed to the U.S. presence in Vietnam as the students, though I doubt that any students recognized me. Most of them were missing class to participate, but the administration did not make a major event out of the truancy, which I thought was very wise.

Other demonstrations occurred when President Richard Nixon

sent U.S. troops into Cambodia in the spring of 1970. The ROTC Building was fire-bombed, but the concrete and brick building failed to catch fire, although a number of stored fire arms were damaged. But the real fire-storm broke when National Guardsmen killed four students at Kent State on May 4, 1970. Campuses erupted across the nation. The next day students raced through Orson Spencer Hall throwing open classroom doors and disrupting classes. About 200 students occupied the editor's office at the *Chronicle,* demanding control of the next day's front page so they could announce a campus-wide strike. The editor refused but, knowing good copy, filled the paper with reports of student meetings and demonstrations.

Four thousand gathered on May 6 for a noon rally south of the Union Building. Catherine Collard, then a student, and other student leaders stirred up the emotions of the crowd. They made five demands: (1) no speaker restrictions, (2) no registration or regulation of literature, (3) no meeting restrictions, (4) no city or state police or National Guardsmen on campus, and (5) no firearms on campus including those of our own police force. Fletcher addressed the meeting but refused to give in to the five demands and could not head off the strike vote. At 12:30 P.M. a fire broke out in the empty World War II frame building on the Union Building green that had been used as a temporary bookstore. We were getting ready to raze it; but if this worthless building could be burned, administrators feared that permanent structures might also come under attack.

Forty-five minutes later at 1:15 P.M., some of about 800 students marched into the second floor of the Park Administration Building. Provost Tom King, Academic Vice President Jerry Andersen, and I advised Fletcher to go home, and gave the same advice to those officed in the Park Building. If they wanted to stay, we told them to keep their doors locked. King conferred with representatives of the state attorney general's office, then ordered the students to vacate the building, warning that, if they didn't, the crowd would be photographed and everyone identified would be suspended. All but eighty-five left the building to join the estimated crowd of 3,000 students outside. I stationed officers at all the outside doors of the building, and they patrolled the crowd, acting responsibly and cautiously so as not to provoke violence. Our decision to choose young, college-trained officers really paid off in this situation. The students finally dispersed when a light rain began to fall. Despite tense moments throughout the day, we did not call in the city police, a gesture which helped calm the crowd.

King then told the eighty-five determined protestors who were sitting on the foyer floor that they must leave or be arrested. They all refused. One of the protesters, Richard L. Young, a law professor, advised his fellow dissidents not to resist but to go peaceably with the officers. Jones and I set up two tables in the basement. Our officers brought the students down to be fingerprinted, booked them, and then transported them to the city jail. The process took until about 8:00 P.M. At the end of the day-long affair, two students appeared at the front door of the Park Building demanding that they too be admitted so they could be arrested. I told them, "I'm sorry, but we don't intend to arrest any more people today." Of the eighty-five, fifty-four were students, two were faculty members, and twenty-nine were nonstudents including four juveniles from local high schools. After being booked into the Salt Lake City jail, most were released on their own recognizance, a few on $300 bail, while only one resisted arrest. Later the charges of failure to disperse and contempt of court were dropped—which I thought was appropriate. Most were conscientious idealists who felt they had to take a stand against an unjust war.

The most serious damage was inflicted early the next morning on the National Guard Headquarters building on Guardsman Way, adjoining the campus. Fletcher called me about 2:30 A.M. reporting the explosion and asking me to go to the scene as a representative of the university to offer what assistance I could. I arrived there about 3:00 A.M., just as the major general in command of the Utah National Guard also showed up. I introduced myself and offered our assistance. He looked at me without warmth and replied rather stiffly, "We will have to be careful, in the future, in our choice of neighbors."

I could hardly blame him. The entire front of the building had been blown out with furniture and equipment scattered all over the street. The police were unable to arrest anyone connected with any of these three incidents, but most people blamed the students. It's true that many students were sympathetic and may have been involved; but it is also true that nonstudent radicals may also have been at work on campus, even though none were identified or charged.

Some faculty and students met on May 8 to demand that our campus police not carry weapons in the daytime and at night must use them only in self-defense or for the protection of human life. Jones produced a report showing that over the past two years, his officers had had to draw their weapons to protect their own lives and those of others thirty-five times. An investigating committee on October 20 approved of our officers going armed at all times, a recommendation the administration adopted.

The extra cost of police services alone during the May riots was $14,800. In the aftermath the university administration had to explain student protests to an enraged downtown community, some of whom were telling us to set up a machine gun on the steps of the Park Building to "mow down" the student demonstrators. Fletcher asked me to mollify one state legislator whom I had known as a bank official when I was in the building business. I described our meeting with some irony:

> With [_____], reasoning must be thrown out. He has very concrete opinions—thoroughly mixed and permanently set. I finally asked if he would like to talk to our *Chronicle* editors and other student leaders, but he refused because "their minds are made up and they won't change." It is my opinion that there is a slight possibility that [_____] might revise his point of view toward the university and the younger generation if one of his own children should suddenly join SDS, grow his hair to his shoulders, and take up the smoking of pot. But on the other hand such an alternative might only lead to disowning his own child and to continue in his own impenetrable way.

Fletcher was so relieved when the campus quieted that he took several carloads of his vice presidents and their wives to Las Vegas for a weekend of relaxation at his own expense. Betty and I rode down with him and his wife, Faye,[2] and all of us enjoyed the floor shows at Las Vegas.

---

2. I rode with Jim in the front seat and, for most of the way, we discussed recent disclosures about the Mormon scripture the Pearl of Great Price, which both he and I thought had just been shown to be an unfortunate choice for one of the four standard works of the church. Joseph Smith had, in 1835, acquired some papyrus documents which, he announced, contained the writings of Abraham. He published a translation in 1842, a narrative that closely resembled the creation story in Genesis 1–2. While chaos was racking the campus, Aziz Atiya, director of our Middle East Center, identified some papers stored in New York as these papyri, long presumed lost. Scholars deciphering them established that they were only common funerary texts found in many Egyptian graves. Scholars had long doubted Smith's story, and the new discoveries amply confirmed their suspicions. Nevertheless, the Mormon church still maintains that the Pearl of Great Price is scripture.

A few months later in the fall of 1970, I met Cathy Collard cashiering in our bookstore. When I asked about her plans, she said she had learned that violent demonstrations were not successful and she was going to law school so she could work within the system. Anyone who has followed her successful career as an attorney for liberal causes knows that she made the right decision.

Another controversy occupied much of my attention during the last two years of my vice presidency—married student housing. On my first day in the office, I had asked Fletcher specifically what he expected of me. That meeting produced a list of nine items, eight of which I had either accomplished or had underway by my report of the following year. My only failure was in increasing married student housing. We had a waiting list of several hundred student families who were desperate for some kind of affordable apartments because we had destroyed the World War II barracks to make the land available for our new buildings. Bruce Jensen and I had met with our planning consultants from San Francisco and had settled on a site south of the two eight-story towers that offered housing to medical students, situated at the base of the foothills and north of Red Butte Creek. It was a logical choice and would have grouped all the new married student apartments in one area.

Unfortunately Kenneth Castleton, vice president for medical affairs, and his medical faculty objected, fearing that our lower rental units would cause the higher-priced medical towers to stand vacant. In my opinion, one Jensen shared, the eight-story Medical Towers were not only a mistake because of luxury features which would make the rents too high, but also because mothers of little children had a difficult time supervising their children on the playgrounds from an eighth-floor apartment. We set the height of our buildings at three stories. Castleton and the medical faculty pressed their case with Fletcher who gave in and instructed Jensen and me to find another site.

This decision set the stage for all kinds of trouble. I opposed it but felt I must be loyal to the boss, even when the brunt of the controversy fell on me. We searched hard for a substitute site and finally settled on the south end of the Research Park which the Board of Higher Education and Governor Rampton had ruled off-limits for anything but industrial research facilities. I warned Fletcher that there might be problems, but he instructed us to proceed. I was a poor prophet. The troubles were much worse than either Jensen or I anticipated.

We learned about an innovative cost-slashing building technique used by the small Hiram Scott College in Scotts Bluff, Nebraska, for its residence halls. Jensen and I took Glen Swenson and some of his staff from the State Building Board and Dale Minson of the architectural firm of Minson & Halander to Scotts Bluff to observe the college's "lift-slab" concept. Its builders poured concrete walls on the ground and, after they hardened, lifted them into position with cranes. The technique had been used for supermarkets and industrial buildings but not for housing. Swenson and I had chosen Minson & Halander to design our proposed housing because Halander was an engineer, and the two partners were willing to try the experiment.

I took Ted E. Davis, our finance vice president, to San Francisco to present Minson and Halander's sketches to regional officials of the federal Housing and Urban Development Agency, hoping for a low-interest loan. The director, amazed at the concept, exclaimed, "We've tried for many years to get California colleges to develop some kind of low-cost student housing, and it takes someone from Salt Lake City to show them how to do it." HUD approved two loans for us: $3 million at 3 percent interest and $4.5 million at 6.3 percent for our two projects. We planned the first on vacant property next to some existing housing west of Foothill Boulevard and the second at the south end of Research Park.

With approval from Fletcher and the Institutional Council, Minson & Halander designed buildings which could be constructed for $11.38 per foot, an unbelievably low figure for such structures; and the State Building Board bid and awarded the project to a construction company. Then all hell broke loose. Although the ASUU and students in general supported the project, the private homeowners south of Sunnyside Avenue enlisted the Sierra Club and residents of the upscale Canyon Crest condominiums at the canyon's mouth to oppose the project on environmental grounds, also claiming that the cheap new housing would lower the value of their homes.

Governor Rampton, supported by members of the downtown community, promised to reserve all of Research Park for its original purpose and announced that he was halting the 320-unit development until the Board of Higher Education could investigate the entire project. Facing this show-down vote, we prepared a report showing that the university (and hence the state) would suffer a $500,000 loss if we were forced to move to another site. John Dixon, the executive vice president who had taken Maxwell's place, supported us to the hilt at the Board of Higher Education's next monthly meeting. After a lengthy discussion and much testimony on both sides, the board voted 14 to 1 that the university, the campus planning office, and I had followed proper procedures and authorized the university to proceed. It was a victory but left a bitter taste for many former supporters of the university. Fletcher may have even forgotten his decision to move the site from near Red Butte Creek. I didn't bring it up and had to take the criticism despite the board's approval.

And there was more to come. Although I had started very early in the process to ensure that the sewer line along Sunnyside Avenue would carry the increased sewage, I found it difficult to pin down George Catmull, the Salt Lake City Commissioner for Streets and Utilities. I had become acquainted with him when we were both building houses in the Granger area, but that relationship did not seem to help. I finally had to make the decision whether to abandon the project and lose HUD's $7.5 million or start building and take my chances on getting a proper sewer connection. I knew I would come under criticism from our Institutional Council; but I also knew that once the buildings were erected, Catmull, Salt Lake City, and the city council would accommodate it. I was in that instance again putting student interests first. Salt Lake City solved its problem by borrowing $223,000 from the University Housing Trust Funds, a loan which it paid back in eighteen months.

And then there were the miscellaneous vice presidential duties. For example, in February 1970 I became the university's Civil Defense Coordinator, a meaningless job unless an international nuclear strike were to occur. In my first few days on the job, I learned that the university would pay my dues at the Fort Douglas Club, a perk for all of the vice presidents and chief administrative officers, so that we would have an exclusive setting in which to entertain important guests and deal with business leaders and legislators.

However, the application blank asked for a picture and asked about religious affiliation. I refused to cooperate with this obvious attempt to obtain racial and religious information but was finally granted membership anyway. The club soon eliminated these provisions. I also represented the administration on a number of committees, among which was one which, thanks to a typographical error, appeared as the "Peach Corps Committee" to which I responded that I would be glad to serve, "especially in September."

While these four crowded years passed rapidly, three different universities had invited me to apply for the presidency of their institutions. I had a temporary interest in only one. In January 1968 Mark Neuberger, secretary for USU's Institutional Council, asked if I had any interest in pursuing that position. I agreed to interview with the council but realized I had little chance when, after the interview, one of the members remarked, "Well, I'll say one thing for him. He's fast on his feet." By March I was one of five finalists, but the choice went to Glen Taggart of Michigan State, who served very successfully for several years. In October 1969 I was considered for the presidency of New Mexico State but I was not deeply interested. Betty would have been very reluctant to move either to Logan or Las Cruces. Finally, in June 1971 I turned down an invitation to become a candidate for the presidency of the University of the Pacific. I had not forgotten my delayed dream of returning to research, writing, and teaching.

During this period Betty completed an M.A. degree in linguistics at the University of Utah and took a two-year job with William Slager of our English department, editing a journal on learning and teaching English as a second language for Native Americans. She very much enjoyed this project and did some work-related travel, including a trip to a native village west of Bethel, Alaska.

During Karen's two-year term of service in India in 1966 and 1967, she met and married another volunteer, Charles Bolton, a philosophy graduate of George Washington University in Washington, D.C. They were married at the American Embassy in New Delhi in November 1966, and the two worked another year in Baswa. Neither Betty nor I could attend the wedding, but we were delighted for Karen and looked forward to meeting Charles. When they returned to Utah in 1967 so that Karen could complete her senior year, we gave them a gala reception in our home. Charles was a man of strength and good humor whom we liked immediately. After Karen's graduation, she and Charles moved to Oakland where she completed her work for a certificate as a medical technician. Later she earned a master's degree in public health at Berkeley.

David paid his own way through the University of Utah by living frugally at home and working as a custodian. After three years of steady but unspectacular work, he suddenly discovered archaeology and a mentor, Jesse Jennings, as a result of work on an Indian "dig" near Salina, Utah, during the summer after his junior year. He came back on fire with enthusiasm. Just at this point, to our dismay, his draft board ordered him to report for a physical. Betty explained to the draft board in Logan, where he was registered, about the problem with his throat. The draft board was adamant, but the medical officer at Fort Douglas released him from any army duty, much to our relief.

Linda was also living at home, working part time at the Marriott Library, and majoring in art. She showed some real skill in that discipline. In 1980 she moved into an apartment on East South Temple with three girlfriends. She pursued a major in art and decided to become a special education teacher, which meant an extra year of school work. For three years in junior high and early high school, Steve ran a paper route. It didn't make him rich but it taught him the virtues of early rising and independent enterprise. We were able to send him to the boys' ranch operated each summer in Teton Valley by our friend Lowell Bennion. Steve worked the next two summers for Wendell Bagley, a Teton rancher, and once told me that after bucking hay bales, he found construction work "a snap."

Jim Fletcher was appointed director of the National Aeronautics and Space Administration in the spring of 1971, and it seemed a good time for me to withdraw from administration by the summer of 1971 and to return to full-time teaching. But Fred Emery, the interim university president for the next two years, had other ideas for me.

17.

LIBRARIAN
AND HISTORY CHAIR,
1971-75

I contemplated leaving administration as a genuine escape, but I failed to reckon with the new president, Fred Emery. Ralph Thomson, director of libraries for many years, was retiring. He had helped search for a replacement, but that individual had, at the last moment, changed his mind. Emery, for whom I have always had a great fondness and sincere admiration, took me to lunch at the Fort Douglas Club, an invitation I probably should not have accepted. He twisted my arm gently to take over the library position just for the two years he had agreed to be president, to effect what administrative reorganization I could and to find a permanent replacement for myself. I was very reluctant but could not turn down Fred Emery, one of the most loyal Utah men I have ever known. My acquaintance with libraries was limited to historical research, not administration; but Emery assured me that my experience in administration would equip me to give the library system new direction and leadership. So I agreed.

Before starting the new job in September 1971, Betty and I took a long-planned, six-week tour of Europe. We landed in Paris, took the Orient Express to Vienna, and then traveled by bus through Yugoslavia, Greece, Italy, Austria, Switzerland, and back to Paris. Then we went by train to Copenhagen, crossed Denmark by rail, took the ocean ferry to England, and flew home from London. It was a very enjoyable trip and gave me a real breather before plunging into the problems of the Marriott Library. Betty was also looking for a new work opportunity, which soon came.

My first action was to upgrade the business manager's position from half-time to full-time. Richard Denman, the current half-time person, turned out to be the most efficient, careful, and innovative business manager I have ever had. It was a joy and a pleasure to work with him. I also made the personnel librarian, Winn Margetts, a full-time employee instead of half-time. Ken Luker, systems analyst, was the third administrator who reported directly to me.

Finally, I was able to persuade Dave Laird, the acquisitions librarian, to become associate director. In some frustration at not being advanced, he had made plans to take a position in Australia but agreed to work with me. The Marriott staff was absolutely delighted because they had such a high regard for him as an individual and a professional librarian, a conviction which I soon shared. Dave taught me the rudiments of librarianship during the first year, then became library director at the University of Arizona. I had hoped that he would become my replacement at Utah, but his heart was in the Southwest. I set up a search committee and, after several months, hired Roger K. Hanson, the library director at the University of North Dakota. I chose Roger because he was committed to using all of the new electronic and computer techniques available to make the Marriott one of the most modern and efficient library systems in the nation. He had a nationwide reputation in the field and was on constant call as a consultant both in the building and operation of university libraries. Our Marriott Library hummed like a well-oiled machine, gratifying our patrons, faculty, and students with its smooth operation. Hanson was very successful as my replacement and only recently retired.

In addition to staffing the key positions, I next had to deal with two sensitive personnel problems. Ken Slack, one of the top officials in the Marriott and an agreeable and competent person, had gotten caught in a situation which was not altogether his fault but which, nevertheless, was affecting his performance and his relationship with the rest of the staff. I had to tell him that he was doing neither himself nor the rest of us any favors by staying on. He eventually agreed and was hired as director of libraries at a West Virginia college where he has had a very successful career. He probably did not thank me at the time for insisting that he look for another job, but his career has benefitted. The other problem was the head of our Catalog Division, whom the staff disliked for his rather arbitrary manner. He left for a better-paying position in one of the Texas colleges. But unlike Slack who just needed a new start, he was unsuccessful in his new job and was eventually forced out. I asked Yvonne Stroup to take over cataloging, and she soon demonstrated keen efficiency and an excellent rapport with the members of her division. She soon reported that the Catalog Division had reduced the time it took to get a book cataloged and the card filed from six to nine months down to three to six months.

Marriott Library, like many university systems, had eight main divisions (acquisitions, special services, general services, processing, humanities, social and behavioral sciences, science, and special collections) with nineteen subdivisions or departments. Some of the division and department heads whom I came to know well, and in no particular order, included my old friend from Berkeley, Everett Cooley (Lyman Tyler and I had persuaded him to leave Utah State Historical Society to become head of special collections and university archivist at the library with an appointment as professor of history); Thomas M. Schmid, acquisitions; Dale Cluff, monographs and later audio-visual; Frieda McCoy, documents; Coy Harmon, assistant to the director; August (Gus) Hannibal, extension (outreach and services to the general public); Beth Oyler, circulation; Lily Fink, binding; Johnny Beaver, building manager; Richard Van Orden, stacks manager; Annie Laurie Bearry, literature; Eloise McQuown, social and behavioral science; Mary Jane Hair, head of social and behavioral science; Edith Rich, science; Marian Sheets, Middle East; and Sue Raemer, my competent and personable secretary.

I worked hard to obtain first-class status for the staff, since some faculty felt that librarians were not scholars equal to those in the traditional disciplines. Nothing can be farther from the truth! In addition to having a master's degree in library science, many of the Marriott people held another M.A. in a discipline and several had Ph.D.s. Furthermore, some of them taught and many also published. After some hard lobbying, with the support of Jerry Andersen, the academic vice president, I convinced the Faculty Senate that our librarians should hold the same ranks and titles as the rest of the faculty, from assistant professor to full professor, with all the rights, privileges and benefits that other members of the academic community had, including sabbatical leaves. The Marriott staff members were ecstatic with their new status. Unfortunately, several years ago the Faculty Senate withdrew that recognition, leaving the librarians with some of the new privileges but newly ghetto-ized in a "special faculty" category. I regret very much this regressive step.

To ensure real participation, I established a weekly staff meeting every Tuesday morning for the eight division heads and the administrative staff—eleven people altogether. Once a month I convened all of the division and department heads, about thirty-five people. And every quarter or on special occasions, we had a general meeting of all the regular staff, excluding only the part-time student help. We also maintained a library advisory board composed of elected representatives from the various sections of the library and chaired by Dale Cluff to meet monthly on promotion and tenure, social activities, or other matters affecting the entire staff. Faculty representing the entire university served on the Library Policy Advisory Board that met monthly under the expert chairmanship of Robert Boehm of the College of Engineering. This board was a great help in effecting necessary changes in library use. For example, it helped me meet three goals: restrict the use of the library for office space, approve the appointment of library representatives from the various colleges, and install an elevator on the west side, omitted by architectural oversight but badly needed by handicapped and elderly patrons who parked in the west lot.

I also started a quarterly newsletter, edited by the capable Gus Hannibal, to inform our own staff and the general university community about what was happening in the library system. Finally, I gave full support to the newly-established Friends of the Library, again under Hannibal's direction. By November 1972 we had 169 members, about eighty of whom were making contributions. It is still a going organization today, very effective in raising money for special book purchases and involving the downtown community in library affairs.

To ensure a comfortable atmosphere in my office, I moved my desk to one side and installed a round coffee table and chairs as a conversational area.

A sensitive issue involving faculty was the long-established custom of some faculty members who checked out books with no intention of returning them on time. There were then 225 faculty and teaching assistants who had checked out 1,213 titles, apparently with no concern about others who might have a need for the works. This was patently unfair and discriminatory toward other faculty and students; in fact, students with overdue books had to pay their library fines before they could reregister. For me, the chief purpose of a university has to be the teaching and welfare of students, so I determined to change the system. With Andersen's support, despite much hollering and writhing from some of the guilty faculty, we instituted a regulation allowing us to deduct unpaid library fines from the salaries of delinquent faculty. Justice was served in this instance, and nearly all of the books were returned immediately.

Another circulation improvement developed when, at the end of my first quarter as director, one day I was astounded to see in the circulation area four large desks staffed by eight student employees who were filing cards from returned books and journals in file boxes which covered every square inch on the desks. Here was inefficiency in its most distressing application. Beth Oyler agreed with me that something must be done to update our circulation system, especially since our collection stood at 1.5 million and was still growing rapidly. Yet we did not have the budget for the logical solution, which was some kind of automated, computer-controlled process. A week or so later I was in Chicago's O'Hare Airport, returning from a meeting of the National Association of Research Libraries, when William Partridge, the U's vice president for development, came in to catch the same plane. For half an hour I explained our circulation problem and asked his aid in raising the money. He was very responsive and came over to inspect the mess. He authorized Ken Luker to study the alternatives; and by July 1972 Luker could recommend an automated system that would cost $106,000 in start-up money and $36,000 for the second year. On November 6, 1972, I met with Partridge and the university budget officer, Leon Robertson; they agreed to fund the project with $69,000 from the University Institutional Funds Committee, with the balance from other sources. The system was in full operation by late February 1973. The University of Utah is one of the leaders in automating all phases of library operations, thanks to the efforts and know-how of Roger Hanson.

Our book losses from theft were much too high, but our patrons were irritated by the security searches at the exits and our employees were also uncomfortable about searching departing partrons. We had some cases of scuffles and even blows as an outraged patron refused to have his belongings searched. I sent Dick Denman on a nationwide tour to inspect check-point systems in other libraries, and he came back with our answer: a small bit of sensitized tape between two pages that energized a buzzer at the exit gate if it had not been checked out. This system drastically reduced theft and eliminated the need for searches. In the intervening twenty years, it has become standard at most libraries.

Another problem was that graduate students and faculty would simply rip out journal articles they wanted instead of taking notes. We tried appealing to their honesty, threatening those we caught with dire punishment, increasing supervision, and establishing rigorous check-in procedures. Nothing worked. Finally, Dick Denman and I installed two photocopiers where patrons could make their own copies at three cents a page in winter and four cents a page in summer, when many more nonstudents and graduate students used the research stacks. It was an experiment, but it solved the vandalism problem almost completely. Soon we added other machines and standardized the price at five cents a page year round. Several commercial duplicating companies complained to Governor Calvin Rampton and to the Board of Regents that we were running a commercial cut-rate operation in competition with them. The assistant attorney general, Henry Nygaard, quieted this fuss by pointing out that parking was so tight at the university and especially near the library that no downtown users could get near our photocopy machines.

In another move to save money in operations which could then be used for acquisitions, we combined the literature and fine arts reference departments, saving both personnel and space, and the social science and behavioral sciences. There was some outcry from aggrieved patrons, but the saving was about $50,000 a year while the same reference personnel were still available. Eventually, Hanson completed the process by combining all of the reference stations into one general reference department on the third floor.

Nearly every major university library faces constant requests to establish small departmental libraries. I gave such requests no welcome. Such duplication is not only costly but also deprives students and faculty of exposure to broader browsing. The only exceptions were libraries in the law school, the College of Business, and the Graduate School of Social Work. The latter two had been in existence for several years; and Ralph Thompson had unsuccessfully tried to close them. Not only were they both close to the Marriott Library, but it cost $70,000 to maintain them. I tried again and, with Andersen's support, was making progress when, at the last minute, the two colleges agreed to grant Marriott Library $7,500 for 1973 and $9,500 for 1974 from their own academic budgets to retain their little collections. Since then Hanson has closed them, effecting great savings to the university and benefitting students who now use the larger Marriott Library collections.

A problem of even greater significance academically was that, for years, the library staff was responsible for approving the form of theses and dissertations. I discovered to my amazement that as many as twenty or thirty were involved, including Sue Raemer's assistant secretary, a very young graduate of the LDS Business College who knew very little about universities and even less about graduate dissertations. There was, therefore, no uniformity in standards, and our astute graduate students shopped around among our staff, looking for someone who would not hold them to rigorous standards in the appearance of the thesis or dissertation. Sterling McMurrin, dean of the Graduate School, and I agreed to hire a thesis editor who would work at the Graduate School. He established an advisory thesis committee of four knowledgeable faculty members as a search committee for this hire, and I transferred some funds from our budget to help the Graduate School pay this person's salary.

Without telling me, Betty applied for the job. Quickly McMurrin and I disassociated ourselves from the process; but we were both delighted when the search committee chose Betty solely on the basis of her credentials which included a recent M.A. degree in linguistics, work as a bibliographer, and her two years as a journal editor. She retired from the position nine years later, leaving this office in apple-pie order. She also served on a national committee of three thesis editors, the other two being from the University of Chicago and Pennsylvania State University, to draw up national criteria for graduate school control of theses and dissertations. This service, I felt, recognized her fine contribution.

As I watched the escalating costs of acquisitions, it seemed senseless for each of the major university and college libraries in Utah to establish duplicate collections. Could new technology help us? I called a meeting of the library directors from Utah State University, Weber State, and Brigham Young University to discuss cooperation. As a result, we established the University and College Library Council of Utah (UCLC), which I chaired, to explore ways of saving money while still offering full service to our patrons. We met monthly, rotating among the four campuses, and adopted four measures: (1) one library would be designated to buy a new collection which would then be made available to the other three institutions. For example, BYU was approved to buy a $75,000 set of British Parliamentary papers, a collection it very much wanted, while the University of Utah agreed to invest in some Middle East documents, one of our specialties. (2) We jointly purchased a van to provide daily delivery service among Logan, Ogden, Salt Lake City, and Provo. (3) We established reciprocal borrowing privileges for all students and faculty at the four institutions with a uniform user's card. (4) We provided microfilm copies of our card catalogs for each library. When I left the library, Southern Utah State College, Westminster College, the College of Eastern Utah, and Dixie College were all clamoring to get into UCLC. In his farewell letter to me on October 1, 1973, Fred Emery singled out for "special commendation" my leadership in taking the initiative "in establishing a cooperative program with the libraries of the other colleges and universities in Utah."

I also became involved in publishing a series of scholarly books. Obert C. Tanner, a longtime friend and great supporter of many philanthropies in Utah and the nation, approached me about his desire to establish a publishing fund under the supervision of Marriott Library in his mother's name. We agreed that Lyman Tyler, Everett Cooley, and I would act as the editorial board for the Annie Clark Tanner Trust Fund with Everett as editor. Obert made an original gift of $100,000, with additional donations later. It has been a most successful venture with some twelve titles published by 1985. Since Cooley resigned as editor, only a couple of works have been published by the fund. The most recent was *A Gentile Account of Life in Utah's Dixie, 1872-73: Elizabeth Kane's St. George Journal* (1995). Our first volume has been a consistent bestseller: *A Mormon Mother,* the autobiography of Annie Clark Tanner. The very fine Northland Press of Flagstaff, Arizona, printed our first five books; since then Everett Cooley worked with Salt Lake City firms. We offer copies at a reduced price to our Friends of the University of Utah Library.

Some minor incidents during my two-year stint at the Marriott

Library included the attempted suicide of a student who jumped spread-eagled from the fifth floor balcony to the third floor of the atrium. Fortunately, he suffered only a ruptured spleen. The president of the United States Volley Ball Association asked us to make Marriott Library the home of their archives, apparently because of the interest shown in the USVBA by our physical education department. We accepted these papers and, as far as I know, still have them.

In June 1973 I formally bade farewell to my enjoyable and stimulating assignment with the library. Once again I looked forward to full-time teaching and writing and returned gladly to the history department; but the chair, Phil Sturges, insisted I become graduate advisor. I accepted this position reluctantly, realizing that each faculty member also owed some administrative service to his department. Phil had been chair for five years and had been, I thought, a good one. I soon learned, however, that during the past year some dissatisfaction had developed with his administration. The faculty complained that he was not accessible except for an hour or two a day. It seemed to me that he had been caught in a bad situation involving the former dean of the college, a member of our department whose administration of the college was less than successful and whose personal problems and rather arbitrary manner had finally forced his resignation. Phil had become unfairly tainted with the same brush. Sensing this dissatisfaction, he asked to resign as of the summer of 1974. The acting dean of the College of Humanities explained how I came to be considered as his replacement in a letter to the academic vice president:

> Although the names of many people were proposed, Dr. Brigham D. Madsen is the only one for whom unanimous support was expressed. The department's confidence in him was evidenced in his being the first choice by a large majority. Even those, however, who gave first priority to others volunteered their respect for Dr. Madsen and their willingness to work with him for the good of the department. They value him as an administrator, as an accessible person who without being willy-nilly will carefully listen to and weigh different viewpoints, and as a leavening and cohesive force within a department that has been fraught with divisions not incapable of constructive resolution. Dr. Madsen has expressed to me his reluctant agreement to accept the chairship, if proffered, for not more than two years, and not to be effective until September 15, 1974, so that he might have the summer to finish other commitments. His willingness to serve is due, I am convinced, to no personal ambition for

more administrative work, in which the whole university knows he has already given most generously and capably. It is his probity and his dedication to the History Department that guide him in making his services available as interim chair.

The acting dean further explained the concerns of the history faculty:

> In synthesized form, the individuals' top priorities seemed to be recruitment, communication about standards and goals, and ways to improve them. Most of their concerns relate not merely to strengthening internal relations—between faculty members and between faculty and students—but also to developing at all levels of instruction, advising, and research the department's potential to achieve greater professional visibility at home and abroad.

Although committed to the chairship for two years, privately I told the faculty that I intended to work with them to find a permanent chair so that I would have to serve only one year. I succeeded, and my replacement, Richard Thompson, took over on July 1, 1975.

I was fortunate in persuading Glenn Olsen, associate professor of medieval history, to become associate chair with special responsibility for the budget. Following my usual administrative practice of making the salary scale of the employees my first priority, I was astonished to learn that the history faculty had the lowest salaries of any department in the College of Humanities and that compensation had not apparently been a strong concern of the previous chairs. Our new dean, Malcolm Sillars, was a marvelous selection, with whom I worked very well. Olsen and I prepared figures showing the abysmally low wages of our faculty, won Sillars's support, and were able to increase salaries dramatically. I shall never forget the particular pleasure of a new assistant professor who received a boost of $2,000, nor has he forgotten it. I was also able to increase the stipends paid our teaching assistants.

I had always felt that the quality of classroom instruction deserved close attention. My own introduction to college teaching was being ushered into a room at BYU and wished good luck. I was determined to help new TAs get ready for their first instructional assignments. Professor Sandra Taylor, an exceptionally good teacher, agreed to direct a week's training for our TAs before school started in the fall of 1974 and to monitor their teaching during the year to help with any special problems. She and I agreed that faculty members who were using TAs should meet their commitment of writing an evaluation of the teaching performance, a responsibility which most of the faculty had ignored. I was very firm about this so that we began to get evaluations of the TAs at the end of each quarter. The week's orientation program each fall quarter was finally abandoned after two years, but not because of any failure on Taylor's part. Unaccountably, the TAs themselves seemed apathetic about the whole program.

Taylor was one of only three women on our faculty of about thirty, and I pushed hard to recruit more women, especially those who would teach women's history. When I left the chair, Shauna Adix, director of the University Women's Resource Center, wrote my successor, "We hope you are as eager to pursue that possibility as Brig was."

To attempt to bring the faculty together, to foster better communication within the department, and to define our goals and objectives, I established a committee with James Clayton as chair to head a year-long effort to come up with a five-year plan. I recognized that our goals might change during that period but still felt that an interchange of ideas and a consensus on recruiting, curriculum, teaching, and scholarship could be very productive. The whole department met several times during the year, while various subcommittees examined special issues under Clayton's expert direction. He drafted the final report, which met with the approbation of nearly all of the faculty and became the standard for our objectives until the new chair instituted another such study.

One innovation that I tried with the help of Phil Sturges and others was to inaugurate open voting in our meetings and especially in our tenure and promotion deliberations. One of our assistant professors had received two or three negative votes, certainly not a significant number, and came to ask me why. I did not have the answer because the ballots were secret. The individual then asked how a candidate could work at improving his or her performance if no specific problems were cited. After a general discussion of the problem, the faculty voted that, in the future, each voter had to cast his or her ballot openly, state the reasons for any negative vote, and place those reasons on the record for the edification and guidance of the candidate. Other departments and officials of the university were critical of this radical departure from traditional practices but, at least until recently, it worked for us. The applicants came to know at once why others might be critical of their performances as teachers and scholars.

In two other attempts to bring cohesion to the department, I started a monthly newsletter to publicize events, to give other information, and to recognize the accomplishments of our faculty. Unfortunately, the publication was later dropped. In the second instance, I inaugurated a spring barbecue and softball game between the faculty and the graduate students/TAs. This annual picnic became a very popular event until some time ago when a serious split occurred in the department, and the administration feared that no one would come, a truly unfortunate circumstance.

As an ex-builder, my construction instincts have always been aroused by a new administrative job, and there were certainly opportunities in the section of Carlson Hall assigned to history. We were short an office, but I found the space by remodeling an extra-large men's room on the third floor. We needed a seminar room, so I contracted with the Law School for the use of its library on the first floor, located a beautiful and large oak table which had formerly been part of the furnishings of the Thomas Library, and convinced Sam Thurman, dean of the Law School, to pay half the cost. I also found the money to purchase a new photocopier to replace the antediluvian model then in use. But most important was our need to bring our TAs from cramped quarters in a classroom in Orson Spencer Hall into Carlson Hall. Room 118 on the first floor at the north end had formerly distributed meals brought from the central campus kitchen. In this remodeled area the TAs could hold office hours and have some space of their own.

One extracurricular activity came my way during this year when President David Gardner asked me to become the first director of the Utah Endowment for the Humanities. With the understanding that I would serve only one year during which I would recruit a permanent director, I accepted. The members of the first advisory board included Gardner, BYU's president, and some other very distinguished Utahns. We were able to hire Delmont Oswald who was just finishing his Ph.D. in European history at BYU as the associate director. He was a fortunate choice and proved an able director until his death in 1997. Oswald and I visited many parts of the state to get the program off the ground. I spent two days in Jackson, Mississippi, as one of three or four speakers for the state's business leaders' conference sponsored by Mississippi's Committee for the Humanities and, all in all, rather enjoyed the year. I served one more year as vice chair of the board, then resigned to concentrate more on teaching and research.

During my year as chair, we conducted a vigorous search for a replacement and settled with satisfaction on Richard Thompson, associate professor of English history in our own department. He was a fine choice. As chair, he introduced some new programs, conducted a good recruitment drive to add five new and very able young historians to the department, administered departmental affairs judiciously, and exhibited impressive common sense. We regretted having to give him up as he returned to teaching full time when Larry Gerlach was chosen as chair. As I left administration for the last time on July 1, 1975, I looked forward with considerable pleasure to spending my last years as a teacher and scholar.

I was sixty years old and had been in education for nineteen years since receiving my Ph.D. from Berkeley twenty-seven years earlier. Of those years, and including my experience in the Peace Corps, I had been an administrator for thirteen, sometimes holding dual appointments. I had never had any instruction in how to become a successful administrator, but a combination of trial and error, common sense, and a certain amount of good luck had provided me with some working rules that seemed effective. About a year after I left the library, a professor of educational administration asked me to address his graduate seminar of about twenty high school teachers and administrators on administration. I sat down and wrote down my perceptions of a good administrator to hand out to the students. For what they are worth, here they are:

MADSEN'S PRINCIPLES OF ADMINISTRATION

1. Choose capable staff members. Do not rely solely on interviews or letters of recommendation when considering applicants for positions but telephone people who know the candidate and his or her work. Always ask what weaknesses the candidate may have.
2. Replace inefficient staff members.
   a. "Elevate" to another position.
   b. Transfer by process of "lateral arabesque" to another

position.

   c. Grant early retirement.

   d. Fire the person.

3. Effect a good organization.

   a. Have no more than six or seven supervisors reporting to you.

   b. Have sufficient staff help:

     (1) Budget director or business manager

     (2) Personnel officer

     (3) Administrative assistant

   c. Choose between check and balance system under which various segments of organization compete and so produce effective results *or* have direct line organization.

4. Delegate authority and responsibility.

   a. Support supervisors with proper budget and in achieving desired changes of operation.

   b. Never go "around" supervisors to deal with their subordinates.

   c. Allow supervisors freedom to innovate and change conditions with only periodic times of evaluation.

5. Encourage proper communication within organization.

   a. Hold a weekly staff meeting with senior supervisors.

   b. Hold a monthly meeting with all supervisors.

   c. Hold a quarterly meeting with all employees within your division, depending on size.

   d. Monthly or quarterly newsletter.

   e. Don't write if you can telephone; don't telephone if you can meet personally with person in his or her office.

   f. Emphasize the importance of "silent body language" in making communication with your staff as comfortable as possible.

6. Establish rapport with staff.

   a. Make informal visits to departments.

   b. Have open door policy with informal office arrangements.

   c. Be ever willing to listen to complaints or reassure those who feel insecure in their positions.

7. Build support for new programs before attempting to put them into effect.

   a. Use proper channels.

   b. Inform key personnel so as to overcome any objections on a one-to-one basis—never go into a large meeting with a new proposal without having laid the groundwork.

8. Protect the boss.

   a. Don't bother him with unimportant details but meet with him only on policy questions.

   b. Warn him of crises which may be heading his way.

9. Stay on the job. It is necessary to leave your desk to publicize your efforts but don't spend too much time perambulating around—"While the cat's away ..."

10. React immediately to attacks from other parts of your organization.

    a. Marshal arguments and then sit down with the aggrieved person and try to convince him or her of the rightness of your position.

    b. "A person is usually down on what he is not up on."

11. Insist on a good secretary. He or she must be very bright, personable, assertive without being aggressive, and, above all, have good judgment.

12. Make your letters and reports to superiors succinct and to the point.

    a. Write only when you have something to say.

    b. Don't send letters starting with "You may be interested in ..." These usually end up in the round file in a hurry.

13. Additional rules:

    a. Don't make promises you can't keep.

    b. Be open and above-board with staff and superiors.

    c. Be innovative but know when to "back off" if the proposals meet with opposition from too many.

    d. Provide ways of "saving face" when subordinates or superiors back themselves into corners.

e. Make decisions promptly but be sure you have relevant facts first.

f. Keep your desk clean and your work organized.

g. Answer correspondence promptly. If some time is required to gather data, reply to writer explaining why there will be a delay.

h. Patience and understanding will ease the burden of administration and a sense of humor can help to keep you from coming to the office on Saturday.

18.

THE SMELL OF CHALK DUST
AND PENCIL SHAVINGS,
1975-84

After numerous detours on the road of returning to teaching and writing, it felt good in the summer of 1975 to see the way clear toward this goal. I still had a number of minor commitments to committee assignments, of course, and I also served in 1977-78 on the Salt Lake County Council for the Aging at the request of my good friend and former student, Shauna O'Neil, who had just taken over the job as director. When a new director was needed for the Hansen Planetarium, I was pressed into service as a member of a three-person search committee to find a replacement, an assignment which resulted in the appointment of Von Del Chamberlain, an excellent selection.

At the university I served on a committee examining the role of the *Chronicle,* the student newspaper, and turned in a minority recommendation that it pay its way without a subsidy. Gardner took the advice of the majority to help the publication with some money each year, a decision which I probably would have made also if I had been in his shoes. Several times I served as chairman or a member of committees for tenure and promotion in my department or college, an onerous and delicate task, but nevertheless an important one. My most important service was chairing the Committee for the Review of Tenured Faculty. Two previous committees had labored long and hard for several years, but their recommendations were very complicated and unnecessarily expensive. I attempted to guide our committee to a simple and direct solution using the chair and a three-person committee from each department. After a hot debate before the Faculty Senate, during which I pointed out in the presence of the student body officers that students, assistant and associate professors, chairs, and deans all underwent periodic reviews, the Senate voted to institute reviews of tenured faculty, a move long overdue. A few days after the decision, a student letter to the *Chronicle* congratulated the Senate for "finally pulling reins on the tenured faculty. It doesn't surprise me that the ad hoc committee which wrote the new bill for faculty review was chaired by a 'Brigham J. [sic] Madsen.' Such an inspired piece of legislation must have been a work of revelation." I received a few complaints from disgruntled faculty and, for two years, served on a committee in the Department of Education to reinvigorate some delinquent tenured faculty. We were able to inject a little enthusiasm and attention to duty into their performance.

I could now give much more attention to my courses. Since about 1977 I had taught an honors course on "Presidential Character" which attracted some media attention during each election year as students rated not only all the presidents and their wives but also the presidential candidates. Part of their assignment was creating a prioritized list of the ten characteristics they desired in a president. In the fall of 1970, after the spring of riots, I proposed to an honors seminar that they examine the reasons for the social revolution which had led to student disruptions and to the great social changes taking place in America. I told them that if they did a good job with each of the chapters they were assigned, I would try to get the essays published. They did, and I did. The University of Utah Press published the book in paperback under the title, *The Now Generation* (1971), with me as the editor. These essays constitute a remarkable and timely analysis from the students' perceptions of what was then happening to our society.

My files contain a number of thank-you notes from students for letters of recommendation I wrote to prospective schools or employers. At the end of every class for years, I announced that I would be glad to write letters of recommendation for any student who needed one, believing that too many students can go through four years of college and yet not come to know a professor well enough to ask for a reference letter. This is a real tragedy in many of our impersonal universities, and faculty should not shirk the need to help students find jobs. I have had students write several years after their graduation asking for a letter of recommendation. I always respond with a letter that

I try to make as unique and helpful as possible, especially emphasizing each student's work record and extracurricular activities.

Teaching, an always-improvable art, depends greatly on the personality, point of view, and character of the individual teacher. In the first day's introduction to my classes in American history, I stressed that I would complete the course right down to the latest pronouncements of our Cowboy-President Ronald Reagan. I reassured them that I would not expect them to remember dates because there are two kinds of people in the world—the majority who cannot remember dates no matter how they try, and a very small minority who remember dates in spite of themselves and usually become historians. In small groups I mixed lecturing with class discussions and always prepared thought-provoking "why" questions to keep the discussion alive and interesting.

In large survey classes ranging from 200 to 800 students, however, I had to lecture, and I don't apologize for doing so. I'm tired of hearing people criticize the lecture method. A well-organized unit lecture, with a beginning, a middle, and a conclusion is one of the most effective means of transmitting knowledge and of interesting students in the subject of history. I have enjoyed a rather good reputation as a "stand-up" lecturer. In my second year at BYU, I tried to get some feedback from my students and my faculty colleagues on how I could improve my teaching performances, but they were all afraid or too polite to give me any constructive criticism. I invited Betty to sit in on a lecture and received some helpful advice: I talked too rapidly and should outline important points on the board. I have followed that procedure ever since.

After some trial and error experimentation with objective quizzes at BYU, I decided to use essay exams exclusively. Today's students can go through an entire four years without ever writing a real paper, a genuine deprivation considering the importance of writing well. As I have always told my students, no matter what occupation or profession they follow, they will be asked to write reports; and on the basis of how well the reports are written, their employers will advance them or keep them treading water. I have always given my classes some practice in organizing and writing good essays under deadlines.

Throughout my nine years as an administrator at the University of Utah, I had taught the survey course in American civilization, usually during first period, which left me the rest of the day to devote to administration. This course was required for university graduation, so many students from the various disciplines knew me. In February 1970 the ASUU Course Evaluation Committee informed me that my ratings for the previous fall quarter had placed me among the eight highest-ranked teachers in the university. The *Chronicle* and the downtown newspapers interviewed all eight of us, one of whom was my good friend, Jack Adamson. I was quoted as saying, "If a teacher doesn't love his subject enough that he would teach it without pay, he shouldn't be teaching." In retrospect, that statement is certainly exaggerated, but it does make a point. I continued, "Historians should make history interesting. ... A teacher should meet students with eagerness and enthusiasm, be informed and relaxed, and have a sense of humor." Two years later I was informed that I was among fifteen finalists for that year's Distinguished Teaching Award. Although some students complained that I (still!) talked too fast and loaded the students down with too much detail, some typical comments were: "The clearest and most interesting professor I ever had"; "He makes history interesting, challenging and comfortable"; and "You could tell that Madsen truly enjoyed his profession because he put everything he had into the lectures." At commencement in June 1977 I was chosen, along with my good friends, Edwin B. Firmage of the College of Law and William Mulder, professor of English, as one of the three recipients of the Distinguished Teaching Award for that year. It was prestigious company, and the $1,000 gift from the AMOCO Foundation was an added bonus. My citation included the following statements:

> Goes far beyond the parameters of adequacy and strives for excellence in his teaching ... availability to students and devotion to the ideals of education are exemplary ... creates a rapport with students, facilitating their personal as well as educational growth ... possesses an extraordinary command of his subject and a commensurate desire to share his knowledge with students ... an exceptional history professor who has created a legacy of intellectually strengthened and grateful students.

Like most citations, it goes overboard, but I do wish I could write as well as the person who composed the statement. I prize that teaching award above any other recognition I have ever received.

Like most university professors and administrators, I have done my

share of speaking and lecturing to both community and
academic groups. I have given
many speeches to the local
service clubs and historical so-
cieties in the state and in a few
other states. Two of the better
received addresses were talks I
gave to the Salt Lake City
Rotary Club: one on July 6,
1976, on "Vignettes of the
Revolutionary Fathers," and
the other on July 21, 1961, on
"Thanksgiving on July 24,
1849." Local groups celebrat-
ing Independence and Pio-
neer days frequently called for
historical topics. Typical lectures of the last few years have
dealt with such topics as
"Chief Pocatello," which was

*Lecturing at the Hinckley Institute of
Politics, University of Utah, 1986.*

delivered in my hometown of the same name, and "Teddy Roosevelt:
The Boy Who Became President," given at Dixie College. Along with
other workers in the academic vineyard, I spent my share of time on local TV stations and, during the national bicentennial (1976), appeared
monthly with G. Homer Durham on the university's station, KUED-
TV, talking about the history of America. Two other appearances were
as speaker at the 86th Annual Utah Statehood Day celebration and as
the commencement speaker at Rowland Hall-St. Mark's School, both
in 1982.

No one has ever asked me to address Congress or the Harvard faculty, and I can see only three formal lectures on my curriculum vitae:
the banquet address at the Ninth Annual Idaho Historical Conference
in Pocatello entitled "Stagecoach Travel on the Salt Lake-Montana
Road"; the Fourth David E. Miller Lecture at the University of Utah
called "Forty-Niners at the Mormon Halfway House: Salt Lake City
in the Gold Rush"; and the Second Dello G. Dayton Memorial Lecture at Weber State College, "Encounter with the Northwestern

Shoshoni[1] at Bear River in 1863: Battle or Massacre?" After my retirement I was invited to present a paper at the Utah Newspaper Project Conference, held at the Marriott Library on November 18, 1983. "The Use of Newspapers in Historical Research," with emphasis on the interest and humor in frontier papers, was published as the lead article in the Ohio College Library Center (OCLC) *Newsletter* of March 1989 at Dublin, Ohio. There was almost too much anecdotal material to be scholarly, but here are two excerpts that give the flavor of these publications.

Corinne's marshal, Dan Ryan, was a two-gun veteran of the Civil War who faced the dangers of his profession unflinchingly. When a drunken brawl began in a saloon after midnight, Ryan

> was called in to make peace and arrest the guilty parties. He [Ryan], in attempting to arrest Paschal, was shot through the left hand with a ball from a navy revolver in the hands of Paschal. Some say it was accidental, while others are equally confident that it was intentional. The Marshal then fired at Paschal, who was on his knees, the ball taking effect in his right breast, making a fearful wound. After the shooting, Paschal walked down to the Osceola Saloon. Soon after entering the house, he fell on the floor, and was picked up by his companions. ... He now lies in critical condition.[2]

In an indirect attack on Mormon female suffrage, the *Reporter* ridiculed a visiting feminist:

> Miss Emma Garrison, a strong-minded female of the Woodhull-Claflin stripe, with a peaked nose, blue stockings, and on the shady side of forty, lectured last evening in the Josephite Hall. Subject, Woman— her work and mission—does it interfere with that of man's? The audience rather thought it did. A collection, after the lecture, netted thirty-five cents in mutilated currency.[3]

---

1. The spelling of Shoshoni/Shoshone is somewhat arbitrary. I and many (though not all) historians prefer *Shoshoni* while many (though not all) anthropologists prefer *Shoshone,* the spelling also used by the Bureau of Indian Affairs, other governmental entities, and the people of Fort Hall. Either is correct and, more importantly, neither is incorrect.

2. *Corinne Reporter,* Nov. 11, 1872.

3. Ibid., Jan. 1872.

Unlike many historians, I have not spent much time writing historical articles for professional journals. Too many years spent in business, government, and university administration focused my interests elsewhere; and during the years I was back in the classroom, I decided to forego articles and concentrate on writing books. Except for some articles in the *Utah Historical Quarterly,* one in *Montana: The Magazine of Western History,* and another in the *Overland Journal,* my other articles have been on minor topics printed in obscure publications. One which appeared in the annual publication of the Utah Academy of Sciences, Arts, and Letters for 1961-62 reveals my particular interest in the instruction of history, "Improving the Teaching of American History: An Imperative."

It was a long time between my first book, *The Bannock of Idaho,* written in 1948 and published in 1958, and my next books which appeared in 1980. During my three years at Utah State University, getting back into teaching was easy but I found it difficult to shift from writing memos to writing history. I had settled on the topic for my next book during the Peace Corps years and, as already mentioned, Betty enthusiastically researched *North to Montana* while we were living in Virginia. I knew the topic broke new ground and that here was an opportunity not only to write about the interesting and colorful subject of wagon freighting and stagecoaching but also to add another important trail to the maps of the western United States.

I organized the book, wrote the introduction and conclusion, and wrote about 60 percent of the narrative. Betty did an excellent writing job with her portion. I sent the manuscript to the University of Nebraska Press whose reader turned it down with the criticism that it was too long and had in it everything but the kitchen sink. I then submitted it to the University of Utah Press where Peggy Pace's unerring ability to detect extraneous material gave it a manageable shape. Then it was accepted for publication. When Peggy asked whose name should appear first, I asked, "If two men had written the book, how would you decide?" She replied that the alphabetical rule would then apply. My answer was that *Betty* came before *Brigham,* so Betty's name should come first.

North to Montana received a highly favorable review from Turrentine Jackson of the University of California, Davis, in the *Western Historical Quarterly,* whose appraisal no doubt helped the book win

Betty and I celebrate the publication of our prize-winning jointly authored book,
North to Montana, *1980.*

some good publicity and eventually two awards. Jackson called it "significant" and the "definitive" history of the Montana Trail. In the summer of 1981 the book placed second in competition for the Best Western Nonfiction Golden Spur Award by the Western Writers of America. Westerners International chose it for their Co-Founders Book Award as the Best Nonfiction Book published in 1980. Betty and I traveled to the Western History Convention at San Antonio in October 1981 to receive the award. I was presented with the plaque adorned with buffalo horns, while Betty was handed the $250 check which came with the recognition. We were pleased.

As a postscript, in August 1994 when the Oregon-California Trails Association held its annual convention in Salt Lake City, I was invited to read a paper on "The Montana Trail: Salt Lake City-Corinne to Fort Benton, 1862-1882." I seized the occasion to "sell" the OCTA on adding the Montana Trail to its official map, an omission which should have been corrected long ago. I can't say that my efforts were rewarded with success, but the battle is not over yet either.

While waiting out the long process of getting *North to Montana* published, I decided to undertake a history of Corinne, Utah, the freight-transfer point on the Central Pacific Railroad for the Montana Trail and an interesting and important locale of non-Mormon efforts to loosen Mormon economic and political control of Utah Territory. I called the manuscript, *Corinne: The Gentile Capital of Utah*. The Utah State Historical Society expressed an interest and published it in 1980 under a partial grant which the society had received to help publish books concerned with railroad history.

Corinne received mostly favorable notices; the Mormon History Association's prize committee considered it but finally decided it was not "Mormon" history. I must confess that I had never considered the book "Mormon" history either, which says something about the mind-set of nearly all Utah historians toward the history of the LDS church. Should *Corinne* then be defined as "gentile" history? I once considered, tongue in cheek, the possibility of organizing a Utah Gentile History Association for scholars who deal in that questionable historical arena. Of course, I wouldn't join, believing that belonging to either group might indicate a bias one way or the other. I am a member of the Utah Westerners, which does show my interest in one very broad area of history. But even here I must be careful always to place my subjects in national perspective and in the context of the history of the United States.

Another book developed out of my 1958 work on *The Bannock of Idaho*. In 1973 Frances L. Horn, a woman attorney with the Washington, D.C., law firm of Wilkinson, Cragun & Barker, invited me to join them as a historical consultant in a suit to recover damages from some accounting claims for the Shoshoni-Bannock tribes of Fort Hall, Idaho. I demurred and suggested they hire a Native American historian; when none could be found, I felt obligated, because I was the only historian who had written extensively about the history of the Fort Hall Reservation, to take on the assignment. My agreement included a recognition that I would attempt to get a book published on the history of the Shoshoni-Bannock and the Fort Hall Indian Reservation. I was to receive $10,000 upon completion of the report and the court case, plus another $10,000 for expenses connected with travel and research. Eventually, I also spent $3,000 of my own to complete the research so that a twelve-year effort yielded me only $7,000 but that was not as important as the opportunity to write the history of these Indians and their reservation.

The accounting claims case was finally settled out of court for about $1.5 million, while my investigation revealed that a more serious claim against the government was its failure to provide irrigation water for Indian farms according to the Fort Bridger Treaty of 1868. This second case, the more important, was finally settled out of court for $5.8 million, 80 percent to be distributed to individual Indian families and the remainder to the tribal council. Horn wrote this council on May 15, 1984, about my part in winning the irrigation case: "His chapters on irrigation and water became the basis for the water claims which will soon yield an award of $5.8 million." This aid to the Shoshoni-Bannock I consider to be one of the most significant contributions of my life. They have been cheated and abused by European Americans for so long that it was satisfying to redress those injustices a little. I came to know some of the tribal leaders well and was invited two different times to attend the day-long annual meeting held each April in the Buffalo Lodge on the banks of the Snake River. This was a signal honor because only three or four white people are ever invited to sit in on the proceedings. Each time they asked me to speak on the early history of their tribes.

I spent only one day in court as a witness for the tribes in 1981 in the district court in Pocatello under Judge Marion J. Callister. The case concerned the attempt on the part of white cattlemen to keep the Indians from pasturing their herds on the forest lands in the Bannock Mountains around Pocatello, a right guaranteed them by one of their agreements with the federal government. I was on the stand most of the day. Callister finally ruled for the Indians but granted some rights to the white ranchers, too.

One of the most unusual spin-offs of this project was a request for permission from Alexander Sudak, a resident of Koscierzyna, Poland, a city situated about thirty miles southeast of Gdansk, to translate into Polish my article, "Shoshoni-Bannock Marauders on the Oregon Trail, 1859-1863," published in the *Utah Historical Quarterly* 35 (Winter 1967). It was published by the Polish Amerindian Friendship Association in a quarterly issue of its magazine, *Tawacin* (1996), possibly a first for the Utah Historical Society and certainly a first for me. This man has an intense interest in American Indian history, encountered my writings someplace, and has been corresponding with me since the early 1980s.

In researching the accounting claims and irrigation case, I eventually amassed about 7,000 documents and 25,000 pages of material, enough to fill a five-drawer legal-size file case. In addition, of course, I had access to almost fifty rolls of microfilm on the Fort Hall tribes from the National Archives. To help organize the material, one summer I hired five graduate students who made index cards for each of the 7,000 items and also wrote position papers on various aspects of the evidence. My final report resulted in the publication of two books by Caxton Printers, Ltd., of Caldwell, Idaho. The first was *The Lemhi: Sacajawea's People,* a paperback published in 1979 and reprinted in 1990.

The second was *The Northern Shoshoni,* a major work that appeared in cloth and paper in 1980. As we approached publication, I learned that some members of the Tribal Business Council members opposed the publication of the two books. I asked for a meeting to convince the council members that the project should go forward. In the confrontation I soon learned, in the rather blunt way in which the Shoshoni-Bannock can address an issue, that they were afraid I would present a pro-Mormon point of view in the two books, a prospect which they very much opposed. After all, as one of them said, my first name was Brigham!

To quiet these fears, I read to them the second paragraph of my chapter on religious developments on the reservation which included the objection of Chief Joseph of the Nez Perce to missionaries working with his people: "They will teach us to quarrel about God, as the Catholics and Protestants do on the Nez Perce Reservation and at other places. ... We may quarrel with men sometimes about things on this earth, but we never quarrel about God. We do not want to learn that."[4] This statement evidently convinced them that I was not attempting to proselyte and that I had been objective about the development of religious movements on their reservation. Knowing the bitter experience some of their ancestors had had on lower Bear River in the summer of 1876 as a result of the failure of a Mormon mission among

---

4. As quoted in Brigham D. Madsen, *The Northern Shoshoni* (Caldwell, ID: Caxton Printers, Ltd., 1980), 195.

them, I could understand their feelings![5] They approved the publication with a unanimous vote. In a footnote to this incident, Frances Horn and Charles Hobbs of the Washington law firm, a consulting engineer, an accountant, and I appeared before the Indian Business Council to present the final results of our investigations in the irrigation case. As the five of us, all dressed in conservative business suits, waited for the meeting to begin, the chair looked at us rather quizzically and said, "You look like a bunch of Mormon missionaries."

The Northern Shoshoni tied for third place in the 1980 Westerners International competition for Best Nonfiction Book of the year. Ironically, it was beaten out by *North to Montana* that year. As the president of the Westerners International wrote me, "You were your own best competition."

In 1982 the Tanner Trust Fund and Marriott Library published my editing of John Hudson's Utah memoir: *A Utah Forty-Niner with the Stansbury Exploration of Great Salt Lake: Letters and Journal of John Hudson, 1848-50.* This was a major editorial project and led to a second book entitled *Gold Rush Sojourners in Great Salt Lake City, 1849-50,* published by the University of Utah Press in 1983. While doing research for the Hudson book at Yale's Beinecke Library, the Huntington, the Bancroft, the U.S. National Archives, and at all the local repositories in Utah, Idaho, and Nevada, I investigated the relevant gold rush diaries and other materials for the second book, a very enjoyable project as well, I believe, as a significant one. Both books have been received well, except for one negative review of *Gold Rush Sojourners* by a historian from a small Connecticut college. I no doubt reveal my western bias by noting that of the few really negative reviews I have received on all my books, nearly all were by easterners who apparently have little appreciation for the country "where the buffalo roam and the deer and the antelope play." The topic still had enough interest that, at the request of the Aztec Club, a group of university faculty and some downtowners, I spoke to them in 1994 on "Gold Rush Sojourners in Great Salt Lake City, 1849-50." In contrast to the

---

5. For a detailed account of this Mormon mission among the Northwestern Shoshone who habitually wintered along the lower Bear River, see *Corinne: The Gentile Capital of Utah,* esp. chap. 9, "Indian Scare," 272-89.

usually tense relations between Mormons and gentiles, the gold rush-
ers and their Mormon hosts usually enjoyed each other's company and
made mutually rewarding exchanges and barters of goods, garden produce, and draft animals.

One of my most interesting projects was *The Shoshoni Frontier and
the Bear River Massacre,* published by the University of Utah Press. I had
shied away from the bloody subject of this massacre but finally decided
to do it when no one else seemed willing to undertake the task. It
turned out to be a major work for me and may rewrite western history
a little. At least Robert Utley, the premier historian of the United
States Army-Indian conflict in the West, who made the initial recommendation that the manuscript be published, felt that I might overturn
some long-held concepts about Utah history. One was the idea that
Mormon-Indian conflicts occurred only in central and southern Utah,
the Walker War being the best known. In reality, there were some
very hostile exchanges north of the Great Salt Lake. The other subject
was, of course, the revelation that when Colonel Patrick E. Connor
and his California Volunteers attacked Chief Bear Hunter's winter
camp of about 450 Northwestern Shoshoni on January 29, 1862, the
engagement was not a "battle" but a brutal slaughter of 250 Shoshoni
men, women, and children.

The reviews, with one exception, were quite positive. Then, to
my pleasant surprise, Westerners International announced that the
volume had been awarded its Co-Founders Book Award for the Best
Nonfiction Published in 1985. I traveled to Great Falls, Montana, to
the Western History Association Conference on October 18, 1986, to
receive another plaque with the usual buffalo horns and the traditional
check for $250. In his letter to me, the secretary of Westerners Inter-
national pointed out that I was the first author ever to receive this
award a second time.

I was also pleased to receive notice that an essay, "Mormons,
Forty-Niners and the Invasion of Shoshoni Country," based on my
book, *The Shoshoni Frontier and the Bear River Massacre,* and written by
one of the editors, appeared in Albert L. Hurtado and Peter Iverson,
eds., *Major Problems in American Indian History* (Lexington, MA: D.C.
Heath and Company, 1994). The article is well-written and factually
correct.

This book played a part in focusing some national attention on this site of the massacre. Allie Hansen of Preston, Idaho, president of the Bear River-Battle Creek Monument Association, and her group had been working for several years to get the site named a National Historic Landmark. I supported her efforts and sent a letter and copy of my book to Walter Echohawk, director of the Native American Rights Fund in Boulder, Colorado. Walter's brother, Larry Echohawk, had become a friend with whom I had worked when he was the attorney for the Sho-Ban Tribes at Fort Hall. (Larry later served as Idaho's attorney-general.) My letter to Walter was prompted by an article in *Harper's* (Feb. 1989) which proposed that skeletons of Indians collected over the years by the Smithsonian Institution and other agencies be returned to the various tribes for proper burials according to native wishes. Echohawk was quoted in the article as saying, "All we're asking for is a little common decency. We're not asking for anything but to bury our dead."[6] I described the massacre at Bear River and how the bodies of the slain Shoshoni were left on the field and asked for his help in getting the site reserved as a sacred resting place for these victims. It will not happen quickly; but thanks to the efforts of many people, perhaps the U.S. Congress will eventually grant the place proper recognition.

On August 5, 1989, I attended the public hearing in Preston, Idaho, called by Dr. Edwin C. Bearss, Chief Historian of the National Park Service, to assess local and regional reaction to the proposal for landmark status. As Bearss wrote in his later official report of recommendation for the site recognition, he expected sharp disagreement among the local people, federal, state, and county officials, and the landowners whether the term to be used should be *battle* or *massacre,* since the degree of culpability borne by the whites is markedly different. He was agreeably surprised to find that the group was unanimous in viewing it as a massacre. In the visit to the site, Bearss asked my advice about where the boundaries should be, and we agreed on about 1,600 acres enclosed by the bluffs on either side of Bear River. I had already sent him a copy of my book which he followed very closely in

---

6. The Northwestern Shoshoni, on June 28, 1996, dedicated a Native American Burial Repository at Pioneer Trail State Park in Salt Lake City, so Walter Echohawk's lobbying is having some positive results.

his report to the National Park Service. I was pleased to read his description of my book as a "heralded publication."

After another public hearing in San Francisco, where Allie Hansen testified, the Department of Interior, in June 1990, finally approved the site as the "Bear River Massacre National Historic Landmark." On October 19, 1990, an official dedication of the site was held; Bearss was done in by a bad plane connection and never showed up, so I was asked on rather short notice to give one of the two main addresses of the day. Several Shoshoni tribal members as representatives of the State of Idaho also spoke. Then a bronze marker was unveiled.

Just four days later Allie Hansen wrote to thank me for my participation and to ask, "According to the Indians, what my group accomplished in the last four years, in no way will help to heal this '127 year old wound.' Why is this the case? Can you help me to understand why it won't? ... I am puzzled." In a two-page letter, I attempted to answer that question, as much for myself as for Mrs. Hansen. I offered two reasons: the strong individualism of the American Indian which sometimes leads them to disregard help from other Native Americans as well as European Americans, and the distrust engendered over two or more centuries with broken promises, outright lies, the destruction of Indian food supplies, the killing of innocent Native Americans by army and militia units, and above all "by our early disdain and contempt for their culture and tribal values and traditions." It was an inadequate explanation but it was as close as I could come.

Allie Hansen and her group are now hard at work to upgrade the monument's status from "landmark" to "National Monument," meaning that the government will purchase the 1,600 acres and build a visitors' center administered by the National Park Service. This recognition is long overdue.

There were a few negative responses to the Park Service announcement of the Bear River event as a massacre, mostly from old soldiers. One of these men, named Tom McDevitt, had published a letter in Pocatello's *Idaho State Journal,* on August 11, 1989, claiming that "it was not a massacre" and then adding a number of additional historical mistakes. Terry Echohawk, Larry's wife, was so upset that she asked me to respond. My letter simply corrected all of McDevitt's errors, leaving his argument considerably weaker.

The second letter came to the National Park Service from Idaho

Representative Richard H. Stallings, enclosing a letter from James F. Varley of Twin Falls. Varley, a retired submarine commander and the author of a well-written and praiseworthy account of General Patrick Edward Connor's military career, *Brigham and the Brigadier* (1989), also took the position that it should be called a "battle" rather than a massacre. In his response to Stallings, Jerry L. Rogers, Associate Director of Cultural Resources for the National Park Service, reviewed the history of the movement for landmark status for the tragedy at Bear River and then noted, "In his definitive and much applauded book titled *The Shoshoni Frontier and the Bear River Massacre,* Brigham D. Madsen ably documents the case for referring to the encounter as a massacre rather than a battle." I must admit that the Park Service was on the spot and, of necessity, chose to support my thesis and theirs; but it was gratifying that they were able to make such a strong case. Incidentally, the National Park Service told me that Varley's letter was the only negative response it had received to the final designation of the site as a massacre.

And I must say I was gratified by one final report, published on March 3, 1988, in the *Deseret News.* ROTC students and their officers from the University of Utah spent the day at the monument. After thorough study of the site, the various positions, and the military activity on the field, one of the officers called for a vote of those who would call it a battle versus those who would call it a massacre. According to the news reporters, "He didn't need to count. The ROTC cadets from the U. of U., the military leaders of tomorrow, call what happened at Bear River a massacre." In this instance the young soldiers outvoted the old soldiers.

In October 1995 a National Park Service team at Denver, under the direction of Dr. Catherine H. Spude, published a Special Resource Study and Environmental Assessment of the Bear River Massacre Site in "response to a joint resolution by the Utah and Idaho state legislatures to consider whether the nationally significant historic site is suitable and feasible for inclusion in the National Park System." Citizens have expressed their opinions on four possible alternatives for recognition at various hearings, and occasional newsletters are being sent out reporting on the project's progress. Eventually, of course, any final action will be taken by Congress.

After I had spent a dozen years supporting Shoshoni-Bannock efforts to achieve justice from the U.S. government and published five books recounting their history, the Fort Hall Business Council, on August 11, 1986, honored me with a formal "Resolution": "Whereas, Mr. Madsen's work has contributed towards the Shoshone-Bannock Tribes claim against the United States Government for which individual members of the tribes have received compensation from the government; now Therefore, Be It Resolved ..., that the Tribe hereby recognizes and honors Brigham D. Madsen for his work done on the history of the Shoshone and Bannock people of the Fort Hall Indian Reservation." The resolution was signed by Arnold Appenay, chair of the Fort Hall Business Council. I treasure this recognition as second only to my Distinguished Teaching Award.

Over the years I had kept a file on Pocatello and finally had enough material to write a 150-page manuscript. A biography of *Chief Pocatello the "White Plume"*[7] was accepted for publication by the University of Utah Press and came out as a paperback in 1986. I dedicated it to my brothers and sisters, and it received the 1986 "Honorable Mention" Book Award by the Idaho Library Association at its annual convention held that year at Sun Valley. Betty and I enjoyed attending the awards banquet at the famous resort. Again this project was one which I felt obligated to do because I had the background and material. It is not an earth-shaking book, but it explores the character and life of the Indian leader who gave his name to my hometown. The book went through two printings.

In all of these literary endeavors, LaVon West was my typist, beginning about 1979 when she was working for the University of Utah's Division of Continuing Education and later as secretary to Paul Cracroft who supervised activities at Kingsbury Hall. No one could ask for a more competent and error-proof collaborator than she. In addition, no one else could read my handwriting!

---

7. I borrowed this name/title from Frederick W. Lander's description, and it should probably be read much like "Hereward the Wake" or "Robin the Hood." Lander, a civil engineer building an army road to California, encountered "Po-ca-ta-ro or the 'White Plume'" on Raft River in August 1859. His diary does not explain why he chose this appellation, but I speculate that Lander compared Pocatello to Henry of Navarre who, in 1590, had worn a white plume on his helmet during the battle in which his Huguenot army defeated the Catholic Holy League. Brigham D. Madsen, *Chief Pocatello the "White Plume"* (Salt Lake City: University of Utah Press, 1986), 8, 9, 41.

Not too many academic honors have come my way and the few that have, in recent years, are as much a reward for longevity as achievement. In 1976 the Institutional Council and President David Gardner selected me as one of three to have a portrait painted by Alvin Gittins, a signal honor which I especially appreciated because I had always had a high regard for Al Gittins as an artist, a scholar, and a gentleman. He completed forty-two such commissioned portraits before his death. I chose to be painted in an informal pose, since I'm almighty tired of rather stiff and traditional subjects that leave the viewer yawning. Al seemed quite fascinated by the way I clasped my hands and insisted on painting me with this feature. Betty thought he didn't show enough hair on top of my head, but the mirror tells me he was probably right. The portrait presently hangs in the Board of Trustees Room on the third floor of the Park Building, a recognition of my role as an administrator. I enjoyed my conversations with Al during the sittings and discovered a kindred soul as we discussed our traumatic experiences as Mormons. About six months before his death, he unexpectedly gave me a painting of a street scene in Taos, New Mexico, a gift which I have been told is quite valuable. It now hangs on our living room wall. I was really touched by his gesture and could respond only feebly by giving him, in return, copies of some of my books.

On June 27, 1979, I received a letter from the ASUU officers inviting me to deliver one of the lectures in their 1979-80 "Last Lecture" series, a real recognition of whatever talents I have as a lecturer. I would have been one of a distinguished group which included President David Gardner, Governor Scott Matheson, and other state and academic leaders. I accepted the invitation, but never heard from the students again.

My peers were a little more responsible as the Board of State History named me to receive the Utah Historical Society's Fellow Award for 1980. It was a complete surprise to me. Then, the following year, I received the Distinguished Service Award of the Utah Academy of Sciences, Arts, and Letters for 1981, accompanied by the Charles Redd Prize in the Humanities and Social Sciences which carried a cash award of $1,500. I was particularly pleased because of my personal acquaintance with and fondness for Charley Redd. One year I was even an also-ran in the competition for the new Rosenblatt

Prize, funded by Joseph Rosenblatt to recognize extraordinary talent as a teacher and scholar. Of the ninety nominations received, the university administration ranked me sixth on the list. Sterling McMurrin was the first recipient, the only real choice which could have been made this first time.

19.

AN ACTIVE RETIREMENT,
1984-90

In July 1984, a few months short of my seventieth birthday, I retired. I had been a member of the University of Utah's faculty for nineteen years, my most productive period as a scholar and writer, even interspersed as it had been with nine years in administration. In retrospect, I have a few regrets about the years away from the classroom spent as a full-time builder and as a Peace Corps/VISTA administrator. On the other hand, those nonteaching years had been an adventure of a different sort, a chance to experience the joys and troubles of the commercial and governmental worlds. I would not have wanted to miss those challenging episodes and what I learned from them.

During my active years at the university, our children were having adventures of their own. After Karen and Charles Bolton moved to Berkeley, Karen worked as a laboratory technician in a hospital while Charley worked for a local political organization. To Karen's distress, which Betty and I shared, the marriage did not last. After the divorce in 1972, Karen in 1977 married Richard Loos, who had custody of his two little sons and daughter by his first marriage. Their daughter Emily was born in January 1978 and Karen spent several years as a warmly affectionate full-time mother and homemaker. Although Richard and Karen eventually agreed to divorce, he met his financial obligations for Emily until she was eighteen and still helps with financial assistance as she attends college. Karen's career during this phase of her life has been with the Northern California Nurses Association, and she is now a highly placed administrator in an agency that assists and monitors physicians, the North American Medical Management Company. She remains involved with Rich's children, and Emily, who is attending the University of California at San Diego, sees her father, brothers, and sister often.

David's college love of anthropology and the mentorship of Dr. Jesse Jennings turned into a passion. He earned an M.A. in 1971 with an almost straight-A average, then a Ph.D. in archaeology from the University of Missouri (1973). He was hired as the first Utah State Archaeologist in 1973, thanks in part to Jennings's vigorous recommendation. In that position until 1994 he brought public recognition to Utah's vast storehouse of ancient peoples and their artifacts. An energetic administrator and creative grantsman, he has been very productive in exploring and cataloging Great Basin finds.

After two unsuccessful marriages and the births of Joshua and Keegan, David met Evelyn Seelinger at the Utah Historical Society where she is an archaeologist in the Antiquities Section. She has a daughter by her first marriage and is a wonderful woman, intelligent, gracious, well-traveled, and a fine homemaker. About 1985 he developed a relationship with Chinese archaeologists beginning to work in Inner Mongolia on the edge of the Gobi Desert, an area much like the Great Basin. He has spent part of six summers on site, has given a short series of lectures at Beijing University, and will spend 1998-99 on two expeditions funded by the National Science Foundation, then write an article illustrated by a National Geographic Society photographer. He is the editor of eleven books on Great Basin archeology and the author of others, three of which received special notice: *Excavation of the Donner-Reed Wagons,* with Bruce R. Hawkins (1980), *Exploring the Fremont* (1989), and *Across the West: Human Population Movement in the Extension of the Numa* (1994). In December 1997 he received a signal honor: an invitation to deliver one of ten lectures at the annual convention of the American Geophysical Union in San Francisco. In the spring of 1998, he was awarded the Governor's Medal in Science and Technology.

Linda graduated from the University of Utah in 1973, then spent that summer with VISTA helping migrant workers at Fruita, Colorado. She worked five years at the Colorado Deaf and Blind School in Colorado Springs, using her training in special education and art. Linda has an exceptional sensitivity to all people who have been ignored and

Our family in 1973.
Back left, Steve, David, and Linda. Front, Betty, Karen, and Brig.
Betty's necklace is a souvenir of a visit to a New Mexico reservation when she was
editing a journal about teaching English as a second language to Native Americans.

overlooked, and an unusual ability to respond to their needs. She obtained an M.A. in special education at the University of Colorado in Boulder in 1975, then returned to the Deaf and Blind School. She has had some wonderful experiences with these youngsters.

In 1978 she married John Dunning, a six-foot, five-inch service station manager, who had served as a Marine medical corpsman in Vietnam and was awarded the Bronze Star when he was wounded. Originally from Haubstadt, Indiana, he returned home to meet ridicule for his patriotic motivations. He moved to Colorado Springs where he met Linda. A couple of years after their marriage, John began experiencing post-traumatic stress symptoms and is now on an almost full disability pension. He and Linda moved to Logan where she taught for a year at Utah State University's experimental special education school, then to Salt Lake City where she taught developmentally disabled children for four years (1980–84), and now teaches gifted students and some resource classes in Jordan School District. John, who has been a bookkeeper and worked for a medical supply house, has also taken courses in history, enjoys reading and discussing military and Indian history, and makes military miniatures. They have a strong and loving relationship but have chosen not to have children because John was exposed to Agent Orange in Vietnam. Linda's avocation, writing, was honored in 1986 with first prize in the Utah Arts Council's short story and in 1995 with first prize in autobiography. She has also received second place awards for a short story and for a nonfiction book. She has written three or four novels, not yet published, including "Shadow Wife," based on her experiences as the wife of a Vietnam veteran, and a biography of Betty titled "Light on a Sensitive Surface." In the spring of 1998, she was one of ten teachers in the Jordan School District to receive a Distinguished Teaching Award.

Steve graduated from Olympus High School in 1973 and announced that he and his childhood sweetheart, Debbie Shakespeare, planned to marry. Neither had yet turned eighteen, but Steve, with typical Madsen independence, turned a deaf ear to our suggestion that they wait a little while. They have had a very successful marriage and have three fine children: Christopher, Trever, and Amanda.

Steve launched into a career as a carpenter in Salt Lake City, then became superintendent of construction, and later an independent contractor on a series of Prowswood condominiums. I cosigned with Steve on the contract, but left responsibility for the project in his capable hands. A man of intelligence and good judgment, Steve has excellent leadership qualities. They relocated to San Diego in 1988 where his firm, Rocky Coast Framers and Construction Company, Inc., recently reached the million-dollar volume mark.

Debbie, intelligent, industrious, ambitious, and optimistic, has been Steve's partner in this enterprise, keeping the company books and providing many happy moments with her irrepressible humor. After the children were in their teens, she completed her R.N. at San Diego State and is now working as an elementary school nurse while pursuing her M.A. in nursing.

Although Betty and I would naturally have liked to have eased more of the bumps and strains that our children have suffered, we could not be prouder of their resilience, industry, and enthusiastic pursuit of their goals. It means a great deal to us that they might be faulted for over-ambition but never for sloth. All four of our children are better individuals in many ways than I am. They are more sensitive to the feelings of others, a characteristic which they certainly learned from their mother, friendly, and diplomatic. They, the spouses they have brought into our family circle, and their children have brought us an immense amount of happiness.

Betty M. Madsen
in an African robe purchased in Nairobi,
Kenya, at the International Women's
Conference in 1985.

For Betty and me, the retirement years brought almost a decade of good years of leisure with the good health to enjoy the luxury of selecting projects instead of dealing with demands imposed by daily schedules. Betty took full retirement in 1981 after a successful nine years as the university's first thesis editor, then spent a year and a half remodeling our kitchen, installing new cabinets, and generally sprucing up the old homestead. After that, she indulged her wanderlust. She visited China, and she and I spent a week in Barbados and three weeks in Spain, Portugal, and Morocco. We also took a twelve-day jaunt to Alaska and made several visits to Karen in Oakland and to Steve's family in San Diego. Betty was an avid traveler, more than I, and I was delighted that she had the time and energy to satisfy this long hunger. One of her most satisfying trips was to Nairobi, Kenya, with Linda to attend the International Women's Conference in 1985. She also wrote portions of her life story, *Fragments: Autobiographical Sketches* (n.d.), 76 pp., addenda i–iv. It is delightful reading, treasured by me and the children.

Among highlights of the post-1984 years for me was the honor of being accepted in June 1987, along with two other faculty members of the University of Utah, as a member of Phi Beta Kappa, mostly due to the efforts of my friend, Sterling McMurrin. I had not been considered for election to the honor fraternity upon receiving my B.A. degree from the University of Utah in 1938 for two reasons: majors in education were not eligible and, even if they had been, my grade point average was not high enough. I probably would have appreciated it more when I was younger, but I still enjoyed the honor a good deal.

I derived considerable personal satisfaction when the Friends of Marriott Library on May 9, 1991, recognized my "generous contributions ... [and] valuable support of the Marriott Library." Since those two years as director were among my most pleasant as an academic administrator, the recognition meant a great deal to me.

On January 4, 1988, I delivered a lecture by invitation on the massacre at Bear River during Statehood Day Activities held in Logan, Utah. After the evening banquet on the first day, as Betty and I were leaving the hall, Governor Norman Bangerter called out, "Brigham Madsen!" I had not remembered ever meeting him but stopped to shake hands. He asked, "Did you teach a survey class in U.S. history at BYU in the fall of such-and-such a year?" I answered that it was quite possible. Grinning, the governor replied, "Well, I was a first-quarter freshman member of that class, and I didn't receive a very good grade." I responded, "Perhaps that was because your major was not history." "Oh," said the governor, "but my major *was* history." Everyone around enjoyed the exchange.

Later, at the evening meeting in the Logan tabernacle, the governor began his address to the crowd by explaining that he had just met Professor Brigham Madsen again after many years but would always remember that Dr. Madsen had given him a low grade in a history class at BYU. When my Stansbury book came out a year later, I gave the governor a copy inscribed: "To Norman Bangerter who chose to give up a career as a student of history to make some history as Governor of Utah."

During the years of busy absorption in administration at the University of Utah, my feelings about the Mormon church stabilized. The U was a good place for a disengaged Mormon, especially because I had not worried about teaching the "wrong" things. Both Betty and I continued to participate in our ward, Betty as ward librarian. I taught priesthood quorum classes, using B. H. Roberts's *Comprehensive His-*

tory of the Church as a text. I refused to use the approved lesson manuals, considering them somewhat juvenile in their approach, and our various bishops were tolerant. In 1971-72 I taught Old Testament for two years, using the latest scholarly texts. By late 1973, as our last child left home, we saw little reason to attend meetings; but we continued to receive home teachers, paid monthly fast offerings for the relief of the poor, socialized at ward parties occasionally, and kept in touch with our neighbors. They didn't understand our inactivity but were tolerant and accepting of us.

Certainly our feelings of disengagement were not aided by another incident that threw our discomfort with the church into high relief. In late 1972 John W. Fitzgerald, a member of my Sunday school class in Olympus Fifth Ward, told me he was to be tried and possibly excommunicated by his stake high council[1] because he had been publishing letters in the *Salt Lake Tribune* criticizing the Mormon church's refusal to grant men of African descent priesthood ordination. He asked me, Sterling McMurrin, Lowell Bennion, and Ray Canning to appear as witnesses for him. We were all there but Sterling, who had to be out of town, but asked me to read his prepared statement to the high council. They listened in absolute silence, without response and without questions, as I read first Sterling's statement, then my own, and then was ushered out. They disfellowshipped Fitzgerald, then later excommunicated him, as he continued to express his opinions; and our statements probably didn't help him a bit. Sterling's letter, as I recall, argued that there should be a place in the church for dissenters and pointed to Fitzgerald's long and faithful service and pride in his pioneer heritage as reasons why his divergence should be accommodated. Mine read:

December 1, 1972
Mr. Jay J. Campbell
Holladay Stake

Dear President Campbell:
Mr. John W. Fitzgerald has informed me that he has been requested to appear before the High Council Court of Holladay Stake on Decem-

---

1. Each Mormon stake has a high council composed of the three-man stake presidency and twelve-man high council. It functions on the local level something like the First Presidency and the Quorum of the Twelve for the whole church.

ber 13, 1972, to answer certain charges concerning his conduct as a member of the LDS Church. He has asked me to appear as a witness in his behalf, and I appreciate the opportunity to speak for him.

Let me introduce myself. For four years, until a year ago, I served as Administrative Vice President for the University of Utah and presently am Director of Libraries and Professor of History at the university. I am a member of the Valley View Eighth Ward in Valley View Stake and teach the Gospel Doctrine Class in that Ward.

I have known John W. Fitzgerald for about fifteen years, having first become acquainted with him when he was a member of my Gospel Doctrine Class in the Olympus Fifth Ward in Salt Lake City. According to your letter of November 12, 1972, the alleged wrongdoing by John Fitzgerald consists of the following:

> 1. "Failure to sustain the Authorities of the Church." Because the exact charge in this instance is not specified, it is difficult to answer properly, but I should like to say that to my knowledge, John Fitzgerald has never, in ward or stake meetings, by word of mouth, or by written communication, ever failed to sustain the Authorities of the Church. He has been a loyal member and remains so today as further indicated by the first two of "Seven Points of Personal Belief" which he has submitted to this Council. Let me read them:

> (1) "I sustain the Leaders of the Church of Jesus Christ of Latter-Day Saints in their positions."

> (2) "I believe the President of the Mormon Church is a prophet as were his predecessors, and as were the prophets of old."

> 2. "Conduct unbecoming a member by holding the Church to ridicule and criticism through your teachings and publications." Having followed rather closely John Fitzgerald's letters and essays published over the past several years in the *Salt Lake Tribune,* I have not detected any sense of ridicule of the Church or its leaders. On the contrary, his statements have been quite temperate analyses of the Church's position in relation to Black members of the faith. There has certainly been national criticism of the Church by nonmembers who have been highly vocal about the Church's practice in withholding its priesthood from Black members. John Fitzgerald is hopeful that the Church leadership will address itself to the possibility of correcting the situation so that the Church he loves will not be subjected to world-wide ridicule.

3. "Advocating false doctrine." Again, the charge is not specific but apparently refers to John Fitzgerald's advocacy of a possible change in the Church's position toward its Black members.

The fundamental issues involved in the case against John Fitzgerald seem to be two:

(4) "I believe in the great concept of Free Agency as it applies in freedom of thought, of conscience, and expression within the limits of good sense and discretion in respect to the rights and prerogatives of others."

(5) "I believe in the right of rational and peaceful disagreement and the advocacy of change as I see the necessity for it."

The basic democratic practice of granting the members of the Church the power to support and sustain or not to support and sustain Church leaders and Church policy is in itself a recognition of the possibility of change as directed by the wishes of a majority of the membership. The very existence of the Church and the right of its missionaries to promulgate its teachings are dependent upon a free country which grants its citizens the rights of freedom of speech, of the press, and of religion. Without freedom of expression by its members there is danger that the Church may stagnate and fall into error inasmuch as its Prophet, Seer and Revelator will be without the guidance which his people can communicate to him as he discerns what is best for the Church. The Mormon people emphasize the importance of education if true salvation is to be achieved, and the very word, education, means the free agency right to choose. But in order to make a rational choice, alternatives need to be presented in a learning situation which must be predicated on the right to speak and write freely on important issues before the Church.

The second issue is evidently concerned with the position of Blacks in the Church. I should like to support John Fitzgerald's view that the practice of withholding the priesthood from Black members is just that, a practice adopted as a result of the slavery controversy in Missouri. As a student of history, it is fairly clear to me that Church teachings concerning Black people developed on a rather informal basis in an attempt to ameliorate the situation of the Church in Missouri when Latter-Day Saint members came under attack by the preponderant slave-holding power structure of the state. Also, the Church wished to ensure that its successful missionary effort in the Southern States would not be impeded by an apparent support of abolitionism. Because of this historic accident, the Church is now hindered in accomplishing its primary mission to preach Christ's gospel of peace, brotherhood, and love to the nations of the world. Today, there are thousands of faithful Latter-Day Saints who expectantly await a decision by the presiding authorities which will remove this stigma of discrimination and will allow the Church to further its missionary effort.

It is my sincere hope that this Council will free John W. Fitzgerald of the charges against him. As an orthodox and loyal Church adherent, he should have the privilege of retaining his membership in order to serve the Church and to continue his advocacy of change within those limits which prudence dictates. The Church will benefit from having such a devoted member.

Sincerely,
/s/ Brigham D. Madsen

I was, of course, arguing my own beliefs as well as arguing for Fitzgerald. My memory of the good brother in North Carolina who was denied the right, earned by his blameless life and faithfulness, of entering the LDS temple, had continued to haunt me despite the lapse of years. I could not consider the policy with anything but abhorrence. Only five and a half years later in 1978, Spencer W. Kimball, then president of the LDS church, announced a reversal of the policy. This "revelation" came far too late to erase the stigma of racism which had tarnished the LDS church for many years, but at least it came! I appreciated the relief and gratitude of many more orthodox Mormon friends and regretted anew such incidents in my own life as the worthy North Carolinian kept from the temple and the slur delivered to acclaimed orchestra leader Dizzy Gillespie. My better memory of growing up in Pocatello where children of all races attended the same school gave me hope that such an experience would be common for my grandchildren. Meanwhile, despite the great good that organized religion, including my own church, can do, I feel that it absolves itself too easily from responsibility for the immense suffering inflicted on millions of people who have not belonged to the "right" church.

A second incident that confirmed my disengagement involved my perception of BYU. Since leaving that institution in 1954, I had simply put it behind me and had not paid much attention to it. In late 1975 a reporter for the national magazine *Science* interviewed me in connection with an article about BYU which was sparked by the Title

IX controversy and the larger question of how much federal regulation the government could apply to private universities. No one before had ever asked me questions about the school for public consumption, and I answered the reporter, John Walsh, rather forthrightly. In his article which appeared in the January 16, 1976, issue, Walsh said I called myself "a nonpracticing Mormon." I had described Ernest Wilkinson's requirement that the members of our department teach LDS church history which "didn't make much sense" to me, offered my unvarnished opinion that real learning in the humanities was not possible at BYU, but praised faculty members who "practiced what you might call bootleg learning." I also commented on the appearance of the students and the campus. "BYU is so ordered, I'm ill at ease when I'm there. I guess it's because democracy is rather untidy and confused," a comment which Walsh had heard from other people. I rather enjoyed giving the interview, but I have never heard from anyone at BYU about the piece. In short, though I felt no animus toward BYU, the church in general, my ward in particular, or Mormons as a group, and certainly felt no compulsion to make a hobby of criticizing Mormonism in public, these experiences of the 1970s showed me that the connecting threads that had frayed and finally parted in the 1950s were severed for good. Betty and I felt considerable peace about our decision to remain cultural Mormons without engaging its religious or doctrinal claims on a weekly basis.

My post-retirement years brought some interesting journalistic opportunities. *Deseret News* writer Carma Wadley aroused considerably more interest in her story (Jan. 5, 1977) quoting the Associated Press's "Top 20 Stories of 200 Years" in comparison with one she'd asked me to compile. My selections agreed with those of the AP except that the AP had included the assassinations of Lincoln and Kennedy and the Great Depression. I enjoyed thinking about these memorable historical events and how I would rank them:

MADSEN'S TOP 20 SELECTIONS

1. The American Revolution
2. Drafting of the U. S. Constitution
3. Civil War
4. World War II

5. The atomic bomb

6. Aviation and the moon landings

7. World War I

8. Development of the steel and automobile industries

9. Development of scientific agriculture

10. The social revolutions of the 1920s and 1960s

11. Changing role of women

12. Pollution of the environment

13. Development of public education

14. Development of television

15. Franklin D. Roosevelt and the New Deal

16. Thomas Edison and the electrification of the nation

17. Louisiana Purchase

18. Brown vs. Board of Education court case which outlawed segregation

19. Vietnam

20. Watergate

A few days later the *Deseret News* (Jan. 12, 1977) printed a letter from a subscriber which said, "With a name like Brigham D. Madsen, I assume he has had at least LDS ancestors, if not parents. Therefore, I was quite surprised that his list of the 'Top Twenty Stories of Our Two Centuries,' did not list the visions of Joseph Smith." I also had a letter from Ernest L. Wilkinson disagreeing with me that the Vietnam War was "one of our worst foreign mistakes." I paid about as much attention to his opinion on this issue as I usually did.

I was once quoted in an article entitled, "Now Opening to Blacks," which appeared in the December 8, 1978, issue of *Awake,* a Jehovah's Witness publication. I have no recollection of giving the interview but still have a copy of a handwritten letter I received in response to my remarks in which I criticized the LDS church's practice of denying the priesthood to blacks. I said, "Church young people were mortified. They would not put up with it any longer." The letter writer asked if I had been reported correctly and then asked, "Are you a member of the Mormon Church? Do you have that priesthood?

Please answer speedily as this could have to do with the Salvation of some persons." Since I failed to answer the letter, I no doubt jeopardized the souls of the unfortunates. In another newspaper article I was once quoted as supporting the Equal Rights Amendment, and received a letter from a downtown businesswoman, a stranger to me, who thanked me for my stand.

While these mild journalistic encounters were without much significance, I feel differently about *Studies of the Book of Mormon,* an edited work. Everett Cooley and Sterling McMurrin were trying to find a historian who would edit a manuscript recently acquired by Marriott Library from the B. H. Roberts family. Roberts, who died in 1933, wrote a lengthy work in the last decade of his life exploring questions about the authenticity of the Book of Mormon. Apologists described his approach as that of a staunch believer who was merely playing devil's advocate. I could not agree. It seemed obvious to me that Roberts had come to doubt the authenticity of the Book of Mormon. The task he set himself, with his usual rigorous standards, was to explain how Joseph Smith had written the book without the aid of gold plates or angels by using Ethan Smith's *View of the Hebrews,* a work that described the American Indians as descendants of the ten lost tribes of Israel. Ethan Smith's book had been published in 1823, seven years before Joseph Smith produced the Book of Mormon. I was already familiar with the outline of this argument from my sessions twenty years earlier with Wilford Poulson.

Being rather foolhardy, a longtime admirer of B. H. Roberts, and rather curious about his findings, I volunteered to edit the *Studies,* even though four prominent Mormon historians who had been approached respectfully declined to touch this sensitive topic and Betty expressed considerable impatience, considering Mormon history to be something of a scholarly waste of time. McMurrin agreed to write a biographical essay on Roberts; I wrote a long introduction, and added explanatory notes and a bibliographic essay. The book appeared in 1985, published by the University of Illinois Press. It was interesting to watch reactions. Most orthodox members simply ignored it, but serious investigators of the origins of Mormonism recognized its importance. Neither Brigham Roberts nor Brigham Madsen increased in favor in some circles.

Both McMurrin and I were interviewed by the *New York Times,* several western newspapers, and some television stations. Two BYU professors, John W. Welch of the Law School and Truman Madsen (no relation to me) of the religion department, rushed to the defense of Mormonism, not by trying to discredit B. H. Roberts but by attacking the messengers who had brought the "bad" news of the Roberts message, Sterling M. McMurrin and me. Under the direction of Welch, the Foundation for Ancient Research and Mormon Studies (FARMS), which he had organized and was directing, began selling, for $4.00, an ad hominem attack on McMurrin and me. Entitled "Did B. H. Rob-erts Lose Faith in the Book of Mormon?", it attempted to discredit us, without seeming to notice that it was also discrediting B. H. Roberts in the process. In addition, FARMS published a fifty-nine-page affair for $3.50, entitled "Finding Answers to B. H. Roberts' Questions and an 'Unparallel,'" and a document entitled "B. H. Rob-erts, His Final Decade: Statements about the Book of Mormon (1922-33)" for $4.50.

After *Studies of the Book of Mormon* had been on sale for a while, Welch was evidently able to persuade LDS authorities that it constituted a serious threat to the historical authenticity of the Book of Mormon. The *Church News* section of the *Deseret News* on December 15, 1985, printed a lengthy article by Welch summarizing the FARMS arguments against us and maintaining that Roberts was only playing the devil's advocate in *Studies.* To ensure that all interested people would get the correct picture of Roberts's *Studies,* the *Ensign* magazine, published by the church for adult members, also published a six-page article by Welch (Mar. 1986), "B. H. Roberts, Seeker after Truth." This unexpected attention by LDS church publications apparently attracted more readers, since *Studies* was number 1 during late 1985 and early 1986 according to the Zion's Book Store list of top-selling LDS books. Since then the University of Illinois Press has sold out two printings of 3,000 copies. Reviewer Richard Sherlock of USU's philosophy department called the book "finely edited," and asserted that it "will be the one that is read in a hundred years." I recall at least one scholar suggesting that *Studies* and Fawn Brodie's *No Man Knows My History* were the two basic books to be read by those interested in the origins of Mormonism.

Before the flurry of attacks by Welch and Madsen had subsided, the B. H. Roberts Society decided to devote an evening to it. This society was an organization headed by certain "liberal" and Mormon faculty members at the University of Utah and local Salt Lake City Mormon "intellectuals." In existence since the 1980s, it stopped meeting in the mid-1990s after sponsoring a decade of lively quarterly debates, panels, or lectures on current topics in Mormonism. Members of the board asked Sterling and me to appear with Welch and Truman to discuss the Roberts book. We accepted at once, happy to have the opportunity to defend our positions against our two BYU protagonists. Then we were told the proposed meeting would have to be canceled because Welch and Madsen refused to appear. We agreed, rather reluctantly, to appear alone and to present our views without the two BYU professors; but to our surprise, the society's directors announced that they were withdrawing their sponsorship of the meeting. To this day we have not been told the reason for this decision.

In the aftermath of this strange development, the Algie Ballif Society of Provo, Utah, a "liberal" Mormon group not related to BYU, asked us to discuss the Roberts tome in one of its regularly scheduled meetings in the City Council Chamber, or meeting room, in the Provo City Hall. We accepted for March 1986 with the understanding that Welch and Truman would also be invited. Eventually, they refused, since Welch said he would be out of town on the appointed day. Later I received a note from the director of an LDS institute. He indicated that he had learned "on good authority" that LDS officials in Salt Lake City had instructed Welch and Madsen to refrain from public appearances with us in any kind of debate. From the point of view of church officials, that made sense.

In preparing for our meeting at the Algie Ballif Society, Sterling and I wrote a two-part paper collectively titled, "Reply to John W. Welch and Truman G. Madsen: A Reply to 'Did B. H. Roberts Lose Faith in the Book of Mormon?,' written by John W. Welch and Truman G. Madsen, and published by the Foundation for Ancient Research and Mormon Studies, Provo, Utah, 1985, $4.00." My part was a sixteen-page paper, entitled, "B. H. Roberts: Studies of the Book of Mormon," while Sterling titled his twenty-eight-page article, "A Reply to Truman G. Madsen and John W. Welch." I read my paper first, and my attitude toward Welch and Madsen can be captured by just one statement from my essay, "There is an old adage about a trial lawyer that when the facts are on his side he uses those facts to present his case; when the evidence is not on his side, he hollers a lot. I submit that in this instance, Professor Welch is hollering a lot."

Richard Poll acted as master of ceremonies and the hall was crowded, with people standing against the walls. There was a long question-and-answer period after the lectures, with a noticeable number of people taking notes (perhaps a few "interested parties" from FARMS and BYU?). We had produced 200 mimeographed copies of our joint papers, which soon disappeared as many asked for copies. A note at the bottom of the title page reads "These papers may be reproduced and distributed without permission. Not to be sold."

Two months later on May 6, 1986, Sterling and I were invited to discuss Roberts's *Studies* at one of the Hinckley Institute's "Books and Banter" sessions at the U. With only a fifty-minute period available, I wrote a much shorter article, while Sterling held forth in his inimitable free-wheeling style. Again, there was standing room only, and I remember one woman, who during the question period, asked, "Did I hear what I thought I heard—that neither of you believe in the authenticity of the Book of Mormon?" When both of us replied that there were no gold plates, only Joseph Smith seated at a table with his face in a hat dictating a work of fiction, the lady could still hardly believe what she heard. As usual, the session was recorded by video-cassette, and a copy is among my papers.

Sterling and I were both pleased in September when the John Whitmer Historical Association, meeting at Graceland College in Lamoni, Iowa, gave me "its Best Book Award for your editing of *Studies of the Book of Mormon* by B. H. Roberts." Graceland, though much smaller, is the equivalent of BYU to the Reorganized Church of Jesus Christ of Latter Day Saints.

In the midst of this controversy, Stan Layton, editor of the *Utah Historical Quarterly,* asked me to drop by his office and read a review he had just received from a BYU professor who had been asked to evaluate my book on the Bear River Massacre. As I read the review in Stan's presence, I could see why he was somewhat embarrassed. The BYU faculty member, whom I had never met and whose name I now can't remember, had found fault with my well-supported assertion that the Mormon citizens of Cache Valley had been quite supportive of the massacre; but his review went far beyond this criticism when he declared, in effect, that my book was perhaps one of the most dreadful pieces of historical research and writing ever to see the printed page. I assured Stan that the reviewer had every right to say what he pleased, so Stan printed it.

Four years after most of the above events took place when the issue might surely presumed to be a dead one, the Friends of the University of Utah Libraries invited patrons and guests to a regularly scheduled quarterly "Sunday Afternoon at the Marriott" in November 1990, a panel discussion on two books: *Studies of the Book of Mormon* and *Autobiography of B. H. Roberts,* newly edited for greater directness (Roberts had written it in third person) by Gary James Bergera and published by Signature Books. Everett Cooley, Bergera, McMurrin, and I appeared on the program. Once again there was a standing-room-only crowd in the Marriott Library Auditorium. Bergera and Cooley read short papers. I read a twelve-page essay in which I shed my role as editor and pointed out the evidence for believing that Roberts meant exactly what he said when he wrote that Joseph Smith was the author of the Book of Mormon without the help of any angels or gold plates. Sterling gave one of his usual and excellent extemporaneous addresses. After the meeting John W. Welch came up to shake hands and to declare that he had enjoyed my remarks.

Some time later Ross Peterson, co-editor of *Dialogue: A Journal of Mormon Thought,* asked the four of us to prepare our presentations for publication. We agreed, and these speeches appeared in the fall 1993 issue.

In another move George D. Smith, publisher of Signature Books, acquired paperback rights from the University of Illinois Press for *B. H. Roberts: Studies of the Book of Mormon.* For this edition, which appeared in early 1992, I seized the opportunity to add a short "Afterword" containing an important note from Roberts to his secretary, Eizabeth Skolfield, dated March 14, 1932, the year before he died. He mentioned that he had intended to present the *Studies* manuscript "to the Twelve and the Presidency" and had "made one feeble effort to get it before them since returning home [from the Eastern States Mission], but they are not in a studious mood."[2] In addition, I cor-

---

2. B. H. Roberts, *Studies of the Book of Mormon,* edited by Brigham D. Madsen, 2d ed. (Salt Lake City: Signature Books, 1992), 369-70.

rected some typographical errors. I also clarified the time frame in which Roberts wrote *Studies.* The appearance of the paperback edition at the same time as the very frank and forthright panel addresses apparently stimulated new interest in Roberts's analysis about the Book of Mormon.

Finally, in addition to the public response, I received a number of calls, visits, and letters from individuals aroused in some way by the book. The first, an anguished note from a university professor outside Utah, is so typical of many who have become shipwrecked after traveling much of their lives on the good ship "Mormon." (Forgive his exaggerated esteem of my editorial prowess):

> My dear friend, what have you wrought?! Your *Studies of the Book of Mormon* is the finest thing I have read this year, maybe in the last several years.
>
> Heretofore I have only known your trail and western publications, but this new publication is in a class by itself—in my opinion far superior.
>
> What brilliant editing and commentary, what industry in research, what felicity of style. Oh, I could go on, and, since you are now emeritus, you know that I know that you cannot get me a job at the U. so this is not flattery.
>
> No, dear friend. I have many troubles of my own. I am full of doubt and I hate it. Innocence has fled. I am thinking and it is painful. I have not yet reached the stage of regret—and I hope I never do—, but I am rethinking everything and not much is really holding up. How sharper than a serpent's tooth it is to have spent a lifetime devoted to something and then begin to wonder—what of the past, what of the present, and, most importantly, what of the *future.* What now. My whole being attuned to one wave length, and that wave length fading out.
>
> Well, "nobody promised me a rose garden," although I thought I was in one for over 50 years; thought never hurt anyone. Maybe I will grow up. I have been so stunted. ... You see I have no "support group," and it is tough to go it alone!! So I reach out to someone like you to help me through the pain of reconsideration.

I hope my answer gave him a little solace. I also received a call and a letter from Dr. Robert D. Anderson, a practicing psychiatrist in Bellevue, Washington. In the 1970s he became disillusioned with his Mormon faith and began an investigation of the origins of the church. The result was an 800-page manuscript entitled, "The Book of Mormon as Autobiography." Anderson used his knowledge and experience in psychiatry and psychoanalysis to describe how, like any good novelist, Joseph Smith used his life experiences as a basis for the book he wrote about the inhabitants of ancient America. It was an up-to-date and much more critical and professional version of I. Woodbridge Riley's pioneering psychological approach to *The Founder of Mormonism* in 1903. I have read the entire manuscript and found it a fascinating and very significant treatise on Joseph Smith's conscious and subconscious use of events in his life in the plot and text of his Book of Mormon. After several months of suggestions, principally from me with help from McMurrin, Anderson whittled the manuscript down to about 400 pages. Anderson was very careful to get the advice and comments from several of his non-Mormon colleagues in psychiatry to ensure that his approach and analysis were fair and professional. The manuscript is scheduled for publication by Signature Books.

The issue resurfaced again in late 1993, when five Mormon scholars were excommunicated and a sixth was disfellowshipped for speaking in public and for publishing their views on feminism, history, scriptural studies, and speculative theology. Others were called in and a few more were excommunicated over the next months, with considerable negative publicity to the church and a steady barrage of articles and letters to the editor in the *Salt Lake Tribune*. After some time had passed, I was "inspired" to write a fourteen-page article entitled, "Reflections on LDS Disbelief in the Book of Mormon as History." I first reviewed the reception that B. H. Roberts's *Studies of the Book of Mormon* received; then summarized the views of archaeologists in their consensus that the first Americans came to the western hemisphere about 11,500 years ago by way of the Bering Strait; referred to the attempt by New England Puritans in the late seventeenth century to keep doubting members active by offering a "Half-Way Covenant"; and concluded with a hope that disbelievers in the Book of Mormon might be encouraged to stay active in their church because of other values offered by the Mormon religion and perhaps a "soft-pedalling" of the new scripture as history. The article seemed too blunt and perhaps too intemperate for publication, but it relieved my mind to articulate my private views during what seemed to be an ill-advised straining toward orthodoxy by the LDS church. I was gratified when *Dialogue: A Journal of Mormon Thought* published this little essay in its fall 1997 issue.

In my opinion, the LDS church faces the possibility of horrendous changes in the next few years. With thousands of able and well-educated young Mormons busy investigating the origins of the church, digging out letters and documents which re-examine the Joseph Smith story and discussing all of these matters at Mormon History Association meetings, the annual Sunstone Symposiums, and other gatherings, and writing about them in *Dialogue, Sunstone,* and many other publications, LDS authorities face the problem of either acknowledging the efforts of the investigators, excommunicating them, or marginalizing them by mounting an enormous effort to produce and maintain a sanitized history, belief in which will become a hallmark of orthodoxy. The revelation in the mid-1980s of Mark Hofmann's forgeries in early church documents seems to have definitively swung church policy, at least for a time, toward the third option. Many members, unfortunately, know only enough to feel that "history is trouble" and to shy away from the whole topic, thereby missing a stimulating and inspiring part of their heritage.[3]

Inevitably, it seems to me, more and more Mormons will be forced to admit that the Book of Mormon is a work of fiction, the product of the very retentive memory and creative imagination of the mind of Joseph Smith. While relegating such fanciful aspects as the Gadianton robber bands and the wooden submarines of the Jaredites to the realm of children's stories, the Book of Mormon does contain passages of merit which teach moral values and serve as important ethical guideposts. In this it can be compared to the Bible's monumental contribution of the Ten Commandments and the Sermon on the Mount, while at the same time delivering its share of such fairy tales as Jonah and the whale. An institution of 10 million members worth billions of dollars is just not going to go away and shouldn't. The Mormon church has many values for its members. The process

---

3. The "Faith in Every Footstep" commemoration of the Mormon pioneer trek reenactment in the summer of 1997, while providing emotional catharsis and entertainment for reporters and members alike, probably confirmed many Mormons in a desire for "pageant" history rather than "real" history.

of transforming a holy work dictated by angels into a rather mundane fictional account of the peopling of a continent by Israelites will take some time to achieve, although the rapidity with which new documents are appearing may hurry the change along. Most church members, especially the older ones, will remain unchanged in their beliefs, but I believe the younger generation may gradually come to accept a more sophisticated and complex view of the church's origins.

In about 1987 Richard D. Poll, who had returned to Provo, Utah, after retiring from a distinguished teaching career at Western Illinois University decided to write a history of the history department at BYU and interviewed me on October 13, 1988. We had a very stimulating conversation but failed to get around to the most important subject—my reason for resigning from the department. I sent him that section of this memoir, then in manuscript, but, as far as I know, the history was never published. That chapter appeared, however, in the spring 1995 issue of *Dialogue,* then being edited by Martha Sonntag Bradley, a former graduate student of mine, and Allen D. Roberts, a historic architect. In 1993 Martha had resigned from her position on the BYU history faculty, expressing disappointment with the lack of academic freedom there. When we ran into each other at a lecture Sterling McMurrin was giving, I mentioned that she might be interested in reading my chapter on my six years at BYU, and the project developed from there.

Dick and I, though perfectly congenial as friends, did not approach history in the same way. I strongly felt that I had not trained at Berkeley to be a professional historian and to devote most of my life to the field of teaching only to be denied the right to teach "the truth, the whole truth, and nothing but the truth." In contrast, Dick wrote that his own philosophy in writing biography is "that I will tell the truth and nothing but the truth but not necessarily the whole truth."[4] It is these sins of omission by "faithful" Mormon historians that result in apologetic accounts of Mormon history. Dick died in April 1994.

I strongly feel that too many Mormon historians overlook embar-

---

4. Richard D. Poll, *History & Faith* (Salt Lake City: Signature Books, 1989), 104.

rassing historical incidents, using as an excuse their concern that it might "destroy the faith" of orthodox church members. The upshot is, in my opinion, a confession of weak faith—and admission that there are no satisfactory alternatives for dealing with difficult historical problems in a context of faith or, equally telling, an admission that faith cannot survive historical challenges. My son David, archaeologist for the Utah State Geological Survey, and I jointly wrote a paper, "One Man's Meat Is Another Man's Poison: A Revisionist View of the Seagull 'Miracle,'" published as the lead article in the *Nevada Historical Society Quarterly* (Fall 1987). The issues we raise are relevant to this discussion. We explained how Native Americans had, for generations, eaten crickets as a high-protein food and that even the Mormon leader Erastus Snow had said later, after the "miracle" had occurred, that "our people had not learned to do this yet [eating grasshoppers, as did the Indians], but had it not been for the providential appearance of the gulls, we would have been brought to the same necessity—to gather up the crickets and salt and dry them to subsist upon."

We had first submitted this quite serious and scientifically-oriented article to the *Utah Historical Quarterly* as a relevant narrative for Utah readers. But the reviewer, a professional Utah historian and a solid member of his Mormon faith, disapproved it on the grounds that it would be inappropriate for Mormon readers and that, besides, the title was an attempt to be "cute."

While the controversy surrounding the Roberts book was ebbing and flowing, I was carrying on with another project: a proposed editing of the journals and documents of Captain Howard Stansbury's expedition of 1849-50 to the Great Salt Lake. One day while I was at work in the Marriott Library, I received a call from my friend, Obert C. Tanner, who since died in October 1993. I had known Obert for a number of years, not as a close friend, but well enough to have gained great admiration for his success as a businessman, for his academic career as a professor of philosophy, and for his concern for people and moral values best represented by his philanthropy and devotion to causes of public concern to all people. He was calling to inquire if I would be interested in writing a biography of the late Apostle Adam S. Bennion, a great friend of Obert's whom he had always liked and respected. I replied that I was flattered and honored Obert thought me capable of such an assignment. He added that he understood the time and expense it would take to complete such a biography and offered to write a check for a generous sum of money.

My answer was that, although I thought Bennion certainly worthy of a full-scale study, I did not think I was the appropriate person to do the work and that besides I was already engaged in work on Stansbury with a further plan to write the life story of General Patrick Edward Connor. He asked that I think it over before coming to a final conclusion, and I assented, for politeness' sake, although I had already come to a firm decision not to tackle the subject of Adam S. Bennion. In the first place I would not be permitted access to LDS records necessary for a balanced and thorough study of the man; second, I wanted to do what I was interested in—the Stansbury and Connor books; and last, and more important, I have always insisted on being free to research and write without feeling obligated to anyone but myself. Later, when I could not reach Obert by telephone, I wrote him declining his invitation and suggested two other historians as possibilities. I never received a reply and hope that he, who had always insisted on his own independence, would recognize that I share the same quality. As far as I know, Adam S. Bennion is still awaiting a biographer.

I continued my work on Stansbury which required trips to the National Archives and to the Bancroft Library where the Dale L. Morgan papers were very helpful. In the 1940s Morgan had become interested in the Stansbury journals but, after some preliminary work, had failed to complete the project. In appreciation for the assistance his papers provided me and because of my admiration for him as a great historian of the West, I dedicated the 890-page book to him.

Exploring the Great Salt Lake: The Stansbury Expedition of 1849-50 turned out to be a monumental task and was finally jointly published by the University of Utah Press and the Tanner Trust Fund, the latter making a large contribution to defray the costs. The reviews were quite favorable. I was pleased that one reader praised the narrative as "fascinating" and gratified when William H. Goetzmann of the University of Texas, the eminent scholar in the field of Western American exploration, commented in his review:

> In bringing a virtual mountain of material concerning the Stansbury expedition to Great Salt Lake in 1849-50 before a modern reading public, Brigham Madsen has done a great service—one that adds mightily to the luster of his many previous works. It is refreshing to see a work of real

and dedicated scholarship in these days of the nouvelle or lightweight contentious western historical journalism.[5]

At the invitation of the *Utah Historical Quarterly,* I wrote an article summarizing the contributions of the Stansbury Expedition to the history of Utah and the West. My essay, "Stansbury's Expedition to the Great Salt Lake, 1948-50," appeared in the *Utah Historical Quarterly* (Spring 1988) where it received the Dale L. Morgan Award for the best article of the year, and was also published as Chapter 3 in *Excavation of the Donner-Reed Wagons,* coauthored by Bruce R. Hawkins and my son, David B. Madsen, and published by the University of Utah Press in 1990. As a spillover project, when the University of Utah received some correspondence and papers to add to its Albert Carrington Collection, I edited eight letters written by John W. Gunnison to Carrington during 1851-53. This article, "John W. Gunnison's Letters to His Mormon Friend, Albert Carrington," appeared in the *Utah Historical Quarterly* in the summer of 1991.

Finally, in May 1991, I delivered a paper, "Dr. James Blake, Scientist: The Stansbury Expedition of 1849-50," at the meeting of the Pacific Coast Branch of the American Association for the Advancement of Science, held at Utah State University.

My most recent book was published in October 1990: *Glory Hunter: A Biography of Patrick Edward Connor,* by the University of Utah Press. As the founder of Fort Douglas and the "father of Utah mining," Connor was an interesting character, especially intriguing to me because Utah historians have unaccountably but studiedly chosen to ignore him. James Fletcher, M.D., of Salem, Massachusetts, a member of the Connor family, sent me a complimentary note. Again the reviews were generally up-beat, the book being phrased as "balanced" and a "fine biography." About a third of the reviewers have objected to my appellation of Connor as a "glory hunter," while another warned, "Readers should not confuse Madsen's work with Frederic Van De Water's 1934 *Glory Hunter,* ... one of the first books to debunk the image of Lt. Col. George A. Custer as a hero. Van De Water's use

---

5. William H. Goetzmann, Review, *New Mexico Historical Review* 67 (Oct. 1992), 4:423-24.

of the term is obviously derogatory; Madsen uses it simply to describe a man who, more than once, turned from civilian life to the adventures of army life."

The biography received the Utah Historical Society's "Utah Military History Award," presented July 12, 1991. There was even a check for $200 to accompany the certificate. At the invitation of the Fort Douglas Museum Association, I addressed the annual meeting in the spring of 1992 giving highlights of Patrick Edward Connor's life. It was well received despite a few reservations on the part of some listeners concerning my critical comments about Connor's anti-Mormon rhetoric and his brutal treatment of Native Americans. In September 1993 the association published the paper as its memento for that year.

My original epilogue was omitted in the published version. I submitted it to the *Utah Historical Quarterly* as a vignette, but it was rejected, so I sent a copy to the Fort Douglas Museum where it was published under the title, "Remembering General Patrick Edward Connor," a review of efforts beginning in the early 1980s to erect a monument in his memory—finally accomplished on October 26, 1986. On February 17, 1991, I delivered a paper on Connor's life at the Books and Authors Lecture Series of the Marriott Library.

An interesting request came from Kent Powell of the Utah State Historical Society asking me and about fifty other Utah veterans of World War II to write a brief sketch of our military experiences. He was interested in my story in particular because of my one-day attendance at the Nuremberg war crimes trial. I wrote a fifteen-page article that Powell shortened and included in *Utah Remembers World War II* with the other vignettes, by Utah State University Press, in 1991.

At this point I should mention what has come to be one of the most pleasant activities of my retirement—the travels of the "Fearless Four" who venture where thousands and thousands have gone before. About 1984 Sterling McMurrin and I decided to ask two other friends, Everett Cooley and Ernest Poulson, to join us in a day's visit to the village of Almo, Idaho, and to the famous City of Rocks on the early California Trail. This first adventure led to semi-annual trips extending to two or three days each. We have now followed the Stansbury route from Great Salt Lake to Fort Hall, traversed the Pony Express Trail from Salt Lake City to the Nevada border, visited the many sites of Indian battles in Wyoming from Fort Laramie north to Custer's Last Stand, traveled over the Ruby Mountains in Nevada to the famous mining area of Eureka, and especially enjoyed a three-day excursion along the Lewis and Clark Trail from Three Forks in Montana and across the Lemhi Pass and along the Lolo Trail to Lewiston, Idaho. There have been other trips, and we looked forward to more. Dick Smoot, who shared our enthusiasm for "history on the hoof," joined us in 1994. Our wives indulged these boyish adventures of their superannuated spouses until they were curtailed by the inevitable limitations of age and ill health. Sterling died in 1996, extinguishing a light in our group. Ernest, Ev, Dick, and I have been joined by Roger Hanson and still continue our summer excursions. During these last years of my life, I am reclining but not declining!

In late 1989 I accepted an invitation from George D. Smith to serve on the editorial board of Signature Books. Unfortunately, after attending only one meeting, I was forced to resign because of health problems. Since 1965 my heart condition has reminded me of its existence with mild angina when I over-exert. Despite these episodes of chest pains, I have led a rather active life, although increasingly frustrated by not being able to proceed at my usual high speed. I would feel so thwarted at not being able to do something I would damn the consequences and proceed at full throttle only to regret my rashness while immobilized by the angina. Nitroglycerin tablets seemed to give the only consistent relief after each episode.

In November 1989, after an increase in the frequency of the episodes, an angioplasty (using a balloon to expand the artery at the blocking point) was performed, but it was not successful. In June 1990 I had successful double bypass surgery. The follow-up tests explained the twenty-five years of angina. The mild heart attack in 1965 had destroyed the blood vessels feeding the interior muscles of both right and left ventricles, thus imposing nonnegotiable limitations on my capacity. A pacemaker in the fall of 1997 corrected a heart irregularity; it took some time to recuperate and additional time to adjust my medication to control some arrhythmia. I still cannot do anything exceptional in the way of physical activity, but as my mother used to say, "I'm just as happy as if I had good sense."

Betty and I tried to deal straightforwardly with our health limitations without dwelling on them overmuch, but her health problems were always more serious, her mobility limited by back pain and by the spinal fusion. In about 1985 she was diagnosed as diabetic, a condition that gradually worsened until she was forced to take insulin shots twice or three times a day. Although she never complained, the shots and the resulting blood testing were the bane of her existence.

Then beginning in the summer of 1992, she suffered a series of health traumas. First hospitalized overnight with a knee infection, she stopped breathing the next morning when a heart valve malfunctioned. The operation to replace it was successful, but her convalescence was lengthy. The next summer she had an appendectomy, and again the incision took months to heal, complicated by a possibly unrelated skin ulcer on her leg. A hysterectomy for cancer followed in 1995. I was able to care for her at home, for the most part, with a daily visit from a nurse, but from that point she was on oxygen twenty-four hours a day.

Uncomplaining, stoical, and determined to resist her health limitations, she was patient and cheerful, winning the admiration of her friends and family. I moved into the role of companion, nurse, cook, and chauffeur, curtailing my own outside activities to be with Betty. I had no hesitations about fulfilling the "for worse" part of a marriage commitment that had had more than its share of "for better," but I was a little surprised that I was not made more restive or frustrated by focusing almost exclusively on Betty and her needs during this period.

Even with the assistance of home health aides, it became apparent that Betty needed more care, particularly at night. In May 1997 we sold our home of thirty-two years and moved to St. Joseph Villa where Betty could get around-the-clock nursing, while I took up residence in the attached senior apartments so that we could still spend most of the day together. We were very pleased with the new arrangement and quite comfortable.

Then, about three weeks later, Betty began developing large sores caused by an inoperable hormone imbalance, a rare condition that produced an excess of calcium in the blood stream. Early on the morning of June 9, 1997, she died. Ironically, it was not any of the major diseases from which she suffered that took her but this ailment that we had never heard of. David wrote the obituary, extolling her public accomplishments including being named 1979 Woman of the Year by the Utah Business Women's Association. At her wish she had a traditional Mormon funeral with a closed casket. She always abhorred viewings.

We had been married for fifty-eight years, and time has not ameliorated very much the shock of losing her, my loving companion of many years.

20.

A WRITER AT WORK

Since my scholarly and writing life will be the last episode in the interesting and fulfilling existence I have led, it seems appropriate to end my autobiography with some reflections on it.

The doing of history may seem like a remote, scholarly activity; but I know that it touches people's lives keenly and intimately. I have already documented this phenomenon in two cases: in describing the Bear River Massacre and in publishing B. H. Roberts's efforts to look squarely at his personal doubts about the authenticity of the Book of Mormon. One more example may be instructive. In the little town of Almo, Idaho, situated just north of the Utah-Idaho border and a few miles from the City of Rocks National Reserve, there stands a monument which has the following inscription:

ALMO IDAHO
Dedicated to the Memory
Of Those who Lost their Lives in a
Horrible Indian Massacre 1861
Three Hundred Immigrants West Bound
Only Five Escaped
Erected by S & D of Idaho Pioneers
1938 435

Through the late 1980s and early 1990s, I had occasional calls and one letter from people in the area asking me if the "horrible massacre" really happened. They inquired because the staff of the Idaho State Historical Society referred their questions to me. In each case I replied that my research over the years had not confirmed the existence of such a dramatic event in the history of the American West. I next received a phone call from a retired rancher in Elba, Idaho, asking again about the fabled massacre. At that point I decided to make a thorough search of the sources to satisfy myself about the truthfulness of the incident with the hope that the Idaho Historical Society would publish my findings in *Idaho Yesterdays*.

My research confirmed my early suspicions that there was no Almo massacre, and I sent the article to the journal editor, who expressed an interest. While the article was undergoing the usual reviews by outside readers, I met the National Park Service Director of the City of Rocks National Reserve who asked me to send him a copy of my manuscript and asked if I would be willing to attend a meeting with citizens of the Almo region to inform them of my conclusions. He hoped to mobilize public sentiment perhaps to give the embarrassing monument a decent burial and remove it from the entrance to City of Rocks Reserve. Shortly I received a letter from him indicating that he had passed out several copies to people in the Raft River Valley and that their reactions were totally negative and perhaps even hostile. He thought it better to dispense with any meetings for the present "to let the dust settle." Myths die hard. After over fifty years of belief in the Almo Massacre, the Almoites were not ready to give up their only claim to some historical distinction.

Then, in September 1994, my four adventurer friends—McMurrin, Cooley, Poulson, and Dick Smoot—and I visited Almo as part of a trek through southeastern Idaho. I left a copy of my manuscript with the Almo storekeeper who wrote me a few days later, "I was told by my employer you are a relative of Chief Pocatello who was responsible for the raids in this area. I'm wondering if this is true and if this had led or influence[d] your decision about the Massacre?" What prompted this inquiry was probably my suggestion at the end of the article that the Almo residents get rid of the present monument and replace it with one dedicated to Chief Pocatello who was born in the Grouse Creek area just south of Almo and thus constituted a genuine claim to fame. That recommendation was obviously a mistake in light of the strong feelings against Pocatello and his warriors, the supposed massacrers. In my reply I assured the writer that my ancestry was 100 percent northern European.

While visiting Almo, I also left a copy of my article with a long-time resident of Almo and the National Park Service historian for the City of Rocks Reserve at its Almo office. She reciprocated by giving me a copy of a paper on the Almo massacre that she had written while a BYU graduate student in history. She had also concluded that "the Almo Massacre is just a legend," but later reports indicated that she, too, was having a difficult time adjusting to the supposed loss of her town's most venerated object.

When my article was finally published in the fall 1993 issue of *Idaho Yesterdays,* the fallout was immediate and drew national attention, much to my surprise. First, the Burley, Idaho, *Southern Idaho Press* asked permission to republish the article in full for its readers in the Raft River Valley. Then the Associated Press representative in Salt Lake City, Bob Mims, interviewed me and reported on the article and the reaction of area residents and others to it. Mims's report, in fuller form, also appeared in the *Salt Lake Tribune* under his name. Later National Public Radio broadcast his account.

In his AP article and radio report, Mims recorded that he had interviewed the following people and gave their individual reactions: Edwin C. Bearss, chief historian for the National Park Service, "defends both Madsen's scholarship and conclusions that the Almo Massacre never occurred"; the historian of the National Park Service in Almo "is not ready to relegate to the realm of fiction the stories told by great-grandparents who settled in the area in 1878"; Keith Tinno, chairman of the Fort Hall Indian Reservation's Shoshone-Bannock Tribe, "heartily agrees [with Bearss]. He sees the monument to the mythical massacre as an affront to his people's honor and history." Tinno approved the suggestion that the monument be replaced with one to Chief Pocatello who was born in the Almo area; and, finally, "the president of the Sons & Daughters of Idaho Pioneers, admits that rededicating her group's marker, as a monument to Pocatello's memory 'would be pretty hard for us to swallow.'"

In his National Public Radio report, Mims interviewed one eighty-three-year-old woman in Almo who objected to some "outsider" (meaning me) interfering in Almo affairs. Another resident expostulated that Madsen was taking them for fools and resented the insult. Other media also interviewed me about the Almo article. Jim French, of KIRO in Seattle, spent about three minutes with me, discussing the fabled massacre. Duane Cardall and his cameraman of KSL-TV interviewed me in my home "office" and gave the interview about four minutes on the nightly news. A reporter for CBS in New York called about the possibility of a story but may have been more interested in using it as a means of getting to Utah to enjoy the ski slopes. I agreed to the interview but never heard from her again.

I received an interesting letter from Merle Wells, an old friend from graduate days at Berkeley, who had had a long and distinguished career as director of the Idaho State Historical Society. Wells attended the January 1994 monthly meeting of the Sons and Daughters of Idaho Pioneers during which the president praised my article as being thoroughly accurate but indicated that her organization would take no action to remove the monument because it now belongs "'to the public'—whatever that means." With the Sons and Daughters of Idaho Pioneers taking no responsibility, and because the monument is on private land, it may stay there forever or until a younger generation of Almoites decides to demolish it. Merle Wells concluded his letter, "Your observations concerning utilization of two graves (that would have to be drilled and excavated in solid rock before dynamite was invented) is particularly valuable. Your article has accomplished its purpose here; now we shall have to see how we make out in Almo."

So ends the Almo massacre for now. It is interesting that while a supposed killing of emigrants was taking place at Almo, a real slaughter of Shoshoni people did happen, just eighteen months later and one hundred miles east, at Bear River. History can play ingenious tricks.

The entire incident points up the political aspects of history but also pinpoints a perception in the public mind that a historian "does" history for effect as politics is "done" for effect. I'd like to put my own modus operandi on the record as a partial corrective to that view.

Of the fourteen books I have produced, five have been editorial projects, and the work of editing documents imposes different requirements on a scholar than the work of writing a history. Some scholars deprecate editing as a lesser and somehow inferior scholastic exercise, but I have found the research and writing involved to be just as demanding as conceiving and writing an original product. I have always treasured the comments of one reviewer of *A Forty-Niner in Utah* to the effect that he found the footnotes more interesting and readable than the text.[1]

---

1. The text for the next few pages, dealing with the writing of history, appeared first in a pamphlet, Brigham D. Madsen, *The Craft of History: A Personal View* (Salt Lake City: Utah Westerners, 1995), 27 pp.

In conducting research for a book on western history, an author must expect to expend a lot of time and effort. That may seem an unnecessary comment, but my observation has been that at least some historians appear to be satisfied with a rather cursory examination of readily available materials. Without an exhaustive search in every possible archive, either in person or by letter, an author runs the risk of presenting a work that is slanted one way or another depending on what records have not been examined. The proper use of imagination to discover new possibilities for evidence is also a given requisite. I tend to be unsatisfied and have very guilty feelings until I have investigated every avenue of research to be sure I have seen every document that might hinge on one side of a question or the other. In sum, it is not possible to deal fairly with a historical subject without doing this kind of research. One reviewer of the Connor biography actually complained that I had wasted time in "prodigious research." Needless to say, I had little respect for any other comments he made.

My tendency to go overboard in research may ensure more objectivity but also means that my first draft is usually too long. However, I would rather deal with that problem than thinness. Proper editorial cutting can eventually achieve a more concise account, and I would prefer that to going back for material that may have been missed, a distasteful task much like disinterring a body once properly buried.

At the same time, having confessed to my obsession for complete research, I also must confess my impatience with scholars who do not seem to recognize that every researcher finally reaches a point of diminishing returns when it is no longer profitable to continue the delicious exercise of running down one more fact. Samuel Eliot Morison presents the dilemma that young graduate students and older scholars share:

> It is a terrible strain, isn't it, to sit down at a desk with your notes all neatly docketed, and begin to write? You pretend to your wife that you mustn't be interrupted; but, actually, you welcome a ring of the telephone, a knock at the door, or a bellow from a baby as an excuse to break off. Finally, after smoking sundry cigarettes and visiting the toilet two or three times, a lame paragraph or two gets committed to paper. By the time you get to the third, one bit of information you want is lacking.

What a relief! Now you must go back to the library or the archives to do some more digging. That's where you are happy![2]

Perhaps many of the perfectionists in the field of historical writing fear that putting something down on paper and publishing it for the world is an exposure they don't want to face.

Another preliminary research task is becoming well-acquainted with the geography of the area under consideration. While this observation again seems rather obvious, too many authors do not pay enough attention to the topography and nature of the locale of their subject. This absolute necessity was emphasized to me by Carl Sauer, a member of my doctoral committee and a world-renowned geographer, and by Herbert Bolton who was a real map man. Bolton insisted that he would accept no finished doctoral dissertation if it did not contain essential maps and if the candidate did not know well the geography of his or her area. The story circulated in Berkeley's Department of History that Bolton forced one student writing on Jedediah Smith to retrace every route he traversed between Utah and California. As Captain John Smith wrote, "For as geography without history seemeth a carkass without motion so history without geography wandereth as a vagrant without a certaine habitation."[3]

With the pleasures of research behind you, what kind of history do you write? Interpretive, revisionist, quantitative, narrative? There can be only one approach for me. I throw in my lot with the writers who choose narrative in history. I subscribe to the proposition: Tell your story with as much imagination, style, and color as you can muster based on the historical evidence gathered. There is no need for long explanatory disquisitions or detailed analyses; if told well, the story will interpret itself. Try renewing acquaintance with some of the "romantic" historians of the late nineteenth century—Francis Parkman, William Prescott, and Washington Irving. I used to read to my western history classes Irving's account in *Astoria* of John Colter's es-

---

2. Samuel Eliot Morison, *History as a Literary Art,* The Old South Leaflets, Series II, No. 1 (Boston: The Old South Association, n.d.), 8.

3. John Smith, *The General History of Virginia* (London: World Publishing Co./Cleveland: G. Rainbird Ltd., 1966), 169.

cape from the Blackfeet. Even blasé seniors and graduate students would sit entranced as they followed Colter who "flew rather than ran, ... he fled on, dreading each moment to hear the twang of a bow, and to feel an arrow quivering at his heart."[4] I shall never be a Washington Irving, but I have at least tried to illustrate that "truth is stranger than fiction."

How to be balanced and fair in writing history is an ever-present challenge. We are all captives of our own experiences, beliefs and, yes, prejudices, which makes an objective approach to history very difficult but also very necessary. In reviews of my Connor book, one scholar insisted it showed a pro-Mormon bias, while others insisted that even daring to write about such a bitter Mormon-hater displayed a pro-Connor and anti-Mormon slant. Perhaps I was fair in my presentation after all. Still another reviewer concluded that my work was not a sympathetic biography. He was right, but the opposite is also true. It is not an unsympathetic biography, either. I don't intend to write sympathetic or unsympathetic accounts. I want to present the good and the bad, and the favorable and the unfavorable—history based on what the evidence reveals. I am here reminded of perhaps an apocryphal story about the strongly nationalist historian George Bancroft who reportedly once revealed his anti-English feelings when describing the Battle of Bunker Hill: "Three times the cowardly British charged up the hill in the face of the American fire."

With research complete and balance in mind, the next task is to organize the prospective book. An outline now becomes imperative and, if the writing bogs down later, then something is wrong with the original outline, which will have to be reconstructed. I recall that one reviewer said that, as a writer, I was "seldom colorful" but "always lucid." A good outline very much aids lucidity, a quality which is a must, even if color cannot be attained.

A historian nearly always faces a decision about whether to follow a chronological or topical format. In my work, I have usually found that it is wiser to start out with a chronological procedure when the early material is rather sparse and to shift to a topical organization as the evi-

---

4.Washington Irving, *Astoria, or Anecdotes of an Enterprize Beyond the Rocky Mountains* (New York: Current Literature Publishing Co., 1912), 131-35.

dence becomes fuller and more complex. A concise, logical approach greatly enhances understanding and interest.

The actual work of writing depends greatly on one's personal style, but I recommend a simple rule. Sit down, pick up the pen (or turn on the word processor), and start putting words into sentences. Do this for a couple of hours. Take a short break. Do it for a couple more hours. Take a short break. Do it ... Some of the prose produced during this period may not be glowing and some of it may need to be junked and rewritten, but writing steadily is the only way to write at all. While some authors insist that writing is real drudgery, the only real drudgery for me is writing the first sentence. After that, placing words in order to tell a story becomes, for me, a pleasure and even a joy.

I always try to keep my audience in mind. Again too many historians write dull and technical papers to read to each other. No wonder that the best historical writing is done by the Bruce Cattons and the Shelby Footes who, as journalists, learned the art of writing for the general public, and for people who don't know a lot about American history but who are interested in learning. Being forced to meet a deadline every day also keeps the journalist busy at writing every day until, lo and behold, his publisher and his readers recognize that he has developed a real style. One of my professors at Berkeley, Charles E. Chapman, wrote two pages in his diary each day just to keep in practice. Others might profit from that example.

Also, in writing, I deliberately avoid stilted historical jargon in favor of plain and simple English. It is not unscholarly to include some human interest material and poignant or even humorous stories occasionally as long as they are relevant and help to illustrate a point. To some of my peers, that smacks of playing to the crowd. I wonder.

Once the writing, rewriting, editing, proofing, and other chores of manuscript production are complete comes the task of choosing a publisher. Perhaps *choose* should be replaced by *find;* beggars can't always be choosers. I have worked with four different publishers and have had pleasant experiences with all. The Caxton Printers, Ltd., accepted three of my books on Indian history, and I especially enjoyed my relationship with Gordon Gipson, managing editor. Everett Cooley, editor-in-chief of the Tanner Trust Fund books, asked me to edit two books and provided funds to aid in the production of a third. The University of Illinois Press hesitated at first to accept me as editor of *Studies of the Book of Mormon* because I had not been prominent in the field of Mormon history. However, we had a mutually pleasant experience on that book, and I have enjoyed a continuing working relationship with Elizabeth G. Dulany, who began as assistant editor and is now associate director. Finally, my close ties to the University of Utah Press have resulted in the publication of five books. It has been my pleasure to work at the University of Utah Press with Norma Mikkelson, David Catron, Peggy Pace, Nana Anderson, and Roger Reynolds.

Having a manuscript accepted is a time-consuming process. After a member of the press has looked it over and has decided it shows some promise, it is sent to an outside reader. If his or her review is positive, a second reviewer gets an opportunity to criticize the offering. At that point the author must try to meet the criticisms raised by conducting a thorough revision. Having completed that rewrite, the press assigns it to an editor. At the University of Utah Press, I usually worked with Peggy Pace, a most competent and knowledgeable editor, now director of the University of Idaho Press. I tend to incorporate too much detail, so Peggy's chief task was to eliminate irrelevancies or overwritten passages. After receiving the edited manuscript from Peggy, I would go through it, checking the results and sometimes reinserting sections but making it clearer why they were essential. The result was, I hope, a much better product.

Selecting a final title nearly always involves an interesting negotiation with the press. The author wants an accurate representation of his work; the press wants a buyer-attracting title. Perhaps the title that best met both criteria for any of my books was *The Lemhi: Sacajawea's People*. Everyone knows about Sacajawea, while Mormon readers are attracted by the Book of Mormon word, Lemhi. The book is now in its second printing.

With the book finally published, the author can bask in whatever immediate recognition comes his way but must wait a long time until the reviews appear. Any author, while gratified by positive reviews, also has to find ways of dealing with negative reviews. I have always appreciated and tried to benefit from sound criticism and have been largely amused by those few that are dedicated to the idea that this or that particular volume is without any merit at all. With the first two or three of my books, I waited apprehensively for the reports of my critics, but these days I sometimes do not even read some of the reviews.

For at least three of my books, a reviewer for each has called it the worst book ever published, a work without any redeeming merit whatever. On the other hand, two of the three also won national awards for excellence, while the third received a local award. Some reviewers seem to be upset that an author has not written the kind of book the critic would have produced if he had the gumption to research and write a book at all.

In short, an author must have enough self-confidence and conviction to shrug off whatever brickbats are thrown at him. If he is satisfied that he has given his very best to the writing of a book and that it was good enough to receive acceptance by readers and a reputable press, that assurance will carry him through.

This disquisition on the craft of history has probably exhausted the patience of all but practicing historians, many of whom would no doubt argue vigorously with me about the proper way to do history. But in summary let me distill my method to certain principles. First, history is an art, not a science. History deals with people, change is the law of life, and seeking the whole truth and describing it must be done in a fair and balanced way. Above all, teaching, researching, and writing history have been, for me, pure enjoyment—to learn, to explore, and to tell the wonderful story of America. As a historian, my honest wish has always been to demolish untruth, to write clearly and truthfully, and to do so without fear of the consequences.

In addition to the precepts of my professional craft, perhaps the best expression of my personal philosophy, including my deep regard for the United States, was captured in a commencement address I gave to the 1982 graduates of Rowland Hall-St. Mark's School of Salt Lake City.

> Graduates of the class of 1982 and parents and friends of Rowland Hall-St. Mark's School:
>
> To the graduates, congratulations upon your completion of the prescribed curriculum to enable you to pursue further studies in preparation for a life career. To your parents, congratulations on their having lived through the occasionally harrowing experience of watching your efforts to develop into mature and thoughtful young men and women.
>
> As I contemplate what I might say to all of you during the fifteen or twenty minutes allotted me during these commencement exercises, I am reminded that it was exactly fifty years ago this month that I graduated

from a small high school in Pocatello, Idaho, and now, looking back over those years, wonder if I have learned anything which may be of value to you. I must be careful to stay within my time limit or I may suffer the opprobrium heaped upon an Independence Day speaker in a Utah town of the 1870s who delivered an oration that, according to the local newspaper, occupied "more time than the laws of patience justified" and who then "retired with the unanimous consent of the house."

There are certain qualities and attributes which, if observed and practiced, may grant you that success which you desire and deserve. Common sense and early training have already dictated them to you, but it may be wise for all of us to be reminded of them on such formal occasions as this. First, don't take yourselves too seriously because if you do, you will soon discover that other people don't. A sense of humor is nothing more than a sense of proportion, and the mountain of yesterday quite often becomes the molehill of today. Preserve your good reputation which is of more worth than the traditional diamonds and rubies. Family pride and tradition will provide important support to you in this endeavor. What is worth doing at all is worth doing well. When you plow a field, do it properly. Don't be content merely to skim over the ground. Or to give us city folks a more apt analogy, when you tune up your sports car, make it hum like the proverbial sewing machine. Don't be afraid to tackle a new task and remember that a seemingly insurmountable mountain can be climbed a step at a time. I have been writing books the past several years and have made the amazing discovery that a long book is written one sentence at a time. Now, for all the other attributes which have not been mentioned, I refer you to the "early to bed and early to rise" aphorisms of Ben Franklin's "Poor Richard's Almanac." The qualities which produce success and personal satisfaction have not changed over the centuries.

As you look forward to college careers or other training, concentrate on learning to speak and write the English language. It is the chief means by which you either succeed or fail in whatever profession you choose to follow. Through a long life, I have had experience as a soldier in World War II, as a building contractor, as a government official in Washington, D.C., and as a university administrator and teacher and have found everywhere I served that it has been necessary to write reports and give oral presentations. On the basis of how well I performed in these assignments, I have been advanced in my fields of endeavor. I shall never know the opportunities that were denied me for my failures.

The ability to speak and write the English language with clarity and precision is a major feature of any success story. Strive to achieve the mastery of Winston Churchill's graceful and powerful "blood, sweat, [toil,] and tears" style of composition. To ever remind me of the force-

fulness of simple English, I have pasted on my file case the pronounce-
ment found in 1 Corinthians 14:9: "So likewise ye, except ye utter by
the tongue words easy to be understood, how shall it be known what is
spoken? for ye shall speak into the air." Also, it goes without saying that
you must train yourselves in the use of computers, for the computer is
transforming the world.

Your generation faces many problems that mine did not even envision, although as I faced the prospect of finding work to finance my
schooling in 1932, I remember that the unemployed made up 23.6 percent of the population as compared to the small percentage of today. My
semester tuition at the junior college I attended in the fall of 1932 was
only $10, but that amount was unobtainable until my father signed a
note for a loan from the school to launch me into my freshman year.

But there is no doubt the problems you face can be horrendous: run-
away inflation; the loss of natural resources, especially a little recognized
but serious erosion of the nation's top soil; more dependence on oil and
other scarce materials from foreign countries; an unfavorable balance of
trade; the pollution of our environment with uncounted numbers of
chemicals insinuating themselves into our lifestyle; and, above all, the
threat of nuclear holocaust. Despite these formidable obstacles, as a historian who has studied other troubles in other times, I am optimistic for
you. I believe that our problems today are solvable. Even the thought of
atomic war is somewhat ameliorated by the realization that the Russian
people, as well as we, fear the same thing. After the Cuban missile crisis of
October 1962 when the world teetered on the brink of a nuclear disaster,
the Russian Premier, Nikita Kruschev later remembered the event:

> When I asked the military advisers if they could assure me
> that holding fast would not result in the death of five hundred
> million human beings, they looked at me as though I was out of
> my mind, or what was worse, a traitor. ... The biggest tragedy,
> as they saw it, was not that our country might be devastated and
> everything lost, but that the Chinese or the Albanians would
> accuse us of appeasement or weakness. So I said to myself: "For-
> get these maniacs. If I can get the United States to assure me that
> it will not attempt to overthrow the Cuban government, I will
> remove the missiles." That is what happened. And so now I am
> being reviled by the Chinese and Albanians. They say I was
> afraid to stand up to a paper tiger. It is all such nonsense. What
> good would it have done me in the last hour of my life to know
> that though our great nation and the United States were in
> complete ruins, the national honor of the Soviet Union was
> intact?

We can only hope that the Soviet leaders of today have the same feelings.

Perhaps the greatest thing you have going for you is that you live in a land of freedom. When the Americans rebelled against the British government in 1776, under the English concept of personal liberty, they were the freest people in the world, and yet they were so sensitive about their rights that they went to war against King George III about whom one critic of the time wrote, "George the Third ought never to have occurred. One can only wonder at so grotesque a blunder." The American Revolution has been called the finest compliment that the English have ever received. We can be grateful for the heritage and practices of freedom which we have inherited from England.

Democracy is not easily or rapidly learned. Furthermore, it is an untidy process. If you want a well-organized, absolutely disciplined society, choose a dictatorship. Fisher Ames, a patriot but a conservative leader of the American Revolution, once compared democracy to the totalitarian kind of state of his day: "Monarchy is like a proud merchant vessel. You get on board and ride the tide in safety and elation until all at once you strike a reef and go down. But democracy is like a raft; you never sink, but dammit your feet are always in the water."

The oldest idea of political philosophy is that ordinary people can't be trusted to govern themselves. Giving the people control of their government is a positive step because if the people of a democracy make mistakes, we make them ourselves. We are not the victims of any dictatorial domination. We American people have had our defeats and our victories, our defects and our assets, our Nixons and our Washingtons, but it is always reassuring that all of us can be openly critical of our country as well as praiseworthy without ending up in a Siberian labor camp. For two centuries, America has been the hope of the world and still is. While the Russians and East Germans had to build a "wall of shame" to keep their people from escaping the "paradise" of their communist countries, in the United States one of our biggest problems is that of illegal aliens trying desperately to get into this land of opportunity and freedom. Our government once even considered building a "tortilla" fence between the United States and Mexico to keep people out.

Not only is our nation a land of economic opportunity where an individual can rise in social and financial status, but, more importantly, ours is a land where the dignity and the freedom of the individual are more valuable than the prestige and power of the state. We can move around where we want; we can speak out; we can exercise all of the precious individual freedoms. The assertion of the great revolutionary leader, Thomas Paine, is still true, "The cause of America is the most honorable that man ever engaged in."

Now, as you graduates face the years of training and wonderful experience ahead, you have many options open to you. Your very graduation this day from Rowland Hall-St. Mark's School, one of the exceptionally fine schools of this state, indicates the probability of your success in whatever vocation or profession you choose. Choose one that is a challenge, one that is interesting as well as financially rewarding. In the future, as the late Sunday evenings of your lives occur and the weekend is over, I hope that you can look forward to your Monday morning job with hope and anticipation. I now give you Madsen's Law: *If you have chosen wisely, and the job is so much fun that you would do it for nothing while, nevertheless, accepting your richly deserved stipend, then your life will be a real adventure.* Certainly, all of you must be concerned with gaining financial security, but to do so at the expense of opportunities to explore this great universe and your potential for service in it, would be a denial of your role as a creative individual.

Although you may not realize it yet, you will become the leaders of your community, and perhaps your state and nation. You have the intellectual and leadership capacity. You have had a good start here at Rowland Hall-St. Mark's. I congratulate you on your graduation and wish you the best of luck as you leave for the fine experiences which await you.

I signed this address "Brigham D. Madsen, Professor of History." This identification was not just a mention of my profession but also a personal statement. I profess history as some profess a personal faith or a love. It has been the means of giving me tools for understanding my world and also for understanding my own experience.

During my over eighty years, I have been an observer and participant in many changes. Born in the year when World War I started, I have lived through the social revolution of the Roaring Twenties. I grew up with the automobile and the airplane, learned the joys of listening to the radio on our Atwater-Kent, suffered through the Great Depression, watched the privations of the mountain people of East Tennessee during those harsh times, rejoiced with the new conditions ushered in by F.D.R.'s New Deal, watched the coming of World War II from our American position of isolationism, served in the military during that war, shuddered with the rest of the world at the detonation of the atom and hydrogen bombs, learned to enjoy the news and documentaries on the new-fangled television, watched Neil Armstrong walk on the moon, went through the wrenching social revolution of the 1960s and 1970s, observed the problems and confrontations which have resulted from the rise of the Third World, applauded the march of civil rights after *Brown v. Board of Education,* and, finally, deplored the advance of desertification which overpopulation has caused throughout the world as the forests and grasslands and topsoil disappear.

Despite the threat of a growing and devastating hunger throughout the world and the fear of a nuclear holocaust, I remain optimistic for my children and grandchildren. The lessons of history teach us that there have always been calamities and problems facing humankind but that people are very resilient, determined to maintain life and pursue happiness in the face of troubles no matter how great. I have had a full life and regret only that I can't live another eighty years to observe the great changes which will inevitably take place. As a builder and a teacher, I have been able to observe my fellow human beings from two different perspectives and have found the panorama to be instructive, interesting, and very worthwhile. Life has been a great adventure.

Appendix

Mormon History and Church Structure

Joseph Smith, Jr., a Vermont farm boy, said that in 1823 he was visited by a heavenly being, the angel Moroni. Moroni directed him to some gold plates that Moroni had deposited in a hill near present Manchester, New York, about A.D. 421, just before his death as the last member of his nation, the Nephites. According to the Book of Mormon, which Joseph Smith said he translated from the plates by aid of a urim and thummim found with them, the American continents were peopled by emigrants from present-day Israel and were thus the ancestors of the present Native Americans. He published this record as the Book of Mormon.

Adherents to the new faith accepted the Book of Mormon as further testimony to the divinity of Jesus Christ and his life as related in the New Testament. Joseph Smith further claimed that God had visited him with instructions that all the present churches had departed from the original teachings of Jesus in a general apostasy. Smith was called to restore Christ's original church through the visitation of Peter, James, and John, who bestowed upon him the Melchizedek priesthood, and by John the Baptist, who conferred the Aaronic, or lesser, priesthood. The Aaronic order is made up of deacons, teachers, and priests, while the Melchizedek has elders, seventies, and high priests. Joseph Smith, already regarded by his followers as a prophet, organized the Church of Christ (later Church of Jesus Christ of Latter-day Saints) on April 6, 1830, at Fayette, New York, and over the next fourteen years produced a stream of revelations, some of which were canonized as a new scripture, the Doctrine and Covenants.

The new church grew rapidly as aggressive missionaries carried its message across the United States and to northern Europe. Settled first at Kirtland, Ohio, in 1831, the Mormons next moved to Far West, Missouri, in 1838, from which they were driven. Their third refuge was Nauvoo, Illinois, a city founded by Smith. Initially, they prospered in their new home, but mob action, spurred by rumors (correct, as they turned out) that Smith had begun to preach and practice polygamy, resulted in his murder on June 27, 1844, as he was held in jail at Carthage, a town a few miles from Nauvoo.

The Mormon church was saved from extinction by the energetic leadership of Brigham Young, president of the Quorum of the Twelve Apostles, who led his followers across the Mississippi River to Iowa and, in 1847, to a new home on the shores of the Great Salt Lake in what was then Mexico. Until his death in 1877, the vigorous and far-seeing Young directed his followers in the settlement of Mormon territory in the Intermountain West and the establishment of Mormonism as a stable and growing religious movement. Conflict with the United States government over the issue of polygamy was finally settled in 1890 when the Mormon leadership renounced public support for new plural marriages and entered the mainstream of American life. Utah achieved statehood in 1896.

The LDS church, with its headquarters at Salt Lake City, is organized into one of two geographical structures, depending on the number of members present. In areas of sufficient populations, eight or ten wards (the equivalent of a Protestant congregation) make up a stake presided over by an unpaid president and his two counselors. All are volunteers who have full-time jobs. In areas of fewer Mormons, branches comprise the districts of a mission, presided over by a man who is called to work full time in that position for three years.

The most dynamic part of Mormonism is its active missionary program carried on by young men and women who carry the message of the Book of Mormon around the world. They do not receive pay for this work and are supported financially by their families or friends.

List of Publications

BOOKS
(ARRANGED CHRONOLOGICALLY)

The Bannock of Idaho. Caldwell, ID: Caxton Printers, Ltd., 1958.

(Ed.) *The Now Generation.* Salt Lake City: University of Utah Press, 1971.

(Ed.) *Agnes Just Reid's Letters of Long Ago.* Salt Lake City: Tanner Trust Fund/University of Utah Library, 1979.

The Lemhi: Sacajawea's People. Caldwell, ID: Caxton Printers, Ltd., 1980.

The Northern Shoshoni. Caldwell, ID: Caxton Printers, Ltd., 1980.

With Betty M. Madsen. *North to Montana: Jehus, Bullwhackers, and Mule Skinners on the Montana Trail.* Salt Lake City: University of Utah Press, 1980.

Corinne: The Gentile Capital of Utah. Salt Lake City: Utah State Historical Society, 1980.

(Ed.). *A Forty-Niner in Utah with the Stansbury Exploration of Great Salt Lake: Letters and Journals of John Hudson, 1848-50.* Salt Lake City: Tanner Trust Fund/University of Utah Library, 1981.

Gold Rush Sojourners in Great Salt Lake City, 1849 and 1850. Salt Lake City: University of Utah Press, 1983.

(Ed.). B. H. Roberts. *Studies of the Book of Mormon.* Urbana: University of Illinois Press, 1985.

The Shoshoni Frontier and the Bear River Massacre. Salt Lake City: University of Utah Press, 1985.

Chief Pocatello the "White Plume." Salt Lake City: University of Utah Press, 1986.

(Ed.). *Exploring the Great Salt Lake: The Stansbury Expedition of 1849-50.* Salt Lake City: University of Utah Press, 1989.

Glory Hunter: A Biography of Patrick Edward Connor. Salt Lake City: University of Utah Press, 1990.

ARTICLES
(ARRANGED ALPHABETICALLY)

"Albert Carrington." In *Utah History Encyclopedia,* edited by Allan Kent Powell, 75-76. Salt Lake City: University of Utah Press, 1994.

"The 'Almo Massacre' Revisited.' *Idaho Yesterdays* 27, no. 2 (Fall 1993): 54–64.

"B. H. Roberts's *Studies of the Book of Mormon*." *Dialogue: A Journal of Mormon Thought*. 26, no. 3 (Fall 1993): 77–90.

"Baseball Champions of Utah Territory." *Salt Lake Tribune*, 16 October 1977.

"Bear River Massacre." In *Utah History Encyclopedia*, edited by Allan Kent Powell, 35–36. Salt Lake City: University of Utah Press, 1994.

"The Bird Life of Great Salt Lake." *Beehive History*, no. 8 (Nov. 1983): 10–13.

"Changing Patterns in Utah Agriculture, 1850–1960." *Utah Science* 23, no. 2 (June 1962): 46–47.

"Chief Targhee." *Upper Snake River Valley Historical Society Quarterly* 1, no. 2 (Fall 1971): 4.

"The City of Corinne: A Vignette." Salt Lake City: Friends of the University of Utah Libraries, 1973. 9 pp.

"The Colony Guard to California in '49." *Utah Historical Quarterly* 51, 1 (Winter 1983): 5–29.

"Corinne." In *Utah History Encyclopedia*, edited by Allan Kent Powell, 117–18. Salt Lake City: University of Utah Press, 1994.

"Corinne, the Fair: Gateway to Montana Mines." With Betty M. Madsen. *Utah Historical Quarterly* 37, no. 1 (Winter 1969): 102–24.

The Craft of History: A Personal View. Salt Lake City: Prairie Dog Press for Utah Westerners Foundation, 1995.

"The Diamond-R Rolls Out." With Betty M. Madsen. *Montana: The Magazine of Western History* 21, no. 2 (April 1971): 2–17.

"The Education of a BYU Professor." *Dialogue: A Journal of Mormon Thought* 28, no. 1 (Spring 1995): 21–40.

"Edward J. Steptoe." In *Utah History Encyclopedia*, edited by Allan Kent Powell, 532–33. Salt Lake City: University of Utah Press, 1994.

Encounter with the Northwestern Shoshoni at Bear River in 1863: Battle or Massacre? Dello G. Dayton Memorial Lecture, May 11, 1983. Ogden, Utah: Weber State College Press, 1984. 32 pp.

Foreword. Robert N. Baskin, *Reminiscences of Early Utah*. 1914; reprinted Salt Lake City: Signature Books, 1998.

Foreword. Daniel Sylvester Tuttle. *Missionary to the Mountain West: Reminiscences of Episcopal Bishop Daniel S. Tuttle, 1866–1886*. Salt Lake City: University of Utah Press, 1987.

"Frolics and Free Schools for the Youthful Gentiles of Corinne." *Utah Historical Quarterly* 48, no. 3 (Summer 1980): 220–34.

"Glory Hunter: A Biography of Patrick Edward Connor." Salt Lake City: Fort Douglas Museum Association, 1993. 32 pp.

"Howard Stansbury." In *Utah History Encyclopedia,* edited by Allan Kent Powell, 529. Salt Lake City: University of Utah Press, 1994.

"Improving the Teaching of American History: An Imperative." *Utah Academy of Sciences, Arts, and Letters Proceedings* 31 (1961-62): 147-59.

"John W. Gunnison: Letters to His Mormon Friend, Albert Carrington." *Utah Historical Quarterly* 59, no. 3 (Summer 1991): 264-85.

"John Williams Gunnison." In *Utah History Encyclopedia,* edited by Allan Kent Powell, 241. Salt Lake City: University of Utah Press, 1994.

"The Military Experience." In *Utah Remembers World War II,* edited by Allan Kent Powell, 111-19. Logan: Utah State University Press, 1991.

"The Montana Trail: Salt Lake City-Corinne to Fort Benton." *Overland Journal* 13, no. 1 (1995): 19-34.

"The Northwestern Shoshoni in Cache Valley." In *Cache Valley: Essays on Her Past and People,* edited by Douglas D. Alder, 28-45. Logan: Utah State University, 1976.

"One Man's Meat Is Another Man's Poison: A Revisionist View of the Seagull 'Miracle.'" With David B. Madsen. *Nevada Historical Society Quarterly* 30, no. 3 (Fall 1987): 165-81. Reprinted in *A World We Thought We Knew: Readings in Utah History. Part 1: Utah Through the Nineteenth Century,* edited by John S. McCormick and John R. Sillito, 52-67. Salt Lake City: University of Utah Press, 1995.

"Reflections on LDS Disbelief in the Book of Mormon as History." *Dialogue: A Journal of Mormon Thought* 30, no. 3 (Fall 1997): 87-97.

"Reply to John W. Welch and Truman G. Madsen." With Sterling M. McMurrin. Mimeographed publication, March 1936. 16 pp. and 27 pp. respectively.

"Shoshoni-Bannock Marauders on the Oregon Trail." *Utah Historical Quarterly* 35, no. 1 (Winter 1967): 3-30. Translated into Polish by Alexander Sudak, reprinted in *Tawacin,* no. 4 (Zima 1996): 12-20 (published in Koscierzyna, Poland).

"Shoshoni Indians (Northwestern Bands)." In *Utah History Encyclopedia,* edited by Allan Kent Powell, 497-98. Salt Lake City: University of Utah Press, 1994.

"The Shoshoni Indians of Utah." *SUP News* 12, no. 4 (July-August 1965): 8-9.

"Stansbury's Expedition to the Great Salt Lake, 1849-50." *Utah Historical Quarterly* 56, no. 2 (Spring 1988): 148-59.

"Tribute: Jack Adamson." Pamphlet for Adamson Memorial Service, University of Utah, October 1975, 21-25.

"The Use of Early Western Newspapers in Historical Research." *OCLC [Ohio College Library Center] Newsletter,* no. 178 (March-April 1989): 19-25.

Index

A

Aalborg, Denmark, 24

Across the West: Human Population Movement in the Extension of the Numa, 340

Adair, Arthur Clinton, 100, 102-4

Adams, J., 2

Adamson, Jack, 266, 322

Addy, George, 199

Adix, Shauna, 313

African-Americans. *See* blacks; Madsen, Brigham D., ethnic/racial tolerance

Agent Orange, 342

Alameda, ID, 22, 45-47, 58, 60-61

Albany, NY, 19

Albertson, NC, 96

Alexandria, VA, 261

Algie Ballif Society, 353

Allen, Frederick Lewis, 57

Allred, Janice Merrill, 31

Almo, ID, 363-70

Almo "massacre," 367-70

Alta Bates Hospital, 148

Altamont, TN, 86

Amager, Denmark, 27

Ambato, Ecuador, 256

America, 167

American Association for the Advancement of Science, 362

American Falls, ID, 124, 129

American Geophysical Union, 340

American Historical Association, 140, 190

American Institute of Architects, 240

American International Development (AID), 261-62

American Revolution, 349

Ames, Fisher, 379

Amherst University, 274

Ammon, ID, 196

AMOCO Foundation, 322

Amos and Andy, 58

Ancient America and the Book of Mormon, 193

Andersen, Jerry, 295-96, 305, 307, 309

Anderson, Andy, 145

Anderson, George, 167, 168

Anderson, Nana, 375

Anderson, Robert D., 356-57

Andrews, Mila, 7

Andrews, William M., 5

Angell, Truman, 19

Angleman, Sidney, 274

Annie Clark Tanner Trust Fund, 310

anti-intellectualism, in Mormonism, 221

Appenay, Arnold, 335

Arecibo, PR, 260

Arizona State University, 253

Armstrong, Neil, 380

Arrington, Leonard J., 249

Ashville, NC, 104

Associated Press, 369

Astoria, 373

Atiya, Aziz, 276, 297

Atlanta, GA, 161

Atlantic Monthly, 117

Atwater-Kent radio, 380

Australia, 304

Autobiography of B. H. Roberts, 355

"Autobiography of an Ex-Builder, The," 236

Awake, 350

Aztec Club, 330

B

"B. H. Roberts, His Final Decade: Statements about the Book of Mormon (1922-33)," 352

"B. H. Roberts, Seeker after Truth," 352

B. H. Roberts Society, 352-53

"B. H. Roberts: Studies of the Book of Mormon," 353, 355

Backman (missionary), 75

Bad Munster, Germany, 168

Bad Tolz, Germany, 168-69, 172, 179-80

Bagley, Wendell, 302

Bales, Willard, 129, **130,** 131

Ballard, Melvin J., 100, 109

Bamberg, Germany, 152, 168

Bancroft, George, 373

Bancroft Library, 140, 330, 361

Bangerter, Norman, 344

Bannock (tribe). *See* Shoshone/Shoshoni-Bannock

Bannock of Idaho, The, 217, 325, 327

"Bannock Indians in Northwest History, 1805-1900, The," 195

Bannock Mountains, 328

Barbados, 343

Barker, Anson, 111

Barnett, John R., 270

Barnhill (of Hampstead, NC), 109, 111

Barton, Peter, 27

Baswa, Rajasthan, India, 266, 301

Batchelor, Earl, 168

Battle of Bunker Hill, 373

Bavaria, Germany, 169

Bay, Paul, 288

Bear Hunter (Chief), 331

Bear River-Battle Creek Monument Association, 332

Bear River Massacre, 330-34, 344, 370

Bear River Massacre National Historic Landmark, 333

Bearry, Annie Laurie, 305

Bearss, Edwin C., 332-33, 369

Beaufort, NC, 96, 109, 111

Beaver, Johnny, 305

Bedwell, Bud, 129, **130,** 131

Beeley, Arthur L., 116-17

beer, 30, 50, 57-60. *See also* Word of Wisdom

Beijing University, 340

Beinecke Library, 330

Bellevue, Washington, 356

"Bells, The," 62

Bennion, Adam S., 360-61

Bennion, Lowell, 302, 345

Benson, Raymond, 62

Bentley, Ellis, 46, 60

Bentley, Harold, 269

Bergera, Gary James, 355

Berkeley, CA, 153, 156-57, 281

Berkeley Ward (LDS), 196

Berlin (historian), 171

Bethel, Alaska, 301

Blackfeet (tribe), 373-74

Blackfoot, ID, 123, 129, 130

blacks, in Pocatello, 55; baptized in Virginia, 85-86; banned from LDS priesthood until 1978, 86, 106-7, 230, 345-48; discriminated against at BYU, 202. *See also* Madsen, Brigham D., ethnic/racial toleration

Bliss, Robert, 288-89

Blue (Chief), 100

Blyler, Bill, 172, 173, 181

Bo-bahoyo, Ecuador, 256

Boehm, Robert, 306

Boise, ID, 210

Bolton, Charles, 301-2, 339

Bolton, Herbert Eugene, 117, 139, 143-45, 193, 373

Bolton, Karen Madsen. *See* Loos, Karen Madsen Bolton

Book of Abraham, 297

Book of Knowledge, The, 48, 54

Book of Mormon, 14, 18, 78, 96, 100, 101, 103, 193, 212, 219-20, 231, 232, 367, 375, 383; historicity of, 351-59

Book of Mormon as Autobiography, The, 351, 356-57

Books and Authors Lecture Series, 363

"Books and Banter," 354

Boone, Daniel, 76

Boss, Gordon, 284

Boston, MA, 1, 2, 15, 253

Boulder, CO, 341

Bountiful, UT, 235

Bowen, Albert E., 194

Bowen, Catherine Drinker, 191, 247

Bower, B. M., 54

Boyd, George, 191-93

Boyden, John, 204

Bradford, Blain, 284

Bradley, Martha Sonntag, 359

Bradt, Carl. *See* Madsen, Carl

Bradt, Mads, 24

Brand, Max, 54

Bremerhaven, Germany, 182

Briggs, Irene, 199

Briggs, John, 17

Briggs, Ruth Butterworth, 17

Brigham and the Brigadier, 334

Brigham Young, the Colonizer, 193

Brigham Young Academy/ University, 39, 100, 132, 167, 186, 188, 190, 194-228, 235, 248, 309-10, 312, 314, 344, 348-49, 352, 354, 359; academic freedom at, 194, 197-98, 221, 225-26, 271, 349. *See also* Madsen, Brigham D., at BYU

Brighton, England, 11

Brill, Sam, 259

Brinton, Reed, 293

Bristol, TN-VA, 77, 79, 83, 84, 90, 92, 100, 104

Brodie, Fawn, 352

Brooks, Juanita, 213

Brown (of Magna, UT), 37

Brown, Arthur, 248, 267

Brown, Charlie, 281

Brown v. Board of Education, 350, 381

Brumbaugh, W. Donald, 270

Brussels, Belgium, 181

Buchanan, James, 7

Burke, Charles C., 164-65

Burley, ID, 369

Burned-Over District, The, 218

Burroughs, Edgar Rice, 54
Bushnell, Lucille, 202
Bushnell, Merrill, 202, 229
Bybee, TN, 78

C

Cahoon, Daniel, 16
Caldwell, Gaylon, 202
Caldwell, ID, 217, 329
Caldwell, L. S., 123, 126
Caldwell, "Lefty," 129, **130**
Caldwell, Vickie, 202
California State Historical Society, 246
California Trail, 363
California Volunteers, 16, 330
Callister, Marion J., 328
Callister, Thomas, 5
Calvert, H. J., 245
Cammack (of Pingree, ID), 129, **130**
Camp Floyd, UT, 7, 16
Camp Pall Mall, France, 167
Camp Pickett, VA, 167, 172
Camp Roberts, CA, 151-57
Campbell (minister), 89-90
Campbell, Dewey, 161, 172, 173
Campbell, Jay J., 345
Camper, Margaret Delilah Julina
    Oakley Whitaker Hill, 88
Canning, Lois, 202, 230
Canning, Ray, 202, 218, 230, 345
Carboni (Berkeley), 142
Cardall, Duane, 369
Carlson (Mrs.), 285
Carr, William, 198
Carrington, Albert, 362
Carruthers, Dick ("One Nail")
    (pseud.), 246
Carter, Annie (Ann) LaRae Madsen,
    20, 42, **45,** 52, 65, 68, **69,** 196

Carter, Denise, 196
Carter, Eldon, 196
Carter, James, 196
Carter, John, 245
Carter, Kathleen, 196
Carter, Peggy, 196
Carter, Robert, 24, 196
Carthage, IL, 384
Castleton, Kenneth, 298
Catawba Nation, 100
Catmull, George, 300
Catron, David, 375
Catton, Bruce, 190, 374
Caxton Printers, Ltd., 217, 329, 375
Cazier, Stan, 249
CBS, 369
Cedar City, UT, 213
Celina, TN, 90
Central Pacific Railroad, 327
Century of Progress Exposition, 74
Chaffin, Lavor, 272
Chamberlain, Von Del, 319
Chapman, Charles Edward, 140, 374
Chapple, Max, 82
Chase, Daryl, 250
Chattanooga Branch, TN, 77, 80
Chaulnes, Germany, 168
Chicago, IL, 74, 162, 182, 265-67, 307
Chief Pocatello the "White Plume," 335
Christensen, Harold, 229
Christensen, LaVonda, 230
Christensen, P. A., 199, 208-9, 226-27
Christian (minister), 89-90
Church of Christ (Campbellite), 78, 89
Church of Jesus Christ of Latter-day
    Saints, doctrines of, 2, 30, 31,
    91, 223, 273; missionaries and
    methods, 75-87, 84-86, 89-92,
    101-2, 104, 252, 263, 384;

practices, 3, 106, 231; structure, 345, 383-84. terms, 95; See also Book of Mormon; Madsen, Brigham D., attitudes toward Mormonism; Smith, Joseph; Word of Wisdom

Church News, 352

Churchill, Winston, 176, 181, 377

Cincinnati, OH, 6-7

Circle Valley, UT, 6

City of Rocks National Reserve, 363, 367-68

Civil War, 324, 349

Clancy, Dick, 256, 257

Clark, J. Reuben, 197, 203-4, 211

Clarkston, UT, 28

Clawson, Rudger, 210-11

Clayton, James, 313

Clayton, William, 4

Clear Creek, OH, 6

Clouse (of Tennessee), 81

Cluff, Dale, 305, 306

Clyde, Ed, 293

Coffin, H. C., 46

Colda (Coldy), South Wales, 11

Collard, Catherine, 295, 298

College of Eastern Utah, 310

Colombia, 255, 259

Colorado Deaf and Blind School, 340-41

Colorado Springs, CO, 340, 341

Colter, John, 373-74

Columbus, GA, 157, 161

Comprehensive History of the Church of Jesus Christ of Latter-day Saints, 220, 344-45

Concord, MA, 253

Connor, Patrick Edward, 16, 330, 334, 361, 362, 371, 373

Conover, A. G., 5

Cook, Melvin, 219

Cooley, Everett L., 188, 248, 305, 310, 351, 355, 363-64, 368, 374

Copeland, Joe, 84

Corinne, UT, 324, 327

Corinne: The Gentile Capital of Utah, 327

Corinne Reporter, 324

Cornwall, Bruce, 197

Cornwall, Jaclyn McAllister, 196-97

Cornwall, Janet, 197

Cornwall, Kenneth, 197

Cornwall, Marie, 197

Cornwall, Michelle, 197

Cornwall, Stephen, 197

Cornwall, Stewart, 197

Coronado, Juan Vasquez de, 140

Costa Rica, 258

Costigan, Giovanni M. D. G., 70-71, 117, 187

Cottam, Walter, 290

Courtland, Leslie, 289

Cracroft, Paul, 335

Craft of History: A Personal View, The, 370

Crampton, Gregory, 247

Crane, Alice (b. 1870), 17

Crane, Alice Davis, 15-17, 20

Crane, Annie. *See* Madsen, Annie Crane

Crane, Brigham, 17, 19

Crane, Carrie, 17

Crane, Charles, 17

Crane, Elizabeth Stewart, **17,** 17-20, 28, 33, 35

Crane, Esther, 17

Crane, Fannie, 17

Crane, Franklin, 17

Crane, George, 11
Crane, Heber, 17
Crane, Hyrum, 17
Crane, James (b. 1866), 17
Crane, James (paternal
    great-grandfather), 11–20, **12**
Crane, Mary, 17
Crane, Rachel Briggs, 17, 18, 20
Crane, Rebecca (b. 1873), 17
Crane, Rebecca Miller, 22
Crane, Sarah, 17
Crane, William, 17, 22
Creer, Leland, 247
Crockett, Allan, 229
Crockett, Eulalia, 229
Cross, Bud, 291
Cross, Whitney, 218–19
Crus Brothers, 245
Cuenca, Ecuador, 256
Curling, 15
Curling, Sanders, 15
Curtis, Bud, 232–33
Curtis brothers (ministers), 90–91
Cushing, Charley, 39
Cushing, Chester Samuel, 38, 57
Cushing, Daniel, 1
Cushing, Francis, 57
Cushing, Heber Carlis, 38
Cushing, Helen Jeannette Murray, 4, 5
Cushing, Henry Ellis, 38
Cushing, Hilda, 57
Cushing, Hosea, 1–5, 212
Cushing, Hosea Philip, 5–6, 9, 38
Cushing, Lucrishey [Lucrezia] Vilate.
    See Hanson, Lucrishey Vilate
    Cushing
Cushing, Lydia. *See* Madsen, Lydia
    Cushing
Cushing, Mary C. Rundlett, 1, 2

Cushing, Mary Emma. *See* Newland,
    Mary Emma Cushing
Cushing, Myrtle. *See* Peterson, Myrtle
    Cushing
Cushing, Philip A., 1
Cushing, Philip Hosea, 38
Cushing, Phoebe Jane, 38
Cushing, Phoebe Nisonger, 6–9, 38, 53
Cushing, Samuel Roswell, 5
Cushing, Sarah Helen, 38
Cushing, William Ellis, 5
Cushing, William Heaman, 39
Custer's Last Stand, 364

D

D-Day, 156, 157
Daley, George, 235
Dalglicsh, Betty, 117–18
Dalgliesh, Harold, 117–18
David E. Miller Lecture, 323
Davis, Charley, 110–12
Davis, Earl, 110, 111
Davis, Elizabeth Cadwallader, 15
Davis, John, 15
Davis, Joseph, 15–16
Davis, Ted E., 281, 299
Davis, William, 15–16
Dayton, Dello G., 188
Decline of the West, 71
Deep Run, NC, 99, 102
Dello G. Dayton Memorial Lecture,
    323
Delta, UT, 116
Dempsey, Jack, 65
de Nevers, Noel, 288
Denman, Richard, 304, 307–8
Denver, CO, 233
Denver & Rio Grande Railroad, 27
Deseret Farmer, 75

Deseret News, 18, 48, 75, 272, 334, 349, 350, 352

Detroit, MI, 289

Dewey, John, 116

Dialogue: A Journal of Mormon Thought, 355, 357-58, 359

Diamond, UT, 9

Dickens, Charles, 11

"Did B. H. Roberts Lose Faith in the Book of Mormon?," 352

Dix, Fae, 272

Dixie College, 310, 323

Dixon, John, 300

Doenitz, Karl, 178-79

Doyle, TN, 89

"Dr. James Blake, Scientist: The Stansbury Expedition of 1849-50," 362

Driscoll, Janet, 255

Dry Creek, TN, 86

Dublin, Ohio, 324

Dulany, Elizabeth G., 375

Dunning, John, 341-42

Dunning, Linda Madsen, 218, **230,** 231, 234, 248, 251, 260, 261, 267, 302, 340-42, **341,** 343

Durham, G. Homer, 323

Dwyer, Thomas J., 162

E

Earl, Boyd, 124, 129, 135

"Early History of the Upper Snake River Valley, The," 141

Echo Canyon, UT, 7, 9, 17

Echohawk, Larry, 332, 333

Echohawk, Terry, 333

Echohawk, Walter, 332

Ecuador, 253, 255, 256

Edison, Thomas, 350

Edwards, William F., 214

Egan, Howard, 4

Elba, ID, 367

Eldredge, Christine, 196

Eldredge, Diana, 196

Eldredge, Kathryn, 196

Eldredge, Kelly, 196

Eldredge, Phyllis Madsen, 20, 42, **45,** 65, 68, **69,** 196

Eldredge, Timothy, 196

Ellsworth, S. George, 188, 248, 249

Emerson, Ralph Waldo, 62

Emery, Alfred (Fred), 275-77, 302-3, 310

"Encounter with the Northwestern Shoshoni at Bear River in 1863: Battle or Massacre?," 323

Engh, Hank, 233

Engh Floral Company, 233

Ensign, 352

Enterprise, UT, 79

Erickson, Martin, 281

Essentials of Church History, 220

Eureka, NV, 364

Evans, Richard L., 293

Evans & Sutherland, 285

Evanston, Wyoming, 63

Excavation of the Donner-Reed Wagons, 340; article, 362

Exploring the Fremont, 340

Exploring the Great Salt Lake: The Stansbury Expedition of 1849-50, 344, 360-62

Eyring, Henry, 191

Eyring, LaReal, 191

Eyring, Le Roy, 191

F

Fairview, ID. *See* Alameda, ID

"Faith in Every Footstep," 358

Fancher train, 213

Far West, MO, 383

Farmington, UT, 272

FARMS. *See* Foundation for Ancient Research and Mormon Studies

Fayette, NY, 383

"Fearless Four," 363

Federal Bureau of Investigation, 292

Federal Home Administration, 236, 238, 240-41, 244

Ferguson, Glen, 253-54, 265

Ferguson, Thomas, 193

Fetzer (army), 169

Fielding, Kent, 199, 204

"Finding Answers to B. H. Roberts' Questions and an 'Unparallel,'" 352

Fink, Lily, 305

Finlayson, James, 27

Firmage, Edwin B., 322

Firth, ID, 129

Fish Lake, UT, 5

Fisher, Albert, 213

Fitzgerald, John W., 230, 232, 234, 345-48

Fitzgerald, Mary, 230

Flagstaff, AZ, 310

Fletcher, Faye, 297

Fletcher, James C., 274-77, 279-81, 283-84, 290-93, 295-99, 300, 302, 362

Foote, Shelby, 374

Fort Benning, GA, 156, 157-67

Fort Bridger Treaty (1868), 328

Fort Douglas, 16, 269, 285, 362

Fort Douglas Club, 300, 303

Fort Douglas Museum Association, 363

Fort Gunnison, UT, 5

Fort Hall Business Council, 335

Fort Hall Reservation (Idaho), 130, 204, 324, 327, 329, 332, 335, 363, 369

Fort Laramie, WY, 364

Fort Sheridan, IL, 182

Forty-Niner in Utah, A, 370

"Forty-Niners at the Mormon Halfway House: Salt Lake City in the Gold Rush," 323

Foundation for Ancient Research and Mormon Studies (FARMS), 352, 353-54

Founder of Mormonism, The, 357

Fragments: Autobiographical Sketches, 343

Frankfurt, Germany, 170-71

Franklin, Benjamin, 377

French, Jim, 369

Freyre, Gilberto, 189

"From Christmases Past...," 48

Frost, Jack, 253

Fruita, CO, 340

Fueston, Verne, Sr., and wife, 87-88; and son, 88

Fulford, Mason G., 111

G

Gainsboro, TN, 78

Gannen, John Swenson, 84

Garden City, ID, 196

Gardner, David Pierpont, 314, 319, 336

Garfield, UT, 200

Garmisch-Partenkirchen, Germany, 172

Garrett, Clarence, 66

Garrett, Oscar, 66

Garrett, Sam, 51, 66

Garrett Freight Lines, 66

Garrison, Emma, 324

Gdansk, Poland, 328

General McClelland, 19

*Gentile Account of Life in Utah's Dixie,
1872-73: Elizabeth Kane's St.
George Journal, A,* 310

George III, 379

George Washington University, 301

Gerlach, Larry, 315

GI Bill, 186

Gifford (army), 170

Gillespie, Dizzy, 202, 348

Gilmore, Robert, 187

Ging (of Utah), 5

Gipson, Gordon, 374

Gittins, Alvin, 336

Glasgow, Scotland, 18

Glory Hunter (George A. Custer), 362

*Glory Hunter: A Biography of Patrick
Edward Connor,* 362-63, 371,
373

Gobi Desert, 340

Goering, Hermann, 179

Goetzmann, William H., 361

Goins, Ed, 55

Gold Hill News, 140

*Gold Rush Sojourners in Great Salt
Lake City, 1849-50* (and
article), 330

Goldsboro, NC, 96, 112

Gomez (carpenter), 147

Gomez, Lefty, 147

Gospel Ideals, 232

Graceland College, 354

Granger, UT, 235, 237, 272

Grant, Heber J., 62, 73, 119

Grass Valley, UT, 6

Great Depression, 60-67, 128, 349,
380

Great Falls, MT, 331

Great Salt Lake, 360, 363, 384

Greenoch, Argylshire, Scotland, 18

Greenville, SC, 100

Grey, Zane, 54

Grouse Creek, ID, 368

Grow, Stewart, 198, 203-4

Guden River, 24

Gulliver's Travels, 48

Gunnison, John W., 362

Guttridge, George, 188

Guyet, Paul, 70

H

Hadlock, Alton, 270

Hair, Mary Jane, 305

Hamilton (army), 169-70

Hamlin (army), 168-70

Hammond, George, 188-89, 195

Hampstead, NC, branch, 96, 98,
100, 108-9

Hampton, Elvon, 264

Hannibal, August (Gus), 305, 306

Hansen, Allie, 332, 333

Hansen, George, 199

Hansen Planetarium, 319

Hanson, Charles, 57, 115

Hanson, Gertrude, 57-58

Hanson, Lucrishey [Lucrezia] Vilate
Cushing, 38-39, 57, 115, 120

Hanson, Roger K., 304, 307, 308-9,
364

Harker, Elmer, 186

Harker, Parley Joseph, 78-87, 89-90,
92, 95

Harker, Rhoda Steed, 79, 92

Harker's Island, NC, branch, 96-97,
105, 109-10, 115

Harmon, Coy, 305

Harmony Church, GA (military camp), 157-58, 161, 165

Harper, Don, 270

Harper, Furnie, 102

Harper, Laurence A., 140, 187-89

Harper's (magazine), 117, 332

Harris, Chester G., 96, 97, 100-101, 103, 109

Harris, Elizabeth, 11-13

Harvard University, 119, 253

Hashimoto, Sam, 55

Hatch, Charles, 178, 179

Haubstadt, IN, 341

Hawkins, Bruce R., 362

Heidelberg, Germany, 179-80

Heizer, Robert F., 195

Henderson, Marion, 99

Herriman, UT, ward, 17-20, 22, 28, 33-35

Hess, Rudolf, 179

Hicks, John D., 186-87

Higham, John, 201

Hingham, MA, 1

Hinkle, Doug, 256

Hiram Scott College, 299

Hire, William, 13

"History as a Literary Art: An Appeal to Young Historians," 190

History of Utah, 117

Hitler, Adolf, 119, 178

Hobbs, Charles, 330

Hodgetts, Herbert L. ("Pink"), 162

Hodson, Paul W., 279-80

Hoffenrichter (professor), 180

Hofmann, Mark, 358

Holbrook (teacher), 47

Holladay, David, 9

Holladay (UT) Stake, 345

Holt (lieutenant), 153, 154, 156

Holt, Grant, 269-70

home construction business, 237-46; bookkeeping, 243; clients, 244-46; design and construction techniques, 240-41; dirt fill, 240; financing for, 237-39; inspections of, 241; land purchase, 239-40; realtors, 243-44

Horn, Frances L., 327-28, 330

Hour of Decision, The, 71

Howard, Alta, 230

Howard, Gordon, 230

Howard, NC, branch, 96, 106

Howells, Sophia, 12

Hudson, John, 330

Hull House, 265

Humboldt State College, 193

Hunter, Milton R., 193

Huntington Library, 330

Hurtado, Albert L., 331

Hyde, William A., 2

Hyer, Paul, 199

I

Idaho Falls, ID, wards, 65, 69, 121, 122, 129, 131, 145, 210-11, 237

Idaho Historical Conference, 323

Idaho Library Association, 335

Idaho State Historical Society, 367, 370

Idaho State Journal, 333

Idaho State University, 66, 117, 141, 187, 264

Idaho Yesterdays, 367, 369

"Improving the Teaching of American History: An Imperative," 325

Indian Business Council, 330

Indians, 5-6, 7-8, 100, 265, 301, 363-64, 383. *See also* individual

tribes; Madsen, Brigham D., ethnic/racial tolerance
Institute of Religion (LDS), 144
Iowa City, IA, 15, 16
Iran, 251, 252, 253
Irving, Washington, 373-74
Ivanhoe, 48
Iverson, Peter, 331

J

Jackson, Ansel E., 162-63
Jackson, MS, 161, 314
Jackson, Turrentine, 325-26
Jakeman, Wells, 214
James, Orten Haight, 16
Japanese Americans. *See* Madsen, Brigham D., ethnic/racial tolerance
Jarvis, Boyer, 275
Jasper, David Westwater, 162, 164
Jefferson, Thomas, 142
Jehovah's Witnesses, 350
Jennings, Jesse, 286, 302, 340
Jensen, Bruce, 286-88, 298-99
Jensen, Christen, 198, 203, 205
Jensen, DeLaMar, 199
Jensen, Soren, 24
Jeremy, Thomas E., 19
John Adams and the American Revolution, 247
"John W. Gunnison's Letters to His Mormon Friend, Albert Carrington," 362
John Whitmer Historical Association, 354
Johnson (sergeant), 154
Johnson, Claris ("Cassicks"), 53, 64
Johnson, Douglas E., 154
Johnson, JoAnn, 284

Johnson, Lyndon B., 262-64
Johnston, Albert Sidney, 7
Jones (teacher), 124, 126
Jones, Dan, 15
Jones, Elroy, 292-94, 296-97
Joseph (Chief), 329

K

Kaiser Shipyards, 145
Kanab, UT, ward, 133, 211
Kane, Thomas L., 7
Kaysville, UT, 27
Kennedy, John F., 227, 252, 259, 349
Kennedy, Padraic (Pat), 266
Kenyon College, 162
Kesler, Frederick, 16
Kezerian, Nephi, 217
Kimball, Camilla, 211
Kimball, Clayton, 288
Kimball, Eddie, 215
Kimball, Heber C., 4, 212
Kimball, L. Kent, 270
Kimball, Spencer W., 211-12, 348
Kimball, William H., 5
King, Martin Luther, Jr., 258-59
King, Tom, 280, 295-96
Kingsport, TN, 92
Kinnaird, Lawrence, 139, 141, 186-89, 193, 195, 246, 264
Kino (Catholic priest), 140
Kinston, NC, 102-4, 106
Kirkham, Francis W., 74
Kirkham, James Mercer, 64-65, 74, 76, 81, 83-84, 95, 98-100, 107, 108, 110-12, 210
Kirkham, Kate Woodhouse, 74-75
Kirkham, Martha Mercer, 74
Kirkham, Oscar A., 74, 210
KIRO-TV, 369

Kirtland, OH, 383

Kitzengen, Germany, 168

Klemme, August, 152-53

Knecht, Robert, 168, 172, 181

Knight, Newell, 220

Knowlton, Bryant S., 142

Knoxville, TN, 76, 81, 85

Kolff, Wilhelm, 284

Koscierzyna, Poland, 328

Kruschev, Nikita, 378

KSEI (radio), 127

KSL-TV, 369

Ku Klux Klan, 58-59

KUED-TV, 272, 323

L

Laager, TN, 80

Laird, Dave, 304

Lamoni, Iowa, 354

Landa, Esther, 272

Lander, Frederick W., 335

Langland (army), 169-70

Lark, UT, 34

Larsen (teacher), 124

Larsen (Larson?), Gary, 256

Larsen, Gerald, 82

Las Cruces, NM, 301

Las Vegas, NV, 297

LaSal, UT, 201, 217

Layton, Stan, 354

LDS Business College, 36, 309

Le Havre, France, 167

Lee, Harold B., 218

Lee, John D., 213

Lehi, UT, 7, 74

Lemhi Pass, 364

Lemhi: Sacajawea's People, The, 329, 375

Lewis and Clark Trail, 364

Lewiston, ID, 364

Lewisville, ID, 79, 212

Library of Congress, 261

Lien, Carsten, 258-59, 262

"Light on a Sensitive Surface," 342

Lincoln, Abraham, 119, 122, 349

Linley, Chesterman C., 154

Lipman, Charles B., 139

Lloyd (missionary), 2

Lloyd, Wesley P., 202

Logan, UT, 35, 247-53, 301, 310, 341, 344

Lolo Trail, 364

Loos, Emily, 339

Loos, Karen Madsen Bolton, viii, 148-49, **149,** 156, 161, **162,** 166, 183, 185, 195, 201-2, 218, **230,** 233, 248, 250-51, 260, 261, 266, 301-2, 339, 341, **341,** 343

Loos, Richard, 339

Los Angeles, 154, 209, 233

Los Angeles State University, 205

Louisville, KY, 74, 75-76, 95, 100, 104

Lucarelli, Dominic, 55

Luker, Ken, 304, 307

Lumbee (tribe), 101, 105

Lunda, NM, 100

Lusk (army), 171

Lyman, Richard R., 99-100

M

Madsen, Alice Fanny, 29, **29**

Madsen, Amanda, 342

Madsen, Anders, 24-25, 26

Madsen, Annie Crane (paternal grandmother), 17, 20-23, 28-31, **29,** 33-35

Madsen, Annie Johanae, 29, **29**

Madsen, Annie (Ann) LaRae (sister). *See* Carter, Annie LaRae Madsen

Madsen, Annie Nielsen Simonsen, 24, 25-26

Madsen, Betty McAllister, viii, 108, 116-17, 119-22, 131-32, 135-39, 142-44, 146, 148-49, 156-57, 161, 166, 172, 181, 183, 185-86, 191, 193, 195, 197-98, 201, 217-18, 226, 229-30, 231, 233-34, 247-48, 251, 253, 261, 263-64, 267, 272, 302, 321, 325-26, 336, 339, 342, 344, 349

education of, 119-22, 138, 301

employment of, 131, 137-39, 303, 309, 343

health of, 217-18, 364-35

parentage of, 132-33

photographs of, **120, 121, 136, 138, 153, 162, 326, 341, 343**

travels of, 250, 303, 343

Madsen, Brent, 196

Madsen, Brigham Andrew, 11, 29, **29,** 31-53, **38, 42, 45, 69,** 73, 92, 112, 131, 135, 145-46, **147,** 149, 156, 196, 200-201, 214, 234-35, 244

Madsen, Brigham Dwaine

BIOGRAPHICAL INFORMATION:

ancestry of, 1-32, 41

childhood and youth of, 40-65

education of, 44-45, 47, 61-63, 65-66, 70; at University of Utah, 115-22; at Berkeley, 135-45, 183, 185-96

employment of, 137-38, 186

as missionary, 30, 41, 73-113; as administrator, 97-98; expenses of, 83

as director, Utah Endowment for the Humanities, 314-15

as teacher, at Stewart Training School, 122

as teacher/principal at Pingree, ID, 122-31

at Kaiser Shipyards, 145-46

military service of, 363, 377, 380; in USA, 149-66, 182; in Germany, 166-82; post-war adjustment of, 185-86; views on, 143, 182-83

at Brigham Young University, 194-228; attitudes about, 225-26; salary at, 186, 195, 199-200, 214; views on Ernest L. Wilkinson, 205, 207-8, 227-28

at Utah State University, 247-53, 260

and Peace Corps, 251-65

and VISTA, 251, 265-68

at University of Utah, 269-322

as faculty, 247

as dean of Division of Continuing Education, 266, 269-75

as deputy academic vice president, 275-78

as dean of the Division of International Education, 277

as administrative vice president, 278-302

as director of libraries, 235, 303-11

as graduate advisor of the History Department, 311

as chair of the History Department, 311-15

as history teacher, 319-22

chair, Committee for the Review of Tenured Faculty, 319-20

retirement from, 339
retirement years of, 339-70

search committee for Hansen Planetarium director, 319

TOPICAL INFORMATION:

as carpenter/building contractor, 1, 51, 66-68, 108-12, 115, 120-22, 146-48, 159, 185-86, 197, 200-201, 229-348, 377

as hobo, 63

as member of the Salt Lake County Council for the Aging, 319

as prospective college president, 101, 264

as public speaker, 62, 322-24, 330

and recreation, 52, 64-65, 70, 160-61, 172, 174, 191

and hitchhiking, 63, 80-81, 96, 104

and National Youth Administration, 66

attitudes toward administration, 270, 315-18

attitudes toward craftsmen and academics, 286, 290

attitudes toward family, vii-viii, 4, 36-37, 40, 41, 50, 55, 68, 69-70, 112, 120, 132-33, 137-38, 143-44, 148, 166, 183, 230-31, 235-36, 342-43

attitudes toward writing/publishing history, 139-40, 190, 195, 358-60, 367, 370-76, 380

attitudes toward Mormonism, 48-50, 73, 88-89, 119, 191-93, 202-3, 219-25, 231-32, 251, 261, 344-49, 357-60

attitudes toward personal/academic freedom, ix, 182-83, 186-87, 194, 197-98, 221, 225-26

attitudes toward teaching, 217, 250, 320-21

attitudes toward United States, viii-ix, 143, 379-80

attitudes toward work, vii-viii, 51-54, 63-64, 67-68

decision-making style, 123

ethnic/racial tolerance, 51, 54-55, 106-7, 126, 164, 202, 243-44, 259, 300-301, 327-35, 345-48, 350, 380

health of, 105-6, 242, 264-65, 267-68, 364

honors of, 250, 322, 326, 330-31, 335-37, 343-44, 354, 362-63

patriarchal blessing of, 2-3

personal values of, vii-ix, 222-25, 376-80

photographs of, **42, 43, 45, 46, 69, 74, 110, 125, 136, 138, 152, 153, 158, 162, 190, 261, 323, 326, 341**

religious toleration of, 51, 66-67, 78

support of ERA, 351

writing style, 372-74

Madsen, Carl (grandfather), 20-31, **21, 29,** 33-37, 54, 92, 186

Madsen, Carl (Charley), 20, 28, **29,** 34, 38, 42, 57, 156

Madsen, Carl, Jr., 33-35, 43-44

Madsen, Charles Rodney (Rod), 45, 68, **69,** 149, 196, 200-201, 214, 234-37

Madsen, Christopher, 342

Madsen, Cindy, 196

Madsen, Danny, 196

Madsen, David Brigham, viii, 20, 166, 172, 183, 185, 195, 218, **230,** 233-34, 247-48, 251, 260-61, 266-67, 290, 302, 340, **341,** 360, 362, 365

Madsen, Debbie Shakespeare, 342

Madsen, Delilah Jean, 29, **29,** 30

Madsen, Desna Gwendolyn, 24, 29, **29,** 30

Madsen, Dora Hibbard, 43

Madsen, Etty Keturah, 29, **29**

Madsen, Evelyn Seelinger, 340

Madsen, Franklin Alonzo, 29, **29,** 57

Madsen, Heidi Stäuble, 196

Madsen, James Emanuel, 29, **29**

Madsen, Joshua, 340

Madsen, Karen. *See* Loos, Karen Madsen Bolton

Madsen, Keegan, 340

Madsen, Lee Self, 196, 236

Madsen, Leone, 57

Madsen, Linda. *See* Dunning, Linda Madsen

Madsen, Lydia Cushing, 11, 33, 37–53, **38, 39, 42,** 65, **69,** 92, 112, 146, **147,** 149, 156, 196, 218, 234

Madsen, Mack James, 44–45, **45,** 65, 68, **69,** 149, 196, 200–201, 214, 234–37, 248

Madsen, Maleia, 196

Madsen, Malinda (Lynn) Annie Elizabeth. *See* Miller, Malinda (Lynn) Annie Elizabeth

Madsen, Mary, 20, 28, **29,** 36

Madsen, Mary Harder, 26–28

Madsen, Michael, 196

Madsen, Niels, 29

Madsen, Paul, 196

Madsen, Pearl, 36–38, 57, 156

Madsen, Phyllis. *See* Eldredge, Phyllis Madsen

Madsen, Steven McAllister, viii, 218, 230, **230,** 234, 248, 251, 260–61, 267, 302, **341,** 343, 345

Madsen, Trever, 342

Madsen, Truman, 352–53

Madsen, William Carl, 29, **29**

Madsen Brothers Construction, Inc., 236

Maeser, Karl G., 211

Magna, UT, 34, 37, 41–43

Major Problems in American Indian History, 331

Malad, ID, 211

Manchester, NY, 383

Manwaring, Winifred, 243

March on Washington (1963), 258

Margetts, Winn, 304

Marquette University, 262

Marsell, Ray, 116

Martin, Thomas, 199

Maryland State College, 253

M*A*S*H, 58

Masters and Slaves, 189

Mather, Cotton, 212

Matheson, Scott, 336

Maxwell, Neal A., 281–82, 293, 300

Mayo, Fitzhugh, 167, 168

Mays, Eli, 81

McAllister, Delos (son), 197

McAllister, Delos R. (father), 132, **132,** 135, 149, 157, 166, 193, 218

McAllister, Diane, 197

McAllister, Ethel Carpenter, 132, **132,** 135, 149, 157, 166, 193, 218, 260

McAllister, Geniel Pratt, 197

McAllister, Karl, 197

McAllister, Lloyd, 197

McAllister, Marcia, 197

McAllister, Neil, 197

McCarthy, Joseph, 216

McConkie, Bruce R., 219

McCoy, Frieda, 305

McDevitt, Tom, 333

McDonald, Howard S., 194-95, 197-98, 203, 204-5

McDonald, Jack, 270

McDonough, Larry, 255-57

McKay, David O., 209, 211, 219, 232

McMurrin, Sterling M., 192, 218, 219, 224, 247, 264, 266, 276, 309, 337, 344, 345, 351-55, 357, 359, 363-64, 368

McQuown, Eloise, 305

McWiggin, Teddy, 15

Meldrum, Clarence, 79-80, 84, 86-87, 88, 90, 100

Merrill, Joseph L., 210

Merrill, Milton R., 248, 249

Michigan State University, 193, 301

Middlebury College, 262

Mikami, Kinya, **125,** 126

Mikkelson, Norma, 375

Mill, John Stuart, 54

Mill Creek Ward (Salt Lake City), 119

Miller, Arlen, 63

Miller, Blaine, 63

Miller, David E., 194

Miller, Malinda (Lynn) Annie Elizabeth, 29, **29,** 63

Milwaukee, WI, 262

Mims, Bob, 369

Mink Creek, ID, 64

Minson, Dale, 299

Minson & Halander, 299

Mississippi River, 384

Miyasaki, Herbert Y., 164

Moe, Edward, 266, 270

Money, Mark, 283-84, 291-92

Monroe (Peace Corps), 257

Monson, Charles, 275

Montana: The Magazine of Western History, 325

Montana Trail, 261, 326, 327

"Montana Trail: Salt Lake City-Corinne to Fort Benton, 1862-1882, The," 326

Monte Vista, CO, 266

Monterey, CA, 149

Monterrey, Nuevo Leon, Mexico, 201

Monticello, UT, 216

Mooney Real Estate, 245

Moore (teacher), 61

Morgan, Dale L., 361

Morison, Samuel Eliot, 190, 371-72

Mormon History Association, 327, 358

Mormon Mother, A, 310

"Mormons, Forty-Niners and the Invasion of Shoshoni Country," 331

Moscow, ID, 115

Moss, TN, 86, 89

Mostofi, Khosrow, 276

Mother in Heaven and Other Essays, 31

Mountain Meadows Massacre, The, 213

Moyers, Bill, 258, 262

Moyle, Henry D., 210-11

Mucha, Judy, 256

Mulder, William, 218, 322

Mulford, Clarence, 54

Munich, Germany, 168, 169

Murmansk, USSR, 178

Murray, Helen Sarvis, 4-5

Murray, William E., 4

Murray, UT, 237, 239, 245

N

Nagode, Jacob, 173

National Aeronautics and Space

Administration (NASA), 126, 302

National Archives, 217, 261, 329-30, 361

National Association of Research Libraries, 307

National Geographic Society, 340

National Guard, 296

National Home Builders' Association, 236

National Park Service, 332-34, 367, 369

National Public Radio, 369

National Science Foundation, 340

Native American Burial Repository, 332

Native Americans. *See* Indians; individual tribes

Nauvoo, IL, 2, 383

Nauvoo Legion, 16

Neckar River, 179

Neff, Andrew Love, 117

Nelson, Jay, 273-74

Nelson, Lowry, 218

Neuberger, Mark, 301

Nevada Historical Society Quarterly, 360

New Delhi, 266, 301

New Mexico State University, 301

New Orleans, LA, 157, 161

New York City, 15, 16, 26, 27, 113, 182, 261, 369

New York Times, 351

Newhope, TN, 86, 92

Newland, George, 57

Newland, Mary Emma Cushing, 39, 57

Newlin (army) 174

Newport News, VA, 167

Newton, Gregory, 253

Nez Perce (tribe), 329

Nibley, Hugh, 208

Nichols, Red, and His Five Pennies, 58

Nielsen, Whitey, 235

Nisonger, Chester, 6

Nisonger, David, 6

Nisonger, Henry, **6**

Nisonger (Niswanger), John, 6

Nisonger, Nancy Gunder, 6

Nisonger, Sarah Slusser, 6-9

Nixon, Alastair, 164-65

Nixon, Richard, 294, 379

No Man Knows My History, 352

Noe (Tennessee convert), 79-80

Noot, Thomas, 14

North American Medical Management Company, 340

North to Montana, 261, 325-27

Northcut's Cove, TN, 77

Northern California Nurses Association, 339

Northern Shoshoni, The, 329-30

Northland Press, 310

Now Generation, The, 320

"Now Opening to Blacks," 350

Nuremberg, Germany, 168, 178-79

Nygaard, Henry, 308

O

Oakland, CA, 138, 141, 302, 343

Oakland State (CA), 194

Oakley, ID, 209

Oberammergau, Germany, 172

Officer Candidate School, 156-66, 173, 277

Ogden, UT, 7, 237, 248, 310

Ohio College Library Center (OCLC) *Newsletter,* 324

Ohio University, 266

Oliver M. Rousseau Company, 146-48

Olpin, A. Ray, 276, 280

Olsen, Glenn, 312

Olsen, Jennings, 219

"One Man's Meat Is Another Man's Poison: A Revisionist View of the Seagull 'Miracle,'" 360

O'Neil, Shauna, 319

Only Yesterday, 57

Oregon-California Trails Association, 326

Oregon State University, 140

Oswald, Delmont, 314

Ottinger, Richard, 263

Outward Bound, 260, 263

Overland Journal, 325

Oxford University, 262

Oyler, Beth, 305, 307

P

"Pa's Salve," 9

Pace, Peggy, 325, 375

Pack, Fredrick Jerusalem, 116

Paine, Thomas, 379

Palm, Franklin C., 140

Palmer, TN, 85

Park City, UT, 216

Parker, ID, 120

Parker, Mayland, 253

Parkman, Francis, 373

Parks, Lester, 92

Parks, Utah, 92

Parkton, NC, 102, 104

Parowan, UT, 216

Partridge, William, 307

Paschal (of Corinne), 324

Paso Robles, CA, 154

Patton, George, 179

Paul, ID, 124

Paxman, Monroe, 202

Paxman, Shirley, 202

Paxson, Frederick Logan, 140

Payson, UT, 7

Peace Corps, 227, 249, 251-65, 269, 315, 325, 339

Pearson (of Alameda, ID), 64

Pearson, Baron, 51, 58, 64

Pearson, Raymond, 51, 58, 64

Pembroke, NC, 101

Penally, South Wales, 11

Pennsylvania State University, 309

Peterson, F. Ross, 127, 355

Peterson, Fae, 229

Peterson, LaMar, 229

Peterson, Myrtle Cushing, 9, 39

Petisco (Peace Corps), 255

Peyton (army), 167

Phi Alpha Theta, 141, 190

Phi Beta Kappa, 344

Phi Delta Kappa, 122

Phi Kappa Phi, 122, 139

Phifers, Ernest, 81

Phillips (teacher), 47

Phoenix, AZ, 98, 99

Pingree, ID, 122-31, 135

Pittsburgh, PA, 266

Piute (tribe), 213

Pocatello (Chief), 323, 335, 368, 369

Pocatello, ID, wards, 2, 43-71, 95, 97, 101, 113, 115, 120, 121, 127, 141, 264, 323, 328, 376

Pocock (missionary), 85-87

Poe, Edgar Allan, 62

Polish Amerindian Friendship Association, 328

Poll, Imogene (Gene), 197

Poll, Richard D., 188, 194, 197-99, 220, 227, 354, 359

Pollock, James (Thomas), 111

polygamy, 17-18, 19, 79, 87, 113, 383, 384

Pony Express Trail, 363

"Poor Richard's Almanac," 377

Porter, Glenn W., 158-59

Porto Viejo, Ecuador, 256, 257

Potter, J. L., 96

Potter, Melvin, 99

Poulson, Ernest, 291-92, 363-64

Poulson, Wilford, 219-20, 351, 368

Powell, Kent, 363

"Preacher and the Grizzly Bear, The," 40

Prescott, William, 373

Presidio (military base), 149, 151

Preston, ID, 332

Prevatt, Willie, 101

Price, UT, 201

Priestley, Herbert Ingram, 140

Princeton University, 191

"Principles of Administration," 315-18

Prohibition, 60, 78, 119

Provo, UT, 39, 195, 197-229, 310, 353, 359

Provo River, 215

Prows, Richard, 235

Prowswood (company), 235, 342

Prudential Federal Savings & Loan, 245

Puerto Rico, 255, 260, 263

Q

Quayaquil, Ecuador, 256

Quest of the Historical Jesus, The, 221

Quinn, Emmett, 288, 289

Quinn, Mildred, 277-78

Quito, Ecuador, 256-57

R

Rabbit Valley, UT, 6

Radke, Mildred, 139

Raemer, Sue, 305, 309

Raft River Valley, 368, 369

Raleigh, NC, 106

Raleigh, Walter, 101

Rampton, Calvin R., 294, 298-99, 308

Randers, Denmark, 24, 25

Ravenscraft, TN, 81

Rawlins, Joseph S., 19

Read, Waldemar, 116

Reagan, Ronald, 294, 321

Red Boiling Springs, TN, 86, 89

Red Butte Creek, 298, 300

Red Springs, NC, 104

Redd, Charles, 201, 216-17, 336

Redd, Katherine, 217

"Reflections on LDS Disbelief in the Book of Mormon as History," 357

Reid, John Lyon, 287

"Remembering General Patrick Edward Connor," 363

Remington, Maurice, 51

Reorganized Church of Jesus Christ of Latter Day Saints, 354

"Reply to John W. Welch and Truman G. Madsen: A Reply to 'Did B. H. Roberts Lose Faith in the Book of Mormon?,'...," 353-54

Rexburg, ID, 210

Reynolds (of Idaho), 46

Reynolds, Roger, 375

Rice, Moyle Q., 250

Rich, Edith, 305

Richards, LeGrand, 210

Richards, Stephen L, 210, 215
Richmond, CA, 145, 196
Richmond, UT, 212
Richwine, Marty, 256-58
Ricks, Joel, 248
Ricks College, 210
Rigby, C., 27
Rigby, ID, 210, 214
Riley, I. Woodbridge, 357
Rim of Christendom, The, 140
Riverton, UT, 21, 28, 29, 30, 33, 36, 37, 42-43, 63
Roaring Twenties, 57-60
Robbins (historian), 171
Roberts, Allen D., 359
Roberts, B. H., 220, 344, 351-58, 367
Roberts, Harold W., 154
Robertson, Leon, 307
Robertson, LeRoy E., 195
Robinson (army), 171
Robinson, Olin, 262-64
Robinson, Thomas, 168-70, 172
Roble, Dan, 256, 257
Rockefeller Foundation, 276
Rockland, ID, 129
Rocky Coast Framers and Construction Company, Inc., 342
Rodeo, CO, 266
Romney, Ida, 211
Romney, Marion G., 211
Romney, Thomas, 144
Roosevelt, Eleanor, 136
Roosevelt, Franklin D., 119, 136, 176, 181, 210, 350, 380
Roosevelt, Theodore, 323
Roosevelt, UT, 131
Ropp, Kenneth, 129, **130**
Rosenblatt, Joseph, 337
Rotary Club, 323

ROTC, 285
Rowland Hall-St. Mark's School, 323, 376, 380
Ruby Mountains, 364
Rutgers University, 193
Ryan, Dan, 324
Ryan, Leo, 262

S

Saar, Germany, 168
Saarbrucken, Germany, 168
Sacramento, CA, 196
Sacramento State College, 194
Sagan, Carl, 223
Sailsberry (of Salt Lake City), 36
St. Anthony, ID, 120
St. Joseph, MO, 19
St. Louis, MO, 7
St. Thomas, Virgin Islands, 263
Salem, MA, 362
Salina, UT, 302
Salley, James, and wife, 78, 100
Salt Lake City, 16, 19, 26, 27, 30, 36, 89, 107-8, 133, 149, 157, 161, 169, 172, 193, 196, 214, 226-27, 229-348, 353, 363, 369
Salt Lake County Council for the Aging, 319
Salt Lake Tribune, 345, 346, 357, 369
San Antonio, Texas, 326
San Diego, CA, 342, 343
San Diego State, 342
San Francisco, CA, 142, 154, 156, 197, 246, 287, 288, 299, 333, 340
San Francisco Chronicle, 142
San Francisco Mime Troop, 294
San Jose State College, 117
San Juan, PR, 263, 260

San Juan County Annual Lifestock Growers Association, 216

San Miguel, CA, 154

Santaquin, UT, 5, 9, 38

Sapp, Billy, 78

Saturday Night Chowder and Marching Club, 202, 218, 229

Sauer, Carl, 189-90, 373

Schaefer, Eulalia, 62

Schaefer, Paul, 142

Schmid, Thomas M., 305

Schweinfurt, Germany, 168

Schweitzer, Albert, 221, 224

Science, 348-49

Scott, Brig, 235

Scott, Walter, 48

Scotts Bluff, NE, 299

Seattle, WA, 258, 262, 369

Seyler (army), 154

"Shadow Wife," 342

Shaefer (University of Utah), 116

Shakespeare, William, 54

Sheets, Marian, 305

Sheik, The, 30

Shelley, ID, 129

Shepherd, Wayne, 293-94

Sherlock, Richard, 352

Shine, Earle M., 165

Shingleton, Tobe, 109

Shoshoni Frontier and the Bear River Massacre, 330, 334, 354-55, 367

"Shoshoni-Bannock Marauders on the Oregon Trail, 1859-1863," 328

Shoshone/Shoshoni-Bannock (tribes), 204, 327-35, 369, 370

Shriver, Eunice Kennedy, 260

Shriver, Sargent, 258, 262-64

Sidlosky, Clem, 256-57

Sierra Club, 299

Signature Books, 355, 357, 364

Sillars, Malcolm, 312

Simmons, James, 100, 108, **111**

Skidmore, Rex, 119

Skolfield, Elizabeth, 355

Slack, Ken, 304

Slager, William, 301

Slover, Robert H., 169-70

Sluiter, Engel, 189

Slusser, Mary Dean, 6

Slusser, Peter, 6

Smith, Alvin T., 38

Smith, Ethan, 219-20, 351

Smith, George D., 355, 364

Smith, Jedediah, 373

Smith, John, 373

Smith, Joseph, 1, 2, 24, 73, 96, 100, 105, 119, 192, 219, 297, 350, 351, 354, 355, 357, 358, 383

Smith, Joseph Fielding, 90, 212-13, 219, 220

Smith, Lorena Madsen, 22

Smith, Lot, 7

Smoot, Dick, 364, 368

Snake River, 121, 124, 211

Snow, Erastus, 360

Songs of Zion, 92

Sons of the American Revolution, 1

Sons and Daughters of Idaho Pioneers, 367, 369, 370

South Ogden, UT, 239

Southern Branch, University of Idaho. *See* Idaho State University

Southern Idaho Press, 369

Southern Utah State College, 310

Southwest Texas State Teachers College, 263-64

Spanish Fork, UT, 5, 82

Sparta, TN, 81, 86

Speedwell, TN, 78

Spengler, Oswald, 71

Spring Creek, UT, 5

Springfield (Grandview), ID, 130–31

Springfield College, 253–56

Spude, Catherine H., 334

"Stagecoach Travel on the Salt Lake-Montana Road," 323

Stallings, Richard H., 334

Stampp, Kenneth, 188

Stanford University, 197, 233, 248, 250

Stansbury, Howard, 360–63

"Stansbury's Expedition to the Great Salt Lake, 1948-50," 362

State of Deseret, The, 144

Statehood Day, 323, 344

Steed, Rhoda. See Harker, Rhoda Steed

Stegner, Wallace, 191

Stephenson (carpenter), 147

Stewart, Annie, 18

Stewart, Helen, 202

Stewart, Maynard Dixon, 202

Stewart, Samuel, 18

Stewart, Sarah Thompson, 17–18

Stewart, William, 17–19

Stickels, Fred L., 164–65

Stock, Bernie, 256–57

Stokes, Ira, 46

Storey, Bascomb, 261, 263

Stroup, Yvonne, 305

Stucki, Carolyn, 199

Studies of the Book of Mormon, 351–58, 367, 374

Sturges, Phil, 311, 313

Stuttgart, Germany, 171

Sudak, Alexander, 328

Summers, Tommy, 129–30, **130**

Sun Valley, ID, 335

"Sunday Afternoon at the Marriott," 355

Sunstone, 358

Sunstone Symposium, 358

"Swearing Elders," 218–19

Swensen, Russel, 198, 221

Swenson, Glen, 292, 299

Swenson, John C., 199, 208

Swift, Jonathan, 48

Sykes, Dave, 256

T

Taggart, Glen, 301

Taggart, Spencer, 141

Talley, Luther, 78

Talmage, James E., 91

Tanner, Annie Clark, 310

Tanner, Obert C., 310, 360–61

Tanner, Virginia, 276

Tanner Trust Fund, 330, 361, 374

Taos, NM, 336

Tawacin, 328

Taylor, Arod, 127

Taylor, Dora, 127, 128

Taylor, Glen, 127–29

Taylor, Golden, 214

Taylor, Helen. See Cushing, Helen Jeannette Murray

Taylor, Lucille, 202

Taylor, Norman, 5

Taylor, Richard, 202

Taylor, Sandra, 312–13

Teggart, Frederick, 144

Tempest, Norinne, 270

Temple of the Rainbow Path, 281

Temple University, 266

Tenby, Pembrokeshire, South Wales, 11, 13, 15

Texas Tech, 264

"Thanksgiving on July 24, 1849," 323

"That Old Feeling," 121-22

Thomas (missionary), 92

Thomas, George, 117-18

Thomas, Sarah, 10-11

Thompson, James Westfall, 140

Thompson, Ralph, 308

Thompson, Richard, 312, 315

Thomson, Ralph, 303

Thoreau, Henry David, 54, 214

Three Forks, MT, 364

Thurman, Samuel, 285, 314

Tinno, Keith, 369

Tintic Mining District, 9

Tip (collie), 234, 251

Tippetts, Twain, 250

"Top 20 Stories of 200 Years," 349-50

Trask, G. D. J., 19

Traver, James, 271

Truman, Harry S., 176-77

Truscott, Lucien, 173, 180

Tucson, AZ, 259

Tunney, Gene, 65

Turner, Frederick Jackson, 140

Twin Falls, ID, 334

Tyler, S. Lyman, 271, 277, 305, 310

U

U.S. Bureau of Indian Affairs, 324

U.S. Constitution, 349

U.S. Department of Interior, 333

U.S. Fidelity and Guaranty Company, 133

U.S. Forest Service, 251

U.S. Housing and Urban Development Agency (HUD), 299, 300

U.S. Navy, 142, 197

U.S. State Department, 141

U.S. Volley Ball Association (USVBA), 311

Udall, Nicholas, 99

Union Pacific Railroad, 9, 17, 44, 47, 49

University of Arizona, 255, 259-60, 304

University of California: at Berkeley, 117, 119, 122, 135-45, 183, 185-96, 198, 246, 248, 302, 305, 315, 370, 373, 374; at Davis, 187, 325; at Los Angeles, 201, 233, 247

University of Chicago, 198, 309

University and College Library Council of Utah (UCLC), 310

University of Colorado, 265, 341

University of Idaho, 115

University of Idaho Press, 217, 375

University of Illinois Press, 351, 352, 355, 374-75

University of Minnesota, 140

University of Missouri, 340

University of Nebraska Press, 325

University of North Dakota, 304

University of Oklahoma, 271

University of the Pacific, 301

University of Pennsylvania, 119

University of Texas, 361

University of Utah, 70, 108, 115, 125, 138-40, 142, 189, 191, 194-95, 197-98, 209, 213, 218, 224, 229, 244, 247, 260, 269-322, 340, 352

American West Center, 271

Associated Students, 294, 299, 336

Behavioral Sciences Building, 282-83, 287

block "U," 287

Board of Regents, 280, 284, 287, 292, 293, 308, 336

building construction at, 279-90

Carlson Hall, 285, 314

Chronicle, 295, 297, 319, 320, 322

Coalition for Student Rights, 294

College of Business, 277

Committee for the Review of Tenured Faculty, 319-20

dance program, 276, 286

Division of Continuing Education, 266, 335

Division of International Education, 276-77

Faculty Senate, 305, 319-20

fountains at, 287

Friends of the Library/Libraries, 306, 310, 344, 355

General Service Center, 286

Hinckley Institute of Politics, 323, 354

Housing Trust Funds, 300

Huntsman Center, 286

Institutional Council, 287, 293, 299, 300, 307, 336

Kingsbury Hall, 335

Law School, 285, 290

Liberal Education Committee, 274

Marriott Library, 285, 289, 302-11, 324, 330, 351, 355, 360, 363

Medical Center, 284

Medical Towers Student Housing, 282

Merrill Engineering Building, 286, 289

Middle East Center, 276, 297

Orson Spencer Hall, 285, 295, 314

Park Administration Building, 285, 289, 295-97

parking at, 288-90

Political Science Department, 276

Press, 320, 325, 330, 335, 361, 362, 375

proposed "university degree" at, 271-72

reentry programs for women, 272-73

Research Park, 284, 292, 298-99

ROTC, 294, 334

security, 292-98

Service Center Building, 270, 291

student housing at, 286, 298-300

Students for a Democratic Society, 294, 297

temporary buildings, 269, 284, 295, 298

Thomas Building, 285, 286, 314

Undergraduate Division, 274

Union Building, 295

VISTA at, 266

Women's Resource Center, 313

University of Wisconsin, 262

University of Wyoming, 167

"Use of Newspapers in Historical Research, The," 324

USS West Point, 167

Utah Academy of Sciences, Arts, and Letters, 325, 336

Utah Arts Council, 342

Utah Board of State History, 336

Utah Business Women's Association, 365

Utah Endowment for the Humanities, 314

Utah Farmer, 75

Utah Forty-Niner with the Stansbury Exploration of Great Salt Lake:

Letters and Journal of John Hudson, 1848-50, A, 330

Utah Historical Quarterly, 325, 328, 354, 360-63

Utah Historical Society, 328, 340, 363

Utah Museum of Natural History, 286

Utah Newspaper Project Conference, 324

Utah Power & Light Company, 291-92

Utah Remembers World War II, 363

Utah State Board of Higher Education, 298, 299, 300

Utah State Building Board, 282, 285, 291, 299

Utah State Geological Survey, 360

Utah State Historical Society, 248, 305, 327, 363

Utah State University/Agricultural College, 35, 36, 127, 144, 188, 196, 209, 247-53, 260, 301, 309-10, 325, 341, 352, 362

Utah State University Press, 363

Utah Technical College, 270, 273-74

Utah Territorial Board of Trade, 17

Utah War, 7, 213

Utah Westerners, 327

Ute (tribe), 5, 203, 266

Utley, Robert, 330

V

Valentino, Rudolph, 30

Van De Water, Frederic, 362-63

Van Nostrand, John, 145

Van Orden, Richard, 305

Vance, B. F., 84

Varley, James F., 334

Venezuela, 253, 255

Veterans Administration, 236, 238, 245

Vietnam War, 289, 341-42, 350; BDM in protest march, 294; demonstrations against at the University of Utah, 294-97; at Kent State, 295

View of the Hebrews, 219-21, 351

"Vignettes of the Revolutionary Fathers," 323

VISTA. *See* Volunteers in Service to America

Vitality of Mormonism, The, 91

Volunteers in Service to America (VISTA), 254, 265, 269, 339-40

W

Wadley, Carma, 48, 349

Wadsworth, Bud, 61

Wahlquist, John T., 117

Walker War, 5, 330

Wallace, Walker, 122

Walsh, John, 349

Wann, Jack, 276

Washington, D.C., 113, 217, 236, 258, 263, 301, 327

Washington, George, 379

"Washington Crossing the Delaware," 48

Washington Terrace, UT, 237

Watergate, 350

Waters, Dan, 293

Wayne State University, 289

Weber State College, 188, 209, 219, 309-10, 323

Welch, John W., 352-55

Wells, Daniel H., 28

Wells, Emmeline B., 27-28

Wells, Merle, 370

Wesleyan University, 262
West, LaVon, 335–36
West Jordan, UT, 38
Western Historical Quarterly, 325–26
Western History Association, 326, 331
Western Illinois University, 359
Western Writers of America, 326
Westerners International, 326, 330, 331
Westminster College, 310
White, Lyman, 2
White, Reed, 46
Wicks, Guy, 70
Wilbur Smith & Associates, 288
Wilkins, Ernest, 218
Wilkins, Maurine Lee, 218
Wilkinson, Cragun & Barker, 327
Wilkinson, Ernest L., 203–5, 207–9, 213–15, 227–29, 350
Willets, CA, 157
Williams (of Pingree, ID), 129, **130**
Willis, Alfred, 110
Willis, Telford, 110, 112
Wilmington, NC, 96–99, 106, 108, 109
Wilson, ID, 130
Wilson, Meredith, 140
Winter Quarters, IA, 4
Wirthlin, Joseph L., 209–10
Wood, Charles B., 89
Woodbury, Angus, 229–30
Woodbury, Grace, 229–30
Woodruff, Wilford, 2
Word of Wisdom, 102, 119, 192, 232. *See also* beer
World War I, 78, 139, 154, 181, 188, 350, 380
World War II, 119, 126, 142, 199, 238, 240–41, 269, 284, 295, 349, 363, 377, 380
World's Fair (1964), 261
Wyoming, 27

Y

Yale University, 330
Yarborough (Peace Corps), 262
Yellowstone Park, 65, 113
YMCA, 256
Young, Brigham, 2, 4, 5, 7, 9, 16, 28, 119, 213, 384
Young, John W., 9
Young, Joseph W., 16
Young, Karl, 199
Young, Les, 255, 257
Young, Levi Edgar, 117–19
Young, Richard L., 296

Z

ZCMI, 89
Zion's Book Store, 352